South Africa's
Resistance Press

This series of publications on Africa, Latin America, and Southeast Asia is designed to present significant research, translation, and opinion to area specialists and to a wide community of persons interested in world affairs. The editor seeks manuscripts of quality on any subject and can generally make a decision regarding publication within three months of receipt of the original work. Production methods generally permit a work to appear within one year of acceptance. The editor works closely with authors to produce a high-quality book. The series appears in a paperback format and is distributed worldwide. For more information, contact the executive editor at Ohio University Press, Scott Quadrangle, University Terrace, Athens, Ohio 45701.

Executive editor: Gillian Berchowitz
AREA CONSULTANTS
Africa: Diane Ciekawy
Latin America: Thomas Walker
Southeast Asia: William H. Frederick

The Ohio University Research in International Studies series is published for the Center for International Studies by the Ohio University Press. The views expressed in individual monographs are those of the authors and should not be considered to represent the policies or beliefs of the Center for International Studies, the Ohio University Press, or Ohio University.

South Africa's Resistance Press

ALTERNATIVE VOICES IN THE LAST GENERATION UNDER APARTHEID

Edited by
Les Switzer and Mohamed Adhikari

Foreword by Guy Berger

Ohio University Center for International Studies
Research in International Studies
Africa Series No. 74
Athens

© 2000 by the
Center for International Studies
Ohio University
Printed in the United States of America
All rights reserved

09 08 07 06 05 04 03 02 01 00   5 4 3 2 1

The books in the Ohio University Research in International Studies Series
are printed on acid-free paper ⊗™

Library of Congress Cataloging-in-Publication Data

South Africa's resistance press : alternative voices in the last generation under
apartheid / edited by Les Switzer and Mohamed Adhikari.
    p.   cm. — (Research in international studies. Africa series ; no. 74)
    Includes bibliographical references and index.
    ISBN 0-89680-213-2 (pbk. : alk. paper)
    1. Underground press—South Africa—History—20th century.
    2. Journalism—Political aspects—South Africa. I. Switzer, Les.
    II. Adhikari, Mohamed.   III. Series.
    PN5477.U53 S685 1999   00-040668
    070.1'7'0968—dc21   CIP

To Mohamed Adhikari's children, Rafiq and Zaheer,

and

To Les Switzer's grandchildren, Nicholas and Alistair;

Garrett; Jessica and Kieran; Casey, Alexander and Tanner

Contents

Part II:
On the Barricades: The Struggle for South Africa

Illustrations

Foreword

From the margins to the mainstream is the trajectory that resistance voices have taken in South Africa in the last century. Where once antiracist representation was on the media fringes, it is now the major force in South African publications. This profound transformation has come about in part because of the journals described in this book. But it has also happened without them: of the many dissident publications analyzed here, almost all were extinct by the mid-1990s or earlier.

Just two survivors of the plethora of publications in South Africa's resistance media entered the twenty-first century. The *Mail and Guardian*, on the one hand, and *East Cape News*, on the other, were still continuing the tradition of vibrant investigative and campaigning journalism in the year 2000. But they kept going only through major changes in ownership: the former *Weekly Mail* newspaper became foreign-owned and foreign-subsidized; the former East Cape News Agencies cooperative turned into a small commercial business.

In addition, after apartheid, these two media platforms no longer stood out as much as they used to, because what they—and the other outlets featured in this book—stood for was simply no longer unique. What used to be in diametrical opposition to unbridled racism became the broad consensus across the postapartheid media. Where courageous dissident journalists previously had to duck, dodge, and dive in order to survive state repression, the new democratic South Africa tolerates all manner of critical media coverage. In these new conditions, the distinctive features of the resistance journalism of the apartheid period were rendered redundant—precisely by their very success.

The paradox, then, is that having been an integral part of the social movement that transformed South African society, the media of that movement were themselves unable to survive the transition. Some publications died early under the dire pressures of the South African police state; others withered later for want of capital and management skill. Still more failed to adapt to the new times and changing audiences following the release of Nelson Mandela and the buildup to the country's first democratic elections in 1994.

The success of the South African liberation movement wrought profound changes in the environment, ownership, staffing, content, and audiences of the mainstream media. The freeing of South Africa lost some heroic voices, but it also led to a mainstream media changed beyond recognition (and it enabled the emergence of a host of brand new broadcasters to boot). The erstwhile "people's" publications did not live to see these changes, but their role in ultimately realizing them was fundamental. These journals were rooted in, and they also reflected, a wider resistance movement. And they also served to further "manufacture dissent"—intensifying on a global scale ever-deepening action against apartheid.

By their contribution to nonracial and democratic discourse, and their professional challenge to both private establishment and state propagandistic mainstream media of the old South Africa, the resistance publications effectively countered the climate and the culture of apartheid. Their inspiration of generations of activists, and their encouragement of new generations of media people, was undeniable. The move by many resistance journalists into the commanding heights of the postapartheid mainstream also directly helped to shape the early twenty-first-century South African mediascape. In short, to understand contemporary South Africa—its transformation as a whole, as well as the changes in the media specifically—one needs to understand the role of resistance journalism in the country during the past thirty or so years.

This is not to suggest that the "end" of South African media history was reached with the end of the apartheid system. Many proponents of the former white establishment media (both English liberal opposition and Afrikaner reformist) contest that they, too, alongside the resistance media, deserve credit for contributing to freedom. Debates continue to rage—long after the burial of political apartheid—about the pace of racial changes in media ownership, control, and content.

What remains generally uncontested, however, is the special part played by the media covered in this book—their historical impact and their living legacy into the twenty-first century. So far, this whole rich history—while lived through by South Africans—has not been widely recorded within the country. Even less has it been reflected upon by many contemporary media practitioners. This is strange, given that it is a very un-African thing to ignore the past from which one is descended. There is thus a gap waiting to be filled, and in this regard, Les Switzer and Mohamed Adhikari have rendered a real service in producing this book.

Once a lonely pioneer researcher into the black press in southern Africa, Switzer has now crowned an illustrious career and a substantial series of publications with this new representation of what would otherwise have been largely a hidden history. He is now joined by Mohamed Adhikari as co-editor, a scholar whose own work does justice to the standards set by Switzer. *South Africa's Resistance Press* will reward any reader interested in the role of media in liberation struggles in general and in understanding the "South African transformation miracle" in particular.

The twenty-first century is, of course, the age of New Media and globalization. But reading the pages of this book and learning about the heroes of "old media" in their specifically local South African resistance form puts things in perspective. History still has enormous relevance to the present.

Guy Berger, Professor and Head of Department
Journalism and Media Studies
Rhodes University Grahamstown

Preface

This book is the third in a trilogy that began twenty years ago with the publication of *The Black Press in South African and Lesotho: A Descriptive Bibliographical Guide, 1836–1976* (1979). *Black Press* was the first attempt to locate, identify, and describe the hundreds of newspapers, newsletters, and magazines projected for the region's subaltern black (African, Coloured, and Indian) communities.

The second publication in this series was *South Africa's Alternative Press: Voices of Protest and Resistance, 1880–1960* (1997). *Alternative Press* focused on the political discourses of South Africa's marginalized black communities—the most extensive and varied archive of this kind in sub-Saharan Africa. These discourses differed substantially from those projected by the establishment commercial press, which was owned and controlled by whites, aimed at or intended for whites, concerned mainly with the political, economic, and social life of the white population, and consumed mainly by whites for most of its two-hundred-year history.

The earliest protest literature can be found in African mission journals in the mid- to late nineteenth century, but an independent African protest press in South Africa can be traced back to the 1880s. South Africa's designated Coloured and Indian communities were represented by their own protest publications from the early 1900s. Marginalized sectors of South

Africa's expanding urban black working-class population were represented by various socialist publications from the 1920s, and a nonracial resistance press would emerge essentially from the 1950s.

As the struggle entered its final stages in the 1980s, a few white-owned establishment newspapers—especially those aimed at black audiences—began to challenge the apartheid order. The boundary lines between antiapartheid mainstream and alternative publications had become less distinct by the end of the decade, which is why the third volume in this series is entitled *South Africa's Resistance Press*. The focus of the book, however, is on alternative political publications inside South Africa from the 1960s to the 1990s and the end of the apartheid era.

The contributors again represent diverse ethnic and cultural backgrounds, and virtually all were either born and raised in South Africa or lived there for long periods of time. Several were associated in one way or another with these alternative publications and were activists in the democratic movement—especially in the 1980s.

Our thanks to George Claassen, Peter Limb, Chris Merrett and Chris Saunders, Keyan Tomaselli, and his colleague Arnold Shepperson for providing photos relating to their chapters. Mohamed Adhikari provided the "Free the Press" photo collage and the photos of *SASO Newsletter* and *SASO Bulletin*. The photo montage of newspapers supporting the UDF, and the photos of *New Age*, *Spark*, and the *Sowetan* were obtained from the Mayibuye Centre for History and Culture in South Africa (University of the Western Cape). Other photos in the introductory chapter, the photo of the Albany News Agency letter, and the photos relating to the *Grassroots* chapter are from Les Switzer's personal collection. Thanks are also due to Bill Ashley, Michele Heddermann, and Dominic Johnson of University Access Services (University of Houston), who prepared several photos for publication.

The business manager of the School of Communication at the University of Houston, Barry Brown, was most helpful in translating computer files from contributors and providing advice on formatting problems. Bob Furnish did a meticulous job in copyreading the manuscript, Leonie Twentyman-Jones prepared the detailed index, and Gillian Berchowitz of Ohio University Press shepherded the manuscript to publication.

The task of editor can be likened to being a gardener in charge of a flower bed. The boundaries must be erected and the flowers planted. A few will grow with a minimum of effort, but many will require careful attention. The soil must be tilled, plants watered, fertilizer applied in the correct quantity, undesirable weeds and insects removed, and shade provided where necessary. Despite the gardener's best efforts, a few flowers don't survive or must be replanted. The ultimate hope is that each flower blooms and the beauty of each one reflects the flower bed as a whole.

We leave it to the reader to decide.

Abbreviations

ANC	African National Congress
ASSECA	Association for the Educational and Cultural Development for the African People
AWB	Afrikaner Weerstandsbeweging (Afrikaner Resistance Movement)
AZAPO	Azanian Peoples' Organisation
AZASM	Azanian Students' Movement
AZASO	Azanian Students' Organisation
BAWU	Black Allied Workers' Union
BC	Black Consciousness
BCCSA	Broadcasting Complaints Commission of South Africa
BCP	Black Community Programmes (ch. 1); Basutoland Congress Party (ch. 3)
BPC	Black People's Convention
CAD	Cape Archives Depot
CAHAC	Cape Housing Action Committee
CLOWU	Clothing Workers' Union
COD	Congress of Democrats
CODESA	Convention for a Democratic South Africa
COSAS	Congress of South African Students
COSATU	Congress of South African Trade Unions
CPSA	Communist Party of South Africa
CUSA	Council of Unions of South Africa

CYL	Congress Youth League
DP	Democratic Party
Ecna	East Cape News Agencies
FOSATU	Federation of South African Trade Unions
GNLB	Government Native Labour Bureau
ICCO	Interchurch Organisation for Development Co-operation
ICU	Industrial and Commercial Workers' Union
IDAMASA	Interdenominational African Ministers' Association of South Africa
IDASA	Institute for a Democratic Alternative in South Africa
IDT	Independent Development Trust
ISL	International Socialist League
IWA	Industrial Workers of Africa
JMC	Joint Management Centre
JODAC	Johannesburg Democratic Action Committee
MARS	Media and Resource Services
MDM	Mass Democratic Movement
MK	Umkhonto we Sizwe (Spear of the Nation)
MPLA	People's Movement for the Liberation of Angola
MWASA	Media Workers' Association of South Africa
NA	Native Affairs
NACTU	National Council of Trade Unions
NAD	Natal Archives Depot
NAIL	New Africa Investments, Ltd.
NAMDA	National Medical and Dental Association
NAP	New Africa Publications
Naspers	Nasionale Pers
NECC	National Education Crisis Committee
NEUM	Non-European Unity Movement
NP	National Party
NPU	Newspaper Press Union

NSMS	National Security Management System
NUM	National Union of Mineworkers
NUSAS	National Union of South African Students
PAC	Pan-Africanist Congress
PFP	Progressive Federal Party
PWV	Pretoria-Witwatersrand-Vaal triangle
RAWU	Retail and Allied Workers' Union
RDP	Reconstruction and Development Programme
Renamo	Resistencia Nacional Moçambicana (Mozambique National Resistance)
SAAN	South African Associated Newspapers
SABC	South African Broadcasting Corporation
SACBC	Southern African Catholic Bishops' Conference
SACHED	South African Council for Higher Education
SACOS	South African Council of Sport
SACP	South African Communist Party
SACTU	South African Congress of Trade Unions
SADF	South African Defence Force
SAIRR	South African Institute of Race Relations
SANC	South African Native Congress
SANNC	South African Native National Congress
SAP	South African Police
SAPA	South African Press Association
SASM	South African Students' Movement
SASO	South African Students' Organisation
SATS	South African Transport Services
SNA	Secretary of Native Affairs
SNS	Standardised News Service
SPROCAS	Study Project on Christianity in Apartheid Society
SSC	State Security Council
SWAPO	South-West Africa People's Organisation
TFP	Tradition, Family, Property

TNC	Transvaal Native Congress
TRC	Truth and Reconciliation Commission
UBJ	Union of Black Journalists
UCM	University Christian Movement
UDF	United Democratic Front
UNISA	University of South Africa
UNITA	Uniao Nacional para a Independencia Total de Angola (National Union for the Total Independence of Angola)
UWUSA	United Workers' Union of South Africa
WACC	World Association for Christian Communication

South Africa's
Resistance Press

1

Introduction

South Africa's Resistance Press in Perspective

Les Switzer

This story begins in the middle years of the apartheid era in South Africa. The events of 1960 temporarily derailed the resistance movement—the Sharpeville-Langa shootings; the banning of the African National Congress (ANC) and the Pan-Africanist Congress (PAC), at the time the two most influential political opposition groups in the country; and the white referendum that resulted in South Africa becoming a republic and leaving the British Commonwealth. The government detained nearly two thousand activists after declaring a nationwide state of emergency in March through August 1960, and those dissidents who escaped this dragnet went underground or fled into exile.

The Congress Alliance—consisting of the ANC, South African Indian Congress, South African Coloured People's Organisation (later renamed the Coloured People's Congress), the white South African Congress of Democrats (many of whom had been members of the Communist Party, which was officially banned in 1950), the South African Congress of Trade Unions, and the Federation of South African Women—was effectively torn apart by these events. The historic Freedom Charter they had drafted in June 1955—a fundamental Bill of Rights for the people of South Africa—was trampled into the ground, where it would lay more or less dormant for almost a generation.

The banned opposition groups regrouped initially in South Africa, formed underground guerrilla units inside as well as outside South Africa, and moved into the first stage of armed struggle. Umkhonto we Sizwe (meaning "Spear of the Nation" in Xhosa and popularly known as MK), the main guerrilla group,[1] was effectively the vehicle of the Congress Alliance. Umkhonto was formed in June 1961, and whites, Coloureds, and Indians as well as Africans were welcomed into its ranks from the beginning. Umkhonto was an independent organization, but Congress Alliance members, especially from the ANC and the South African Communist Party (SACP), played crucial roles in obtaining the financing, in organizing the guerrilla camps (initially in Tanzania), and in training recruits.

Umkhonto units inside South Africa carried on an intermittent campaign of urban sabotage directed against noncivilian targets for almost three years between 1961 and 1964. Aided by informers, forced confessions, intercepted plans, ill-conceived public statements (the major one by PAC exile leader Potlake Leballo, which resulted in the mass arrest of PAC activists in April–June 1963), raids on hideouts, and the apparent success the security police had in infiltrating outlawed organizations, the underground guerrilla movement inside South Africa was all but destroyed. Peasant unrest in the African reserves was contained for the most part without spilling over into the urban areas, and by the mid-1960s there was little overt resistance in the countryside. Police raided Umkhonto's headquarters in South Africa—on a farm in the future white suburb of Rivonia, near Johannesburg—in July 1963 and captured most of the leadership. The Rivonia trial, which ended in June 1964 with life sentences for Nelson Mandela, Walter Sisulu, and other leaders of the Congress Alliance, was followed by more arrests, detentions, bannings, and trials in a concerted campaign to wipe out all vestiges of independent black political activity in South Africa.[2]

South Africa under Apartheid

The National Party was at the height of its power during the 1960s and early 1970s.[3] The post–World War II economic boom continued, and the government under prime ministers Hendrik Verwoerd and his successor B. J. (John) Vorster faced little white or black opposition to its policies. This was the era of grand apartheid—the era in which the master plan for segregated white, African, Coloured, and Indian communities was gradually implemented. The key to erecting the edifice of apartheid was control over African labor. During the "repressive" period (1960–1976), as Stanley Greenberg puts it, the state would attempt to reclassify, redistribute, and ultimately relocate the entire black labor force in South Africa.[4]

This development coincided with a radical reorganization of the authority structures inside the rural African reserves. Ethnicity would be employed to discourage racial solidarity between people of color and prevent participation in a nonracial society. Each African ethnic group would be categorized as a national unit with its own language, culture, and history. Each group, in turn, would be allocated a specific territory, and even the segregated urban African townships outside the reserves would be further segmented along ethnic lines.

The African reserves—referred to as Bantustans, then homelands, and ultimately national states—would house the bulk of the African population. The boundaries of all African reserves would now be drawn (or redrawn) and fixed, and the movement of Africans within designated white urban areas and between rural and urban areas would be strictly controlled. Africans in urban areas would be housed in townships sealed off from surrounding white suburbs and situated wherever possible close to existing reserves. Permanent resident rights for Africans in the cities were eliminated for all but a privileged minority, and vigorous attempts were made to prevent African families (women in particular) from entering the designated white urban areas.

South Africa's African labor policy was dictated by the need to maintain a small but permanent industrial work force in the urban areas, establish select categories of migrant contract workers to serve the (white-controlled) capitalist sector in town and countryside (especially the mines, commercial farms, and state-owned corporations), and contain so-called redundant or otherwise unwanted African workers, as well as contract workers and their families, in the reserves. The labor control system was to be modernized, and to achieve this goal the state had to consolidate the reserves, establish a cadre of African political collaborators with enough authority to control the residents, and devise new development strategies to feed and employ the redundant population. The state did not succeed, and the reserves finally collapsed: more than any other single factor, this led to the breakdown of the apartheid system.[5]

The political, economic, and social costs of apartheid's black labor policies during this period, of course, were enormous. First, the attempt to establish parallel bureaucracies for administering African, Coloured, Indian, and white South Africans placed an immense financial burden on the government and ultimately on the white taxpayer.[6] Second, a massive increase in police, security, and prison forces was necessary to enforce the African labor control measures, supply low-wage African workers to white commercial farms (most of which were mechanized by the end of the 1960s), and move un-wanted African workers in white urban and rural areas to "resettlement" camps in African reserves.[7] Third, the government removed millions of Africans from the core only to lose control over this "surplus" labor force in the periphery. The lower echelons of the labor control network broke down completely in the African reserves. A costly and flawed strategy to promote agricultural and industrial development inside and adjacent to the reserves ultimately failed. Unemployment soared and hundreds of thousands of desperate African migrants left the reserves, bypassing white and black administrative and policing authorities. By the early 1980s so-called squatter communities had been established in and around all of South Africa's major cities.

There were other internal factors at work in the generation after 1960 that contributed to the demise of apartheid. The African population increased from about 68 percent of the total in 1960 to about 74 percent in 1990, while whites, Coloureds, and Indians together decreased from about 32 percent in 1960 to about 26 percent in 1990. The state's draconian labor control measures did achieve a slight decrease in the *percentage* of the African population living in white-proclaimed urban and rural areas, but the *number* of Africans living in these areas increased rapidly—especially in the cities. The official African population living in white urban areas increased by more than two million between 1960 and 1980—from about 29 percent to about 33 percent of the total African population (with unofficial estimates of up to 50 percent if peri-urban, refugee "closer resettlement" communities in adjacent reserves are included).[8]

Many scholars argue that apartheid policy contained the seeds of its own destruction. Manufacturing's contribution to the gross domestic product (GDP), for example, was greater than mining and agriculture combined by the mid-1960s, and manufacturing employed more people than any other sector of the economy by 1970.[9] While South Africa's economic future clearly lay in manufacturing and allied services, employers argued that continued growth would require a better educated, more skilled, and permanent urban African labor force. So the labor control measures could not really halt the movement of Africans to the cities, and a better-educated African population in town and countryside (in part, to service a bureaucracy to administer the reserves and the labor control measures) could not be implemented without a major reallocation of available resources and a reform of apartheid policies.

Reforms were gradually implemented in the 1970s and accelerated in the 1980s—especially under Pieter Willem (P. W.) Botha, who replaced John Vorster as prime minister in September 1978, and Frederick Willem (F. W.) de Klerk, who replaced Botha in August 1989. The state in essence tried to deracialize and depoliticize the linguistic and social practices of apartheid to make it more palatable to domestic and foreign critics. Repressive measures would be applied to a few targeted areas and relaxed when and where they could not be defended. The plan was to phase out direct coercion—such as arbitrary searches and arrests of Africans in the streets and in their homes—delegate responsibility to white employers and recognized African authorities in upgraded urban townships and developing reserves, and provide incentives for privileged strata within the black (African, Coloured, Indian) community to support the state in its efforts to maintain the apartheid order.

Pass law prosecutions were declining by the 1970s. More funding was made available for African education, especially for secondary and tertiary education—albeit mainly in the reserves. The number of African high school graduates expanded rapidly from the early 1970s—doubling to more than 11,000 in 1978 and soaring to 83,000 in 1984—although African primary and secondary schools remained vastly overcrowded, the teachers undereducated and "underqualified" (80 percent in 1985, according to the government). The number of Africans allowed to enter so-called white universities also increased rapidly— from 309 in 1974 to 788 in 1980, and there was enormous growth in total African university enrollment.[10]

The 1970s experienced an upsurge in labor unrest after a decade of relative inactivity—punctuated by the 1973 Durban strikes, which went on for two months and involved more than 61,000 workers in brick-making, textile, and other industries. The workers were relatively successful in their wage demands, and the number of strikes, work stoppages, and boycotts increased dramatically during the 1970s and 1980s. The government-appointed Riekert and Wiehahn Commissions tried to placate both employers and workers by making a concerted attempt to deracialize the industrial relations system— expanding the number of technical and trade schools for Africans, accepting Africans in skilled jobs formerly reserved for whites,[11] easing restrictions on housing and the movement of Africans in cities, and extending full trade union rights to Africans. These recommendations, presented in 1979, were gradually implemented by the government in the next decade.

Economic and political factors beyond South Africa's control would play a major role in weakening the apartheid state's resolve. Some scholars suggest that the South African economy, like the economies of other so-called developing nation-states, could no longer function as a self-contained entity with increasing government intervention in all aspects of economic (as well as political and social) life—guaranteeing subsidies for exported goods and high tariffs on selected imported goods, maintaining exchange controls and import substitution policies, propping up a vulnerable, relatively noncompetitive, domestic capitalist sector (outside the mining industry), and encouraging domestic wage policies designed to sustain a privileged, racially stratified professional-managerial and labor force. The international economy was also increasingly under the influence of U.S.-inspired neoclassical economic policies encouraging free trade, free movement of labor, and free competition in a privatized capitalist sector relatively free of government control.

This new world economic order was "at war," as Norman Etherington puts it, "with fundamental concepts of apartheid."[12] Apartheid for these critics would not be able to withstand pressures to reform from the global economy's chief representatives —transnational corporations and banks. The new order was punctuated by metropole-dominated pricing policies, floating exchange rates and currency markets, and control over a considerable portion of the world's resources, investment capital, and new technologies for moving capital in various forms (including cultural capital like information and entertainment) back and forth across national frontiers.

South Africa's economy was showing signs of stress by the mid-1970s—burdened by the increasing costs of apartheid, ill-conceived economic policies (designed, for example, to decentralize the industrial sector and promote more protected, capital-intensive local businesses), poor export performance (especially in manufacturing exports), a small domestic market (due mainly to the low incomes of African consumers), increased foreign debt and decreased capital (especially foreign capital) investment, falling mineral prices (especially gold), and soaring oil prices.[13] The general decline in South Africa's economic fortunes had a tenuous reprieve in 1979 and 1980, but it was based entirely on a sudden increase in the price of gold in 1978. When the gold price fell again in July 1981, the economic outlook took another turn for the worse.

South Africa's economy was in a downward spiral by the 1980s. The value of the rand in relation to the U.S. dollar, for example, plummeted—from $1.29 in 1980 to $0.35 in 1985.[14] Economic sanctions imposed by the United States, the British Commonwealth (except Britain), the Nordic countries (Sweden, Norway, Denmark), the European Union, and even Japan in 1985–1986 were now having an impact on South Africa's imports and exports. South Africa was barred from importing computers as well as oil and military equipment, and embargoes were placed on key South African exports like coal, steel, agricultural produce, gold coins, textiles, and uranium oxide. Dozens of colleges and universities, twenty-three states, and more than seventy cities in the United States by the end of 1988, for example, had embarked on a "divestment" campaign designed to force American corporations to divest themselves of South African stock and force those who had operations in South Africa to withdraw from the country. Foreign firms still in South Africa began pulling out of the country—about 309 companies between 1984 and 1989.[15]

The government was now unable to obtain foreign capital from any credit agency, and the South African economy in the 1980s could not generate enough domestic capital to offset the combined impact of sanctions on imports and exports and lost foreign investment. A crisis of sorts was reached in September 1985, when the major international banks refused to grant any more extensions on debt repayments and South Africa was forced to default on its foreign debt.[16] According to Anton Lowenberg and William Kaempfer, "industrial growth," which had averaged an estimated 6.3 percent to 7.4 percent a year between 1964 and 1974, declined to 5.1 percent between 1974 and 1980, and was −0.1 percent between 1980 and 1984.[17] The real gross domestic product per capita—a key indicator of economic performance—also declined steadily, showing a negative growth rate by the early 1980s, as South Africa entered a prolonged period of economic recession.[18]

Meanwhile, 1960 witnessed the dramatic decolonization of much of sub-Saharan Africa, when fourteen ex-French colonies along with Nigeria, Somalia, and the former Belgian Congo were granted independence. Although the UN General Assembly did vote in 1966 to revoke South Africa's trusteeship over the former German colony of South-West Africa (renamed Namibia in 1968),[19] southern Africa was largely under European control in the 1960s and early 1970s. In essence, Namibia remained a South African colony, and the Portuguese colonies in southern Africa, Angola, and Mozambique, remained Portuguese. African opposition groups posed no real threat to the settler regime in Rhodesia during this period. The three British "protectorates" bordering South Africa—Basutoland (Lesotho), Bechuanaland (Botswana), and Swaziland—were granted independence between 1966 and 1968, but since they were essentially South Africa's client states they posed little threat to the apartheid government. Indeed, South Africa contributed relatively little military or financial aid to fight anti-apartheid forces beyond its borders before the mid-1970s.

South Africa's vulnerability to guerrilla attacks became more of a reality when the Portuguese government was overthrown by a military coup in 1974, and Angola and Mozambique were granted independence in 1975 (along with Guinea-Bissau in West Africa). Civil conflict erupted between opposing political groups in both countries. South Africa began spending vast sums of money on military forays in the form of large-scale air and ground attacks into Angola, and in commando raids directed against suspected ANC guerrilla installations in Lesotho, Botswana, Mozambique, Rhodesia/Zimbabwe, and Zambia. South Africa also began financing allegedly anti-marxist insurgent nationalist groups in Angola (UNITA, or the National Union for the Total Independence of Angola) and Mozambique (Resistencia Nacional Moçambicana, or Renamo). In addition, South Africa took advantage of its economic dominance in the region to extract some compliance with its political policies.[20]

South Africa's relations with its neighbors formed part of the Botha government's planned "total strategy," which was conditioned by the belief—labeled a "total onslaught"—that South Africa was a major target of the communists and the ANC was a puppet of the Soviet Union. In the climate of the Cold War in the decade following the 1976 Soweto uprising, South Africa did win a sympathetic hearing and some political support in some Western countries—especially from the United States under Ronald Reagan and the United Kingdom under Margaret Thatcher. And South Africa was able to force the ANC to abandon bases and staging areas in Zambia, and closer to home in Swaziland (a nonaggression pact signed with South Africa in 1982) and Mozambique (a nonaggression pact, the Nkomati Accord, signed with South Africa in 1984).

Nevertheless, the Rhodesian civil war, which had been dragging on for about fifteen years, dramatically shifted in favor of the African nationalists after Mozambique became independent in 1975 (providing guerrilla troops inside Rhodesia for several years with a permanent base of operations across the border). South Africa's efforts to secure a favorable settlement when Rhodesia gained majority rule four years later ended in failure. The avowedly marxist Zimbabwe African National Union under Robert Mugabe won the elections and renamed the country Zimbabwe in April 1980.

As the civil war in Angola dragged on, South Africa turned northern Namibia, where most of the country's population lived, into a virtual armed camp. South Africa was carrying on a protracted campaign against the South-West Africa People's Organisation (SWAPO), the main guerrilla force seeking independence for Namibia, and at the same time using the territory as a staging area for troops fighting over the border in Angola against a government (under the marxist-oriented MPLA, or

People's Movement for the Liberation of Angola) that supported SWAPO.

Angola became a nightmare for South Africa akin to Vietnam for the United States—draining the country of much-needed resources, demoralizing its troops, and eventually ending in military reverses at the hands of Cuban forces sent to aid the MPLA government. With air superiority, the Cubans essentially succeeded in forcing South Africa out of Angola and into a negotiated settlement. South Africa signed a set of accords in December 1988 that would give Namibia its independence in exchange for the withdrawal of Cuban troops from Angola. SWAPO, under Sam Nujoma, won the elections for an independent Namibia in March 1990.

South Africa's aggressive actions against its neighbors were prompted in large part by the ANC's success in reestablishing itself as a viable organization in exile—helping to orchestrate the worldwide antiapartheid movement from London, securing bases in Africa for military training, establishing credibility on the diplomatic circuit, and raising money from a wide range of sources to finance its operations (major donors included the Scandinavian countries, especially Sweden, the Soviet Union and its allies, and the World Council of Churches from 1969). ANC attempts to wage war against the apartheid state had little impact before the late 1970s, but compared to other exile groups the ANC (and its major ally in exile, the SACP) was better organized, and its leaders better educated, politically more sophisticated, more secure financially and apparently less vulnerable to corruption. Non-Africans were finally admitted as ANC members at the 1969 Morogoro (Tanzania) conference (although non-Africans were not elected to serve on the national executive committee until 1985), and the ANC's reading of the Freedom Charter's "revolutionary message," as Tom Lodge puts it, "remained noticeably conservative (and realistic)."[21]

The Labor Movement

The most significant response against apartheid inside South Africa during the 1970s and early 1980s was generated by workers aligned with a revived black trade union movement and students aligned with the Black Consciousness (BC) movement. There were two major trends in the growth of the trade union movement at the time—epitomized by the Federation of South African Trade Unions (FOSATU) and the Council of Unions of South Africa (CUSA).

FOSATU was an avowedly nonracial federation of independent trade unions established in April 1979. Some FOSATU union officials were whites (including the first secretary-general of FOSATU), who had been members of NUSAS (National Union of South African Students) during their student days and were involved (especially at the University of Natal) in wage campaigns launched by a NUSAS-sponsored organization called the Wages Commission. They had established industrial service organizations to help black workers organize unions and remained members of these unions after they were organized. FOSATU organized tight-knit, exclusively workers' groups at the shop floor level, encouraged the development of broadly based industrial unions, and focused on educating its workers in democratic procedures and on pursuing their economic interests, but initially it stayed clear of political involvement. By the early 1980s, FOSATU was one of the largest umbrella trade union bodies in South Africa.

The other major trade union federation was the Council of Unions of South Africa, which linked working-class interests to race and insisted on black leadership of the trade union movement. Many members were allied to BC groups, and CUSA was not so much concerned with organization as it was "with the traditionally BC strategy of encouraging assertiveness among its members."[22] CUSA claimed a membership that was half the size of FOSATU in 1982, but its adherence to BC positions appeared out of step by the mid-1980s. After walking out of unity talks with FOSATU in August 1985, CUSA lost its major union, the National Union of Mineworkers (NUM), the biggest and most powerful trade union body in South Africa. NUM rejoined the unity talks, which led to the formation of a new union federation called the Congress of South African Trade Unions (COSATU) in November 1985.

The Black Consciousness Movement in the 1970s

The origins of Black Consciousness lay in the political vacuum created in the mid-1960s after the main opposition groups had been banned and armed resistance crushed by the state. The history of the BC movement has been well documented and needs little repetition here other than to note that it developed essentially in two stages during the 1970s.[23]

The first stage, between 1969 and 1972, was generated by an attempt to establish an alternative to the dominant, nonracial, liberal discourse that had engaged generations of African nationalists. It was devoted primarily to deconstructing the language of subordination and constructing a new language, a new ideology based on the identity of being an alienated black person in a white-dominated culture. BC tried to raise up "a culture of the oppressed," Robert Fatton suggests, "as a means of transforming the whole of [black] society into a new and superior ethical order."[24] As Steve Biko, the most prominent spokesperson of the BC movement in the 1970s, put it, "Black Consciousness is an attitude of mind and a way of life. . . . Its essence is the realisation by the black man of the need to rally together with his brothers around the cause of their oppression—the blackness of their skin. . . . At the heart of this kind of thinking is the realisation by blacks that the most potent weapon in the hands of the oppressor is the mind of the oppressed."[25]

Biko was a leader of the South African Students' Organisation (SASO), formed in December 1969 by black students attending mainly segregated universities and teaching colleges created during the apartheid era. SASO remained the major BC organization, but attempts were made to expand the movement's support base beyond students with the launching of the Black People's Convention (BPC) in 1971. Two years later BPC had forty-one branches throughout the country and perhaps 4,000 members, although most were former students. The BC movement at the time operated in the open and espoused nonviolence. Indeed, the apartheid regime tolerated and in some cases actually encouraged BC activities during these years.

Black Community Programmes (BCP), launched in 1972, was an attempt to reach out to rural communities. Education and health were priorities, and BCP's main influence was in the Ciskei region of the eastern Cape. BCP operated three small health clinics and held numerous classes in literacy, homemaking, and health education.[26] But these were no more than pilot projects designed, as Anthony Marx puts it, to "convince blacks that they could solve their problems on their own, without the aid of whites."[27] For some Black Consciousness adherents, BCP's emphasis on the need for material services was in conflict with BC's focus on the need for ideological commitment. In addition, BCP needed money to support its projects, and obtaining funds from religious groups (mainly European church groups and the South African Council of Churches, the main Protestant coordinating body in the country) and even some white-owned conglomerates (including the Anglo-American Corporation) contradicted the BC movement's emphasis on self-reliance. Nevertheless, BCP helped increase membership in affiliated BC groups and employed virtually all the full-time employees: BCP had a staff of fifty, for example, in 1978, another 400 workers who were indirectly dependent on the organization, and a yearly budget of more than R500,000.[28]

In an attempt to incorporate black workers into the BC movement, the Black People's Convention launched a new trade union—the Black Allied Workers' Union (BAWU)—in 1972. Some students in SASO were skeptical that uneducated workers would be drawn to BC's ideological messages, but BAWU contributed to its own demise by focusing on consciousness-raising seminars instead of the workers' material grievances. BAWU remained small (not more than 1,000 card-carrying members) and nonconfrontational, being involved in only one of the hundreds of strikes initiated by black trade unionists between 1972 and 1976.[29]

The second stage in the evolution of the BC movement between 1973 and 1977 was conditioned by issues that effectively made the apartheid regime more vulnerable and hence more likely to resort to repressive measures to contain internal dissent. The economy slipped into recession in 1975–76, and the recession was accompanied by a dramatic halt to the creation of new jobs and a dramatic increase in unemployment —especially among African industrial workers.

The recession was paralleled by an increase in the rate of inflation. The cost-of-living index, for example, rose on average by about 12 percent a year between 1974 and 1976—the two main increases, food and transportation, being significant items in black household expenditure. In addition, the government had attempted to freeze housing for Africans in so-called white urban areas since 1968, and the shortage of African housing in the cities had assumed massive proportions by 1976. Local African municipal authorities—now under the jurisdiction of twenty-two regional Bantu Administration Boards—were unable to obtain funds from the central government or the white municipalities. To cover their own operating expenses, the administration boards began increasing township rents and service charges in 1975–1976. Urban African workers, who had won wage increases for almost a decade, were now experiencing a rapid deterioration in their modest living conditions.

South Africa also became more susceptible to international pressure to reform its apartheid policies during the 1970s. It was generated in part by events surrounding the decolonization of Angola and Mozambique in 1974–1975, by protests and demonstrations inside South Africa in support of the struggles in these ex-Portuguese colonies and in Rhodesia, and by a resurgence in guerrilla activity primarily by the ANC inside South Africa from the later 1970s.

The number of BC activists in South Africa during these years may not have been significant, but BC's ideological impact cannot be underestimated. SASO began recruiting younger students, and branches at the primary and secondary school level existed in seven cities by early 1972. As the rhetoric of Black Consciousness began to pervade urban township culture, numerous other youth groups were established—the most important being a national umbrella organization called the South African Students' Movement (SASM), which was created in April 1971 (it was then called the African Students' Movement) by students at high schools in Soweto, a huge cluster of African townships near Johannesburg. SASM soon had branches at other schools in the Transvaal, in Cape Town, in Durban, and especially in the eastern Cape.

The South African government began to crack down on the BC movement. Banning orders were issued against Steve Biko; his chief lieutenant, Barney Pityana; and six others in March 1973. Abraham Tiro, a student leader who had fled to Botswana, became the movement's first martyr when he was assassinated in February 1974. Security police stepped up their harassment of activists and a more concerted attempt was made to curb BC activities (such as confiscating the land and buildings of the Federal Theological Seminary, located near Fort Hare in the eastern Cape and a focal point of BC liberation theology). A seventeen-month treason trial was held for nine BC leaders that finally ended in December 1976 with relatively short prison sentences (five or six years) for the defendants.

The Soweto uprising of 16 June 1976 would subject South Africa once again to international scrutiny. It was initiated by a student protest march against the use of Afrikaans as a language of instruction in Soweto schools. Orchestrated to some extent by SASM and its action committee, the Soweto Student Representative Council, the protesters broadened their attack to include all apartheid authority structures, and violence soon spread throughout the country. More than 600 persons—mainly young and black—would be killed and 3,000 wounded during the next eighteen months. More than 2,000 had been detained by mid-1978, and a number would be killed in detention (including Biko), but perhaps 5,000 others left South Africa to join the ranks of the ANC and (to a much lesser extent) other exile organizations. Eighteen organizations were banned in October 1977, along with the *World* and *Weekend World* (newspapers aimed at the African market and distributed mainly in Soweto), as police and security forces tried to destroy the BC movement in the same way they had tried to destroy the ANC and other opposition groups in the previous generation.[30]

It did not work. On the international front, diplomatic relations with several key allies, including the United States under then president Jimmy Carter, were severely strained in the wake of the Soweto uprising. The UN General Assembly had already suspended the South African delegation's credentials in 1974 and given the ANC and PAC observer status. In November 1977 the UN Security Council adopted a mandatory arms embargo against South Africa—an embargo that would have an impact on South Africa's fighting capabilities in Angola, for example, ten years later. The antiapartheid movement in the United States and Europe gathered momentum from the late 1970s. The boycott of South African sports and entertainment figures further isolated the country from the outside world, while corporate shareholders passed resolutions, disrupted board meetings, and staged protests against companies with ties to South Africa.

On the domestic front, the 1976 Soweto uprising helped to mobilize mass participation against apartheid for the first time since the Sharpeville massacre in 1960. Mass participation also ended the possibility of middle-class control over the direction of the struggle. Many BC activists moved away from race-based assertiveness toward the nonracial position of the ANC, toward the Charterists (those who adhered to the principles enshrined in the 1955 Freedom Charter), and to issues of identity more concerned with social class (see below). Those still anchored to the Black Consciousness tradition found a home with the Azanian Peoples' Organisation (AZAPO), launched in April 1978, and the National Forum, an umbrella organization for an estimated 200 to 300 BC-oriented groups launched in June 1983.

AZAPO was by far the strongest of the BC organizations created after the 1976 Soweto uprising. While more militant than its predecessors, the organization was weakened by personal and ideological dissension. AZAPO tried to incorporate class analysis into its platform by redefining the working class in South Africa on the basis of color—"a race of workers" who were black—but the continued emphasis on ideas and attitudes "designed to create an exclusive racial assertiveness," as Anthony Marx points out, "came increasingly under fire as no longer being an appropriate goal."[31] The BC movement would have a more lasting ideological impact on black communities than the political impact new BC organizations would have in the post-1976 era.

The Charterist Movement in the 1980s

The Botha government's reform initiatives expanded to the political arena in the early 1980s with a temporary easing of banning and restriction orders, which allowed some veteran activists of the previous generation to return to public life. Existing censorship legislation affecting the press was also somewhat relaxed, which allowed more opportunity for mainstream commercial newspapers to cover opposition news and a more congenial climate for launching a new generation of dissident, antiapartheid publications. Attempts to silence these journalists and their publications by other means, however, increased dramatically during the 1980s.[32] Envisaging a new political dispensation for Africans living in the urban areas, the government introduced the Black Local Authorities Act in 1983—designed to establish "new" African councils in all urban African townships with essentially the same powers as so-called white municipalities.

The most significant political reform attempted by the Botha government, however, was a new constitution for South Africa. The plan was first made public in 1977, widely discussed within the National Party, first presented to white voters in 1982, and approved in a whites-only referendum in November 1983. The constitution provided for a tricameral parliament—a legislative branch with separate chambers for whites, Coloureds, and Indians. African political rights would remain restricted to the Bantustans-cum-homelands and the urban township councils. A new and powerful executive branch would consist of a state president and a president's council, which would replace the Westminster-style prime minister and cabinet. Members of the executive branch would be selected by electors drawn from the three parliamentary chambers. The white-Coloured-Indian population ratios at the time (4:2:1) ensured that whites—and the National Party—would retain control of both branches of government.

Pretoria's attempt at political reform did not end with the Black Local Authorities Act and the 1983 constitution. As pressure for change mounted inside and outside South Africa, there were intense discussions within government and National Party circles in the mid- to late 1980s to craft a new constitutional dispensation that would allow urban Africans access to political power. But these "tortured" attempts at "constitutional engineering" were doomed to failure, because "the reform strategy's primary objective," as Robert Price puts it, was "to avoid a loss of [white] control."[33] It was a classic case of too little, too late.

The reform era initiated by the Botha government only served to deepen the levels of alienation of the disenfranchised population. It took seven years before the new constitution, initiated in Parliament in 1977, was actually implemented, and there was a similar time lag between recommendation and repeal of other apartheid legislation—like the laws regulating African movement between town and countryside, laws restricting Africans from getting jobs and living in the western Cape, laws preventing blacks from entering "white" public parks, toilets, hotels, and restaurants, laws preventing marriage and sexual relations between designated racial groups.

Attempts to evade sanctions by rerouting goods to countries in Asia and Latin America that were less likely to adhere to these restraints on trade and establishing phony companies in third countries to ship South African goods abroad did little to boost South Africa's exports. The Botha government in the 1980s also tried to gain a certain measure of self-sufficiency—what Pretoria called "inward industrialisation"—with lavish promises of support to white entrepreneurs in manufacturing and black entrepreneurs working largely in the informal sector, but this renewed attempt at import substitution was a failure. In any event, it would not have solved South Africa's economic problems.

When Pretoria finally moved to start building houses and improve basic services in the urban African townships in the 1980s, the prolonged economic recession limited these efforts to a few of the most depressed townships, where the emphasis was mainly on improving conditions for the small, impoverished African middle class. Attitude surveys among urban Africans between 1977 and 1985, for example, suggest a rising tide of anger against government policies from all social groups—including skilled workers, white-collar workers, and professionals, who were the main beneficiaries of these reforms.[34]

New youth groups linked mainly to a revived Charterist movement emerged as a "central category in political opposition," as Jeremy Seekings puts it, in the years following the Soweto uprising. He suggests that youth organized in overtly political groups was a relatively new phenomenon in South Africa during this period. While the BC movement never really recovered after the state crushed the 1976–77 uprising, it served to rejuvenate the ANC at home and abroad. Student protest veterans who remained in South Africa were recognized as a key constituency by the ANC, which was far better equipped than the PAC and other exile groups to assist these activists in rebuilding credible opposition groups that in turn could work with parents in developing community civic groups and with workers in organizing trade unions. Seekings categorizes members of youth groups between 1979 and 1984 as relatively well educated products of Bantu Education—most had completed high school—with women as well as men playing an active role in opposition activities. They were politically articulate and committed to fighting all forms of apartheid authority.[35]

Among the first groups to emerge that were openly aligned with the ANC was the Congress of South African Students (COSAS), which was launched in June 1979 in the Transvaal by former students who were not interested in issues affecting the schools so much as maintaining the momentum of protest eclipsed by the state's crackdown on BC organizations in 1977.[36] COSAS remained a youth rather than a student-based organization until 1982, when membership was finally limited to students—mainly high school students. COSAS was most popular among students in urban African townships in South Africa's industrial heartland in the southern Transvaal—the so-called Pretoria-Witwatersrand-Vaal triangle (PWV)—and in the eastern Cape after school boycotts again erupted in various parts of the country in 1980. The Azanian Students' Organisation (AZASO), which was created initially by the BC-aligned Azanian People's Organisation for black students in tertiary education (at university or in the technical and teacher-training colleges), was taken over by students aligned with the Charterist movement in June 1981.

COSAS and AZASO were two examples of national student groups, but many student and other youth groups were more localized and their constituents more concerned with issues in the schools, workplace, and community. They often represented specific religious, sport, or other social interest groups, and they played a major role in helping to organize and energize the hundreds of grassroots civic groups that began to proliferate in communities all over the country from the late 1970s. These civic groups—serving a wide variety of constituencies in terms of age, gender, social class and status, religious orientation, ethnic group identity, geographical location—would anchor the resistance movement in the next decade.

Mass protests were now being organized at the local, regional, and national levels. The event that sparked the first nationwide political confrontation since the school boycotts of

1980 was the 1983 constitution. African, Coloured, and Indian communities all over the country were urged to unite in opposition against the new African urban councils and the new tricameral parliament. Delegates representing primarily civic, student, youth, women, and worker organizations—87.5 percent of 575 organizations—attended the first conference of a new United Democratic Front (UDF) in Mitchell's Plain, a Coloured township outside Cape Town on 20 August 1983. The UDF would be the umbrella body for these and a growing number of other affiliate organizations—a coalition of essentially independent interest groups, whose leadership and strength lay in individual communities.

The UDF from the beginning associated itself with the exiled ANC and the inclusive, multiclass, nonracial Charterist movement, even though the Freedom Charter itself was not officially adopted until 1985. The only criteria for admission to the UDF was adherence to a nation that included all the people of South Africa (as against the divisive strategies of Afrikaner nationalism and PAC-motivated Africanist ideology, and the ethnic nationalism of tribal authority figures), opposition to apartheid, and adherence to the main tenets of a nonracial democracy. The symbols, slogans, and protest songs, the honorary "patrons"[37] as well as the officers elected to lead the UDF embodied, and were empowered by, this historic tradition. The present would be linked inextricably with this past in the struggle for a democratic South Africa.

The security police were unable to suppress or even to keep track of all UDF activities, because the UDF to a large extent remained a decentralized federation of autonomous organizations—an alliance of hundreds of small groups, who remained closely tied to their local constituents and facilitated grassroots participation in the struggle. This was a deliberate strategy—maintained to make government action against the resistance movement more difficult. Each affiliate specialized in a particular area of political work—campaigning on civic issues like housing (e.g., Durban Housing Action Committee); mobilizing designated Indian (e.g., Natal Indian Congress) and white (e.g., Durban Democratic Association) communities; mobilizing youth (e.g., South African Youth Congress), women (e.g., Federation of Transvaal Women), and students (e.g., National Union of South African Students); organizing a particular geographical area (e.g., Port Elizabeth Black Civic Organisation); organizing special-interest groups like war resisters (e.g., End Conscription Campaign) and even detainees (e.g., Detainees' Co-ordinating Committee).

The UDF's goal was mass mobilization and not ideological conformity to any specific tradition. The UDF tried but failed to bring BC organizations under its wing, and the trade unions, wary of its loose organizational structures, for the most part also rejected a formal affiliation. On the other hand, the UDF's nonracial approach appealed to a broad spectrum of white donors inside and outside South Africa, which ensured that substantial funding was available. The UDF, for example, had a yearly budget of more than R2 million by 1987, and more than R200 million had been donated to affiliate organizations.

The fund-raising efforts of popular UDF religious leaders like Desmond Tutu, Allan Boesak, and Beyers Naude; informal contacts with the ANC and its list of European and U.S. donor agencies; and contributions from wealthy South Africans who formed a support group called Friends of the UDF "made possible," as Anthony Marx suggests, "the type of political activity for which the UDF had been formed." Halls and public-address systems were rented for mass rallies, while UDF even sold tickets for concerts it sponsored through electronic Computicket outlets in the country's major shopping malls.

Publicity campaigns on a scale never before experienced in South African opposition politics saturated South Africa's black townships with pro-UDF print and visual media. The newsletter *UDF News* circulated widely in white areas and received considerable notice in various media outlets overseas. In addition, the UDF was able to provide funding and legal expertise to defend detainees and provide a variety of services to impoverished urban and rural communities. The UDF alone had about eighty full-time activists on the payroll by 1987, and there were scores of other part-time and full-time staffers employed by affiliated groups. By this time, black communities especially in the urban areas were politicized mainly around the banner of the UDF—effectively diminishing what little impact BC-affiliated groups like AZAPO still had in these townships.[38]

The UDF was unusual in the stress it placed on accountability between leaders and their constituent communities and on campaigns that stressed the linkages between national and local issues. The support given to the refusal to pay higher rents in Soweto and Alexandra—the two major African areas in Johannesburg—was linked, for example, to low wages and unemployment, and the threat of eviction was acted upon by boycotting the businesses owned by township councillors. A similar strategy was used in the successful boycott of the 1983 urban African council elections.[39] Strikes and stayaways, consumer and local-election boycotts also broadened the participant's political consciousness. Thus students involved in a new wave of school strikes in 1983 and 1984 quickly recognized that their educational grievances were linked to other grievances affecting the community as a whole, and they joined civic groups and trade unions in protesting the community councils and the tricameral parliament.

Police fired on workers and students striking against rent hikes in African townships east of Johannesburg,[40] and a month-long battle ensued in August-September 1984 that signaled a dramatic shift in the struggle. Sixty people were killed and thousands detained, and these events sparked a virtual civil war for control of South Africa's black townships lasting almost two years.

The insurrection, as it was called, differed from other uprisings in its geographical and social diversity and intensity. In contrast to the 1976 Soweto uprising, for example, which was essentially confined to youth in the urban metropolitan areas, grassroots civic organizations affiliated to the UDF had now been established in the smaller cities and towns, and in villages throughout the countryside. Except for a small elite of businessmen, traders, and administrators serving the urban town councils and rural African reserves, "the insurrection drew support and participation from virtually the entire social spectrum of black South Africa."[41]

The urban black townships, in particular, became virtually ungovernable between 1984 and 1986. Trade union bodies like COSATU and the National Union of Mineworkers became more committed to the ANC and the political struggle (and the number of workdays lost in 1986 increased by 950 percent over the figures for 1983), consumer boycotts against perceived black collaborators and white-owned businesses escalated, and the number of students boycotting the schools, especially the post-primary schools, soared (from about 10,000 in 1983 to almost 700,000 in 1985). The rent strikes initiated in five African townships on the East Rand had spread to fifty-three African townships nationwide two years later. Rent strikes eliminated the main source of income for the urban African township councils, and thirty-five had ceased to function by July 1986.

Mass rallies were also a feature of the insurrection years, and many were organized around funerals for those killed in clashes with police and security forces—the government having banned outdoor political meetings in 1985. Crowds estimated at anything from three or four thousand to 50,000 were in attendance—listening to speeches, singing freedom songs, wearing ANC and Umkhonto we Sizwe insignia, raising flags of the SA Communist Party or the Soviet Union, displaying pictures of Nelson Mandela and other political leaders, and draping the coffins with ANC colors in mass demonstrations of defiance against all forms of apartheid authority.

The youth as a social category, according to Jeremy Seekings, were transformed in the mid- to late 1980s. The number and size of youth groups soared. The figures are not verifiable, but the South African Youth Congress (launched in March 1987), for example, claimed a membership of 500,000. While relatively well educated, politically articulate students or ex-students were still at the core of these organizations, membership broadened dramatically to include thousands of "youth"—usually males in their twenties and thirties—who were less educated, not sophisticated politically, often came from poor families, and were unemployed. They were more defiant and more likely to use the youth group as a cover to engage in criminal activities. As violence escalated, females withdrew or were excluded from participation. As the youth became more diversified, tensions within youth groups increased—as did tensions between younger and older community activists.[42]

Under the leadership of the UDF and affiliated civic organizations, black township communities initiated their own governmental structures with a layered tier of UDF national and regional executive committees, township area coordinating committees, and, at the local level, area and street committees. These committees were responsible for providing township services such as garbage collecting, sewerage and water supply, setting curfews for drinking establishments (shebeens), and creating people's parks. They also sought to settle domestic disputes, punish petty criminals, and impose discipline where needed. Special "people's courts" dealt with more serious criminal cases and political crimes, although there was much controversy over these kangaroo courts—especially in cases involving the "necklace" method of killing suspected apartheid collaborators (by setting fire to automobile tires doused with gasoline and placed around the necks of victims). The best-organized committees were in the eastern Cape, but the street committee system, as it was called, had spread to black townships in the Transvaal and the western Cape by 1986.

The committee system also worked to organize and coordinate strikes and boycotts at the local level, and served as a catalyst for other structures set up to provide educational and health services to the urban black population. To replace apartheid education and provide schooling for tens of thousands of boycotting students, UDF organizations eventually organized a National Education Crisis Committee (NECC) in March 1986. The NECC did provide alternative educational structures in many communities, even though it was limited in terms of what could be provided. Community-based responses to health problems led to UDF-sponsored health clinics and training facilities for first-aid workers. An alternative National Medical and Dental Association (NAMDA) was actually formed as early as 1982, and five years later NAMDA was planning a national health service—to replace the government's ministry of health—that would provide primary care for South Africa's black population.

The insurrection produced Africans, Coloureds, Indians and even Whites in all walks of life who were willing to confront the apartheid regime. As many scholars have noted, these years witnessed a liberated consciousness at work against the enemy. And, as orchestrated by the UDF and its allies, the ANC reemerged as "the embodiment of the tradition of liberation and the leading organization in the struggle to overthrow apartheid and white minority power."[43] Although the resistance movement still included organizations with an exclusive, Africanist orientation, most opposition groups inside South Africa had declared themselves publicly in support of the ANC and the Freedom Charter by the late 1980s.

The legislative power of South Africa's parliament by this time had been undermined by new agencies created by the Botha government as part of its "total strategy" policy. Soon after Botha took office in 1978, the State Security Council (SSC), a purely advisory body on intelligence matters, was made a key government agency and placed at the top of a new organizational structure called the National Security Management System (NSMS). The Botha government's obsession with state security was given virtually free reign in nine regional policy-making bodies called Joint Management Centres (JMCs), which by 1986 had been further subdivided into sixty sub-JMCs operating in major metropolitan areas and 448 mini-JMCs operating in local areas, including the African townships. The NSMS—a pyramidal, chain-of-command structure with the State Security Council at the top and the mini-JMCs at the base of the pyramid—virtually replaced Parliament as the key decision maker in governing South Africa. The SSC emerged as the most powerful single government policymaking agency during the insurrection crisis of the mid- to late 1980s. These "securocrats" (a reference to the elite planners within the NSMS) would orchestrate an end to the insurrection.[44]

The government declared a partial state of emergency in July 1985—the first one since Sharpeville in 1960—covering mainly areas in the eastern Cape and the Transvaal. The second state of emergency was imposed nationwide in June 1986—the first since the insurrection had begun ten months earlier. Successive states of emergency would be imposed every year thereafter until 1990. While the securocrats preached the rhetoric of reform—of reviving and restoring the community councils as viable local government units, improving living conditions in the townships and reestablishing a group of "moderate" leaders who would be given the opportunity of helping to devise a new constitutional dispensation for Africans—in practice they were intent on crushing the insurrectionists and dismantling the UDF and its allies.

The army was brought in to supplement the police force, and key UDF-controlled townships were essentially placed under military occupation. Thousands of relatively young African men recruited mainly from remote rural reserves were brought in, given a few weeks of training, and designated a municipal police force to help the town councillors reimpose apartheid rule in the townships. Eight months after the first state of emergency was imposed, more than 29,000 persons had been detained—far more than in previous crises like Soweto (when 2,430 were detained) and Sharpeville (when 11,500 were detained). The goal of the authorities was to eliminate not only the UDF leadership at the national level but also UDF-affiliate leaders at the regional and local levels; activists in the civic, student, youth, women's, and teachers' organizations; organizers of key, high-profile campaigns like those in support of political detainees and those opposed to the military draft; and young "comrades" involved in the street committees and the people's courts.

Acting under the Public Safety Act, numerous BC organizations (including AZAPO) and thirty-two UDF-aligned organizations were prohibited from engaging in any activity whatsoever and thus effectively banned early in 1988. While trade unions were not included in this list of "restricted" organizations—the authorities were apparently fearful of the impact nationwide strikes might have on an already shaky economy—COSATU, as the biggest confederation of trade unions, was banned from engaging in overt political activity.

These actions were accompanied by a wholesale assault on the civilian population. The municipal police (nicknamed *kitskonstabels*, or instant police) recruited from the rural areas— with few social ties to the urbanites and virtually no training or experience in policing—were particularly brutal. They were joined by alienated, often uneducated and unemployed vigilante groups and self-proclaimed, paramilitary "self-defence militias" intent on wreaking vengeance on those who had participated in the insurrection. They were essentially criminals whose activities had been curbed by the street committees, town mayors, councillors, and allied traders, owners of small shops and some professionals who were part of the apartheid community council system pushed aside by the UDF, traditional leaders whose authority was undermined by UDF organizers, and even some UDF malcontents who had personal grievances to settle.

There were much-publicized incidents like the bombing of COSATU's headquarters in Johannesburg in May 1987 and the virtual civil war that erupted in Natal as the powerful Zulu homeland leader, Chief Gatsha Buthelezi, and his Inkatha Party used the states of emergency to launch a reign of terror on UDF groups in the region. The majority of victims, however, were hidden from public view, because the South African press was barred from covering virtually any activity in these townships under a set of emergency media regulations issued in June 1986. Bombings, arson attacks, the ransacking of homes and offices of UDF adherents, systematic physical assaults, rape, and murder were conducted almost daily for perhaps two years in black townships throughout the country—with virtually no attempt by the authorities to arrest the perpetrators of these crimes.[45]

From the perspective of the Botha government, a surface calm appeared to return to the black townships, and there was a slight upturn in the economy in 1987 and early 1988—raising hopes that South Africa would be able to withstand international sanctions. But such confidence was short lived, as the economy again nose-dived, the government's "inward industrialization" program was not working, and two years of naked repression was not winning the war in the black townships. The UDF may have been effectively outlawed, but the level of alienation against the apartheid regime among all social groupings in the urban townships was such that little organization was needed to ignite resistance to government policies.

The organizational focus of opposition simply shifted to churches (associated mainly with the South African Council of

Churches and the Roman Catholics) and especially the trade unions, which had a combined membership of more than 1 million out of an estimated 4.6 million Africans in nonagricultural jobs in 1988. COSATU, by far the largest trade union coordinating body, was now closely identified with the ANC and the Charterist movement. Unions associated with COSATU were tightly organized, democratic, and their leaders accountable, and they now filled the political vacuum to some extent vacated by restricted UDF-affiliated organizations.

The trade unions would play a major role in maintaining the momentum of the struggle in its final stages. And COSATU in particular would demonstrate its capacity to mobilize workers in so-called political strikes in support of community grievances. Already in 1986, for example, it was estimated that 75 percent of the workdays lost to strikes were the result of workers supporting community-inspired protests—only 25 percent were disputes over wages, benefits, or working conditions. Massive strikes affecting the vital manufacturing sector of the economy not only cost the government tax revenue and hundreds of millions of rands in lost production, but the workers were willing to sacrifice their own economic interests by proclaiming their support for international sanctions. Worker demands could no longer be separated from political demands at this point in the struggle.[46]

The UDF began coordinating activities with COSATU behind the scenes, circumventing its restricted status by operating under a new name, the Mass Democratic Movement (MDM). Although the MDM was not a formal organization, it became an alliance of the ANC, COSATU, UDF, and UDF-affiliated organizations. Initiating a Conference for a Democratic Future in December 1989, the MDM sought to unite all antiapartheid organizations in opposition to the government. Although Africanist-oriented groups withdrew in protest against representatives from the homeland governments, the conference suggested that political and trade union bodies were working more closely with each other than at any other time since the 1950s.

So the UDF was by no means dead—even during the worst months of repression. More than 600 political prisoners participated in a well-organized and disciplined hunger strike in February 1989, and another campaign was launched to publicize the fact that a disproportionate number of detainees were children—40 percent were under the age of eighteen—being held without trial and often without access to attorneys. School boycotts involving students, parents, and teachers, moreover, continued unabated between 1987 and 1989.[47] An attempt by the securocrats to revive the African township councils was also a complete failure. Township elections held in October 1988 produced no candidates in some areas, despite widespread publicity, more detentions of activists, and a ban on antielection rallies. Voter turnout was only 11 percent in Soweto, which had the heaviest concentration of urban Africans in southern Africa. Even in townships where the government had built houses and tried to improve living conditions, there were very few candidates and virtually no voter turnout.

Rent strikes in the African townships seem to have continued virtually unabated; indeed, despite the states of emergency, strikes of all kinds escalated in 1987 and 1988. In commemoration of the 1976 Soweto uprising, COSATU launched in June 1988 probably the most successful nationwide general strike in South African history. It lasted three days, and 70 percent of the workers in South Africa's key manufacturing sector alone did not go to work.

While the white population were still largely insulated from events in black areas, white anxiety increased as confidence in government's ability to control the violence eroded. Wave after wave of strikes and boycotts in South Africa's urban black townships was accompanied by a dramatic increase in the number of ANC guerrilla attacks against various industrial targets, against police stations and government facilities, against suspected collaborators, and for the first time against so-called soft targets in crowded shopping malls and office buildings—in a bid to bring the war closer to the white civilian population.[48]

White support for apartheid diminished dramatically during the 1980s. Young men refused to serve in the army, the white emigration rate was rising, and more and more English- and even Afrikaans-speaking politicians (especially after 1986), students, journalists, businessmen, and other members of the white elite were ignoring the government and holding meetings with the ANC in London, Lusaka (Zambia), and Dakar (Senegal).

The National Party itself was under pressure from right-wingers increasingly disenchanted with the Botha government's reform measures, and many of them bolted to form the Conservative Party in 1982. Seven years later the Conservatives became the official opposition party with 23 percent of the parliamentary seats (and 31 percent of the white vote) in the 1989 elections. Afrikaner politicians to the left of the National Party also bolted to form a lobby group called the National Democratic Movement. Dissident National Party members along with the liberal, largely English-speaking Progressive Federal Party (PFP) formed a new, openly multi-racial party in April 1989 called the Democratic Party, which won 20 percent of the parliamentary seats (and 20 percent of the white vote) in the 1989 elections—a 9 percent gain in seats over what the PFP had accomplished in the 1987 elections.

Thus the National Party's majority in Parliament had gradually whittled away—from a high point of 81 percent of the parliamentary seats in the 1977 elections (with 66 percent of the white vote) to a low of just under 57 percent in the 1989 elections (with 48 percent of the white vote). Even within the

National Party, opinion polls suggested that by the end of the 1980s only 23 percent of the MPs and less than one-third of the white electorate remained committed to the Verwoerdian vision of grand apartheid. This would become a factor in pushing apartheid leaders toward the negotiating table in the early 1990s.[49]

Growing disillusion with the policies of the securocrats triggered a split between hard-liners and those within the Botha government who wanted to reopen communication links with black opposition groups and reestablish political and especially economic relations with the international community. The Angola-Namibia accord reached at the end of 1988 was somewhat of a triumph for this faction, because it sent a clear signal to the outside world that South Africa was withdrawing from its decades-old attempt to destabilize African governments in southern Africa. The dramatic end to the Cold War, with the breakup of the Soviet Union and the fall of communist governments in Eastern Europe in 1989 and 1990, diminished the influence of apartheid ideologues, who had maintained the ANC and its allies were part of a communist conspiracy.

P. W. Botha himself suffered a stroke and was replaced as National Party leader by F. W. de Klerk in February 1989. Botha was finally forced to resign as state president in August, and de Klerk was elected by the party caucus to replace Botha as state president in September. It was, in retrospect, a decisive turning point in the long quest for majority rule.

Toward a New South Africa in the 1990s

Talks with ANC leaders, including "secret" meetings between Botha and other key government officials and the imprisoned Nelson Mandela, had already started even before de Klerk took over as state president. In the first few months of de Klerk's administration, the National Security Management System, which had virtually governed South Africa in the mid-late 1980s, was dismantled. Walter Sisulu, ANC secretary-general, and seven other lifers were released from prison. More segregation laws, like mandating separate beaches for designated racial groups, were finally overturned after years of conflict (with the repeal of the Separate Amenities Act in 1991).

The stage was also set for de Klerk's historic announcement at the opening of Parliament in February 1990 unbanning the ANC, the South African Communist Party, and the Pan-Africanist Congress; lifting all restrictions on the UDF, COSATU, and thirty-one other organizations; releasing many political prisoners; and suspending the death penalty. The formal release of Mandela after twenty-seven years in prison, on 11 February 1990, sent an unmistakable signal to the world community that the National Party was ready to negotiate a political settlement.

The government and the ANC began holding formal talks in May 1990 and in June the state of emergency was lifted in all provinces except Natal, where fighting between ANC/UDF cadres and Chief Buthelezi's Inkatha continued. Although de Klerk ended the emergency in Natal in October, the Inkatha Freedom Party, as it was now called, would battle the ANC and its allies for control of the province for years to come.

The ANC formally announced an end to the armed struggle in August 1990, as all political prisoners were released and those outside the country allowed to return. By the end of the year, ANC president-general Oliver Tambo and other long-term exiles had returned to South Africa. The National Party announced in October 1990 that it was opening membership to all races, as did the Inkatha Freedom Party. The Mass Democratic Movement was no longer necessary, since the ANC had emerged as the most popular political party in the country. The UDF, after eight years of turbulent history as a surrogate for Congress, formally disbanded in March 1991. Mandela officially succeeded the ailing Oliver Tambo[50] as ANC president in July 1991 at the first legal national conference held in South Africa since Congress was banned in 1960.

The de Klerk government repealed virtually all the remaining apartheid laws in 1991, including those affecting land (Native Land and Trust Act of 1936), residence (Group Areas Act of 1950), and racial classification (Population Registration Act of 1950). In December 1991, "after more than a year and a half of talks about talks," as Mandela himself put it, "the real talks began."[51] The Convention for a Democratic South Africa (CODESA) would now form a new arena of struggle between the National Party and the ANC—the two major protagonists —for the next two and a half years. The debates went on at a hall in Johannesburg's World Trade Centre, while boycotts, protest rallies, marches, periodic outbursts of violence, and assassinations (the most tragic being that of Chris Hani, a former Umkhonto we Sizwe leader, secretary-general of the SACP, and one of the most popular figures in the ANC) continued in various parts of South Africa. Gradually a compromise was hammered out around a government of national unity that would embrace all political groups that had participated in the talks. The first truly democratic election in South African history was held on 27 April 1994, and the African National Congress emerged as the majority party. It was the beginning of a new era.

This collection of essays celebrates the contributions of scores of newspapers, newsletters, and magazines that confronted the state in the generation after 1960 and contributed in no small measure to reviving a mass movement inside South Africa that would finally bring an end to the apartheid era. This marginalized press had an impact on its audience that cannot be measured in terms of the small number of issues sold, the limited amount of advertising revenue raised, or the relative absence of effective marketing and distribution strategies. These journalists rendered personalities, events, and issues visible that were too often invisible and provided a voice to alienated communities that were too often voiceless. They contributed immeasurably to broadening the concept of a free press in South Africa. In no small way, the guardians of the new South Africa owe these publications a debt of gratitude that cannot be repaid.

South Africa's resistance press evolved in three distinct phases in the last generation of the apartheid regime. The first two phases are explored in three chapters by Peter Limb, James Zug, and Mbulelo Mzamane and David Howarth.

Phase one of the resistance movement inside South Africa really represented the end of a period of protest that began more than eighty years earlier. Virtually all African nationalist newspapers, which were the dominant organs of alternative news and opinion before the 1940s, had been bought out, closed down, or depoliticized in the aftermath of the Great Depression and merged with a new captive black commercial press controlled by white entrepreneurs. The only independent African nationalist publications to survive in South Africa in the 1950s and early 1960s were a few pamphlets and short-lived newsletters like *Inyaniso* (subtitled *Voice of African Youth*), *Isizwe* (Nation), *Africanist*, and *African Lodestar*—produced mainly for a limited audience of political activists in South Africa's urban African townships.

The resistance movement between the 1940s and early 1960s was represented mainly by socialist newspapers both allied to and independent of the Communist Party (banned in 1950). The ANC and Congress Alliance found an outlet in publications like *Liberation* (1953–1959) and *Fighting Talk* (1942–1963) that were nonracial, nonsectarian, and perhaps more representative of left-wing working and middle-class interests at the time. This tradition would essentially end when *Spark*, the last of a long line of newspapers in the *Guardian* stable, was shut down permanently in March 1963.[52]

Two case studies in this book illustrate the strengths and weaknesses of the protest-cum-resistance press before the mid-1960s. In chapter 2, Peter Limb seeks to interrogate a common assumption among academics and even activists that the ANC press before Congress was banned from South Africa in 1960 focused mainly on issues that were of concern to its largely middle-class audience. He offers an analysis of selected newspapers associated with Congress between 1900 and 1960 to suggest that more coverage was given to workers' grievances than is generally recognized. And those who wrote for these newspapers showed "a level of engagement with worker struggles that suggests a more complex set of attitudes toward labor."

Limb examines selected African nationalist newspapers in three periods (1900–1920, 1920–1940, and 1940–1960) and suggests that there was considerable coverage of workers' conditions during each of these periods. He argues that as African workers moved in increasing numbers to the cities and joined trade unions in the 1940s and 1950s, surviving independent African nationalist newspapers—like *Inkokeli ya Bantu* (People's Leader, 1940–1942), *Izwi lase Afrika* (Voice of the People, 1941–1942) and *Inkundla ya Bantu* (People's Forum, 1938–1951) became more militant in the support of workers' rights. Journalists were more often in direct contact with workers, who were represented "as exploited victims of an oppressive system." Workers, however, played virtually no role in running these newspapers, which "mass-produced editorials on industrial moderation as much as on the plight of labor." The plight of individual workers was "rarely portrayed," and "press images of working lives did not capture the vibrancy of working-class culture." The ANC and its press, moreover, never recognized an independent role for workers in the African nationalist movement.

There were very few publications sympathetic to the ANC and other African nationalist organizations inside South Africa that catered to African workers between the 1960s and 1980s. The multilingual *Workers' Unity*—an irregular monthly and quarterly published in Cape Town with sections in English (entitled *Morning Star*), Afrikaans, and various African languages —was the organ of the African Textile Workers' Industrial Union and a supporter of the South African Congress of Trade Unions. It survived as a trade union newspaper for about ten years between 1953 and 1963. Perhaps the best-known trade union publications in the 1970s were launched by NUSAS-sponsored wages commissions and produced independently under various titles at universities in Johannesburg, Durban/ Pietermaritzburg, and Cape Town—newsletters like *Abasebenzi* (Xhosa for "Workers"), *Isisebenzi* (Zulu edition) and *Basebenzi/ Basebetsi* (Zulu/Sotho edition), and *Umanyano* (Unity).

Several newsletters were initiated by trade unions in the 1980s. Publications sympathetic to the ANC included *CCAWUSA News*, organ of the Commercial Catering and Allied Workers Union of South Africa; *NUM News*, organ of the National Union of Mineworkers; and *FOSATU News*, organ of the umbrella Federation of South African Trade Unions. Another example was the *South African Labour Bulletin* (April 1974 to date), a monthly published in Durban by the Institute for Industrial Education (a nonprofit agency concerned mainly with urban African workers), which was also linked originally to NUSAS and the wages commission. The *SALB* supported FOSATU in the 1980s and 1990s.

James Zug in chapter 3 provides a detailed account of the final years of the *Guardian* (1937–1963)—now called *New Age* (1954–1962) and *Spark* (1962–1963)—probably the most significant socialist newspaper in South African history. Closely aligned to the ANC and its allies by the 1950s, its multiracial work force led in part by women, the weekly soldiered on in the midst of unremitting harassment and acts of violence from police and security agents. Beatings, shootings, raids, deportations, detentions, bannings, trials, jailings, and imprisonment were almost common occurrences, and Zug paints a vivid picture of the newspaper's struggle to stay alive during these turbulent years.

Virtually no other publication provided sustained coverage of opposition politics inside and outside South Africa, as well as the activities of Umkhonto we Sizwe guerrillas, after the ANC and other dissident groups were banned in 1960. While most coverage was devoted to boycotts, protests, and police raids in the cities and urban black townships, unrest in the countryside—highlighted by the peasant revolt in Mpondoland in the northeastern Transkei reserve in the early 1960s— linked *Guardian* staffers and sympathizers with events in the rural areas. Although *Spark* was finally blown out in March 1963, all this newspaper "had fought for," as Zug suggests, "reaped a bountiful harvest in the distant future of the 1990s."

Phase two of the resistance press inside South Africa is associated with the Black Consciousness movement and its press during the 1970s. Unlike African nationalist and socialist newspapers of the previous generation, BC publications did not provide news, opinion, and entertainment of general interest to its audience. *SASO Newsletter,* official organ of the South African Students' Organisation, was the most significant of these publications. *Black Review* and its companion, *Black Viewpoint,* both irregular annuals, were initiated by Black Community Programmes, but they had a very brief life. And only one issue of *Black Perspectives,* a scholarly journal designed for academics and professionals, was ever published.

As Mbulelo Mzamane and David Howarth point out in chapter 4, however, the stress on transforming consciousness, overcoming fear, and building racial pride was not limited to political and literary journals produced by the Black Consciousness movement. The ideology of Black Consciousness became a potent force in mobilizing black communities to mass action—especially among students and youth—even if the BC press had a relatively limited audience. These ideas were also found in the so-called captive black commercial press—especially in newspapers like the *World* and *Weekend World* that BC helped to reinvigorate.[53]

They argue that Black Consciousness revived resistance inside South Africa and made a very significant ideological contribution to the antiapartheid movement. BC ideology was not simply a separatist racial and cultural discourse—it referred "to certain universal values in its construction of a black identity" that would represent "a novel articulation of ideological elements in South Africa." It was not only "the young and impressionable" affected by these ideas, "but blacks in various walks of life." Through the writings of BC leader Steve Biko and his colleagues, this counterhegemonic discourse raised political awareness and constituted a major theme in African township art, song, and theater, in sport and in the churches.

Phase three of the resistance movement inside South Africa —the period covered by most case studies in this book—focuses on alternative newspapers during the 1980s and early 1990s, when the struggle was mediated primarily through the UDF and its affiliate organizations. The UDF used the media— white-owned commercial as well as resistance publications— to inform people about its activities, to establish contact with a wider audience, and to build new relationships that crossed gender, class, racial, and ethnic boundaries. The commercial press provided extensive coverage of escalating protest but did not provide its readers with the kind of political conscientizing favored by the UDF. The UDF increased its efforts to recruit support among disaffected white voters from the late 1980s and used a variety of media for this purpose—until white-controlled media outlets began providing widespread coverage of opposition politics from the end of the decade. UDF media—in the form of T-shirts, buttons, posters, pamphlets, a national newsletter (with a circulation of 25,000), advertisements in commercial newspapers announcing upcoming events, calling for the release of Nelson Mandela and reprinting the Freedom Charter, UDF-sponsored choral groups and jazz concerts—penetrated white as well as black markets, and reached African peasants even in remote rural areas.

South Africa's mainstream commercial press by the 1980s was controlled by four newspaper chains—accounting for 95 percent of daily newspaper readers and 92 percent of Sunday and weekly newspaper readers (in terms of circulation) in South Africa. The two English-language chains were the Argus Printing and Publishing Company and Times Media, Ltd. (formerly the South African Associated Newspapers group). The two Afrikaans-language chains were Nasionale Pers and Perskor. Argus and Nasionale Pers towered over their rivals, and English-language chains were the dominant presence in the newspaper world—with fourteen dailies (versus five Afrikaans dailies) and about 80 percent of an estimated 1.3 million readers in 1991. Four of the eight Sunday newspapers were owned by Argus/Times Media, three were owned by Nasionale Pers/Perskor, and one was regarded as "independent."[54] A number of these newspapers (Afrikaans as well as English), while still catering to a mainly white audience, became much more critical of the apartheid regime during the 1980s. The *Sowetan*, a newspaper intended mainly for Africans in Soweto and other urban townships in South Africa's industrial heartland, displaced the *Star* in 1991 as the largest daily in terms of circulation. Both were owned by the Argus company.[55]

Other protest outlets in the 1980s stemmed from left-wing academic and student journals, newsletters, newspapers, and pamphlets produced at white-designated universities. In addition, individuals and teams of white and black activists produced literacy texts for adults and newsletters for workers, and published oral narratives, personal memoirs, and revisionist histories documenting the struggle. Among the more interesting of these publications were magazines like *Africa South, Learn and Teach, Learning Roots,* and *Reader,* and Luli Callinicos's two-volume people's history of South Africa, entitled *Gold and Workers, 1886–1924* (1980) and *Working Life, 1886–1940* (1987). Information, ideas, and attitudes were also communicated through a variety of literary, musical, and performance texts performed in urban African townships and informal settlements.

The community press would play a central role in chronicling the history of the struggle during this period, disseminating the tactics and strategies of specific organizations, and helping to build a level of defiance in town and countryside that sustained and broadened the resistance movement. Table 1.1 offers a profile of some existing community newspapers when the insurrection in South Africa's urban black townships was at its height.

Jeremy Seekings in chapter 5 provides a convincing portrait of how media were used by the United Democratic Front and its affiliate organizations to mobilize, recruit, organize, and conscientize an ever-widening audience of black and white South Africans. He offers a profile of the UDF's own press, highlighted by national and regional versions of the *UDF News,* critically examines coverage of UDF activities by the white-controlled commercial press, and provides examples of support given to the UDF by other alternative publications and interest groups.

Seekings notes that most UDF-sponsored media production between 1983 and the second half of 1985 was geared to various antiapartheid campaigns conducted at the regional level.

Table 1.1

Resistance Newspapers, 1987

Name	Source of Finance	Claimed Circ.	Frequency	Target Area	Audience
Speak	Sales/funding from Oxfam, German Catholic Church, some small funders	7,000	One edition every two months	All parts of S.A. but mainly Durban and Johannnesburg	Zulu- and English-speaking women. Bought mainly by men
Weekly Mail	Sales and local investors	20,000	Weekly	All parts of S.A.	Left-wing intellectuals and academics: mainly white
South	Sales and donors	20,000	Weekly	West and East Cape	Readers classed African, Coloured, Asian
Indicator	Advertising	20,000	Twice monthly	Black areas in PWV	Readers classed African, Coloured, Asian
Saamstaan	Cebenco Vaskenati	18,000	Monthly	Southern Cape; Karoo; Transkei; Netherlands	Xhosa, English, and Afrikaans speakers in target area
Grassroots	Subscribers, church groups, pledges	English: 32,000 Xhosa: 18,000	Monthly	Western Cape (distributed through NGO Black Sash)	Low-income readers classed African, Coloured, Asian
New Nation	Southern African Catholic Bishops' Conference	60,000	Weekly	All Parts of S.A.	Mainly working class, from all Christian denominations

Southern Cross	S.A. Catholic hierarchy; advertising; sales	12,500	Weekly	All parts of S.A.	English-speaking Catholics
UmAfrika	Mariannhill Mission; foreign funding; sales	12,000	Weekly	Mainly Natal; parts of Transvaal and Transkei	Zulu and Xhosa speakers; also missionaries
Al-Qalam	Muslim Youth Movement; Muslim advertisers	16,000	Monthly	Southern Africa; ~100 foreign subscribers	Muslim public
Muslim News	Advertising	25,000	11 editions a year	All parts of S.A.; mainly West Cape.	98% Muslim; 2% other
Upbeat	World Universal Service, Interfund, Misereor. SACHED is publisher	30,000	10 issues a year	Through branches of SACHED to schools and youth groups	Schoolgoers
COSATU	Union affiliates and money raised independently	250,000	6 times a year	S.A. and Namibia. Distributed through affiliates	Workers in South Africa and Namibia
Saspu National Saspu Focus	Churches, affiliates			Banned	
Umtapo Focus	Foreign funders; subscriptions; individual sponsors	2,000	6 times a year	Durban and area; few to Johannesburg and Cape Province	Mainly students and trade unionists

Source: I am grateful to Keyan Tomaselli and the Centre for Cultural and Media Studies, University of Natal, for supplying this table.

As violence in South Africa's urban black townships mounted, the UDF began shifting to a longer-term strategy that was designed to sustain the struggle by improving the leadership cadre and the organization of local and regional affiliates. UDF media focused more on news about the UDF, especially in a new journal called *UDF Update* (launched in July 1985), and on political education, especially in a new journal called *Isizwe* (launched in November 1985).

UDF newsletters and pamphlets evoked the term "people's power" as a framework for "liberating" the townships, but the restrictions imposed on UDF activities by successive states of emergency in the later 1980s had an impact on UDF publications. When the UDF was effectively banned in February 1988, and the organization resurfaced as the Mass Democratic Movement, political education continued in an intermittent journal called *Phambili* (launched in April 1988).

Seekings also documents the shifts in UDF's targeted audience. The UDF was initially concerned with mobilizing Coloured and Indian opposition to the 1983 constitution and with building an organizational base among mostly urban Africans participating in the township revolts of the mid-1980s. Although individual white activists had always participated in UDF activities, the UDF began to make a serious impact on the white community as the violence escalated. UDF "calls to whites," for example, were reflected in a Cape Town newsletter (later a magazine) called *Upfront* (launched in mid-1985).

As the resistance movement broadened between 1989 and 1991, the mainstream white-controlled commercial press simply ignored government restrictions and began to report extensively on UDF/MDM and other dissident activities. *Seekings* concludes that "the UDF's access to the commercial media . . . and its own capacity to produce publications . . . helped the UDF forge fragmented networks and organizations into a nationwide movement [and] raise morale . . . reduce the space in which the government could maneuver, [and] recruit new layers of activists into political action and organization."

While more and more community newspapers were launched as the antiapartheid struggle escalated during the mid-1980s, in the eastern Cape an alternative source of news and opinion was to be found primarily in a network of local news agencies under the wing of the regional East Cape News Agencies (Ecna). Franz Krüger, one of the founders of Ecna and later group editor for the network, begins chapter 6 with a brief, critical overview of the mainstream press in the eastern Cape to demonstrate how ineffective it was in providing news about the impact of apartheid policies in the region—the most impoverished in South Africa—or about the conflict raging between the police and security forces and the antiapartheid opposition. These newspapers effectively controlled the flow of news out of this highly politicized region to other media outlets in South Africa—including the main national news agency, the South African Press Association.

In retrospect, the birth of an alternative regional news service seems almost inevitable, but constant harassment from South African and homeland security police made the task of maintaining these agencies extraordinarily difficult. (The Ciskei and Transkei, the two "independent" African homelands in the eastern Cape, each had their own security forces.) Four local news agencies were launched between 1982 and 1987—Veritas (based in King William's Town), elnews (based in East London), Albany News Agency (Grahamstown), and Port Elizabeth News (which tried several names before finally sticking with Pen).

Krüger describes in detail how the local agencies were started, who the main personalities were, what kind of news values and news stories they offered, and how they survived during the 1980s and early to mid-1990s. Ecna established a central office with Krüger as regional coordinator in early 1990, and the regional news service expanded rapidly thereafter. The new agency, Standardised News Service (SNS), started early in 1991, had twenty-four subscribers by the end of the year. Subscription rates were established for these clients, which Krüger says included alternative community newspapers, specialized publications, some mainstream newspapers (especially from the Argus group), a few independent radio stations, some foreign correspondents, and even a foreign embassy. Although other clients were still serviced on an individual basis, most revenue was now obtained from the SNS. As the subscription list expanded, the technology improved, and there was more news coverage, the price for the service rapidly increased. Nevertheless, Ecna still depended on "overseas donors" to remain financially solvent.

Throughout South Africa, Ecna was recognized as a major source for news about the eastern Cape region by the early 1990s. The staff had expanded to seventeen members, and Ecna was involved in community development and "high-quality design work for both community and commercial clients." Ecna would survive into the postapartheid era without overseas funding, but most community projects had to be abandoned and the staff reduced. Ecna today has returned to its journalistic roots and serves primarily newspapers in the eastern Cape region.

Chapters 7 and 8 focus on two of the most important community newspapers—*Grassroots* and *South*—both published in Cape Town and aimed largely at Coloured and African readers in the Cape peninsula–western Cape region. These case studies provide considerable insight into the activities of journalists working within the communities they served during the crucial decade of the 1980s.

In her study of *Grassroots*, Ineke van Kessel shows how the newspaper chronicled "the everyday struggles of ordinary people"—ranging from demanding more washing lines and how to prevent nappy rash to lower rents, rising costs of living, unemployment benefits, pensions, and the history of past struggles. Those who worked for the newspaper did not see themselves primarily as journalists but as community activists "with an unashamedly propaganda mission. While the commercial press presumably anesthetized its readership with 'sex, sin, and soccer,' the community media meant to conscientize their readers . . . to promote change through collective action."

Van Kessel comments on the contradictions within this community—the "racial divide" between Africans and Coloureds, the "ideological, religious, linguistic, generational, and socioeconomic" fault lines—a community described by *Grassroots* as "the oppressed and exploited majority" in the western Cape. The community newspaper's project was to raise political awareness and build bridges across these divides, to promote as well as broaden the horizons of populist, community-based organizations, and to function as a catalyst between the interests and concerns of local and national organizations associated with the UDF and the wider Charterist movement.

Grassroots was launched in early 1980, and the activists who were in control effectively shut down the newspaper ten years later, in August 1990—unable to survive without foreign subsidies and unwilling to transform a "struggle paper" into a professional, general-interest commercial newspaper. Van Kessel charts the development of *Grassroots* as a progressive community newspaper, but she notes that it never developed "an editorial formula to deal with conflicts and crises *within* progressive [community] organizations."

Coloured identity was negated in the effort to direct Coloureds toward a nonracial, working-class consciousness. Although *Grassroots* played "a key role in forging a community of young, educated activists," it did not succeed in unifying the Coloured community behind the UDF/ANC banner. And *Grassroots* did not have even a minor impact on Africans in the western Cape, where the vast majority were poorly educated or illiterate residents of urban townships and squatter camps "beyond the reach of newspapers." As a "product of a particular youth culture," van Kessel concludes that *Grassroots* "could hardly have made a lasting imprint on the worldview of a broad section of people in the western Cape." Nevertheless, the "ideals of popular participation have outlasted the utopian images of People's Power and continue to inspire a new breed of community media: the community radio stations of the 1990s."

Mohamed Adhikari has written a meticulous account of *South*, the other celebrated western Cape weekly during the 1980s. Intended essentially for Coloured readers, it was launched in March 1987. Adhikari offers comparisons between *South* and other community newspapers in the region at the time, and he suggests that *South* was less dependent on foreign donors, not as constricted by local community concerns, and reported more widely on issues of regional and national importance.

Adhikari places *South* in the context of South Africa between the mid-1980s and early 1990s, and he notes that most of the media activists who worked for the newspaper had professional experience on other alternative or mainstream commercial newspapers. *South* promoted the policies and activities of the UDF both in the region and nationwide, but there was no formal relationship with the front and staffers would criticize its activities on occasion. These media activists "jealously guarded" their "editorial autonomy," and "the editorial integrity of the newspaper was maintained."

Adhikari describes the tensions of trying to operate a newspaper "along democratic lines and eliminate as far as possible the usual hierarchies of the workplace"—while also adopting a professional attitude toward news reporting and adhering to a weekly production schedule. In addition, *South* was under constant internal and external surveillance during the late 1980s (there was at least one police spy on the staff for two years), and the newspaper itself was banned in May and June 1988. Adhikari maintains that "one of the great strengths of *South* lay in its ability to draw on a team of people who were committed to the antiapartheid struggle and who were prepared to make sacrifices for the newspaper."

South was intended for a nonracial, working-class audience, even though it was read primarily by the Coloured middle classes. The activists who worked on the newspaper, however, regarded "any recognition of Coloured identity . . . as a concession to apartheid thinking." This "facade" would only be lifted in the early 1990s, when "it became more acceptable to use racial terms and ethnic labels in public discourse." Nevertheless, the newspaper could not attract enough readers or advertisers to survive as a commercial publication.

South never really adapted to the shifting political climate. *South* was given a facelift with a new, more commercial layout, and the newspaper tried to broaden its audience and attract more Coloured readers with major changes in news content—focusing on consumer issues, sports, advice columns and entertainment, some international news, and a classified advertising section. A tabloid free sheet called the *Southeaster*, funded entirely by advertisers, was also launched in February 1994, but it only exacerbated financial (and managerial) problems at *South*.

South finally closed down in December 1994—unable to compete with the establishment commercial press and unable to sustain a readership within the Coloured community to support the newspaper. Adhikari maintains that *South* had a much greater impact on the antiapartheid movement in the western Cape than its circulation would indicate, but in the end the newspaper was "a product of the antiapartheid struggle and . . . never succeeded in creating a space for itself outside the struggle."

Chapters 9 and 10 focus for the most part on newspapers that were intended for a larger audience—*New Nation,* the *Sowetan, Vrye Weekblad,* and the Afrikaans alternative press. In chapter 9, Keyan Tomaselli seeks to contrast *New Nation,* a national newspaper created by the Southern African Catholic Bishops' Conference (SACBC) and aimed at a multiracial audience, with the *Sowetan,* a commercial newspaper owned by the Argus group and aimed at an urban African audience.

Membership of South Africa's Roman Catholic churches was mainly African by the 1980s, and *New Nation,* launched in January 1986, sought to provide this religious community with regional and national coverage of the struggle. The racial identity of its audience closely resembled the racial identity of South Africa's population—23.4 percent of the readers being white, Coloured, or Indian and 76.6 percent African. While *New Nation* was subsidized mainly by the church, it also sought advertisers in an ongoing but ultimately futile effort to achieve financial autonomy.

New Nation had freelance stringers throughout the country and tried to represent activists in all geographical areas, but in practice news content was dominated by stories from South Africa's industrial center in the southern Transvaal—the PWV metroplex—where most of the readers were. *New Nation,* with its offices in Johannesburg, focused on news related to UDF/ MDM and affiliated groups, trade unions associated with COSATU, church organizations, and pressure groups like the Black Sash that adhered to the Charterist position.

The *Sowetan,* launched in February 1981, was really the successor to the Argus-owned *World/ Weekend World,* which was banned in 1977, and the Argus-owned *Post/ Weekend Post,* which ceased publication in 1980 after the authorities refused to reregister them as newspapers and warned Argus that they would be banned. Tomaselli points out that Argus company personnel were essentially liberals in the South African tradition, who "understood the repression of blacks in terms of race rather than class." Argus adhered to the government's "racial classifications" in all categories of life, and the black staff of the *Sowetan* "tended to absorb this mind-set."

Thus the *Sowetan* in the 1980s analyzed struggle issues in racial terms, provided as much if not more coverage to BC groups as to UDF/MDM groups, and produced editorials sympathetic to the BC position. The *Sowetan's* readers—also living mainly in the African townships of Soweto and the surrounding PWV region—were in the top two income groups (with incomes of more than R500 a month) according to surveys, and the newspaper provided extensive coverage to African business groups. As Tomaselli puts it, "While the *Sowetan* was clearly antiapartheid, its position with regard to big business and the capitalist system as a whole was one of support."

Tomaselli compares the journalistic practices, news and advertising content, and news values of both newspapers. As a weekly, *New Nation* was more interested in issues than events and carried a far greater proportion of news devoted to politics, community civic activities, labor, and religious activities. As a daily, the *Sowetan* carried a much higher proportion of general-interest news and "followed conventional commercial reporting procedures that emphasized deadlines and news retrieved from a variety of sources—often managed news from the wire services."

The authorities seem to have been particularly harsh on *New Nation* during the repressive years of the late 1980s. Three issues were banned in February to August 1987, the newspaper itself was the first to be banned for three months (March–June 1987), and the editor (Zwelakhe Sisulu) spent 735 days of the first 1,056 days of *New Nation's* existence in detention.[56] *New Nation* and its major patron, the SACBC, were also subjected to severe criticism from a right-wing

Catholic lay movement called Tradition, Family, Property (TFP) that was spearheaded by thousands of white Portuguese who fled to South Africa from Angola and Mozambique after those countries were granted independence. TFP, backed by the apartheid government, accused the newspaper of being a "surrogate" for "the forces of communist imperialism" in South Africa. *New Nation* was forced to spend considerable time and money in defending itself and the SACBC against attacks that were sustained for most of the history of the newspaper.

In the South Africa ushered in by de Klerk's reforms, an African-owned company called New Africa Investments, Ltd., bought the *Sowetan* from the Argus company in 1993. Even though many staffers "remained within the orbit of the evolving Black Consciousness movement," the new owners, apparently under pressure from the ANC, ensured that the *Sowetan* would support Congress in the future. *New Nation* was also sold to New Africa Investments by the SACBC, which stopped funding the newspaper, in 1995. *New Nation* was forced "to tone down [its] socialist content," but the newspaper only lasted for about two years before it folded in May 1997. The *Sowetan* was a commercial success, according to Tomaselli, because the newspaper "managed its affairs by submitting to the demands of whatever market player obtained the greatest return for its investment."

Several militant, antiapartheid Afrikaans publications were also launched during the 1980s. In chapter 10, George Claassen undertakes the rather daunting task of both providing a profile of the mainstream commercial Afrikaans press and examining the emergence of new Afrikaans organs of news and opinion that challenged, confronted, and ultimately played a significant role in undermining the apartheid order. He focuses on four of these publications—*Die Suid-Afrikaan, Vrye Weekblad, Saamstaan,* and *Namaqua Nuus.*

Claassen begins with a sketch of establishment Afrikaans newspapers—stressing the "symbiotic relationship between Afrikaans publishing houses and the National Party" before the 1980s—and the birth of right-wing publications opposed to the party's modest reforms of apartheid policies. Claassen then examines *Die Suid-Afrikaan* (launched in Spring 1984) and *Vrye Weekblad* (launched in November 1988) and their various offshoots—the two most representative Afrikaans alternative publications in the last decade of apartheid rule. The list of leading writers and financial supporters, especially in the case of *Die Suid-Afrikaan*, "reads like a who's who of white and black, mostly Afrikaner, verligtes"—enlightened Afrikaners without "political links" who embraced "an open society, equality and a peaceful settlement in South Africa."

Both *Die Suid-Afrikaan*, a magazine, and *Vrye Weekblad*, a newspaper, tried to deconstruct the Afrikaans language in an effort to divorce it from apartheid ideology. They used new terms to undermine racial categories: readers of *Die Suid-Afrikaan*, for example, were called Afrikane ("from Africa"), which included all South Africans, instead of Afrikaners (Africans), which was limited to white, Afrikaans-speaking South Africans. "This was a significant linguistic innovation," as Claassen suggests, "because many conservative white Afrikaners refused to allow Coloured Afrikaners—now the majority in the Afrikaans-speaking community—to be called Afrikaners." *Vrye Weekblad* would go even further with its use of "a colloquial mix" of oral, slang Afrikaans, English and various African languages, which was "more adventurous, far more abrasive, and even reckless." As Claassen puts it, *"Vrye Weekblad* opened up the sounds and faces of Afrikaans to its readers—the Afrikaans of the Cape Flats, the Afrikaans of Namibia, the Afrikaans that had long been marginalized because it did not belong to the official Afrikaans of the rulers."

Die Suid-Afrikaan lasted more than ten years—the final,

two-month edition was dated December 1995/January 1996 —but the subsidies had dried up and the magazine did not have enough subscribers to continue publishing. *Die Suid-Afrikaan* was essentially aimed at the Afrikaner professional and literary elite, but the intellectual content of its articles, supplements, and special editions was "free of academic jargon" and the various issues discussed "stimulated debate about South Africa's political and social problems as no other Afrikaans publication ever did."

Vrye Weekblad under its long-time editor Max du Preez was a self-styled crusading newspaper that broke new ground in the Afrikaans press by publishing stories, interviews, and photos of banned individuals and organizations, exposing the horrors of security police "death squads" and "documenting planned terrorism by right-wing groups," and revealing the existence of a secret "Third Force" that was deliberately sabotaging the peace process after talks with the ANC and other unbanned organizations began in the early 1990s. *Vrye Weekblad's* brand of advocacy journalism was calculated to place the newspaper on a collision course with the apartheid regime. Indeed, *Vrye Weekblad* itself made headlines in other publications for continually defying the censorship laws.

Claassen chronicles the life and times of the newspaper and assesses its role in the Afrikaans-speaking community for more than five years (the last few months as a news magazine) before it finally folded in February 1994. In addition to political reporting, the newspaper's book pages and supplements, according to Claassen, "were the best in Afrikaans publishing at the time." *Vrye Weekblad* was also involved in popular music— sponsoring a European-African arts festival in 1991 and producing a supplementary jazz magazine entitled *Two Tone*, which "introduced its mainly white, Afrikaans-speaking readers to black culture in South Africa."

Although *Vrye Weekblad* was an innovator in layout and design (its advertising posters alone are now collector's items) and tried to reach a wider audience, four out of five of the mainly white readers were university graduates (and half of them had more than one degree). This was not the case with *Saamstaan* and *Namaqua Nuus*, two community newspapers aimed mainly at Coloured and African working-class readers. *Saamstaan* circulated mainly in the southern Cape–Karoo region and *Namaqua Nuus*, as the title suggests, circulated mainly in the northwestern Cape–Namaqualand region.

Saamstaan was launched in February/March 1984 initially to protest the 1983 constitution and its tricameral parliament. Originally a project of the *Grassroots* community newspaper, *Saamstaan*, which was published mainly in Afrikaans with some English and Xhosa stories, "quickly established itself as a voice of the local, mostly poor, working-class community." *Namaqua Nuus*, originally a project of *Die Suid-Afrikaan*, "concentrated more on hard local news for towns in its distribution area." Launched in September 1988, it was also published mainly in Afrikaans.

Saamstaan (literally, Let us stand together) was far more confrontational than *Namaqua Nuus*, and the militant rhetoric of its Coloured and African journalists made this newspaper even more vulnerable to attacks from the security police. Whereas "*Namaqua Nuus* reporters could talk to the police and get comments from them on news events," according to Chris Gutuza, a mentor for both newspapers, "this was out of the question at *Saamstaan*, where the police were . . . part of the system against which the newspaper was fighting."

Both newspapers were distributed free until after 1990, when "donor money started drying up." *Namaqua Nuus* did carry advertisements from early 1989 and had a small classified section, but it was not enough to sustain the newspaper. The

Nuus survived for slightly more than six years before it closed down in October 1994, and *Saamstaan* ceased publication two months later.

No summary of the resistance press in South Africa would be complete without at least mentioning some other publications involved in the struggle in the last three decades of the apartheid era. They include national student newspapers like the *National Student* and later *SASPU International*, local student newspapers like *Inquiry*, popular journals aimed mainly at academic and student activists like *Work in Progress*, publications representing religious communities other than Christian such as Durban's Muslim newspaper *Al-Qalam* and Cape Town's *Muslim News*, small newspapers and newsletters serving local communities like *Ilizwi LaseRhini* (the Grahamstown Voice), "homeland" publications like *Isaziso* (Bulletin), a Transkei weekly in English and Xhosa under the courageous editorship of Maxon Vuyani Mrwetyana,[57] and publications representing the many antiapartheid pressure groups like *SASH* (published by the women's group Black Sash) and *Out of Step* (published by the End Conscription Campaign).

Most of the newspapers featured in this book were at least partially subsidized by external funding agencies. When that subsidy was gradually withdrawn in the years immediately leading up to the 1994 elections, very few alternative publications survived. The last chapter features a publication that was not subsidized. Christopher Merrett and Christopher Saunders focus on the *Weekly Mail* between 1985 and 1994—the "flagship" in the struggle against apartheid during those years and the only alternative newspaper that continues to thrive in the postapartheid era. The *Weekly Mail* was launched in June 1985 by a group of dissident journalists left jobless by the demise of two liberal mainstream newspapers, the *Sunday Express* and especially the *Rand Daily Mail.* The new *Weekly Mail* with its "social-democratic" political perspective "became in a

The cover of a "Free the Press" booklet produced by South Press Services, depicting front pages of selected newspapers from South Africa's resistance press in the 1980s.

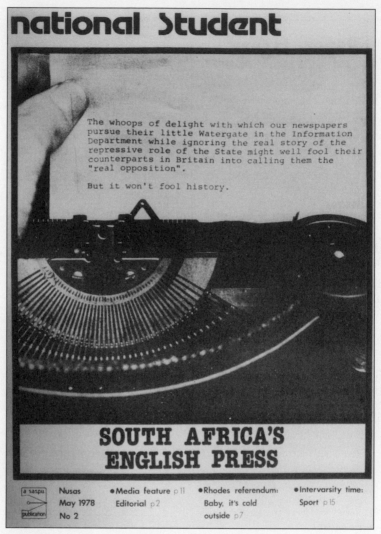

National Student, an intercampus newspaper produced by the National Union of South African Students, was one of two official student publications in South Africa banned permanently in May 1979.

Inquiry

Vol 3 1980

GRAHAMSTOWN
The Unsettled City

Published by
Rhodes University Department of Journalism   and   The South African Institute of Race Relations

A few academic departments in South Africa's universities produced intermittent publications that covered local struggles. This issue of *Inquiry*, entitled "Grahamstown: The Unsettled City," was produced by Rhodes University's Department of Journalism in 1980 and banned for possession as well as distribution.

Ilizwi LaseRhini 5c

Grahamstown Voice   March 1984 Vol 8 No 1

Lumkela i'passport' yase Ciskei

KWINYANGA kaFebruary iRhini Council iye yavumela oonomazakuzaku baseCiskei ukuba baze kwiholo zoluntu ngenjongo zokunika abantu ipassport yaseCiskei. IGRACA engumlomo wabantu iye yakhupa amaphepha icebisa abantu ukubaiifoto zabo zakufakelwe isitampo saseCiskei. Nakwiintlanganiso zeGRACA ezathi zalandela abantu bayikhaba ngawo omane le nkqubo imdaka neyantlukwano.

IFUMANEKA NJANI IPASPOTI YASE MZANTSI-AFRIKA?

Nawuphi naumntu oMnama waseMzantsi - Afrika uvumelekile ukuba athathe incwadi yokuhambele amazwe ebizwa ngokuba yi South African Travel Dokument.

Le ncwadi ikuvumela ukuba ungene kumazwe anje ngala alandelayo: Bophutatswana. Lesotho, swaziland, Zimbabwe. Transkei and Ciskei. Le ke yeyona ncwadi abantu abaMnyama baseMzantsi-Afrika ekufuneka befune yona ukuze bakwazi ukuhambela amanye amazwe kunye namanye amazwana.

Qaphela!

Lumkela ukuthatha incwadi yokuhambela amazwe evela eCiskei okanye evela koonozaku-zaku baseCiskei abavelaeBhayi.

Kanti lumkelanokuqhathwa apha aRhini ngabantu abasebenzela iCiskei okanye abo bancedisa ekuqhubeleni phambili lo msebenzi umdaka wokuphelisa ubumni bakho apha eRhini naseMzantsi-Afrika kwilizwe lakho lokuzaiwe.

(hamba.ku "page 2")

UDF publicity secretary Terror Lekota. Signature campaign news on pages 8 and 9

INSIDE: Civic News p3 and 5   Toivo p7   Buses p4

Ilizwi LaseRhini/Grahamstown Voice was the product of a collaborative effort between Rhodes University students and local African township residents. Published mainly in Xhosa, it was typical of the many newsletters produced by or for black communities at the local level.

minor way a newspaper of record"—issuing a weekly "Apartheid Barometer" that documented people who were detained and publications that were banned, covering events in the African townships, exposing the activities of the security forces inside and to a lesser extent outside South Africa, and providing "deeper coverage than the mainstream press on extraparliamentary organizations, labor and trade unions, and the nonracial sport movement."

The *Weekly Mail* quickly "acquired a reputation," Merrett and Saunders suggest, "as a newspaper that challenged the legitimacy of the regime and documented an emerging protest culture." They provide numerous examples of how the newspaper was able to sustain this reputation during the worst years of repression and continue to fulfill its mission of "giving its largely white readers an idea of what was happening in the black townships, of what blacks were thinking and how they were suffering." While other alternative publications faced severe police harassment and even closure during the states of emergency, the *Weekly Mail* "drew attention to censorship, while keeping sufficiently within the law to survive." The newspaper was forced to suspend publication for one month, November 1988, but a "Wail dammit" sympathy campaign gained support from businesses with international connections and with the foreign diplomatic corps. Outside pressure, especially from the British government, apparently offered some measure of protection from the security police and other forms of government interference.

Weekly Mail's readership was mainly white "slumpies," as they were called: "slightly left, upwardly mobile professionals." The newspaper cost R3 an issue by 1992, which was high even for the mainstream press, and circulation was rarely above 20,000 an issue. Nevertheless, the newspaper "had an influence out of all proportion to its circulation." While the *Weekly Mail* focused on political news, it also had "a sizeable arts section."

The editors were pioneers, moreover, in the use of desktop technology in editing, laying out, and designing the newspaper.

While committed to a democratic South Africa, the *Weekly Mail* always remained independent of specific opposition groups—a rarity in the resistance press during this period. Although the newspaper supported the UDF/ANC alliance, for example, it did not hesitate to cover "some of the less savory aspects of the liberation struggle." Because the *Weekly Mail* apparently never received overseas funding, it was largely dependent on advertising to survive as a commercial newspaper. Thus the *Weekly Mail* accepted human rights advertisements from the Shell company in violation of the sanctions campaign, for example, even though the same advertisements were rejected by *New Nation*.

The *Weekly Mail* briefly sought to retool itself as a daily following de Klerk's reforms, but that newspaper folded in less than three months in September 1990. The collapse of the *Daily Mail*, according to Merrett and Saunders, had significant ramifications for the *Weekly Mail*. The newspaper had moved to new offices, acquired new equipment, and owed a large sum of money to the *Daily Mail*'s printers, a subsidiary of the Argus company. While the *Weekly Mail* would retain its reputation as a probing, investigative newspaper, the "editors were less prepared to take risks" in the early years of the post-apartheid era.

The *Weekly Mail* began an association with the *Guardian*, a British daily, and the *Guardian*'s weekly international edition was integrated with the *Weekly Mail* edition in 1992. Renamed the *Weekly Mail and Guardian* in July 1993 (later shortened to the *Mail and Guardian*), the newspaper would continue to be "jealously protective of its editorial and financial independence." The *Weekly Mail* worked hard "to demystify the ANC" for its white readers, although the *Mail and Guardian* would become more critical of the ANC-led government after the April

1994 election. As Merrett and Saunders conclude, "The *Weekly Mail* not only worked for a new democratic order; it helped, in a small way, to bring it about."

Notes

1. The guerrilla arm of the PAC was Poqo (a Xhosa word meaning "pure" or "alone.") Poqo was more violent and more visible than MK inside South Africa during the 1960s. T. Lodge, *Black Politics in South Africa since 1945* (London: Longman, 1983), 241.

2. For a more detailed assessment of the resistance movement in urban and rural South Africa during this period, see Lodge, *Black Politics in South Africa*, chaps. 10–11. The term *black* in this book refers to apartheid South Africa's racially designated African, Coloured, and Indian (or others of Asian origin) population. The term *white* refers to apartheid South Africa's racially designated European population. While discussion of these terms now seeks to identify all persons in South Africa as Africans—some being black Africans and some being white Africans—racial identities, and ethnic identities among Africans (especially the Zulu), persist in the postapartheid era. Most opposition groups within the antiapartheid movement until at least the mid- to late 1980s, moreover, were organized along racially designated lines.

3. Two recent studies provide a useful analysis of the main political protagonists during the period. For the National Party, see D. O'Meara, *Forty Lost Years: The Apartheid State and the Politics of the National Party, 1948–1994* (Athens: Ohio University Press, 1996). For African opposition groups, see T. G. Karis and G. M. Gerhart, *From Protest to Challenge: A Documentary History of African Politics in South Africa, 1882–1990*, vol. 5, *Nadir and Resurgence, 1964–1979* (Bloomington: Indiana University Press, 1997).

4. See S. B. Greenberg, *Legitimating the Illegitimate: State, Markets, and Resistance in South Africa* (Berkeley: University of California Press, 1987).

5. I make this argument with specific reference to the Ciskei reserve as a case study in my book *Power and Resistance in an African Society: The Ciskei and the Making of South Africa* (Madison: University of Wisconsin Press, 1993), chap. 10.

6. The last vestiges of Coloured and Indian, as well as African, voting rights in South Africa's provinces—namely the Cape and Natal—were also abolished. The Coloureds were to be represented by a consultative body called the Coloured Persons Representative Council (est. 1968) and the Indians by a South African Indian Council (est. 1964). Restrictions on the migration of Africans to the western Cape, declared a Coloured "labor preference" area, were enforced. Indian "labor preference" areas were also envisaged for parts of Natal, and Indians remained barred from living and working in the Orange Free State.

7. While hundreds of thousands of Coloureds and Indians and even some whites (who were usually well compensated) also had to vacate areas designated for other population groups, Africans were the main victims. The removals were conducted on a scale unparalleled anywhere else in Africa. In the metropolitan areas alone, more than 3.5 million Africans were forced to leave their homes between 1960 and 1983, and almost 2 million others were scheduled for "resettlement." Africans jailed for pass law violations, for example, soared to 621,600 a year on average between 1965 and 1970, and it was estimated that 4.1 percent of the total African population (10.2 percent of the working-age population) was actually in jail in 1969 and 1970. Greenberg, *Legitimating the Illegitimate*, 48; L. Platzky and C. Walker, comps., *The Surplus People: Forced Removals in South Africa* (Johannesburg: Ravan, 1985).

8. R. Hunt Davis Jr., ed., *Apartheid Unravels* (Gainesville: University of Florida Press, 1991), 4 ("Introduction: Apartheid Unravels"); Switzer, *Power and Resistance*, 346 (table A10.1a). The number of Africans migrating to the cities accelerated during the 1980s. By 1991 about 58 percent of the African population were living in urban or peri-urban areas (39 percent of these were living in South Africa's thirteen metropolitan areas). SAIRR, *A Survey of Race Relations in South Africa, 1991–1992* (Johannesburg: SAIRR, 1992), 330.

9. The proportion of economically active Africans in manufacturing rose from 7.9 percent in 1960 to 14 percent in 1980. A. W. Marx, *Lessons of Struggle: South African Internal Opposition, 1960–1990* (New York: Oxford University Press, 1992), 193.

10. The number of Africans in universities in South Africa increased from 515 in 1961 to almost 3,000 by 1972. Five ethnic universities had been established for Africans in the reserves-

cum-homelands by the 1980s—one for designated Xhosa in the Ciskei (at Fort Hare, the only nonracial university created specifically for Africans in the preapartheid era); one for designated Xhosa in the Transkei; one for designated Zulu in Zululand; one for designated Sotho, Venda, and Thonga (University of the North) from the Orange Free State and the Transvaal; one for designated Tswana in Bophuthatswana. A new university called Vista, headquartered in Johannesburg, was launched for Africans in urban metropolitan areas in 1981. Some Africans by that time were also being admitted to graduate programs at Afrikaans-language universities and to certain professional programs, such as the University of Natal Medical School. The total African university enrollment had increased to 18,289 by 1980 (including Fort Hare but excluding other homeland universities), although at least 60 percent of these students were studying by correspondence through the University of South Africa (UNISA). Total African university enrollment had soared to 100,632 a decade later—and the number of Africans enrolled in the technical colleges (technikons) had increased from 545 in 1980 to 16,283 in 1990. Africans enrolled at traditional white-designated universities had increased more than sevenfold, to almost 7,500 (excluding UNISA), between 1980 and 1990. Compulsory education was required of Indians (from 1973) and Coloureds (from 1976) but not Africans. Marx, *Lessons of Struggle*, 41; M. Lipton, *Capitalism and Apartheid: South Africa, 1910–84* (Totowa, N.J.: Rowman and Allanheld, 1985), 61; SAIRR, *A Survey of Race Relations in South Africa, 1981* (Johannesburg: SAIRR, March 1982), 379; and SAIRR *Survey, 1991–1992*, 217–18, 222.

11. Africans had been allowed training as artisans in the reserves and adjacent border areas from 1971, and job reservation was abandoned in some white industrial unions (like steel and engineering) in 1978. The job color bar was abolished in all nonmining industries in 1981.

12. N. Etherington, "Explaining the Death Throes of Apartheid," in *Peace, Politics, and Violence in the New South Africa*, ed. N. Etherington (London: Hans Zell, 1992), 116.

13. OPEC, the consortium of leading oil-producing countries, raised the price of crude oil five times between 1971 and 1975. OPEC also agreed to impose an embargo on oil exports to South Africa in November 1973, but it was not really effective until the fall

of the shah of Iran in 1979. The UN from December 1975 also adopted yearly resolutions calling for a worldwide embargo on the export of oil to South Africa. On the impact of the oil embargo, see A. D. Lowenberg and W. H. Kaempfer, *The Origins and Demise of South African Apartheid: A Public Choice Analysis* (Ann Arbor: University of Michigan Press, 1998), chap. 8.

14. James Cobbe, "South Africa and SADCC: Economics of the Southern African Region," in Davis, *Apartheid Unravels*, 171.

15. R. M. Price, *The Apartheid State in Crisis: Political Transformation in South Africa, 1975–1990* (New York: Oxford University Press, 1991), 65–69, 220–33.

16. De Klerk achieved a renegotiation of part of the international debt in 1989—a gesture that undoubtedly helped advance the reform process.

17. Lowenberg and Kaempfer, *Origins and Demise of Apartheid*, 206 (note 13). These are value-added estimates based on 1975 prices. The authors conclude that apartheid was "enormously expensive and ultimately unsustainable," and that "South Africa's rulers brought upon themselves the collapse of apartheid . . . although external events were important in accentuating domestic weaknesses" (196).

18. South Africa experienced a nearly 5 percent increase in GDP per capita in 1980, but GDP shrank below zero in 1982 and stood at −4 to −5 percent by 1985. The government, deeply committed to funding regional and domestic military and security forces in the 1980s, could not implement its own plans to establish middle-class communities in the urban African townships. The money was simply not available to build schools and houses and electrify the townships without a radical reallocation of existing resources. Price, *Apartheid State in Crisis*, 157–59.

19. The vote was ratified by the International Court in 1971.

20. For analyses of South Africa's strategy in southern Africa from the mid-1970s, see Price, *Apartheid State in Crisis*, 38–45, 92–95; Pearl-Alice Marsh, "Decolonization in Southern Africa and the Labor Crisis in South Africa: Modernizing Migrant Labor Policies"; Cobbe, "South Africa and SADCC"; Allen Isaacman, "Conflict in Southern Africa: The Case of Mozambique"; and Patrick O'Meara, "South Africa's Contradictory Regional Goals," in Davis, *Apartheid Unravels*, 142–64, 165–81, 182–212, 213–27.

21. Lodge, *Black Politics*, 301.

22. Marx, *Lessons of Struggle*, 199.

23. The following paragraphs on the BC movement are based on G. M. Gerhart, *Black Power in South Africa: The Evolution of an Ideology* (Berkeley: University of California Press, 1978), chaps. 8–9; S. C. Nolutshungu, *Changing South Africa: Political Considerations* (Cape Town: David Philip, 1983), chaps. 5–8; R. Fatton Jr., *Black Consciousness in South Africa* (Albany: State University of New York Press, 1986); Marx, *Lessons of Struggle*, chaps. 2–3.

24. Fatton, *Black Consciousness*, 67.

25. S. Biko, *I Write What I Like* (London: Bowerdean Press, 1978), 91–92.

26. Biko worked for BCP in its Durban office for seven months before he was banned in March 1973, after which he directed BCP activities in the eastern Cape for more than two and a half years from his home in King William's Town. BCP's biggest health clinic was located five miles outside King William's Town.

27. Marx, *Lessons of Struggle*, 55.

28. Nolutshungu, *Changing South Africa*, 191, 203 (note 16).

29. BC groups had limited contact with black workers. SASO created the Black Workers' Council in 1972 to organize workers, but their main achievement was the Union of Black Journalists, a small group limited almost entirely to newspaper men and women working in Johannesburg.

30. Black Community Programs was not banned until July 1978.

31. Marx, *Lessons of Struggle*, 87, 101.

32. See esp. chaps. 6–10; T. Lodge and B. Nasson, *All, Here, and Now: Black Politics in South Africa in the 1980s* (Ford Foundation and the Foreign Policy Association: South Africa UPDATE series, 1991), 32.

The Botha government did try to constrain the press with a Commission of Inquiry into the Mass Media—the so-called Steyn Commission (Justice M. T. Steyn was chair of the commission)—appointed in June 1980. The Steyn Commission's first report, published in April 1980, dealt with relatively noncontroversial press security matters. The Steyn Commission's second report, published in 1982, was highly critical of the press. There were two major proposals in the report—one to control journalists by licensing them like doctors and lawyers and establishing a register of licensed professionals that they would be compelled to join, and one to control the press by establishing a new, legislated press council that newspapers would be compelled to join. The Steyn Commission report triggered a storm of protest and the proposals were essentially dropped. The government did pass a Registration of Newspapers Amendment Act (Act 98 of 1982) that required all publications registered as newspapers to be members of a press council (the bill initially proposed a government-controlled press council but after more protests this was changed to a voluntary, nongovernment press council). Newspapers that refused to join could lose their registration certificate—without which they could not operate. The mainstream newspapers formed their own Media Council in 1983, so they were exempted from the original legislation embodied in the Publications Control Act (1974). The two major journalist associations—the mainly white South African Society of Journalists and the mainly black Media Workers' Association of South Africa—and most of the alternative newspapers launched during the 1980s, however, refused to join the new council. Radical newspapers were vulnerable because the government (in practice, the minister of home affairs) could withhold registration of a newspaper (under the Newspaper Registration Act) that refused to cooperate with the Media Council. For a summary of regulations affecting the press, see G. S. Jackson, *Breaking Story: The South African Press* (Boulder: Westview, 1993), chaps. 5–6.

33. For more detail on the government's attempts at political reform during the 1980s, see Price, *Apartheid State in Crisis*, 134–46. The separate parliaments would have exclusive control only over certain domestic matters, such as education.

34. Ibid., 153–54 (and table 5.1). The "truly angry" respondents in these surveys rose from 39 percent of the total in 1977 to 66 percent in 1985.

35. J. Seekings, *Heroes or Villains? Youth Politics in the 1980s* (Johannesburg: Ravan, 1993), chap. 2.

36. COSAS adopted the word *Congress* to emphasize its pro-ANC stance, although underground ANC supporters from Botswana had advised against it. Jeremy Seekings, e-mail communication to author, 29 June 1999.

37. Three UDF "patrons" were profiled publicly as the leadership cadre—Allan Boesak, Albertina Sisulu, and Archie Gumede—but the real organizers of the UDF were to be found in the myriad of resistance groups being formed at the local community level. Boesak, a

senior churchman in the Dutch Reformed Church, had emerged as a key theological opponent of apartheid by the 1980s. During these years he also served as president of the World Alliance of Reformed Churches and as vice president of the South African Council of Churches. Boesak was instrumental in calling for the creation of the UDF, and he became the patron of UDF activities in the Cape. Albertina Sisulu, wife of jailed ANC leader Walter Sisulu, was prominent in the ANC Women's League and president of the South African Federation of Women. She became the UDF patron in the Transvaal. Gumede, a lawyer who had been active in the ANC during the 1940s and 1950s, reemerged as the patron of UDF activities in Natal.

38. On the success of fundraising and services provided by the UDF, see Marx, *Lessons of Struggle*, 138–46; on fighting between the UDF and AZAPO, 172–75.

39. Price, *Apartheid State in Crisis*, 182.

40. The strikes occurred in African townships on what is called the East Rand—Rand in this instance being a short term for the Witwatersrand, which embraced Johannesburg and its environs.

41. For details of the 1984–1986 insurrection, see Price, *Apartheid State in Crisis*, 192–215.

42. Seekings, *Heroes or Villains?* chap. 3.

43. Price, *Apartheid State in Crisis*, 198.

44. Ibid., 86–87, 252.

45. Journalists who did not obey the regulations were subject to a R20,000 fine or ten-year prison sentence, and the offending newspaper or magazine could either be closed down or the publication suspended. Foreign journalists were denied visas and work permits to enter the country in a bid to prevent all print and especially television coverage of township activities. On efforts to destroy the resistance movement between 1986 and 1988, see Price, *Apartheid State in Crisis*, 251–65.

46. The tensions between ANC/UDF- and PAC/BC-oriented organizations in the political arena were mirrored by tensions between COSATU and its counterpart, the National Council of Trade Unions (NACTU), in the trade union arena. While the ideological differences between the two groups were never as polarized as government and mainstream media depicted them, COSATU and NACTU (formed in October 1986) were not able to resolve their differences.

The political affiliation of members and officials within NACTU was mainly with AZAPO or the banned PAC, and whites were specifically excluded from the executive committee. On trade union activities in the political arena during these years, see Marx, *Lessons of Struggle*, chap. 6.

47. Price, *Apartheid State in Crisis*, 268, 270. According to government reports in 1988, for example, 400,000 African high school students alone boycotted classes, and 917 African primary and secondary schools experienced "unrest and disruption."

48. ANC guerrilla attacks inside South Africa rose more than 600 percent in four years (from 45 in 1984 to 281 in 1988). Ibid., 269 (fig. 8.2).

49. Ibid., 236–45 (esp. figs. 7.5 and 7.6).

50. Tambo had suffered a debilitating stroke in London in 1989 and he died in April 1993. The ANC gave him what amounted to a state funeral.

51. N. Mandela, *Long Walk to Freedom: The Autobiography of Nelson Mandela* (Boston: Little, Brown, 1994), 517.

52. For case studies of protest publications during this era, see Switzer, *South Africa's Alternative Press: Voices of Protest and Resistance, 1880–1960* (Cambridge: Cambridge University Press, 1997), esp. chaps. 7–11.

53. Two researchers working independently of each other, for example, concluded that the *World* had become a "serious" political newspaper during the Black Consciousness era. Cf. T. M. French, "The *World*: A Content Analysis," (Rhodes University, Department of Journalism and Media Studies, 1977, unpublished paper); F. St. Leger, "The *World* Newspaper 1968–1976," *Critical Arts: A Journal for Media Studies* 2, 2 (1981): 27–37.

54. Jackson, *Breaking Story*, 31–33. Although *Ilanga*, a Zulu-language newspaper in Durban, was not owned by the major newspaper chains in 1991, it was not really "independent," as Jackson assumes. *Ilanga* was bought by an Argus subsidiary (World Printing and Publishing Company) in 1962, and the newspaper's title was shortened from *Ilanga lase Natal* to *Ilanga* in 1965. The newspaper was placed under the direct control of the Argus company in 1976. L. and D. Switzer, *The Black Press in South Africa and Lesotho: A Descriptive Bibliographic Guide, 1836–1976* (Boston: G. K. Hall, 1979), 39. *Ilanga*,

closely linked to Chief Buthelezi and the Inkatha movement in the 1980s, was bought by Inkatha in April 1987.

55. Jackson, *Breaking Story*, 32. On developments within the mainstream press in the postapartheid era, see the case study by Sean Jacobs on the media's response to the 1999 election. S. Jacobs, "The Media," in *Election '99: South Africa*, ed. A. Reynolds (Cape Town: David Philip, 1999).

56. Zwelakhe Sisulu was released in December 1988 under a restriction order that was three pages long. C. Merrett, *A Culture of Censorship* (Cape Town: David Philip, 1995), 127. I thank Keyan Tomaselli for bringing this point to my attention.

57. Mrwetyana's newsletter was a constant thorn in the side of the ruling Matanzima brothers. *Isaziso* under different titles—*Isaziso* (March 1976–August 1978), *Isizwe* (January–July 1979 and April 1991–March? 1994)—provided perhaps the only ongoing critique of the Transkei government at the time. Mrwetyana himself was assaulted, detained, and eventually forced into exile in Lesotho. Personal communication from Mrwetyana.

Part I

IN TRANSITION: FROM PROTEST TO RESISTANCE

2

"Representing the Labouring Classes"

African Workers in the African Nationalist Press, 1900–1960

Peter Limb

African workers in South Africa had few mediators to communicate their grievances—given the oppressive social system, the silence of the white press, and the fragile nature of black trade unions. Newspapers associated with the African National Congress (ANC), however, encouraged public awareness of the conditions of African workers. A study of how workers were represented in the African nationalist press reveals not only a general sympathy for their harsh conditions but also a level of engagement with worker struggles that suggests a more complex set of attitudes toward labor than hitherto acknowledged by historians.

The ANC and African Workers: Theoretical and Historiographical Themes

The ANC has been viewed by historians as essentially middle class, a nationalist elite with few organic links to workers. Many ANC studies share the notion, at times ill-defined, of its elite nature. The early ANC was drawn from "the new 'middle class'" (Walshe) with "petty bourgeois leaders" (Cobley). The ANC of the 1950s only reluctantly involved workers (Feit), and its leaders, drawn from the "lower middle class," feared being driven back into the ranks of workers (Lodge). The tendency to paint the early ANC as middle class is not restricted to those outside the ANC. Benson, who worked with Congress, claims that before the 1952 Defiance Campaign the ANC was "an élite party of middle-class intellectuals." ANC historian Meli refers to its early leaders as "definitely not working class." Yet these writers acknowledge the increasing significance of workers within Congress. Lodge, for example, concedes that ANC growth increased in the 1950s to the extent that it acquired a working-class base.[1]

Conceptions of ANC-worker ties are changing. Regional studies suggest that ANC links with workers were more substantial at local levels.[2] They pay more attention to labor influences in Congress and gradually are pushing back the date of these contacts.[3] Despite a reluctance to abandon prevailing notions of the ANC as middle class, its resonance with Africans in working-class occupations is more often conceded.[4] Class-reductionist characterizations of Congress, which leave little room for appreciation of the ANC as a *movement* with all its ramifications—branches, members, supporters, traditions—or for the conscious decision making of members, are slowly making way for the (re)discovery of the "organic" nature of the ANC.[5] Odendaal, for instance, argues that the ANC was closer to communities than historians have assumed.[6]

In reexamining these contacts, African journalism assumes added significance in the context of the paucity of early ANC written records and of formal history writing by Africans. With few publication outlets, many early African writers turned to newspapers. This often accorded with cultural preferences. Xhosa historians, argues Peires, favored "the form of the newspaper article . . . [which was] closer than books to the form and spirit of the traditional Xhosa *ibali* [tale]." Exclusion from higher education, and later the rigors of exile, ensured that genres such as journalism continued to predominate in African writing.[7]

Concern with African workers characterized the work of writers and journalists such as R. R. R. and H. I. E. Dhlomo, and Alex La Guma, who also were ANC members. ANC leaders also made use of the press to draw attention to workers' rights. Leftist ANC members, such as Moses Kotane and Johnny Gomas (who were also members of the Communist Party), penned many articles on workers for the pro-ANC press.[8] Hence, the press is important as a source for measuring the variation of ANC concern with African workers.

Nationalism, Legitimacy, Representation, and the Press

Nationalism rarely emerges without involvement of both elites and masses. Lonsdale demonstrates this dialectical relationship in his study of the role of "ordinary Africans" in nationalism. Davidson argues that the "labouring poor" gave nationalists "ground to stand on." Anderson conceptualizes the nation as an "imagined" political community in which intellectuals, making use of tools such as the press, play a pivotal role in developing nationalism, notably in colonies (such as South Africa) with a stunted indigenous bourgeoisie.[9]

The ANC drew support from a wide range of black social strata. This relates to its emphasis on African national unity. Founding member Pixley Seme called for a Congress that "more than fairly represented . . . every section" of the people.[10] While tempered by its liberal demand for incorporation into public life, Congress attacked rigid state controls that created barriers to African nationalism. These political barriers combined with the economic leveling of diverse black social strata to induce cross-class alliances.[11] The petty bourgeoisie dominated Congress but were forced to return, repeatedly, to the need for cross-class unity. Hence, the ANC variety of nationalism could not afford to be separate from African workers.

Although the ANC claimed to be a legitimate African movement, Congress had to confront rival imperial, state, and ethnic authorities—each claiming a measure of legitimacy.[12] The ANC also laid claim to an inherited African past. It used various tools to claim legitimacy,[13] and one tool was the press. In the discussion below, I explore the extent to which the African nationalist press represented African workers and was a legitimate vehicle for their aspirations.

Labor history shows that competing social classes "brandish their own representations" and "act with certain representations of themselves and others in mind."[14] It is arguable that the proletariat can represent itself. The African proletariat in the first half of the twentieth-century, however, was too small and poorly resourced to secure effective self-representation. I use *representation* to refer to how writers depicted or claimed to speak on behalf of workers. I focus on the nature and accuracy of worker representations rather than on the frequency of press coverage of their struggles.[15] This coverage transcended mere portrayal—there was a real sense of political representation. Denied involvement in Parliament, the ANC sought to represent African aspirations where it could, which included the press.

To avoid subjective preconceptions, interpretation of the press record must be alive to the multiple composition of texts and to the fact that the representation of themes in the press always involves the influence of the press itself. The duality of power implicit in settler society created a deeply ambiguous context in which African political culture developed. ANC writers employed irony and metaphor, so their texts must be scrutinized to transcend merely apparent meanings. These news reports were often based on factual accounts of specific events, and there was little elaboration of individual personalities. The ANC nationalist press's representation of labor, however, tells us both about ANC views on workers and about the perilous state of African workers, and thus helps us to better understand ANC and labor history.

Congress, the African Press, and African Workers, 1900–1920

In the late nineteenth century, an elite of educated, Christianized Africans took shape whose leaders began to express, through newspapers and organizations, early forms of national consciousness. A loosely structured South African Native Congress (SANC) was started in the Cape in 1898 and a Natal Native Congress in 1900, while the Transvaal Native Vigilance Association was started in 1902.

These regional bodies focused on land and franchise issues but also expressed sympathy for African workers. The SANC protested to the Cape government against unfair "labour Clauses" in 1906, for example, urging that they be "totally repealed." It criticized the hostility of the "capitalistic press" to black rights. It defended consumption of "kaffir beer" by African workers, who might "feel the need of something to quench their thirst after violent exertions." Such early forays into labor issues created an impression. A writer in Bloemfontein's white-owned newspaper, *The Friend*, for example, noted that if these African congresses "were granted power to control and supervise Native labour . . . we would soon find this country on the highway to prosperity."[16]

Regional pressure groups gave way, in the face of the Union of South Africa's white-settler colonies in 1910, to the South

African Native National Congress (SANNC, later the ANC), formed in 1912. Members stemmed mainly from the petty bourgeoisie but also included some wage earners. Thomas Zini, a migrant worker who represented the Cape Peninsula Native Association, took part in the SANNC's founding conference. Among delegates to the 1914 SANNC conference were Africans "kicked out of Government service to make room for the white man." The first SANNC meeting passed resolutions for increased compensation for injured miners and reduced mine death rates. Congress appointed a minister for labour and a secretary for mines, and held meetings with government on the need to extend compensation to laborers.[17] But the SANNC remained small and without an effective nationwide apparatus. Hence, many workers probably knew little about it, though most urban Africans lived in close proximity to each other: the identity of Congress, once established in a location, could easily spread by oral means or via the press.

Many early African newspapers helped nurture African nationalism.[18] They were marginal commercial ventures, modest in size and generally moderate in tone. Yet they confronted a social system that discriminated against Africans, and their news reports, notes Switzer, show "a sustained, albeit muted, level of protest."[19] Government publicly stated its preference for African groups conducting their deliberations through the African press rather than by "secret plotting." However, privately officials objected to press criticism. The minister of native affairs in 1906, for example, attempted to deny John Dube (the key African political figure in colonial Natal) permission to establish a "larger scale" Natal Congress "until the native press . . . adopt[s] a more respectful and proper tone towards the Government and the white race."[20]

The circulation of the early African press was low and literacy rates remained low. An educated elite controlled this press, but at times they also sought to represent workers. In these columns, some of the earliest representations of workers by those who were to become ANC leaders are discernible. Regional differences could be pronounced here: in the eastern Cape a newspaper linked to the SANC attempted to speak on behalf of African workers; in the mining town of Kimberley newspapers edited by ANC activist Sol Plaatje often reported on strikes; and on the Rand the organ of the Transvaal Congress developed a reputation for militancy.[21]

"Voice of the People" or Voice of the Workers?
Izwi Labantu *and African Workers*

Editors of *Izwi Labantu* (Voice of the People, 1897–1909), published in East London, included Nathaniel Umhalla, George Tyamzashe, and especially Allan Kirkland Soga. All were active in the Cape SANC, along with Walter Benson Rubusana, one of the leading figures in Cape African politics, and the newspaper essentially reflected SANC interests and concerns. The secretary of native affairs noted in 1903 that SANC "representations . . . accord with the views expressed in . . . [*Izwi,*] whose editor appears to be closely associated with the organization." A 1902 SANC meeting gave thanks to *Izwi*'s editor. Soga at this time saw the SANC's role as one of confronting "all questions affecting the social problems and welfare" of Africans.[22]

This emphasis on welfare is evident in Soga's editing of *Izwi*, in which he also expressed ideas betraying some understanding of the significance of class struggle and of African labor's position in society. He foreshadowed post-Union South Africa as "a glorious country for corporation pythons and political puff-adders, forced labour and commercial despotism." He saw growing labor conflict as "a phase of the coming struggle between capital and labour." Efforts to extend the limited

African franchise beyond the Cape foundered on the "superior strategy of the . . . capitalist class . . . playing their game for cheap labour."[23]

"Native Labour" was an oft-repeated headline in *Izwi*. The newspaper condemned the whipping of mine laborers and the "chapter of horrors" of their exploitation, and drew attention to the fleecing of migrant laborer wages by labor agents and to their lack of redress. East London workers were "pigging it in ram-shackle tin shanties." In an ironic commentary on the "progress" supposedly underpinning elite beliefs, *Izwi* noted, "'Higher Civilisation' . . . consigns the poor . . . to the lowest sinks." The high loss of lives in the coal mines was ascribed to "conditions imposed by unfeeling capitalistic systems." *Izwi* prophesied that "the next war will be between labour and capital." The "daily trudge of six miles" faced by East London laborers was criticized. This concern brought some indirect contact with workers. Headmen in charge of migrant laborers en route to Cape Town, for example, called on the editor to complain about conditions. *Izwi* criticized the harsh treatment of Namaqualand laborers and argued that any labor "shortage" was due not to "corpulent" blacks but to low wages. Congress was urged to redress the absence of African representation on the Chinese and Kaffir Labour Commission.[24]

However, Soga was ambivalent in his support of worker grievances. He perceived that the African laborer's "mouth is closed" due to "ignorance of the English language," but he was not prepared to go beyond exposure of labor conditions to a more direct representation of their interests. Soga refused to publish "letters sent to us for publication complaining of evil treatment" in the mines "as the interests affected [were] too great . . . to be satisfactorily dealt with in the press." Soga put greater faith in political representation, claiming that labor complaints should first be supported by "reports of some responsible body or committee like the Vigilance Association" (there were no African unions at this time). He was not prepared to "risk injuring the larger interests of labour during these depressing times."[25]

Izwi carried items from the *Labour Leader* (Britain) and the *New York Socialist* on workers' conditions in different countries. Soga believed blacks and whites would "come to recognise that their economic salvation rests with socialism."[26] Nevertheless, there were contradictions in his populist socialism. *Izwi* was kept alive in 1898 and 1899 by empire builder and arch capitalist Cecil Rhodes, and Soga contributed to the Rhodes memorial fund after Rhodes's death in 1902 to mark "all that this great Englishman has done" for Africans. In East London, Soga worked to establish a haven for the "more respectable" African. *Izwi* urged Africans to show "respect and good conduct in all their official and business relations with their [white] superiors," though the newspaper hastened to stress the "great importance . . . of safeguarding the health . . . of our labouring classes."[27] Such contradictory language indicates the vacillation of petty bourgeois ideology. However, it also betrays a tactical decision on how to survive in a hostile milieu.

Izwi ceased publication in 1909. Soga took part in the formation of the SANNC and edited the pro-SANNC *African Native Advocate* (1912–13). By 1920, however, he had abandoned his socialist and ANC leanings, as well as journalism, to join Walter Rubusana's conservative Bantu Union and to work as a civil servant.[28]

Other African newspapers, at times, also took up the plight of workers. During the South African War (1899–1902), the Natal newspaper *Ipepa lo Hlanga* (Paper of the Nation) reported strikes and predicted postwar efforts to push down wages. *Ipepa* (1894–1904) challenged the widespread notion that the African worker "has no right . . . to sell his labour at the best possible market." *Ipepa* stressed that Africans "as people are looked upon by many as camels or any other beast of burden."

Whether these reports signaled merely a desire for moral upliftment of workers, a more general empathy for Africans as a race, or genuine concern for workers, is unclear.[29] Workers' issues even filtered through the pages of John Dube's *Ilanga lase Natal* (Natal Sun, 1903–), which epitomized the ambiguities inherent in attempts by African elites to use the discourses of colonialism in the service of African nationalism. *Ilanga* warned, for example, of attacks on African jobs and argued that labor "shortages" could be solved by "giv[ing] higher wages to those working underground."[30]

Koranta ea Becoana, Tsala ea Batho, and African Workers

More consistent representations of workers appeared in two newspapers edited by Solomon Plaatje, the first SANNC secretary-general. Plaatje is portrayed by historians as a moderate, a supporter of the British Empire, and an anticommunist. *Koranta ea Becoana* (Bechuana Gazette, 1901–8), published in Mafeking (now Mafikeng), was owned by SANC figure Silas Molema and edited by Plaatje. The masthead read: "The Amelioration of the Native: Labour, Sobriety, Thrift and Education," but the newspaper disclaimed "social equality with the white man" in favor of "political recognition as loyal British subjects." Such ideas were common among Africans of the day. Plaatje's opposition to radical socialism led him to accept help from the De Beers mining company,[31] but he was not unaware of African workers' conditions or unsympathetic to their plight. His less well-known reporting of industrial issues while an editor raised questions about the situation of African labor.

Historians of *Koranta* hitherto have neglected its attitude to labor,[32] but, as with *Izwi,* "Native Labour" was a frequent news headline. In 1902 and 1903 prominence was given to those who opposed plans by "insatiable Rand mine . . . capitalists" to indenture Chinese labor. Plaatje linked such plans directly to moves by magnates to lower African wages in order "to obtain the cheapest labour in the world at our expense." He denounced claims by a white writer that African laborers were lazy, and he attacked "the greed" of Rand mine magnates for "wrongfully and illegally withholding the just wages of their labourers." The British secretary of state for colonies, Joseph Chamberlain, was congratulated on his rejection of the proposal by mine capitalists that Africans work for virtually nothing. Mine owners should "discharge their obligations towards the employees."[33] *Koranta* printed reports on the mistreatment of mine laborers. And when the government relied only on the views of mine magnates to investigate such mistreatment, *Koranta* took up the issue, supplying its own evidence on harsh mine conditions.[34]

Koranta frequently denounced the harsh and discriminatory treatment of African laborers—exploitation of unpaid apprentices, refusal to employ certain ethnic groups, and high industrial accident rates. The latter was a "butchery" occurring "with terrible frequency," even at Kimberley-based De Beers. It pricked Plaatje's conscience, causing him to reflect that "we have at times used our columns for the cause of [De Beers's] mines." He mused that the best advice one could give to laborers was to "steer clear of . . . Kimberley diamond mines." Noting De Beers's huge profits, Plaatje commented, "our people may pride themselves . . . that their black muscles are [its] pillar." Kimberley capitalists were denounced: De Beers's "promiscuous distribution of monetary gifts [dividends] . . . very often overlooked the interest of the most loyal and harmless (though important) section among its labourers."[35]

"Loyal and harmless (though important)" sums up Plaatje's attitude to African workers. He recognized them as vital to the economy. Mines "did not happen to grow. They were dug by black men." *Koranta* was their defender—"organ of the majority of [De Beers] employees. . . . [and] representing the labouring classes"—whose role it sought to explain and defend. Africans wanted "fair pay, for they have to do all the hard work"; whites sought to restrict Africans to occupations that would never "improve our position." Plaatje affirmed that "we want our Natives to teach our Europeans the dignity and happiness of educated labour." But if he posed as a defender of African workers, Plaatje revealed his own distaste for African workers' involvement in class struggle: "Unlike any class of labourers the world over, [African labor] can produce a spotless record of years of loyal and faithful service." *Koranta* also claimed to be "the first native organ that held up the personality of Booker Washington," an advocate of black capitalism, as an "emblem of emulation" by youth.[36] While *Koranta*'s labor reporting was not limited to the Rand and Kimberley, its circulation of only one to two thousand copies and the low literacy levels of African workers limited the newspaper's penetration of working-class communities.[37]

Plaatje gained added insight into the tribulations of migrant laborers when in 1909 he briefly was forced by the financial demise of *Koranta* to work as a labor recruiter. The following year he returned to journalism as editor of the self-styled "independent race newspaper" *Tsala ea Becoana* (Friend of the Bechuana), later retitled *Tsala ea Batho* (Friend of the People, 1910–15), published in Kimberley.[38] After Plaatje became SANNC secretary in 1913, *Tsala* increasingly was viewed by its readers as an organ of Congress.[39]

Tsala often carried reports on strikes, letters from mine employees, and expressions of concern for the welfare of African wage earners. Plaatje (and his subeditors after he went overseas in 1914) criticized the retrenchment of African interpreters and post office workers in favor of less skilled white employees. Plaatje attacked the meager pensions accorded to African employees and their "niggardly wage," and he published letters from workers voicing grievances in the newspaper.[40] *Tsala* also carried mining company advertisements, as well as Native Recruiting Corporation policies, suggesting it was read by at least some African mine workers.

Plaatje helped forge closer relations between Congress and the African Political Organisation, which claimed influence among Coloured workers. He condemned "selfish white labour agitation" and state policy for squeezing Coloureds out of work. Yet, he opposed strikes. Some Africans, notably "women and some of the chiefs," favored a general strike. But, he warned, "when the strike is declared and those women begin to jeer at the pusillanimous laborers who hesitate to join, we will have the whole quarter million out on strike. . . . Many . . . will be shot."[41] *Tsala* detailed proceedings of meetings of government and ANC leaders on protection for migrant workers. News reports featured calls by white farmers for forced labor, parliamentary debates on rail workers' wages, industrial color bars, and white digger demands to expel Xhosa laborers from Kimberley. *Tsala* also covered matters of everyday interest to African workers, such as assaults committed by white miners against laborers.[42]

Tsala editorials opposed to strikes undeniably expressed moderate views. However, the mere presence of such views does not prove aloofness from workers. African newspapers were scrutinized by government, so they tended to modify editorial expression in the same way that declarations of imperial loyalty often accompanied ANC protests.[43] *Tsala*'s pages reveal not only the opinions of editors but also the central ideas of Congress and the diverse social classes supporting it. "Middle class" movements influenced Plaatje, but they in turn were responding to other influences, including the growing social presence of African workers.

Plaatje could not avoid worker issues in Kimberley, with its heavy preponderance of mine laborers, and his sympathetic reporting about workers probably was related to his need for readers. However, he remained essentially a nationalist: reports on workers were couched in terms of the interests of Africans in general. Nothing in his columns suggests that he favored an independent role for labor. Nevertheless, the "Friend of the People" was, as *Bantu World* eulogized in 1932, "a thorn in the flesh of the oppressors and exploiters."[44]

Abantu-Batho *and the Reporting of African Workers*

Abantu-Batho (The People, 1912–31) was closely associated with Congress. It became the official organ of the Transvaal Native Congress (TNC) in 1918 and the official organ of the national ANC in 1928.[45] *Abantu-Batho* staff included Levi Mvabaza, Daniel Letanka, Cleopas Kunene, Robert Grendon, Saul Msane, Herbert Msane, T. D. Mweli Skota, Jeremiah Dunjwa, Richard Selope Thema, C. S. Mabaso, and B. G. Phooko. All were Congress members. Many were involved in labor protests. By 1916, Mvabaza was active in the International Socialist League (ISL). Writing in *Abantu-Batho*, he persistently took up the cause of workers.[46] Mvabaza, Letanka (TNC chair in 1916), and Dunjwa (TNC secretary) were involved in strikes on the Rand between 1918 and 1920. Mvabaza and Letanka were arrested with ISL leaders after a 1918 strike by African workers.[47]

At this time the first documented African workers' organization, the Industrial Workers of Africa (IWA) emerged out of meetings between ISL and TNC activists. Police files that include translations from *Abantu-Batho* indicate that some IWA leaders were TNC members. Herbert Msane, apparently briefly an *Abantu-Batho* editor, wrote an article on Ethiopianism for the ISL's organ, the *International*. He became an enthusiastic IWA member and printed socialist leaflets in Zulu in October 1917. Police found that Msane had not yet used *Abantu-Batho* as a vehicle for the IWA, but in a November issue of *Abantu-Batho* he gave one of the earliest defenses of unionism by an African writer. Msane also proposed a secret committee of TNC and ISL leaders to plan a general strike in July 1918.[48]

Robert Grendon, a black teacher and journalist who periodically edited *Abantu-Batho*, reportedly "expressed a keen interest" in the ISL. He addressed an ISL public meeting in June 1916 on "the race problem of Africa and its connection with the working class movement." Grendon was less radical than Herbert Msane. His talk invoked nostalgically the "better" rights of Africans in the Victorian Era.[49] Yet, in October 1918 he strongly defended African strikers in *Ilanga lase Natal.* Referring to successful struggles of white workers and Indian passive resisters, he wrote, "The Native has learnt two important lessons during the last few years. . . . It is now his turn to question the laws laid down for the control of his industry and toil." Grendon not only drew attention to this rising class consciousness of African workers but also urged political solidarity: "the White Socialist is in principle a brother to the Black Socialist."[50]

Other *Abantu-Batho* staff, such as Mabaso (a teacher, clerk, and shopkeeper) and Dunjwa (an interpreter and teacher, who joined *Abantu-Batho* in 1913 as Xhosa editor) also took an interest in labor. Dunjwa, elected TNC secretary in 1919, exposed the harsh conditions of African laborers after visiting the mines.[51] Phooko, a member of the editorial board, in 1916 urged the director of Native Labour to consult with African labor. He warned that if laborers, who had been "unearthing the gold that fills the Capitalist's coffers at very little or no consideration of their services," should "down tools one day, the whole superstructure of beautiful White South Africa would come down in a terrible crash."[52]

Abantu-Batho condemned the 1913 Natives' Land Act, which had reduced Africans to "penury and want."[53] In one celebrated news report, *Abantu-Batho* targeted the state of workers, who did "the unskilled labour and all kinds of drudgery. . . . They are the mainstay of the country's industries . . . and the least paid." Conditions of women workers were singled out for particular scrutiny. "Some employers are so inconsiderate and almost brutal that they do not care even for their female native servants to be housed properly, if at all." Female workers, the newspaper was "told," were "extremely overworked." Laundry workers endured a "sweating-system of a most shameful character," often without food breaks—a basic need also denied office workers. Details of working hours and wages were cited. It was a "fallacy" that Africans could survive on low wages. African workers were warned "against collaboration" with white labor following the refusal of white craft unions to support African workers. In the face of these problems, *Abantu-Batho* urged the TNC "to inquire into the question of how natives are employed" and, "[i]n the absence of organised labour among natives," it urged that the inquiry "be directed to hours of work, rate of pay, and general treatment, particularly of women."[54]

Nevertheless, *Abantu-Batho* was attacked by the ISL in its newspaper, the *International*, as being "edited (consciously or unconsciously) under the aegis of the Native Affairs Dept. and the Capitalist class." While the *International* conceded the above news report "sounds at last the initial rumblings of a spontaneous, indigenous class-conscious industrial movement," *Abantu-Batho* was characterized as a "humble henchman of the capitalist press."[55]

Despite this criticism, *Abantu-Batho*, as far as can be determined from surviving copies,[56] consistently exposed exploitation of African labor. It spoke out against work contracts imposed on domestic workers and featured protests against passes for African women. One correspondent noted that "all the work that should have been done by our wage labourers [is] now done by prisoners who are imprisoned for nothing but passes."[57] The imposition of passes was termed a "war of extermination." Another correspondent wrote that the question of women's passes had produced "the greatest unrest" he had known.[58] *Abantu-Batho* carried extensive reports in 1917 and 1918 of efforts by women to organize themselves. It publicized the views of Charlotte Maxeke, for example, a social worker and a founder of the women's wing of the ANC, who had contacts among working women. She argued that women could not rely on men: "they must get themselves ready for the struggle."[59]

During rising labor agitation in 1918, *Abantu-Batho* reported joint TNC-IWA meetings and the comments of TNC leaders on the harshly repressed July "bucket" strike of Johannesburg municipal workers, and described the response of miners in a way that suggested possible firsthand contact with them. "At the Ferreira compound all the natives refused to go to work. . . . At Roodepoort the Municipal Boys refused. . . . At Randfontein they tried to refuse." *Abantu-Batho* explained that many strikers were refused permission to attend a TNC meeting that decided against industrial action. It was publishing this information because "every worker must read so that he may know." The implication that many workers read the newspaper undoubtedly was wishful thinking, but it does suggest that *Abantu-Batho* claimed a worker readership.[60]

Abantu-Batho continued to support TNC and worker militancy, reporting antipass protests in 1919[61] and the 1920 African miners' strike. Mine conditions were so harsh that Africans "were not going to put up with this any more." African workers had "intelligence enough to know which side [their] bread is buttered on." They were "beginning to wake up. . . . finding out that they are slaves to the big capitalist."

The TNC convened mass meetings in support of the 1920 strikers, condemned the police for beating the workers, and "formulated demands for a weekly minimum wage."[62] The TNC and its newspaper established a reputation among African workers as a defender of their interests.

Abantu-Batho's coverage of workers was more sympathetic than most other African newspapers—like *Imvo Zabantsundu* (Native Opinion, 1884–), published in East London by the Cape's most famous African politician at the time, John Tengo Jabavu. *Imvo* regularly criticized Congress leaders as radicals. It reported a range of African demands but gave scant attention to workers. It described African strikes in 1913 as a "bad example" and in 1918 urged striking African municipal workers to obey the prime minister's advice "to be quiet and go on with their contracts."[63]

Congress, the African Press, and African Workers, 1920–1940

ANC leaders continued to express sympathetic, if ambiguous, attitudes to workers between the world wars. Yet, as discrimination intensified they sought allies, including workers. Closer ANC-worker relations were aided by the formation of the first African trade unions, a rise in African literacy,[64] and the establishment by intellectuals associated with Congress of a number of newspapers that espoused support for African workers.

On labor issues, African newspapers in this period tended to divide into two broad categories, moderate and radical.[65] Those more closely associated with the ANC gave more sympathetic attention to African workers. By 1931 there were nineteen African newspapers, including several linked to Congress. Yet by the mid-1930s, most independent ANC-aligned publications had either collapsed or been taken over by the white-owned media conglomerate Bantu Press. Even so, the estimated circulation of commercial newspapers such as *Bantu World* at this time was only 2,500.[66]

In the 1920s the first African trade unions launched publications, and the Communist Party of South Africa (CPSA) ventured into vernacular publishing, indicative of a rising black membership. These newspapers—normally English was combined with various African languages—were read by organized workers and African nationalists, but their circulation was slight. The CPSA press in the early 1930s was enveloped in sectarianism, attacking ANC leaders in vituperative terms and becoming, in the opinion of prominent CPSA figure Moses Kotane, so turgid that it was "no more sold and read by the masses."[67]

By 1951 the number of African newspapers had declined to seven, all white-owned. Advertising profits, tapping rising urbanization, fueled press monopoly and moderated political journalism,[68] while state efforts to assert political hegemony by encouraging a compliant African middle class increased.[69] Nevertheless, in this period white media domination was challenged by the resilience of an ANC-aligned, nonracial press that sought to represent a national constituency, a growing portion of whom were workers.

The first African labor union, the Industrial and Commercial Workers' Union (ICU), was formed in 1919. After a meteoric rise it declined rapidly a decade later. ICU leaders, such as Clements Kadalie, claimed to speak on behalf of black workers, but their credentials to do so were no more impressive than those of ANC leaders.[70] The history of the ICU organ, *Workers' Herald* (1923–28), is well detailed. Switzer argues that essentially it was reformist, seeking "to represent the African worker as one who aspired to middle-class values" but making "common cause" with workers as repression intensified.[71]

Less well known is the ICU's first organ, the *Black Man*

(1920). Its editor, S. M. Bennett Ncwana, was sporadically active in the ANC and ICU, and wrote for *Abantu-Batho*. His eclectic ideological perspectives included Garveyism and Christianity.[72] In 1920 he supported socialists Reuben Cetyiwe and Hamilton Kraai at a Ndabeni ICU. He launched a number of ill-fated Garvey-inspired business enterprises, while in the pages of *Black Man* he sought to articulate the demands of African workers.[73]

Black Man promoted Pan-African unionism. Devoted to the "organisation of industrial workers throughout the African continent," it attacked the labor recruiting system as "pernicious to the working classes," denounced "hand-to-mouth wages," condemned De Beers for trafficking in convict labor, and even endorsed some strikes. The newspaper boldly demanded "new conditions for farm labourers, a reasonable minimum wage for our women . . . reconsideration of salaries of ministers and teachers of our race."[74] It adopted a critical attitude to Congress, attacking "interference" by Cape Congress leaders Rev. H. R. Ngcayiya and Simon Jordan in a strike, and warning against ANC leaders "allow[ing] themselves to be tantalised by fertilised flattery purposely invented to divert . . . plans from pure industrial to political camouflage."[75]

African World (Cape Town, 1925–26) was founded by western Cape ANC president James Thaele with the Garveyist slogan "Africa for Africans."[76] Subtitled "Mouthpiece of the Cape A[NC]," it gave Congress critical support: ANC resolutions were endorsed, but leaders were warned "not [to] permit themselves to be classified with the pliable," a reference to the role of ANC figures in government-sponsored "Native conferences."[77] In true Garveyist style the newspaper was aimed at "large businesses owned by blacks."[78]

Thaele's experience as an editor of the *Workers' Herald* (from 1923 to 1925) increased his sensitivity to the workers' cause. If not overtly working class in tone, *African World* nevertheless attempted to articulate worker demands. It called for "equal pay for equal work—is it asking too much?" A belief in the dignity of labor was combined with faith in the ANC's historic role: "Through labour may our comrades subdue their difficulties. . . . The A[NC], with its well advised leaders and comrades stands [as] a bright star to the thinking man of Africa."[79]

African World employed a radical rhetoric that combined Garveyism with anticapitalism. It attacked the "political combination of the bourgeoisie into monopolistic organisations and their plutocratic domination of the state machine." Just what *capitalist* meant to African nationalists is problematic. To some, it appears to have been synonymous with white domination. *African World* told its readers that "constitutional agitation and the cultivation of race-pride" were required to free Africa "from the incubus of European capitalistic control." It urged the ANC, "as a government in embryo" of all Africans, to unite with the ICU to promote "'Passive Resistance' and a Strike. . . . with a view to bring to a standstill. . . . within 24 hours the Mining Industry."[80]

African World was less supportive of actual strikes. Commenting on the 1925 British seamen's strike that affected South Africa, the editor argued that "a struggle of this kind at all times is a thing to be deplored." Sympathy with strikers was possible as Africans had "no appeal from the civil and economic tyranny," but "we must . . . not [be] drawn into the quarrel." Reform of industrial systems was needed, but *African World* specifically rejected communists, "who would destroy these" systems.[81] Nevertheless, *African World* published articles by radicals such as Bransby Ndobe, Thomas Mbeki, Josiah Ngedlane, and Stanley Silwana, and reproduced articles from the CPSA press. The result was a lively political discourse. Mbeki invoked "that long and winding highway known as History" to compare the persecution of ANC-ICU activists with the fate of Socrates. Silwana stressed the violence underlying past and present empires. Leir Stebe, mixing metaphors, argued that it "is high time we should be out of the White men's capitalistic control. . . . [O]nward with the African Empire"[82]

Abantu-Batho continued to support African nationalism during the 1920s. It called for the unity of African forces to fight "white domination" and gave support to African struggles in Kenya and Swaziland.[83] The militant ANC president Josiah Gumede purchased a controlling share in the newspaper in 1929 in an effort to provide Congress with a viable organ. In 1930 and 1931 he and fellow editor Daniel Letanka maintained an often radical editorial approach. Attracted by growing communist support for national liberation, they printed articles by prominent communists[84] and, inspired by Garveyist anti-imperialist rhetoric, speeches from *Negro World.*[85]

The role of the editors had much to do with *Abantu-Batho* support for workers in the early 1930s. Gumede, even when ousted as ANC president in 1930, continued to espouse the cause of African labor.[86] ICU leader A. W. G. Champion and his colleague Jim London joined the staff in 1931. Samuel Masabalala, a Port Elizabeth workers' leader in 1920, and (ex-communist) T. W. Thibedi were also associated with the newspaper.[87] Sesotho editor Daniel Letanka had been jailed after a strike in 1918. Reminding readers of this fact, *Abantu-Batho* contrasted the "heroic age" of the 1918–20 protests with the inaction of ANC leadership a decade later. Letanka died in 1932 "penniless . . . after years of supporting himself on his small income" from *Abantu-Batho.*[88] His long association with the journal helped lend its reporting and editorializing a more consistent radicalism that condemned the "class of traitors among our . . . leadership."[89]

Abantu-Batho closed in July 1931, and many of its staff left to join *Bantu World.* Nevertheless, its influence helped ensure the survival of radical African nationalism. Gilbert Coka, a radical journalist, spoke of a "tide of nationalism, led by the truly national newspaper *Abantu-Batho.*" ANC historians highlight the impact of its demise. Govan Mbeki argues that after its closure the ANC "relied almost entirely on the spoken word to get its message across."[90]

Abantu-Batho's printing press was used to print the *African Leader* (1932–33), launched as an unofficial ANC organ and which, in turn, incorporated *Ikwezi Le Afrika* (Africa Morning Star, 1928–32), another pro-ANC newspaper.[91] The *African Leader* gave prominence to new ANC president Pixley Seme's moderate presidential statements on ANC policy, although it also claimed to have "not deviated in any way from the policy of" *Abantu-Batho.*[92]

While the left-wing views of Gumede were conspicuously absent from its pages, some ANC members used *African Leader* to expose the misery of workers. Editors, including ANC secretary T. D. Mweli Skota, were skeptical of Seme's reliance solely on self-help: "not all [ANC] members . . . can be trader. . . . Some must for all time fill the role of worker. . . . The workers as a class have problems peculiar to their class. . . . They will always need an organisation such as the A[NC] to champion . . . political emancipation." Despite its claim to speak on behalf of workers, the *African Leader* agreed with *Bantu World* editor Selope Thema "that there can be no nation of workers." The *African Leader* rationalized its moderate policy, claiming that while the ANC had been formed in times of mass protests, "the conditions which called for mass organisation no longer exist."[93]

Unemployment was an issue that no newspaper could avoid in the early 1930s and the *African Leader* was no exception. Halley Plaatje, ANC chief undersecretary, wrote that there was nothing "to bring out real spite and hatred like being told on asking for relief work that your government provides only for . . . white skins." Other correspondents also drew attention to how unemployment hit black workers more than it affected white employees.[94] At this time, the *African Leader* saw an ANC role in industrial organization: "Congress should within its ambit have a number of trade unions grouped together into a federation controlled and guided by the National Executive."[95] Yet, in practice, the ANC could not lead the workers and neither could the *African Leader*, which ceased publication in 1933.

Izwi Lama Afrika (Voice of Africa, 1931–32), published in East London, devoted much space to local issues, and declared it would "endeavour to do away with . . . [the] radicalism which is the bane of this country."[96] This conservatism did not prevent *Izwi* from raising problems affecting workers, protesting moves to increase taxation of Africans, which fell most harshly on "the poorest class."[97] It accused employers of underpaying Africans, urged a minimum wage, supported office workers denied pensions by the East London Council, attacked the disparity in wages between white and African Council workers, and condemned the use of convict labor.[98]

Part of the reason for this stance was *Izwi*'s belief that the revival of trade in the midst of the Depression depended "upon the increase of the Natives purchasing power." Another was the prior ICU experience of lead writers like Bennett Ncwana, then secretary of the East London Non-Europeans Unemployment Committee. He argued that due to racial discrimination Africans suffered more from the depression, and low African wages endangered the "money market." His simplistic solution was for black and white to work harmoniously.[99] Working with the municipal department of health, *Izwi* requested readers to circulate the journal "among Native Labourers and Domestic Servants," who apparently were seen as a threat to public health and not regarded as subscribers.[100] Such manifest ambivalence toward workers was compounded by *Izwi*'s relatively weak ANC ties and its support for the white-controlled Joint Councils.[101]

Umlindi we Nyanga (Monthly Watchman, 1936–41), also published in East London, expressed a similar ambivalence toward workers. Controlled by white business interests, it was edited by eastern Cape political leader Richard Godlo. His ANC ties may have been a factor encouraging editorial concern for African workers' interests. Workers and political activists used the letters columns to draw attention to issues such as inadequate wages and adult education for workers. Articles in support of African trade union demands were reprinted from the radical *Guardian.* Infant mortality and juvenile delinquency were "inextricably interwoven with . . . inadequacy of wages." Union campaigns were covered and a strike by miners reported sympathetically.[102]

In these newspapers, some link was seen, consciously or unconsciously, between the struggles of workers and readers. Yet strikes made ANC moderates feel uncomfortable. Similar trends are apparent in other white-owned newspapers aimed at African readers. ANC members at times edited and wrote for these publications, which courted African workers and with relatively greater financial resources sometimes produced striking representations of African industrial life—though these journals distanced themselves from African political and workers' bodies.[103]

Imvo Zabantsundu in the previous decade had little sympathy for the ANC and even less for workers. This attitude changed in 1921 when Alexander Jabavu became editor. In 1925 he was elected an ICU vice president and in 1926 told an ICU conference that state policy was ostracizing African workers.[104] Unlike his father, Jabavu expressed loyalty to "the famous" ANC. Under his editorship, *Imvo* expressed concern that African union leaders appeared more interested in self-aggrandizement than in "fighting the battles of the exploited race." *Imvo* printed a letter of the eastern Cape Native Farmers' Association calling on white farmers to raise laborers' wages. The exile without trial of ICU leader Champion evoked sympathy in its pages.[105] Yet, this newfound support for workers waned considerably by the end of the decade, and *Imvo* was absorbed by the Bantu Press in 1935.

The Native Recruiting Corporation and the Transvaal Chamber of Mines established *Umteteli wa Bantu* (Mouthpiece of the People) in 1920, supported by SANNC moderates like Saul Msane and Isaiah Bud-M'belle, who were worried by TNC radicalism.[106] *Abantu-Batho* claimed in 1931 that *Umteteli* "was solely organised by the Chamber of Mines with the object of killing *Abantu-Batho* who at the time had appealed with success to the mine natives who are at the mercy of the uncrowned kings of the Compounds."[107]

According to former editor Harold Kumalo, whites wrote many *Umteteli* editorials. Still, it devoted considerable space to African worker conditions, and criticized state and white labor policies directed against their interests. At the same time, it studiously avoided any commitment to union demands and furiously derided communism. This orientation helped it recruit moderates, including ANC figures like Marshall Maxeke, Selope Thema, and H. S. Msimang. Occasionally it joined *Abantu-Batho* in condemning attacks on Africans. Both newspapers supported African worker objections to attempts by the mining companies to stop paying them with gold. But whereas *Abantu-Batho* urged African workers to "refuse to be paid in paper money," its rival stopped short of recommending protest action.[108]

The white-owned Bantu Press founded *Bantu World* in 1932. Selope Thema, who remained an ANC member, became editor.[109] He was aware of the "dependent and servile" nature of African labor, but his view of workers was condescending. If Africans were treated justly, "nowhere in the world" could "be found more docile workers."[110] The African petty bourgeoisie were the main communicators of opinions in *Bantu World*,[111] but it did report on labor conditions. Yet, such reports often were comments by white liberals and not black union leaders. An article by Edgar Brookes, for example, agreed that African teachers were "overworked and underpaid." His naive solution was recourse to faith in God and the liberal Joint Councils.[112]

Despite editorial moderation,[113] *Bantu World* exposed poor working conditions, advocated higher black wages, and reported efforts by workers to raise their wages. The "long rows of pathetic shanties" and equally long hours of work of diamond laborers were described.[114] Correspondents, some of them clearly workers, spoke out on labor matters.[115] Trade unionists contributed: Philemon Tsele urged union unity, and Gana Makabeni called for the unionization of unorganized workers. When African teacher wages were cut by 10 percent in 1932, their union was implored "to take the only right way—DIRECT ACTION." Meat Workers' Union Secretary P. Ramutla explained the rationale for unions. Readers debated the value to workers of the Transvaal Mine Clerks' Association. *Bantu World* saw that working conditions were "agitating the minds of the African workers and should be tackled seriously." However, while strikes were reported, often without comment, there was no attempt to directly support strikers.[116]

The white-owned African press thus monitored African workers' conditions. Why it bothered to do so at all was partly because of key journalists with ANC links, such as Selope Thema. In the next two decades, as ANC ties with these journalists grew weaker, the white press progressively abandoned African workers.

"Get the Paper Around": Labor in the ANC-Allied Press, 1940–1960

Rapid African urbanization and the growth of African unions began to translate into a greater working-class influence on the ANC and its allied press during the 1940s. ANC policies were publicized mainly in the CPSA's *Inkululeko* (Freedom, 1939–50), edited from 1945 by ANC-CPSA activist Edwin Mofutsanyana,[117] and in the independent socialist newspaper, the *Guardian* (1937–63).[118]

Several ANC-linked newspapers also supported African worker rights in the early 1940s. *Inkokeli ya Bantu* (People's Leader, 1940–42) sought to "champion the cause of the African people." Its editors included Stephen Oliphant, western Cape ANC secretary. Due to the war, the newspaper avoided publishing "anything likely to cause undue hardship or embarrassment" to the state.[119] Such self-imposed restrictions inhibited its capacity to articulate worker grievances, but it did not ignore workers. *Inkokeli* covered debates on labor rights, for example, in the Natives' Representative Council, where the councillors were mostly ANC members. Selope Thema (on reimbursing miner expenses), Richard Godlo (on higher wages), Richard Baloyi and Thomas Mapikela (on union recognition) were among those urging better working conditions.[120]

Inkokeli certainly did not advocate socialism, but it did represent workers as "the backbone of the wealth of the country." Nonrecognition of African unions was "systematic and discriminating." The ANC was urged to get more involved in strikes and unions: in all such matters "Congress should intervene on their behalf . . . if only to let the authorities . . . understand that these [working] people have leaders who are ever watchful and ready to speak on their behalf."[121] *Inkokeli* promoted a variety of "African trade unionism" in which workers were urged to "organise their trade unions on African lines" and to refuse non-Africans membership.[122]

Inkokeli criticized government for neglecting "the all embracing issue" of wages. Domestic workers' conditions were a "disgrace." Many skilled Africans received only "labourers' wages." Low African teacher wages were condemned. Workers were victims of fraudulent self-help schemes but could not turn for protection to a native affairs department that was "the last body the Africans think of." The solution, thought *Inkokeli*, lay "in an honest attempt on the part of the ruling classes to remove the stigma" of passes. This approach is perhaps indicative of a petty bourgeois ideology. Yet, similar appeals appeared in more radical newspapers.[123]

Izwi lase Afrika (Voice of the People, 1941–42) was the "official organ of the Cape African Congress" and edited by its secretary, Bennett Ncwana. While essentially a moderate organ of African nationalist opinion, the journal printed Cape ANC resolutions on matters affecting African workers. And it gave some attention to worker grievances: Africans received "hand-to-mouth wages," and "African working classes" doubted "whether a Parliament that was always coercing the poor black and never restraining the employers was really possessed of heavenly wisdom."[124]

Inkundla ya Bantu (People's Forum, 1938–51)[125] was more forthright in its support of African workers. Repression of strikes demonstrated the "unreasonableness" of nonrecognition, and the newspaper urged recognition of African trade unions. *Inkundla* printed articles on unions by both communist Moses Kotane and anticommunist unionist J. D. Nyaose. It saw the 1946 African mineworkers' strike as caused by government refusal to recognize the African Mine Workers' Union. The editor even called at the union's office to get their side of the strike and published the union's grievances. Other strikes were reported, and low African teacher wages especially highlighted.[126]

Such reporting reflected not only the solidarity of an oppressed people but also *Inkundla*'s support for ANC policies.[127] This alignment was influenced by its editors: the prominent political activist Govan Mbeki and (from 1944) Jordan Ngubane (Natal leader of the Congress Youth League, or CYL). In 1941 the editor urged ANC president A. B. Xuma to rouse the "professional and working classes" and enlist *Inkundla* in the task. *Inkundla* criticized a lack of "solid work" by the ANC in the townships but supported Congress during a difficult time in 1943 when a rival African Democratic Party was formed. Xuma expressed pleasure at this support and urged members to "get the paper around."[128]

Inkundla articulated a broad, inclusive variety of African nationalism. Columnist "Kanyisa" [Ngubane] declared that "we have never concealed our dislike for Communism. . . . But we shall never raise our arm against the Leftists just because Malan says we must." When radical unionists Stephen Tefu and Naboth Mokgatle were arrested, *Inkundla* protested, invoking Africans' right to "self-determination." Workers tended to be subsumed under this rubric of the African nation. Ngubane eschewed class struggle. He argued that only teachers could guide African struggles. Yet at times he gravitated toward proletarian tactics. He argued in 1946 that "unionism remains the spearhead of the national liberation movement" and urged unions to unite with Congress.[129]

In the late 1940s, the ANC became more militant. Its 1949 Programme of Action spelled out tactics such as boycotts and strikes to realize ANC aims. This militancy brought greater contact with workers, and many joined the ANC in the defiance campaigns of the early 1950s.[130] Congress in 1949 also endorsed African nationalism "as a basis of the fight for national liberation." This nationalism was promoted by the CYL, formed in 1944. The CYL—often depicted as remote from workers, though founder Anton Lembede saw it as infused with "modern socialistic ideas"—used *Inkundla* to urge the end of industrial color bars, to demand the "constitutional right of African workers to organise themselves," and to declare solidarity with the 1946 strikers.[131]

The ANC's 1949 Programme also saw the need for a national press, but that aim was not realized. *Inkundla*, the last remaining African newspaper linked to the ANC, folded in 1951. The Cape ANC newsletter, *Inyaniso*, wrote in 1954 that Congress had for years acknowledged the need for its own organ, but it was "well nigh impossible to establish a newspaper from scratch today . . . due to the great monopoly" of the white press.[132]

In the 1950s, Bantu Press newspapers abandoned their nationalist pretenses and uniformly criticized the ANC and union militancy. *Bantu World* continued to report socioeconomic issues of interest to workers, but its coverage of African politics became muted. *Umteteli* reported social news of concern to mine workers but rarely supported African unions or Congress. *Imvo* periodically protested African housing conditions but deplored the "wild behaviour" of squatters and supported recognition of African unions only as a means to avoid unrest. When miners protested poor conditions, *Imvo* ran a series about "the good life" on the mines.[133]

Congress nevertheless found diverse ways to communicate with supporters through leaflets, and short-lived newsletters like *Inyaniso, Izwi La Lentsoe La*, and *Lodestar*, through public meetings, and a few pro-ANC newspapers—notably the *Guardian*, which itself became a symbol of antiapartheid resistance. The banning of the CPSA in 1950 ended the legal communist press, but the *Guardian* continued to champion labor struggles until it was forced to close down in March 1963.

Articles on workers' grievances by ANC leaders such as Walter Sisulu and Dan Tloome also appeared in Congress Alliance publications such as *Liberation* and *Fighting Talk*, and in union journals such as *Workers' Unity*. Left-wing journalists employed *Drum* to expose the harsh treatment of African farmworkers in the press.[134] This was a difficult time for the African press. Yet, without the ANC's principled and programmatic support for African workers' rights, journalists may have been less inclined to take up workers' issues.

THE AFRICAN WORLD

Price 3d.

N'KOSI SIKELELA IAFRIKA

Africa for Africans!   **Europe for Europeans!**

The only Weekly National Organ, printed in the English and Bantu languages.

VOL. I. No. 2.   MAY 30, 1925.   [Registered at the G.P.O. as a Newspaper.]

The Policy of Divide and Rule.

An aspiring youth one day said that the "British Empire is an Empire which is based upon the policy of exploitation of physically weaker races and upon the policy of brute force." This statement, true as it is, it is somewhat too limited in that it refers to Great Britain alone to the exclusion of the other Capitalists' Governments, such as Germany, France, America etc; the only difference is the degree to which this "brute force" is carried and the method of its application as well as the serpentine diplomacy on which it is being meandered. In America, for instance it takes the form of burning, popularly called lynching while at the same-time "democracy" is preached and carried to a certain extend, for you are safe in America as long as you keep in your place. The American whiteman can tolerate and give you all the educational, the religious and and all the other equalities but not *social equality*, and political equality in their

superlative degree.

Hence the doctrine of the Ku Klux Klan of the "nigger must keep in his place" and the often repeated slogan of "imperium within imperio cannot exist."

France and Germany are doing it through the subtle inter-colonial systems of using the Black man as a cannon fodder in the wars in order to bring into materiality their schemes of territorial expansion.

But it is left with Great Britain to show and to use the worse possible method of this *brute force*, indeed the most destructive, the most un-Christian, the most heathenish. It is a combination of all that is bad fancied or real!

Thanks be to God, the Omnipotent, the Omniscient and the Omnipresent that Great Britain, the one time "mistress of the sea" for we sometime read in Latin Brittania *undas gurbenat* she is no more. She has suffered of late, a political disintegration of the worst-kind, to the extent that she is now simply called a Common Wealth of nations instead of the colourless capitalistic concoction of "an Empire on whose soil the sun never sets!" The policy

Great Britain has re-sorted to in order to realise her imperialistic dreams is unchristian, in that it is the policy of divide and rule.

The ministers as angels, wolves in sheep-skins are agents of this malice.

Governors under Crown systems are working hand in hand with missionaries. The system has caused a great deal of havoc amongst the unfortunate uncivilised backward races throughout the British Colonies. This divide and rule policy has constituted and aggravated the caste system already in vogue in India among the Indians.

The method there is this: as it is with us here in Africa the whiteman marries an Indian woman and the off-spring is called Eurasian. The Eurasian problem in India is as much as the native and coloured problem is in all the British possessions.

The second phase of this brute force is the autocratic power given to the dominions by Great Britain for no other purpose but that of racial extinction even as she has done with the Maories of Australia. In India and in Africa where there is a preponderance of all that is non-European she has introduced opium, alcoholic drinks and daily measures as we see here in the Union.

The *African World* (1925–1926), subtitled "Mouthpiece of the Cape Congress," persistently attacked what it termed the "capitalists" and was generally sympathetic to African worker struggles.

African Leader (1932–1933) supported the ANC's moderate political stance at the time but drew attention to harsh African labor conditions.

Inkokeli

YA BANTU

(THE BANTU LEADER)

A MONTHLY MAGAZINE

Published by The African National Publishing Co., 168 Loop Street, Cape Town.

Circulating throughout the Union and the Protectorates of Southern Africa.

A Journal for the free thought and free expression on matters affecting Africans.

Vol. 2.　No. 4.　PRICE 3d.　　　　CAPE TOWN.　　　　FEBRUARY, 1942.

"God in His wisdom planted Herbs for all the ills of man"

The Natal Herbs

SPECIALISTS IN HERBS.

If your complaints require Herbs, you could do no better than consulting, or writing to the above firm which specialises in . . . . . .

Herbs of Superior Quality

Herbs stocked for all complaints. Numerous Testimonials of gratitude filed from grateful people who testify of the quality of the Herbs supplied by

THE NATAL HERBS

and what they have proved to them.

A TRIAL ORDER IS SOLICITED FROM YOU

All correspondence to be addressed to BOX 1829, Cape Town.

222 HANOVER ST., CAPE TOWN.

FIRM FAVOURITES FOR OVER 40 YEARS.. FLAG

THE FLAG

CORK TIPPED AND PLAIN CIGARETTES

The pro-ANC *Inkokeli ya Bantu* (The Bantu Leader, 1940–1942) often provided a forum for African workers and their trade unions in the Cape at a time when these unions lacked their own press.

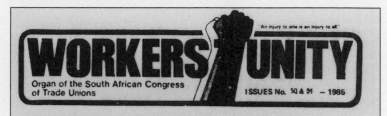

WORKERS UNITY

"An injury to one is an injury to all"

Organ of the South African Congress of Trade Unions

ISSUES No. 50 & 51 — 1985

TRADE UNION UNITY
A major workers victory

A trade union is a mass association of working people. For it to be able to challenge the power of the capitalist bosses, it has to be united and organised on the industrial principle, but for such unity to be lasting, it must be based on principles; it has to be arrived at on the basis of equality and mutual respect for one another. The aim should not be to form a federation for the sake of a federation. The ultimate objective should be to unite the workers through the federation. Unless and until all the oppressed and exploited workers of our country are involved in these talks with the unity of purpose in mind, trade union unity would not be easy to achieve.

The desire by the majority of the unions to form a trade union federation cannot be doubted, but what we are doubting is weather all the unions share a common objective. Since the 1981 Langa Summit Meeting, we have been closely following the developments in the unity talks, not as observers, but as participants in our own right. Indeed, the talks have shown qualitative developments.

In spite of all the good work that has been done so far, there remain a number of unresolved questions. To quote only a few:
* What is the basis of this unity we are talking about?
* What is the role of the Feasibility Committee vis-a-vis the industrialisation of the general workers' unions?

Contd on page 12

CONTENTS

	Page
Trade Union Unity	1 & 12
Unemployment	2 - 3
International	4 - 5

May 1st poster	6 - 7
Industrial Courts	8 & 9
Renegade British workers	9 & 11

Workers against-Apartheid	10

Exile newspapers like *Workers' Unity* championed worker struggles in the 1980s.

Conclusion

The banning of the ANC in 1960 saw the African nationalist press forced underground. Nevertheless, with the resurgence of the black trade union movement, the revival of political resistance, and the renaissance of the alternative press in the 1970s and 1980s, workers' interests and needs became much more visible in mediating the news of South Africa.

Mention of the ANC in the press often was illegal between 1960 and 1990, but Congress Alliance exile publications continued to be issued—most notably *Sechaba* (1967–90) but also *Workers' Unity, Mayibuye,* and *Dawn.* In these publications, African worker struggles were given considerable prominence. Underground leaflets were distributed inside the country. An ANC leaflet in 1970, for example, specifically called for worker mobilization as the key to taking "back our country." The journal of Umkhonto we Sizwe in 1983 called for "united action for the creation of one [trade union] federation." Underground revolutionary comic strips made direct reference to workers and their relationship to the ANC.[135]

As urbanization and African literacy rose[136] and labor unrest accelerated, there was growing sympathy for the struggles of African workers and nationalists from a repoliticized, white-owned black press and a burgeoning alternative press.

The African nationalist press throughout its history represented African workers as exploited victims of an oppressive system. In other ways, workers were poorly represented. They did not significantly participate in the running of the press, and neither Congress nor its allied press envisaged an independent political role for workers. The message of the press often was ambiguous: it mass-produced editorials on industrial moderation as much as on the plight of labor. It rarely portrayed workers as individuals. The scant press images of working lives did not capture the vibrancy of working-class culture. This inability to represent workers more accurately is related to press ownership and editors' ideologies.

The labor reporting of the pro-ANC press does suggest that its staff were in touch with sections of the working class. Given the neglect of African demands in the white press and limited labor coverage in publications not allied with the ANC and its allies, the political newspapers supporting Congress were one of the few news outlets for African labor. They became a medium through which some workers were able to communicate their feelings to a wider community.

Notes

1. P. Walshe, *The Rise of African Nationalism in South Africa* (Johannesburg: Donker, 1970), 243; A. Cobley, *Class and Consciousness: The Black Petty Bourgeoisie in South Africa, 1924 to 1950* (New York: Greenwood, 1990), 170–72; E. Feit, *South Africa: The Dynamics of the African National Congress* (London: Oxford University Press, 1962), 1–9, 26–36; T. Lodge, *Black Politics in South Africa since 1945* (London: Longman, 1983), 2–10, 110; M. Benson, *South Africa: The Struggle for a Birthright* (London: Faber, 1964), 164; F. Meli, *South Africa Belongs to Us: A History of the ANC* (London: Currey, 1989), 37–44; T. Lodge, "Political Organizations in Pretoria's African Townships, 1940–1963," in *Class, Community, and Conflict*, ed. B. Bozzoli (Johannesburg: Ravan, 1987), 401–17.

2. W. Hofmeyr, "Rural Popular Organization and Its Problems: Struggles in the Western Cape, 1929–1930," *Africa Perspective* 22 (1983): 26–49; P. Delius, "*Sebatakgomo* and the Zoutpansberg Balemi Association," *Journal of African History* 34 (1993): 293–313.

3. H. Sapire, "African Political Organisation in Brakpan in the '50s," *African Studies* 48 (1989): 183–207; J. Cherry, "The Making of an African Working Class, Port Elizabeth, 1925–63" (M.A. thesis, University of Cape Town, 1992).

4. Bozzoli argues that the ANC of the 1950s was able to successfully enter the mind of some wage earners. B. Bozzoli, with M. Nkotsoe, *Women of Phokeng* (London: Currey, 1991), 239–41. H. Bradford

is one of few to warn against "strait-jacketing of struggles within extremely schematic categories . . . [such as] 'petit bourgeois.'" Bradford, *A Taste of Freedom: The ICU in Rural South Africa* (New Haven: Yale University Press, 1987), 15–16. The harshness of laborers' lives stands in sharp contrast to the "easy" lives of clerks. Yet, a racially ordered society impeded the upward social mobility of *all* African wage earners, lending credence to Stedman Jones's emphasis, in a different context, on the lack of a "great political, cultural and economic divide" between middle and working classes. G. S. Jones, *Languages of Class* (Cambridge: Cambridge University Press, 1983), 183–85.

5. P. Limb, "The ANC and Black Workers," in *Peace, Politics, and Violence in the New South Africa*, ed. N. Etherington (Oxford: H. Zell, 1992), 284–305.

6. A. Odendaal, *Vukani Bantu! The Beginnings of Black Protest Politics in South Africa to 1912* (Cape Town: D. Philip, 1984), 286, 8–21; Odendaal, "'Even White Boys Call Us 'Boy': Early Black Organisational Politics in Port Elizabeth," *Kronos* 20 (1993): 3–16.

7. P. Morris, "The Early Black South African Newspaper and the Development of the Novel," *Journal of Commonwealth Literature* 15, 1 (1980): 15–29, 16; J. Peires, *The House of Phalo* (Johannesburg: Ravan, 1981), 176; T. Couzens, introduction to *R. R. R. Dhlomo* (Grahamstown: NELM, 1975); B. Bozzoli and P. Delius, "Radical History and South African Society," *Radical History Review* 46 (1990): 13–46, 16.

8. R. R. R. Dhlomo, "The Black Bolshevik Factory" (*Sjambok*, 7 March 1930), in *R.R.R. Dhlomo*, 61–65; B. Peterson, "*The Black Bulls* of H. I. E. Dhlomo," *English in Africa* 18, 1 (1991): 25–49; J. Gomas, *One Hundred Years: "Emancipation of Slaves"* (Cape Town: CPSA, 1934).

9. J. Lonsdale, "Some Origins of Nationalism in East Africa," *Journal of African History* 9 (1968): 119–46; B. Davidson, *The Black Man's Burden: Africa and the Curse of the Nation-State* (London: Currey, 1992), 163–66; B. Anderson, *Imagined Communities* (London: Verso, 1983), 13–15, 137.

10. P. Seme, "The Native National Congress," *Tsala ea Batho*, 17 July 1915.

11. P. Jordan, "The South African Liberation Movement and the Making of a New Nation," in *The National Question in South Africa*, ed. M. Diepen (London: Zed, 1988), 110–24, 112.

12. A. Ashforth, *The Politics of Official Discourse in Twentieth-Century South Africa* (Oxford: Clarendon, 1990), 43.

13. T. Lodge, "Charters from the Past: The African National Congress and Its Historiographical Traditions," *Radical History Review* 46/47 (1990), 161–88.

14. D. Reid, *Paris Sewers and Sewermen: Realities and Representations* (Harvard University Press, 1991), 87. See also S. Hall, ed., *Representation* (London: Sage, 1997).

15. On frequency analysis see L. Switzer, "Moderate and Militant Voices in the African Nationalist Newspapers during the 1920s," in *South Africa's Alternative Press: Voices of Protest and Resistance, 1880s–1960s*, ed. L. Switzer (Cambridge: Cambridge University Press, 1996), 147–88.

16. Cape Archives Depot (CAD), Native Affairs (NA) 544/579: "Rules of the Native Congress," *Izwi Labantu* 16 June 1903; SANC telegram, 3 July 1903; Secretary of Native Affairs (SNA) "Memorandum on SANC," 28 April 1906, 25 July 1902; *Izwi*, 14 April 1906; editorial, *Koranta ea Becoana*, 4 July 1903.

17. Odendaal, *Vukani Bantu!* 272–78; Walshe, *Nationalism*, 34; letter of J. S. Kokozela and T. G. Diniso (Kimberley branch secretaries), *Tsala ea Batho*, 14 March 1914, 6 April 1912.

18. L. Switzer, "The Beginnings of African Protest Journalism at the Cape," in *Alternative Press*, ed. Switzer, 57–82.

19. L. Switzer, "The African Christian Community and Its Press in Victorian South Africa," *Cahiers d'études africaines* 96 (1984): 455–76, 464.

20. Natal Archives Depot [NAD], SNA 991/1906, J. Dube to Native Affairs, 29 March 1906, and NA replies, citing S.A. Native Affairs Commission Report 1903–5 s.324–25

21. The other main African newspapers of the period, *Ilanga* and *Imvo*, are treated in R. Hunt Davis, "'Qude maniki!' John L. Dube, Pioneer Editor of *Ilanga Lase Natal*," in Switzer, *Alternative Press*, 83–98, and Switzer, "Beginnings of African Protest," 59–63, respectively, though neither deals at any length with labor issues.

22. A. Odendaal, "African mobilisation in the Eastern Cape, 1880–1910" (Ph.D. diss., Cambridge University, 1983), 170–71, 196; CAD NA 544/579: Soga to Civil Commissioner, East London, 25 April 1906; SNA, "Memorandum SANC," 25 July 1902; SNA 1/237, 4 July 1903: "Native Congress, Indwe . . . ," "Meeting at King

Williams Town," 1902; "Intlanganiso Ye SANC," *Izwi*, 14 October 1902.

23. Odendaal, *Vukani Bantu!* 69, 95 (citing *Izwi*, 1 May 1906); *Izwi Labantu*, 23 February 1909.

24. *Izwi Labantu*, 8 February, 16 March 1909, 6 May, 4 November 1902; "Native Labour," 29 September, 13 October 1908, 8 February 1909, 9 July, 6 August, 3 September, 3 December 1901, 19, 26 May, 21 July, 24 November 1908, 13 January 1909, 13, 20 February, 1906. The regular printing of mining company advertisements directed at laborers suggests some workers read (or had read to them) the newspaper. Local labor recruiters, such as a Mr. Shingler, also advertised for workers in *Izwi Labantu* (e.g., 2 March 1909).

25. *Izwi Labantu*, 29 September, 13 October, 19, 26 May, 21 July 1908, 16 March 1909.

26. *Izwi Labantu*, 29 September, 19, 26 May, 21 July, 27 October 1908.

27. *Izwi Labantu*, 6, 27 May 1902, 21 July 1908, 3 December 1901; Odendaal, "Mobilisation," 199, 218–19.

28. "Liquidation," *Izwi*, 16 April 1909; "Bantu Union," *Black Man*, November 1920.

29. Odendaal, *Vukani Bantu!* 61; *Report of the South African Native Affairs Commission 1903–5*, 3:539, 544; *Ipepa lo Hlanga*, 14 December 1900, 14 June 1901, 17 July 1902, cited in P. Warwick, *Black People and the South African War, 1899–1902* (Cambridge: Cambridge University Press, 1983), 163, 172, 144.

30. Hunt Davis, "'Qude maniki!'" 87; *Ilanga lase Natal*, 10 April 1903, cited in Davis; *Ilanga lase Natal*, 29 May 1903, cited in Warwick, *Black People*, 172; S. G. Rich, "Keeping Them Ignorant," *International*, 21 July 1916 (citing *Ilanga lase Natal*).

31. B. Willan, "Sol Plaatje, De Beers, and an Old Tram Shed: Class Relations and Social Control in a South African Town, 1918–19," *Journal of Southern African Studies* 4 (1978): 195–215; Willan, *Sol Plaatje: South African Nationalist, 1876–1932* (London: Heinemann, 1984), 218ff.

32. Willan, *Plaatje*, chaps. 5–6. This tendency is continued by Plaatje, *Selected Writings*, ed. B. Willan (Johannesburg: Ravan, 1996); however, a different selection of texts could demonstrate a more labor-conscious Plaatje.

33. Editorials, *Koranta ea Becoana*, 20 June, 25 July 1903; "Asiatic Labour," 29 August 1903; 31 December 1902, 11 April, 7 February, 4

November 1903; "Native Labour," 17 January 1903; "Hats Off for the Colonial Secretary," 24 January 1903; "Labour," 4 November 1903. *Koranta* did print a Sylvester Williams article attacking Chamberlain and "his gold-worshipping confrères": "Mr. Chamberlain," 18 July 1903.

34. *Koranta ea Becoana*, 11 October, 15 November 1902.

35. *Koranta ea Becoana*, 2 December, 28 October 1903.

36. Editorials, *Koranta ea Becoana*, 25 July, 2 December 1903; 18 April, 24 January, 29 August 1903; 28 October, 18, 11 November, 4 April 1903; "The Labour Problem," 27 June 1903.

37. *Koranta ea Becoana*, 7, 14 March 1903; Willan, *Plaatje*, 109, 125.

38. Willan, *Plaatje*, 137; L. and D. Switzer, *The Black Press in South Africa and Lesotho: A Descriptive Bibliographical Guide, 1836–1976* (Boston: G. K. Hall, 1979), 61–62.

39. *Tsala ea Becoana*, "S.A. Native Congress," 17 February 1912; 2 August 1913; 17 October 1914; P. Seme, "Native National Congress," 17 July 1915; "Native Land Bill," 10 May 1913; 26 July 1913. Circulation increased from 1,700 in 1910 to 4,000 in 1913.

40. *Tsala ea Becoana*, 2 December 1911; 17 February 1912, 17 July 1915; letter of "Native Sufferer," 25 October 1913; letter of E. Monye, 10 May 1913; letters of G. Matlhako (Bultfontein mine) and A. I. Kipalisa (Nourse mine) 5, 19 July 1913; "'Benefit' Societies," 30 August 1913; "Native Wages on Their Mine," 18 April 1918.

41. *Tsala ea Becoana*, S. Plaatje, "Along the Colour Line," 3 January 1914; "The Coloured Man's Chance," 17 January 1914; Plaatje, "Along the Colour Line," 10 January 1914.

42. *Tsala ea Becoana*, 14, 28 November 1914; 23 January, 15, 22, 29 May 1915; 3, 17 September, 24 December 1910; 30 August 1913; 21 February, 7 March 1914.

43. *Tsala ea Becoana* was "carefully read by the heads" of several state departments: "Native Papers and Missionaries," 21 March 1914. *Tsala* was "widely read" in North West Cape, Western Transvaal, and Orange Free State: Z. K. Matthews, "Solomon Plaatje," *Imvo Zabantsundu*, 24 June 1961.

44. *Bantu World*, 25 June 1932. In the 1920s, Plaatje largely withdrew from ANC politics, but his continued sympathy for African workers is evident in his graphic description of the wretched conditions of Lichtenburg laborers. Plaatje, "Native Life at the Alluvial Diggings," *Daily Dispatch*, 7 May 1927.

45. TNC Constitution s.19, NTS 17/326; Switzer, *Black Press*, 25; Carter Karis Collection 2:Xl13: 96/1.

46. *Abantu-Batho*, 18 July 1918. Mvabaza worked as a location "wardsman" in Port Elizabeth before becoming coeditor of *Abantu-Batho* in 1913: Odendaal, "Mobilisation," 263; *Political Profiles*, 107.

47. *Abantu-Batho*, 15 May 1919, tr. in Transvaal Archives Depot (TAD) 7204 17/326; *Imvo Zabantsundu*, 16 July 1918. Letanka worked as an interpreter, then on *Abantu-Batho*. T. D. Mwlei Skota, ed., *The African Yearly Register* (Johannesburg: Esson, 1932), 147.

48. H. Msane, "The Ethiopian Movement," *International*, 21 July 1916; reports on "Internationalist Socialistic Meeting," 19 July, 15, 22 November 1917, tr. of H. Msane, "IWA," *Abantu-Batho*, 22 November 1917; South African Police (SAP) to Secretary of Justice (JUS), 31 July 1917, "*Industrial Workers of Africa* enroled," [November 1917?], JUS 3/527/17; "IWA," 13 June 1918, in TAD, Government Native Labour Bureau (GNLB) 281, 446/17/D48. IWA meetings continued to be advertised (*Abantu-Batho* 4 July 1918, JUS 3/527/17), but its leaders gravitated to Cape Town and it eventually dissolved into the ICU around 1919.

49. *International*, 2, 9, 16 June 1916. On editorial tussles between Grendon and the more moderate Kunene, see C. Lowe, "'The Tragedy of Malunge,' or, the Fall of the House of Chiefs," African Studies Association, Boston, 1993, 3–11, 77–79.

50. *Ilanga lase Natal*, 11, 18–19 October 1918, cited in T. Couzens, "Robert Grendon: Iris Traders, Cricket Scores, and Paul Kruger's Dreams," *English in Africa* 15, 2 (1988): 49–91, 50, 77, 82.

51. *New Dictionary of South African Biography* (Pretoria: HSRC, 1995), 61–62.

52. [Phooko], "Firm and Just, or, Just and Firm," *Abantu-Batho*, reprinted in *International*, 15 December 1916.

53. *International*, "Modern Voortrekkers," 15 December 1916, citing *Abantu-Batho*, 30 November 1916.

54. *Abantu-Batho*, "Native Drudgery," November 1916, cited in *International*, 1 December 1916.

55. *Abantu-Batho*, "Beware of Labour Cranks," November 1916, cited in *International*, 19 October 1917: harsh criticism of a sometime ally but typical of contemporary ISL views.

56. Extant library runs of *Abantu-Batho* are limited to a few years (1920, 1930–31) and preclude any systematic analysis of consistency of approach to workers.

57. *Abantu-Batho*, M. Poseka, "About Native Women's Passes," 13 December 1917, tr. in SAP to JUS, 20 December 1917; *Abantu-Batho*, "Passes for Women," 20 December 1917, cited in JUS 3/527/7.

58. *Abantu-Batho*, 6 December 1917, tr. in SAP Ermelo to SAP Pretoria, 12 December 1917: JUS 3/527/7.

59. *Abantu-Batho*, 20 December 1917; reports of detectives on meetings, 18 January 1918; *Abantu-Batho*, M. Poseka, "About Native Women's Passes," 13 December 1917: all in JUS.

60. *Abantu-Batho*, 18 July 1918; 4 July 1918, tr. in JUS, file 3/527/17.

61. NTS 7204 17/326: tr. of *Abantu-Batho*, 15 May 1919, NA 1217/14/D.110, tr. of TNC notice in *Abantu-Batho*, 15 May 1919, NA 1217/14/D.110; *Abantu-Batho*, 3 April 1919 in TAD DNL 309 125/19048, cited in P. Bonner, "Transvaal Native Congress 1917– 1920: The Radicalisation of the Black Petty Bourgeoisie on the Rand," in *Industrialisation and Social Change in South Africa*, ed. S. Marks and R. Rathbone (London: Longman, 1982), 270–313, 300.

62. *Abantu-Batho*, February 1920; *International*, 27 February 1920; *Star*, 18 February 1920; *Rand Daily Mail*, 20, 27 February 1920; *Cape Argus*, 23, 26 February, 1 March 1920.

63. *Imvo Zabantsundu*, "Threatened Revolution," 15 July 1913, 9 July 1918; "Native Nationalists," 24 December 1918; 16 July, 17 September, 19, 27 November, 3 December 1918.

64. From 9.7 percent in 1921 to 21.3 percent in 1946. Switzer, "Beginnings of African Protest," 2, 10.

65. See Switzer, "Moderate and Militant Voices."

66. The so-called carry-on readership (literates reading to nonliterates or passing the newspaper on to other literates), however, would probably be much in excess of this figure. E. Rosenthal, *Bantu Journalism in South Africa* (Johannesburg: Society of the Friends of Africa, 1949); A. Friedgut, "The Non-European Press," in *Handbook on Race Relations in South Africa*, ed. E. Hellmann (Cape Town: Oxford University Press, 1949), 484–510.

67. *Umsebenzi*, 12 December, 2 May 1930; 11 May 1935; 7 April 1934. ANC-CPSA members, despite their criticism, estimated that many Africans still looked to the ANC as a champion of their rights. J. B. M[arks], "Natives and Organisation," *Umsebenzi*, 16 February, 4 May 1935; B. Bunting, *Moses Kotane* (London: Inkululeko, 1976), 58.

68. L. Switzer, "*Bantu World* and the Origins of a Captive African Commercial Press in South Africa," *Journal of Southern African Studies*

14 (1988): 351–70; I. S. Manoim, "The Black Press, 1945–63" (M.A. thesis, University of the Witwatersrand, 1983), 1, 40–50. In 1932, J. D. Rheinallt Jones and advertisers "evolved a scheme" to "improve" and supply news to the African press, enabling "their policies (moderate and co-operative) to be protected." The scheme failed. "Minutes of a Meeting of the Executive Committee, SA Institute of Race Relations (SAIRR), 4 March 1932," in SAIRR, "Records Relating to the Joint Councils of Europeans and Natives, 1929–40," University of the Witwatersrand, W. Cullen Library.

69. K. Tomaselli, R. Tomaselli, and J. Muller, "The Political Economy of the South African Press," in *The Press in South Africa*, ed. K. and R. Tomaselli and J. Muller (London: Currey, 1987), 39–117.

70. ICU Secretary Kadalie worked only briefly, as a teacher and as a clerk; ICU *yase* Natal leader A. W. G. Champion worked as a mine policeman and then went into business.

71. L. Switzer, "The Ambiguities of Protest in South Africa: Rural Politics and the Press during the 1920s," *International Journal of African Historical Studies* 23, 1 (1990), 87–109; idem, "Moderate and Militant Voices," 152–77.

72. Marcus Garvey's ideas of race pride, black business, and black solidarity spread in South Africa from about 1920. Garveyism influenced ANC leaders such as Plaatje, Josiah Gumede, and Mweli Skota. H. D. Tyamzashe, editor of the *Workers' Herald*, wrote for Garvey's *Negro World*. See R. Hill and G. Pirio, "'Africa for the Africans': The Garvey Movement in South Africa, 1920–40," in *The Politics of Race, Class, and Nationalism in Twentieth-Century South Africa*, ed. S. Marks and S. Trapido (London: Longman, 1987), 209–53; Cobley, *Class and Consciousness*, 183–88; *Negro World*, 4 November 1922; 17 November 1923; 2 August 1924.

73. P. Wickins, *The Industrial and Commercial Workers' Union of Africa* (Cape Town: Oxford University Press, 1978), 66, 41; TAD, NA 39/362: memo of 29 July 1926, and "Non-European Political Organizations in the Union," mimeo [1926]; *Black Man*, August 1920.

74. "The Recruiting System," *Black Man*, 1, 2 (August 1920); 1, 3 (September 1920).

75. "Our Demands," "ICU and Mr. Simon Jordan," *Black Man*, 1, 4 (October 1920).

76. *African World* 1, 1 (23 May 1925); "UNIA Stands Uncompromisingly for Manhood Rights on Behalf of 400,000,000 Negroes," 30 May, 13 June 1925.

77. *African World* 8, 22 August, 23, 30 May, 27 June, 11, 25 July, 1925, 9 January 1926. Subeditor Arthur Ndollo (ANC choir conductor) and assistant editor Johnson Dlwati (W. Cape assistant secretary) also were ANC figures.

78. *African World*, 23 May 1925; "The Significance of Garvey," 8 August, 23 May 1925.

79. *African World*, 10 October 1925; J. Nduma, "The Onlooker," 23 May 1925.

80. *African World*, 23 May, 12 September, 1925; 9 January 1926; 4 July, 22 August, 27 June, 30 May 1925.

81. *African World*, "The Shipping Strike," 12 September 1925; 26 September 1925.

82. *African World*, J. Ngedlane letter, 3 October 1925; B. Ndobe, "Makhoa a Kotula Lipelaelo," 13 June 1925; T. Mbeki, "The Spirit of Self-Determination," 4 July 1925; S. Silwana, "The Iniquities of Legislators," 26 September 1925, 24 October 1925; L. Stebe "Black Man Bound for the African Empire," 20 June 1925.

83. *Abantu-Batho*, 14 June 1923 (Swaziland Archives RCS 486/23). Thanks to C. Lowe for this source.

84. *Abantu-Batho*, A. N[zula], "The Tyranny of the Pass Laws and Pin Pricks," 25 September 1930; C. Baker, "Imperialism in Practice," 4, 11 September 1930.

85. *Abantu-Batho*, 1, 15 May 5, 17 June 1930; Skota, *Register*, 439.

86. H. S. Msimang ascribed Gumede's fall to his failure to consult with his executive and his inclination to seek guidance from "outside." Msimang, "Why Mr. Gumede Failed," *Umteteli*, 31 May 1930. In 1931, Gumede decried legislation that discriminated against African workers. Gumede, "Minutes of Evidence," Native Economic Commission, 10 April 1931, 6825ff. At a 1934 ICU meeting, he moved resolutions on African wages and unemployment. NA 49/328.

87. *Abantu-Batho*, 7 May 1931; [Champion], "The Story of My Exile," *Abantu-Batho*, 16 April 1931; Thibedi, "Meqoqo le Basebetsi," *Abantu-Batho*, 11 June 1931.

88. Skota, *Register*, 171; "Lefu la D. S. Letanka," *Bantu World*, 7 May 1932; *Political Profiles*, 58.

89. *Abantu-Batho*, "You May Not See Us Again Alive," 7 May 1931; "Alive Again," 11 June 1931; 25 June 1931. The 1930 prospectus for *Abantu-Batho*'s sale listed the directors as: Gumede (farmer), S. Matseke (shoemaker), Letanka (journalist), and Masabalala (journalist). *Abantu-Batho*, 1 May 1930.

90. *Umsebenzi,* 21 July 1934; G. Mbeki, *The Struggle for Liberation in South Africa: A Short History* (Cape Town: D. Philip, 1992), 89.

91. Switzer, *Black Press,* 27, 38. *Ikwezi* was chiefly concerned with the rights of African property owners but drew attention to the way in which poor people were penalized by the sale of African houses by location authorities, and reported favorably on efforts for ICU unity. *Ikwezi Le Africa,* "Sale of Location Houses," "Trade Union Unity," 27 June 1931.

92. *African Leader,* 19 November, 31 December 1932; 29 April, 18 March 1933.

93. *African Leader,* 11 February, 1 April 1933.

94. H. G. Plaatje, "The Native Mind," *African Leader,* 18 February 1933; K. Thaele, "ANC," ibid., 18 February 1933. See also D. Taabe, "Unemployment," ibid., 11 March 1933.

95. *African Leader,* "Some of the Opportunities Lost," 1 April 1933.

96. *Izwi Lama Afrika,* 14 August 1931, 8 May 1931.

97. *Izwi Lama Afrika,* "We Protest," 5 June 1931; "Native Service Contract Bill," 12 February 1932.

98. *Izwi Lama Afrika,* "Complaints against Employers," 12 June 1931; "Location Native Staff," H. D. T[yamzashe], "Location Roads," 3 July 1931; "Native Revenue Account," 2, 18 January 1932; "Permit System," 14 August 1931; "Convict Labour," 12 February 1932.

99. *Izwi Lama Afrika,* Bennett Ncwana, "Cape Native Franchise," 14 August 1931; "Natives Are Starving," January 1932; "Native Unemployed," January 1932.

100. *Izwi Lama Afrika,* "Fighting Dirt," January 1932.

101. Switzer, *Black Press,* 47; *Izwi,* 19 June 1931, 27 February 1932. Some articles supported the ANC. "Musa" urged Africans to take greater interest "in fighting organisations" such as the Independent ICU and the ANC. Musa, "The Hemming-in-Process," 14 August 1931.

102. *Izwi,* 15 February 1936; H. D. Tyamzashe, "What the White Man Doesn't Know, But Should Know, about the Native," 16 April 1936; 15 May, 15 June, 16 August 1936; 15 December 1937; 15 March 1938; 16 January, 15 February 1939; 15 April 1939; "Bantu Trade Union Movement," 15 May 1939; "Africans on Strike," 15 November 1939.

103. The missionary-controlled *Izindaba Zabantu* ran a series, for

example, on the virtues of Catholic socialism. See "People's Banks" by Bernard Huss in *Izindaba Zabantu* in 1927.

104. *Workers' Herald*, 28 April 1926.

105. *Imvo*, "Native Labour Unions," 9 May 1922; 25 April 1922; "The Industrial Crisis," 28 February 1922; letter of Eastern Cape Native Farmers' Association, 9 March 1920; "Garveyism," 31 March 1922; 23 December 1930.

106. Willan, *Plaatje*, 251–53.

107. *Abantu-Batho*, 12 February 1931.

108. Switzer, *Black Press*, 110; *Umteteli*, 7 August 1920; *Abantu-Batho*, 20 July 1920; K. Breckenridge, "'Money with Dignity,'" *Journal of African History* 36 (1995): 271–304, 279.

109. *Bantu World*, 23 April, 7, 14 May 1932. Hyman Basner stated that it "was child's play for the Chamber [of Mines]" to buy African newspapers that "immediately . . . took on a liberal instead of a militant nationalist complexion."

110. R. S. Thema and J. D. R. Jones, "In South Africa," in *Thinking with Africa*, ed. M. Stauffer (London: SCM, 1928), 36–65.

111. Switzer, *"Bantu World,"* 351–52.

112. E. Brookes, "Bantu Teacher Is Overworked and Underpaid," *Bantu World*, 4 June 1932; 18 August, 15 October 1938, 24 August 1935, 14 March 1936, 3 March 1934.

113. *Bantu World*, see editorials, 17 August 1935, 14 March 1936; 24 February 1934.

114. *Bantu World*, R.R.R. Dhlomo, "The Mine Tragedy," 4 June 1932; F. Le Mas, "The Black Workman's Story," 18 September 1937; "Increase the Blackman's Wage," 13, 20 July 1935; "African Workers Ill-Treated," 23 October 1937; "Farmers and African Labour," 21 August 1937; HLP, "Life at Diamond Diggings," 16 January 1937.

115. "Dorcas," a domestic worker, wrote that teachers "despise us." Another worker, Norah Molao, emphasized loyalty to employers. *Bantu World*, letters from "Dorcas," 5 February 1938, and N. Molao, 30 November 1935; G. Khumalo argued that "employers will always pay very little to the poor workers." Letter of G. Khumalo, *Bantu World*, 17 July 1937.

116. *Bantu World*, 6 August 1938, 4 January, 5 December 1936, 16 October 1937, 3 March 1934, 23 January 1937, 9 April, 28 May, 4, 11 June 1938; 7 May 1932; letters of P. Ramutla, 15 October 1938; Lekoko, 29 May 1937; J. Gubevu, 10 July 1937; J. Mantshongo, 19

March 1938; 23 October 1937; "Forty African Strikers Raid Factory," 27 February; 16 October, 18 September 1937.

117. *Inkululeko*, 10 July, 14 August, 18 September, 9 October 1943. See E. Jones, *"Inkululeko:* Organ of the Communist Party of South Africa, 1939–50," in Switzer, *Alternative Press*, 331–72.

118. See L. Switzer, "Socialism and the Resistance Movement: The Life and Times of the *Guardian*, 1937–52," in Switzer, *Alternative Press*, 266–307.

119. Switzer, *Black Press*, 43; *Inkokeli ya Bantu*, November, December 1940, July 1941.

120. *Verbatim Report of the Proceedings of the Natives Representative Council, 25 November–6 December 1940*, 1:xxvi–iii, 356–62; *Inkokeli ya Bantu*, July, January 1941.

121. *Inkokeli ya Bantu*, "The Lot of the African Worker," June 1941; "Congress and the Coal-Workers' Strike," July 1941; "Echo of the Coal Strike," August 1941.

122. *Inkokeli ya Bantu*, September, June 1941, March, April, May 1942; "Native Trade Unions," June 1942.

123. *Inkokeli ya Bantu*, "The Black Man in the Towns by the Black Man in the Street," November, December, March, April, February, 1941, January, June 1942; *Inkokeli ya Bantu*, November 1941, January 1942, July, March 1941.

124. *Izwi Lase Afrika*, 1, 1 (14 November 1941); "Cape African Congress Report"; "Cape African Congress: Address by Rev. J. A. Calata," 21 November 1941; "Miners' Phthisis Commission," 16 January 1942. Bennett Ncwana later called for the ANC to "establish a chain of African controlled newspapers." *Inkundla ya Bantu*, 14 April 1951.

125. *Inkundla* first appeared under an English title, *Territorial Magazine*, but in June 1940 it was given the Zulu-Xhosa title *Inkundla ya Bantu*—a shift in format that was welcomed by its readers. L. Switzer and I. Ukpanah, "Under Siege: *Inkundla ya Bantu* and the African Nationalist Movement, 1938–51," in Switzer, *Alternative Press*, 215.

126. *Inkundla ya Bantu*, 31 July 1944; April (2d fortnight), May (2d fort.) 1946, 17 April 1945, August (2d fort.) 1946, October (1st fort.) 1946, 5 June 1947, 17 July 1948.

127. Switzer and Ukpanah, "Under Siege"; Ukpanah, "Yearning to Be Free: *Inkundla ya Bantu* (Bantu Forum) as a Mirror and Me-

diator of the African National Struggle in South Africa, 1938–51" (Ph.D. diss., University of Houston, 1993), 125, 167–70, 191–95, 328–33.

128. *Inkundla*, 1 February 1941, 8 May 1947; Xuma to D. Sibeko, 9 November 1943, *Xuma Papers*.

129. *Inkundla*, 20 October, 2 June, 25 August, 16 June 1951; Ukpanah, "Yearning," 147; K. Eales, "Jordan Ngubane, *Inkundla ya Bantu* and the ANC Youth League, 1944–51" (B.A. [Hons.] thesis, University of Natal, 1984), 110; *Inkundla*, 17 July 1944, (2d fort.) April 1946.

130. "Programme of Action . . . ," in Karis, *Protest to Challenge*, 2, 337–39.

131. ANC, "Memorandum of Resolutions . . . 1949" and "CYL Manifesto," March 1944, in Karis, *Protest to Challenge*, 2, 302–8; A. Lembede, "Some Basic Principles of African Nationalism," *Inyaniso*, February 1945; Lembede, "Policy of the Congress Youth League," *Inkundla*, May 1946. The CYL also published a monthly in English entitled the *African Advocate* in 1947, but it lasted only about seven months. Switzer, *Black Press*, 26.

132. "Maintaining Contact with the People through the Newspapers," *Inyaniso* 1 (1954). *Inyaniso* was "cyclostyled" in New Brighton by Mokxotho Matji, ANC Cape secretary and a factory worker.

133. Manoim, "Black Press," 169–80, 223–25; Switzer, *Black Press*, 122–23, 110–11; *Imvo*, 6 January, 21 September, 2 February, 17 August 1946, 18 December 1948.

134. D. Tloome, "Lessons of the Stay-Away," *Liberation* 32 (1958); W. Sisulu, "Alliance of the Trade Union and Liberatory Movements in Africa," *Workers' Unity*, August 1955. See also E. Mphahlele, "Guts and Granite!" *Drum*, March 1956.

135. M. Shope, "SACTU's Role in the Developing Struggle," *Sechaba* 2, 8 (1968); "The ANC Says to Vorster and His Gang: Your Days Are Coming to an End!" leaflet, [ANC, 1970]; editorial, *Dawn*, 9–10 (1983): 2; *The Story of Simon and Jane* (n.p.: ANC, [1976]).

136. Urban African literacy tripled between 1951 and 1970 to reach two-thirds of the adult urban population. See C. Charney, "Black Power, White Press: Literacy, Newspapers, and the Transformation of Township Political Culture," African Studies Institute, University of the Witwatersrand, May 1993, seminar paper, 3–4.

3

"Far from Dead"

The Final Years of the *Guardian*, 1960–1963

James Zug

It was the last time they were happy.[1] Years later, when they looked back at that night, they realized it had been the end of something. Events steamrolled their lives in the months that followed so completely that the joy and optimism they had felt on New Year's Eve 1960 seemed impossible. Massacres, torture, exile, life imprisonment—the world tipped over and disconnected.

Like every year, the *Guardian* celebrated the 1960 New Year at Brian and Sonia Bunting's cottage above Clifton Beach in Cape Town. Nearly 200 old friends and colleagues crowded into steamy rooms, where the talk of politics and cigarette smoke thickened the summer air. They danced to a gramophone, drank champagne by the case, and reminisced about Lionel Forman, the senior staff writer who had died nine weeks before at the age of thirty-one. Late in the evening, the party thinned out. A gaggle of people walked down to the beach and skinny-dipped in the cool Atlantic surf. One couple wandered up the hill in hopes of summiting Lion's Head for sunrise. At daybreak, the house grew quiet, and Brian and Sonia climbed into bed for a few hours of sleep. Although it was New Year's Day, work beckoned. It was a Thursday and the *Guardian* would be appearing on the streets of Cape Town that afternoon.[2]

Every Thursday since February 1937 had been the same in that way, for the *Guardian* was as regular as the sun. Started by an eclectic group of young trade unionists, university professors, and disgruntled communists, the *Guardian* had become in the 1940s the leading voice of the South African freedom struggle. Nonracial, radical, and led in part by women, the newspaper had closely allied itself with the African National Congress by the 1950s. Its headquarters were in Barrack Street in Cape Town, with branch offices in Johannesburg, Durban, and Port Elizabeth. Circulation, which had topped fifty thousand during World War II, averaged in the mid-thirties in the 1950s, and most Congress leaders advised, fund-raised, sold, and wrote for the weekly. Under the apartheid regime, the *Guardian* suffered heavily for its stubbornly left-wing policies. The Security Branch arrested, watched, deported, raided, beat, shot, tapped telephones, intercepted post, and harassed those working on the newspaper. The government charged eight staff members and the newspaper itself with a capital crime, treason, as part of the mammoth four-year Treason Trial (no one discussed how a newspaper would be executed). Twice, in 1952 and 1954, the newspaper was banned, but each following Thursday a replica under a new title appeared.

Such reincarnations would prove more difficult in the 1960s, the fourth and final decade graced by the ink and newsprint of the *Guardian*. Three months after the Buntings' New Year's Eve party, the newspaper, called *New Age* at the time, was suspended for five months during a state of emergency. The government banned the ANC, the weekly's political raison d'être, and threw the liberation movement into disarray. In 1962, Pretoria again banned the weekly, and again a new version, *Spark*, emerged the following Thursday. Three months later the government pounded *Spark* out of existence by house-arresting almost the entire editorial staff.

The Briefcase and the Banana

The year started off badly. On 21 January 1960 the worst mining disaster in South African history occurred. A mine shaft in Coalbrook, in the Orange Free State, collapsed, killing more than 400 miners.[3] Two months later the boom was lowered. The police, in a small Transvaal town called Sharpeville, fired on an anti–pass law demonstration led by a new political movement, the Pan-Africanist Congress (PAC). Sixty-nine people were gunned down, many shot in the back. Rioting broke out across South Africa. The next day Chief Albert Lutuli, the ANC president, publicly burned his pass and declared 28 March to be a national day of mourning. As a national strike, the twenty-eighth was an overwhelming success, with the entire country brought to a standstill. That night thousands of bonfires lit up the Johannesburg skyline. In Orlando teenagers danced through the streets, tearing down telephone poles, and singing *thina silulusha*—"we are the youth."[4] In Cape Town the male migrant workers in Langa and neighboring Nyanga, two African townships, went on a general strike. The police responded by closing off the two townships.[5] The government halted the Treason Trial—the defense's second witness, Lutuli, had just taken the witness chair—and suspended the pass laws.

As the crisis worsened, the focus shifted to a single man, the twenty-three-year-old PAC leader in Cape Town, Philip Kgosana. After moving from Pretoria to Cape Town in 1959, Kgosana studied economics at the University of Cape Town but lived in a cubicle in one of Langa's hostels with a canning worker. To earn money he sold *Contact*, the Liberal Party's fortnightly. By early 1960, Kgosana had become the PAC's chairman for the city, and, after the Sharpeville massacre, he found himself the de facto leader of the liberation movement. As such, he got caught in the middle of a long-standing feud between Patrick Duncan and Brian Bunting. Duncan, the Liberal Party leader and editor of *Contact*, and Bunting, the editor of *New Age*, had fought numerous political battles in the late 1950s. Duncan loathed communism and often attacked the ANC and its allies for supporting the Soviet Union. Once he refused to run a Congress of Democrats advertisement on the grounds that the COD, made up largely of radical white political activists, was a "totalitarian organisation."[6] Bunting, in return, denounced the Liberal Party for its rejection of universal suffrage.

After Sharpeville, any pretense of civility disappeared as both men rushed to gain Kgosana's support. Duncan had the early advantage, due to his prior contacts with Kgosana. Every day after the massacre, Kgosana visited *Contact*'s offices to discuss the political situation, and on 23 March he attended one of Duncan's formal dinner parties.[7] When Kgosana was arrested on 25 March during a march he led to Caledon Square, Cape Town's police headquarters, Duncan intervened to have him released.[8] Kgosana initially agreed with Duncan's antipathy toward Barrack Street. He told the strikers in Langa early in the week to "be careful of *New Age*. . . . Let us close our ears to what the newspapers say and continue with our dynamic program."[9]

New Age, in its 24 March 1960 edition, covered the Sharpeville massacres—"Mass Slaughter"—and the Langa violence in depth, but its reports begged for a profile of the new student-turned-leader.[10] Duncan scoffed at *New Age*, calling its coverage of the PAC in Cape Town "absurd."[11] Bunting repeatedly sent interview requests to Kgosana, who initially turned them aside. But on 24 March the PAC leader, when visiting Duncan's offices, decided to exercise some independence or at least media savvy. He telephoned Barrack Street to arrange a time for an interview and later described the scene when he asked to speak with Bunting: "When Duncan heard the name 'Bunting' he grabbed the receiver from my hand and slammed it down in a wild fury. . . . He was so agitated with my having contacts with communists. . . . Bunting roared with laughter when I told him about my debacle with Duncan."[12] That night Duncan recorded a different interpretation in his diary:

> I spoke to him about Bunting. I said the PAC campaign was his campaign, and he must run it the way he wanted, but if he were to work closely with Bunting, he would have to count us out. I reminded him that Sobukwe had split with the ANC over the question of communist domination and told him that the Liberal Party was firmly anti-communist. He was extraordinarily nice about it and thanked me for the advice. "I am still young," he said, "and shall be always grateful to you for advice when you see any way in which you think we are going wrong."[13]

Either way, Kgosana left Duncan's offices, walked over to Barrack Street, and gave a long interview to Bunting.[14]

Neither Bunting, Duncan, or Kgosana could have predicted what happened next. At three in the morning on 30 March 1960, the South African government secretly declared martial law. Police swept into homes across the nation to arrest hundreds of activists.[15] At dawn they raided Langa, arresting hundreds of workers, beating others, and forcing strikers onto buses to take them to work. Furious, Langa residents spontaneously marched to Caledon Square. The news of the march reached Barrack Street, and the entire staff of *New Age* walked over to Caledon Square and watched the estimated 30,000 protesters from the roof of a building across the street.[16] "History was being made" remembered Brian Bunting. "We knew that. We stood on the roof and gasped at the crowd coming down Buitenkant Street. There were so many. We had never seen so many Africans together, all at once. And they were so orderly and quiet. Kgosana was so cool and efficient."[17] On the steps of the police station, Kgosana spoke to the people and negotiated with the police commander. Some onlookers later claimed Duncan pushed his way to the front and advised Kgosana to accept the commander's promise of an audience with the minister of justice if he sent the crowd home.[18]

At five in the afternoon, after cooling his heels with Patrick Duncan in *Contact*'s boardroom, Kgosana and five other PAC officials returned to meet with the minister.[19] Instead of meeting with the minister, they were arrested and thrown into solitary confinement. The government that evening went on the radio and publicly announced what many already knew: South Africa was in a state of emergency.

Martial law went into effect and detention without trial was legalized. The police shut down the townships, imposing a curfew, turning off electricity, water, and telephone service, and physically driving workers back to the factories.[20] The pass laws, suspended after Sharpeville, were reinstated on 6 April. Pretoria banned the ANC and the PAC. Beginning with the predawn raids on 30 March, the Special Branch arrested anyone connected to the liberation movement, all national and regional executive members of the various congresses, as well as anyone who had ever been politically active. The police arrested more than 2,000 African political activists (under a statute dubbed Section Four), as well as 18,000 so-called idlers, or African men who they considered troublemakers.[21]

For *New Age* the state of emergency was a disaster. On Thursday, 31 March 1960, only hours after the official proclamation, the Security Branch arrested most of the editorial staff. Brian Bunting, Durban branch manager M. P. Naicker, Port Elizabeth branch manager Govan Mbeki, Cape Town columnist Alex La Guma, and Johannesburg fund-raiser and circulation manager Ivan Schermbrucker led the list of fifty-five *New*

Age editorial, administrative, and sales staff members arrested and held in jail.[22] That same day the weekly appeared with the Kgosana interview and reports on the township violence. The Security Branch hurried around the country, confiscating copies from street sellers.[23] Chaos faced the few staff members not among the fifty-five arrested. Some scrambled to go into hiding. Albie Sachs, a young lawyer who wrote the international news feature, reconstructed the scene on 31 March 1960:

> I recall going up the office the day after the march . . . and everybody was gone this time. It was just me. In the office we had some photographs of the march. The regulations had come out which made it illegal for anybody to publish anything that caused alarm or whatever. I couldn't decide what to do. . . . We had very little material and didn't have any fillers. I decided to plan the next edition, alone. I remember really scraping the barrel to fill it—I mean it was eight pages. I used the heading "Go Home In Peace," which Kgosana had said, and I wrote a very careful editorial. . . . That's the dream, you know, of the young reporter, that something happens to the editor and you've got to bring out the paper in the midst of all the turmoil. But now suddenly I had a whole newspaper and dramatic events.[24]

Sachs telephoned Caledon Square to see if *New Age* was allowed to publish. The police said yes, so he laid the edition out and on Tuesday, as scheduled, took the copy to the Pioneer Press plant for printing. That same day, 5 April 1960, the minister of justice issued a *Government Gazette Extraordinary* special proclamation ordering *New Age* to cease publication for the duration of the emergency. "A systematic publishing of matter which is, in my opinion, of a subversive character," was the minister's reason.[25] Detectives raided all four *New Age* offices and ordered them closed. For the first time since February 1937, the weekly was not going to meet its Thursday appointment.

Late in the afternoon the police arrived at Pioneer, just as the press was beginning to churn out the 7 April edition. About

100 copies had come off the duplicate plate, with the ink still wet on the newsprint. The police stopped the press, seized all the copies, and dismantled the type. But Len Lee-Warden, the owner of Pioneer and an MP at the time, snuck one copy away.[26] Besides Sach's careful editorial, the missing 7 April 1960 (vol. 6, no. 25) edition had a full page of reporting on the Treason Trial, which was still in progress, an Eli Weinberg photograph of mourners at Congress leader Ida Mntwana's funeral, an article on Malawian leader Hastings Banda, and news of ANC leader Oliver Tambo's dramatic escape to Bechuanaland. Concerning the Langa march, Sachs ran a large, three-column front-page photograph of Kgosana and two full pages inside of pictures of the day. Sachs managed to insert a little levity: the minister of justice wrote a Guest Editorial on the emergency regulations, and a photograph of three newspaper-reading PAC members waiting to surrender at Caledon Square on 28 March showed them "engrossed in *New Age*'s accounts on the Monday shootings."

A pathos permeated the pages of the vanished edition. Forcibly removed from the reading public, the 7 April 1960 edition symbolized what the state of emergency meant to South Africa. Because of the weekly's disappearance, the events following the dismissal of the Langa marchers from Caledon Square were lost to most South Africans. Few knew what really happened that day. Few knew that Kgosana had been tricked and was imprisoned. Few knew of the thousands in jail or underground. The stories, the pictures, the truth, were sadly bundled up with the hundred copies of *New Age* and taken away.

The five months that followed were somnolent ones in a political sense. The thousands of politicals sat in jail, putting on Shakespeare plays, practicing ballroom dancing, or writing novels.[27] Thousands more fled the country, some permanently leaving in order to set up the ANC in exile, others slipping over the border into Swaziland to wait out the emergency. Inside South Africa, a smattering of activists went into hiding and tried to organize opposition against the apartheid regime. The opposition coalesced into an ad hoc three-man secretariat —the Emergency Committee—that ostensibly ran the Congress: Michael Harmel, the long-time Johannesburg correspondent for the weekly, Ben Turok (*New Age* staffer Mary Butcher's husband), and Moses Kotane, the communist leader. These men, on the move every few days, wrote statements, organized the distribution of flyers, bulletins, and leaflets, decided who should leave the country, and attempted to figure out the direction and pace the movement should take. Because the government refused to say publicly who was in jail, the committee issued the "African National Congress Voice," a bulletin listing the names of detainees. The bottom line of the bulletin advised readers, "Read it. Study it. Pass it on. But do not get caught with it, or tell anyone where you got it."[28] In June, after heated discussions, they issued a leaflet announcing the existence of the South African Communist Party.[29]

Below this secretariat came a random gaggle of activists for whom Wolfie Kodesh, a veteran *New Age* staffer, acted as the conduit to the committee. Kodesh ferried Kotane, Harmel, and Turok to secret meetings in his dark Volkswagen van— disguised as a dry-cleaning van—and brought them messages, food, clothing, and bottles of whiskey. When not busy caretaking the committee, Kodesh secured new safe houses and found duplicating machines to produce leaflets. The police were watching his apartment, so he too was on the run. It was a scary but exhilarating adventure, as Kodesh remembered:

> I got a phone call from Bram Fischer [Communist Party leader] saying he had just been told by some chap that there was going to be a raid within hours. I phoned Cape Town and Port Elizabeth and alerted them, and then I went into hiding. . . . I was the liaison between those in hiding and those who had managed to get

away. I had a number of disguises. . . . I wore a hat, for instance, a thing I never do. I grew a beard, you know, and wore a tie. I even got a false shoe to make me a bit taller. It wasn't comfortable. I sort of limped, so I chucked it away. . . . It was bloody cold, winter, you know, and I had to sleep on the Observatory Golf Course. They had patrols going round all over Johannesburg, not only in the townships. You didn't know who they knew of your friends and relations.[30]

By the middle of August 1960 the government started releasing detainees. Some of those underground returned from hiding, and some in Swaziland, like Ruth First, came back to South Africa but remained underground. Most *New Age* staff members pushed for the weekly to reappear as a sign of defiance.[31] Bunting refused. "We always wanted to be legal," he recalled, "to give the government no legitimate cause for banning."[32] His refusal, it turned out, was a wise decision, for in October 1960, Pretoria charged Kodesh and Cape Town business manager Fred Carneson with subversion, alleging that the 31 March 1960 issue contained statements that violated the emergency regulations. Kodesh and Carneson, as directors of the firm that published the weekly, countered by arguing the edition had already been printed before the emergency was declared. *New Age* won the case.[33]

Back at Barrack Street *New Age* scrambled to get ready for publication once the emergency was lifted. Staff members, like birds coming back after a winter migration, flocked to the offices to get the news, see old comrades, and set about repairing the *New Age* nest. They cranked up the fund-raising machine, and a drive among Indian shopkeepers in Natal wiped out a £3,000 debt.[34] Albie Sachs, with great pride, returned a briefcase to Brian Bunting: "When Brian was taken away, I noticed he had a very, very nice briefcase with an expensive lock. I walked out with the briefcase and hid it somewhere, thinking I had saved some vital things from the police. Several months later, at the end of the Emergency I gave it back to Brian and said, 'Here you are, Brian, here is your briefcase with all those important documents.' He opened it up. Inside was nothing but a sandwich and a banana, one very ripe banana."[35]

Nicetime Girls and Dynamited Pylons

On 31 August 1960 the government lifted the state of emergency. Eight days later, on Thursday 8 September, *New Age* returned to the streets and villages of South Africa. Five months of proscription, fifty-five staffers in jail, and the banning of the ANC were not enough deterrence for the weekly. Barrack Street's unique spin on South African politics was back. "Freedom Is within Our Grasp: Govt. Received Terrific Setback from Emergency," trumpeted the opening page of the first edition. A picture of a smiling Nelson Mandela and Duma Nokwe walking home in Soweto after being released ran below *New Age*'s logo, a long article told of *New Age*'s banning, and two pages detailed the experience of those detained, including a report on what the Special Branch asked during interrogations.

Brian Bunting informed all far-flung correspondents that "*New Age* Letter Box Is Now Open Again." Four enormous photographs of the Langa March—"Pictures from Our Banned Issue"—accompanied a report on the historic day. A full page looked at the latest court proceedings from the Treason Trial, another examined the "Battle for the Congo," and Alex La Guma's regular "Up My Alley" column rated the prison warders he met while in jail. "Liberation is near," readers were told in the editorial, and they were exhorted, "We must not get used to tyranny. We must not let freedom go by default."[36]

"*New Age* Was Snapped Up in the Townships," read the headline of a Robert Resha account of selling the newspaper in Johannesburg. Resha, an ANC leader and *New Age* sportswriter, toured the city on the first Friday after the emergency. People flocked to buy the newspaper, and African sellers went through more than double their usual stock. Outside Retsies, a popular African café on Pritchard Street run by ANC veteran Elias Moretsele, Resha encountered a mob of newspaper readers. "It was difficult to see who was selling and who was the buyer of *New Age*, for everyone seemed to have a copy or two. I spoke to three persons who had more than one copy each. They were stocking up for their friends." Resha walked to Market Street, where he "met a few Treason Trialists selling *New Age*. 'How is it going?' I asked. 'We think we should have taken more copies to sell,' was the reply." After selling his usual two dozen in Mofolo township, Resha ran into Hosiah Tsehla, an Alexandra *New Age* seller, who told him, "People were longing for *New Age*. I have not seen the African people so happy for a long time. When they see *New Age*, they seem to feel that freedom is just around the corner."[37]

Quite a corner it was, before freedom hove into view. The newspaper had been set back just as much as the government. The first—and last—interruption in the newspaper's twenty-six-year history threw Barrack Street, as Bunting wrote in the first postemergency issue, "into complete confusion."[38] On the surface a veneer of stability gave the illusion that all was well. Every Thursday *New Age* appeared, and the main editorial staff remained intact. Underneath, however, swirling currents of exile and arrest swamped the newspaper. Much like the situation in 1950, when the Communist Party was banned, the scene after the emergency was suddenly different. The banning of the ANC destroyed *New Age*'s intricate system of correspondents and financial backers, especially among Indian shopkeepers in rural Natal and Transvaal. Few people were left, according to Ruth First, who could alert *New Age* "when some new vicious scheme of the police and the administration came to light."[39] Key contributors to the newspaper, like Wilton

Mkwayi, Sam Kahn, Winnie Kramer, and Tennyson Makiwane, had gone out of the country, never to return to their desks.

The aftermath of the Sharpeville massacre had forever altered the political landscape. After long and bitter discussions and with sizable misgivings, some activists within the ANC and the newly titled South African Communist Party turned to a campaign of guerrilla warfare and sabotage. On 16 December 1961, six days after ANC president Albert Lutuli accepted the Nobel Prize for Peace in Oslo, the campaign opened. Umkhonto we Sizwe (Spear of the nation), the armed wing of the ANC and SACP, dynamited electrical power pylons in Johannesburg, Durban, and Port Elizabeth. War had been declared.

Blurry and indistinct, the lines between the banned ANC, Umkhonto we Sizwe (MK), and *New Age* crossed and recrossed. One of the few legal entities functioning in the country, *New Age* thrust a powerful, public fist in the sky. "The paper became, after the bannings, the standard-bearer, if you like, of the entire liberation movement in South Africa," said Fred Carneson. "There it was, like a bloody pole stuck on top of the hill. A fortress, it was. Everybody saw it. It was an enormous source of encouragement."[40]

Based in London, the ANC needed *New Age* more than ever to keep its name in the limelight, to encourage the now heavily discouraged membership, and to provide a conduit for policy statements. The newspaper covered ANC leaders abroad, including the opening of Congress offices in Algeria and a 26 June celebration in Dar es Salaam.[41] Messages from Yusuf Dadoo detailed the ANC's Government in Exile plans, and the weekly printed his postal address in London so birthday messages could reach him.[42] Oliver Tambo wrote bylined articles describing his hopes.[43] On 24 August 1961, *New Age* ran a three-column photograph of Tambo and other ANC leaders at a Tanganyika conference.[44] The weekly reprinted ANC leaflets which had been illegally produced and distributed in South Africa, as well as ANC statements and reports like one from the 1962 ANC conference in Lobatsi, Bechuanaland—the first official ANC conference since 1959.[45] Barrack Street interviewed ANC leaders still in the country, like Walter Sisulu and Duma Nokwe, and sometimes asked them to write bylined articles.[46] When Dr. A. B. Xuma, the former ANC president, died in 1962, the newspaper ran a lengthy obituary.[47] With a puritanically small amount of salacious detail, *New Age* reported on female police spies hired to entrap ANC men, "attractive nicetime girls who attend house-parties in an apparent mood of gaiety."[48]

Symbolically, it was vital for Albert Lutuli, the nominal head of the ANC, a well-respected elder statesman and an inspiration for millions of Africans, to be featured in *New Age*. Lutuli, still confined to Groutville, north of Durban, kept closely in touch with the weekly. Ebrahim Ismail Ebrahim, a young staff member, made monthly train journeys to Groutville to collect statements and discuss politics with Lutuli, who had a subscription to *New Age*. Throughout the early 1960s, Lutuli wrote comments for the weekly, sent letters to the editor, and posted "Africa Day Messages." Barrack Street ran his three-page Nobel Prize acceptance speech in full, and he sent *New Age* a statement of thanks to all those who sent messages of congratulations.[49] Before the crucial 1961 white general election, Lutuli sent long "election surveys" giving the official ANC point of view. Barrack Street sold a framed picture of Lutuli for five shillings and in 1962 printed Lutuli's final public statement before it became illegal to print anything written or spoken by him.[50]

Although it was dangerous, *New Age* supported Umkhonto we Sizwe. MK's original manifesto ran in 1961 and its "First Anniversary Message" was proclaimed in New Age in January 1963.[51] Eli Weinberg, the weekly's photographer, shot MK slogans painted on city walls and MK notices plastered on telephone poles.[52] Barrack Street ran pictures of the many sabotaged buildings and electricity pylons. The Thursday after the 16 December 1961 bombings saw a cheeky juxtaposition on the front page: Bunting placed a photograph of a damaged pylon with the headline "A New Phase in South Africa" next to a photograph of a man planting a flag on top of Mount Kilimanjaro to celebrate the independence of Tanzania with the headline "Birth of a Nation."[53]

Explanations for the acquisition of such news from an illegal, covert movement were duplicitous. For the initial Umkhonto declaration in December 1961, *New Age* said it was "telephoned to look out for the announcement" in posters on walls "near newspaper offices." A heading above another Umkhonto statement claimed the story's source was "[i]n a proclamation from this underground organisation which found its way into newspaper offices." Sometimes "a copy of the leaflet was sent to the Johannesburg office of *New Age*," or a letter was "received through the post," or "the statement was slipped under the door of the Johannesburg office of *New Age*."[54]

Shamelessly fibbing, *New Age* in fact functioned as an essential part of Umkhonto. The newspaper's four offices provided a cover for clandestine work. Daytime political discussions, dropped messages, forwarded documents, and covert planning sessions now took place at Barrack Street and *New Age*'s three branch offices. In Durban a so-called Daily Committee ran the underground Congress movement for Natal; each morning at eight it met at *New Age*. MK meetings were also regularly held there. Ebrahim recalled, "We'd meet each other there and then go out. I think that everyone met there, ANC people met there. MK was always having somebody meet there. And of course, everything was underground—if it doesn't concern you, you don't worry about it."[55] Most of the staff at *New Age* broke the law every day. Staffers worked for the weekly by day and built bombs by night. Govan Mbeki, the Port Elizabeth branch manager, sat on Umkhonto's High Command and spent only one day a week laboring for the newspaper—devoting the other six days to underground work.[56] Mbeki later recalled one result of MK's emphasis on secrecy. He had a contact on New Brighton's advisory board who was secretly funneling him information for scandal-raising *New Age* stories about government corruption in the townships. Not knowing this man was Mbeki's contact, some MK comrades asked Mbeki if they could blow his house up for being a collaborator. Mbeki sternly said no. "They complained to Jack Hodgson in Johannesburg and accused me of being arbitrary. Luckily, Jack agreed with me, and we left the man alone. It was an example of too much discipline, unfortunately a too-rare disease."[57]

More comical was Ebrahim's confrontation with MK silence. M. P. Naicker, the Durban branch manager, had no idea Ebrahim was in Umkhonto, even though both men were members of the underground SACP and MK, and had worked together since the early 1950s.[58] In late October 1962, an MK cell consisting of Ebrahim, Ronnie Kasrils, Billy Nair, Bruno Mtolo, and Coetsie Naicker, M. P. Naicker's brother, dynamited three electrical pylons in Clairwood. The explosions plunged Durban into total darkness for a night. The next morning a nonchalant Ebrahim walked into *New Age*'s office. When the news of the sabotage in Clairwood came on Radio South Africa, M. P. Naicker and Ebrahim discussed covering the story. Ebrahim recalled:

> It came over the news, so I told M. P., "I'm going to go and find these places and take some photographs." I just wanted to see how good a job we had done. He agreed. So I went and when I got there I started asking the people around there where the pylons were. I knew where the place was because I had led the group there the night before. I made sure a lot of people had to direct me, so nobody would think that I would know the place. . . . I got

to the place and there were some workmen. I took the photographs, and I was satisfied—the pylons were completely down.[59]

On 8 November 1962 two large photographs of the fallen eighty-foot pylons ran on the front page of *New Age*.[60]

Nelson Mandela's association with *New Age* was further proof of the weekly's direct connection to the armed struggle. By the late 1950s the Xhosa prince-turned-Johannesburg-lawyer had become the de facto leader of the liberation movement, and now, for fourteen months, he helped run Umkhonto from underground. Nicknamed the Black Pimpernel, Mandela was in direct contact with many *New Age* staffers: Ruth First brought British reporters to interview him at a safe house after a failed May 1961 general strike.[61] In August 1961 he used the pages of the weekly to battle with a new political rival, Ntsu Mokhehle. The leader of the Basutoland Congress Party, Mokhehle tried to kick out the many ANC members who had fled to Basutoland and were joining the BCP. Despite being underground and hounded by the largest manhunt ever launched by the South African police, Mandela gave "a written statement" addressing the situation "that reached the *New Age* office on Monday morning this week." Defending the ANC, Mandela reminded Mokhehle of a meeting they had only eight months before in which they "agreed to work for complete unity and harmony." Mandela denied having ever left South Africa, calling the allegation he fled after the May stayaway "devoid of all truth and most reckless."[62] When Mokhehle contacted a Johannesburg newspaper to further abuse the ANC, Mandela wrote another statement ("sent in to *New Age* over the week-end") that argued "Mr. Mokhehle is taking advantage of the illegality of the ANC to make frivolous accusations against it in hope that no voice will be raised in its defence." In reference to his present status underground, he added, "As for my own personal position, I would like to point out that not for one single moment have I left the country since the May strike. South Africans have fed and sheltered me."[63] (An interesting coda to the story was that when Mandela was inaugurated as president of South Africa in 1994, one of his well-wishers was the prime minister of Lesotho, Ntsu Mokhehle.)[64]

Defending the ANC through the pages of *New Age* was easy for Mandela since he was living with Wolfie Kodesh. In the middle of July 1961, due to a mix-up at a political meeting, Mandela went home with Kodesh and stayed with him for two months. Unlike the emergency, when he had to sleep on a golf course, Kodesh had rented a safe house under an assumed name, and he and Mandela lived there. A routine was quickly established. At 5 A.M. the two men jogged in place for an hour. Kodesh then drove into town and worked at *New Age* until lunchtime, when he would tell Ruth First, the Johannesburg editor, that he was off to do a story. He would double back to the flat to spend the afternoons talking and planning, with the blinds tightly drawn. Kodesh lent Mandela a copy of Clausewitz's classic treatise, *On War*, which Mandela read avidly.[65] In the evenings they traveled to meetings and once went to an abandoned brickyard to test a new bomb. "I fear that I took over his life," Mandela later remembered, "infringing on both his work and pleasure. But he was such an amiable, modest fellow that he never complained."[66]

In January 1962, Mandela left Kodesh and slipped over the border into Bechuanaland. For the next half year he toured around Africa and Europe, meeting with presidents and foreign ministers and holding long planning sessions with ANC executives. The weekly scooped the story of Mandela's departure from South Africa when Tennyson Makiwane sent in a story of Mandela's arrival in Addis Ababa for a conference. "Will Return on Completion of African Tour," assured the headline.[67] On 1 March 1962, *New Age* ran a photograph of "Tambo and Mandela Reunited," the two leaders smiling in the Ethiopian sun. In July the Black Pimpernel slipped back into the country, but a month later the police captured him in Natal. When Wolfie Kodesh drove to tell Winnie Mandela of her husband's arrest, she barely recognized him. "He was white as a ghost," she said of Kodesh, "his hair was standing on end. I noticed he hadn't shaved and was wearing a dirty shirt and trousers as if he'd jumped out of bed. You could see something drastic had happened."[68]

"Release Nelson Mandela," trumpeted *New Age* on 16 August 1962, the first of many calls for his freedom. The weekly ran pictures of Mandela, of Winnie, of protesters at Durban's city hall and of a slogan spray-painted on a Durban fence: FREE MANDELA. Winnie Mandela, the newspaper said, "has asked *New Age* to appeal to people to repudiate any person starting wild rumours about the arrest of her husband." The weekly gave lavish coverage to his subsequent trial, statement from the dock, conviction, and sentencing.[69]

We Know and Can Identify Our Kidnappers

One of the justifications for the ANC's turn to armed struggle was that rural African consciousness had been reradicalized. The countryside, especially in Mpondoland, was in revolt, and MK, so went the argument, would ride the waves of anger and mobilization. Mpondoland, an isolated, mountainous region in northeastern Transkei, came under Cape colonial rule in 1894 and under South Africa rule after 1910. Pretoria sought to exert greater control over the region after the National Party came to power in 1948, and the Mpondos were in open rebellion by 1960. They stopped paying taxes, burned huts of government informers, and boycotted shops in the district capital of Bizana. Pitched battles between armed Mpondos and policemen, involving tear gas and shotguns, left scores dead. In

October 1960 an estimated 5,000 Mpondos marched through the streets of Bizana, led by an elderly man carrying a black flag in mourning.[70] Unable to quell the uprising, the government declared a state of emergency for the district in November 1960, outlawing meetings, closing the roads, and permitting detention without trial. Migrant workers coming home for the December holidays found themselves in jail for having entered the area without a permit. The police beat some of those jailed, and, for the first time, administered electric shocks to prisoners.[71] The government sentenced thirty Mpondoland leaders to death.

Among the peasants jailed during the rebellion was a man named Anderson Khumani Ganyile. Expelled from Fort Hare in January 1960, Ganyile, a twenty-five-year-old ANC Youth Leaguer, returned to Bizana and soon was detained for four months during the Sharpeville state of emergency. Upon release in August 1960, he became one of the leaders directing the Mpondoland revolt.[72] He acted as an interpreter for Rowley Arenstein, a Durban lawyer representing the Mpondos taken to court.[73] A protégé of Govan Mbeki's while at Fort Hare, Ganyile kept closely in touch with *New Age*, often exchanging telegrams and letters with Mbeki in Port Elizabeth. In October 1960, Mbeki, Eli Weinberg, and Joe Gqabi, a reporter and assistant photographer in Johannesburg, toured the region and met with Ganyile. "Civil War in the Transkei: Murder and Arson as People Fight Bantu Authorities," headlined the 22 September 1960 Mbeki article. Weinberg's accompanying photographs still remain masterpieces of photojournalism, with horseback Mpondos, sjamboks raised high in salute, etched against the dark Transkei hills.[74]

On 7 November 1960, while selling copies of *New Age* outside Bizana's magistrate court, Ganyile was arrested.[75] The government immediately deported Ganyile via Johannesburg to a detention camp near Mafeking. On 9 November, Joe Gqabi followed Ganyile on the Mafeking-bound prison train and, at a whistle-stop in Krugersdorp, managed to conduct a brief, shouted interview.[76] In January 1961, Ganyile escaped from the camp and fled across the Cape into Basutoland. *New Age* celebrated Ganyile's freedom with a photograph of him and John Motloheloa, a former *New Age* seller in Cape Town who had been deported to Basutoland, outside a Maseru cafe.[77]

The next word from Ganyile was a note scrawled on a scrap of paper which arrived at *New Age* in Durban: "Kidnapped in Basutoland 26/8/61 at 10:30 A.M. by six policemen from the Union. We are three and now in KD [Umtata] and we appeal to friends. We know and can identify our kidnappers. Yours, Powers." The South African police, crossing an international border in violation of Basutoland's sovereignty—again a first for the apartheid regime—had kidnapped Ganyile, nicknamed Powers, and smuggled him back into South Africa.[78] They were holding him in solitary confinement in Umtata, the capital of the Transkei. Ganyile's only hope was for *New Age* to publicize the case. Naicker wrote an article on the kidnapping that filled the front page. Naicker and, interestingly enough, Patrick Duncan traveled to Basutoland to see Ganyile's hut, where they found blood on blankets left behind.[79] Nelson Mandela, in Bechuanaland at the time, called Ganyile "one of the country's rising freedom stars."[80] A demonstration was held in Cape Town outside Parliament. In London the matter was raised in the House of Commons.[81]

Eventually, under international and local pressure, the government freed Ganyile and allowed him to return to Basutoland. Eric Louw, the minister of foreign affairs, apologized to the British government. On 8 February 1962, Ganyile's full-page article "How I Was Kidnapped" ran in *New Age:* "Yes fascism was at the door," he wrote. "The long and the short of it is that they started throwing stones at the door and windows. Bottles and an ax were the only weapons we had to defend ourselves." The Ganyile incident exposed the lengths Pretoria was willing to go to suppress its opponents—and *New Age's* continued ability to rouse a reply.[82]

Working in a Minefield

Ganyile's experience, unfortunately, was not unique for *New Age*. After Sharpeville, a jail cell rather than a newsroom desk became the regular destination of a *New Age* reporter. In his first four months at *New Age*, Brian Somana was incarcerated four times. Walter Sisulu had persuaded the young insurance agent to join *New Age* as a reporter and photographer, but he soon missed the quiet life of premiums and deductibles.[83] Once Somana took photographs of a group of handcuffed Africans at the Johannesburg railway station and was arrested under the Prisons Act of 1959, which forbade articles or photographs about prisons or prisoners (a law passed in part because of unceasing *New Age* muckraking about prison conditions). Somana was acquitted on that charge but still fined £4 for abusive language.[84]

Govan Mbeki overshadowed all others in his tendency to wind up in jail. In 1961 he was arrested in Pretoria's first attempt to try former Congress leaders on charges of furthering the cause of the ANC. After a trial in Johannesburg the charges were withdrawn for lack of evidence. In January 1962 the police arrested Mbeki and held him for five months, three in solitary confinement, before charging him with instructing men in the making of homemade explosives and for possession of potassium chlorate and potassium permanganate. Mbeki was acquitted after a state witness, who had been beaten into a confession, withdrew his testimony.[85] (While in jail, with a pencil and rolls of toilet paper, Mbeki wrote the bulk of his book on the Mpondoland uprising, *South Africa: The Peasants' Revolt.*

Ruth First edited the manuscript and it was published in 1964 while Mbeki was on Robben Island.) Afterward, Mbeki thwarted the police regularly when they tried to arrest him on pass law offenses; as *New Age* branch manager he signed his own passbook, so his papers were always legally in order.[86]

Harassment, if not arrest, was a fact of life. Ruth First visited South-West Africa (a territory then administered by South Africa) in 1961 and, after four days of unhampered research and interviewing, was discovered by the Security Branch. They descended like flies. "The scrutiny never faltered," she wrote. "The trail to the dry-cleaner and the shoemaker, the skulking next to the telephone booth, both ends of the road and every exit of the hotel patrolled, detectives following me to the airport, to the post office to buy stamps, watching me at breakfast, interviewing people I'd seen."[87] In Cape Town, Brian Bunting awoke one night to find his car, parked in his driveway, burning in a blaze of smoke and flame.[88] Alex La Guma received a threatening phone call from self-named members of the Ku Klux Klan in 1961.[89] In July 1962, Pretoria, incensed by the publication in Nigeria of La Guma's *A Walk in the Night*, prohibited him from publishing any writings. On 28 June 1962, "Up My Alley" appeared for the final time. Below his usual heading was stamped a single word: PROHIBITED.[90]

Turbulence from Umkhonto we Sizwe buffeted the newspaper's staff. A number of employees left the country. Joe Gqabi crossed into Bechuanaland in March 1962 and, along with Wilton Mkwayi, was a part of the first MK training group that met with Mandela in Tanzania in June 1962.[91] Robert Resha left in June 1961, and Tambo immediately appointed him the ANC's ambassador for Africa, stationed in Dar es Salaam.[92] Inside South Africa most staff members neglected the weekly, as they spent most of their energy writing leaflets and blowing up electrical pylons.[93] In November 1962, Govan Mbeki went underground when he saw Security Branch detectives coming to his New Brighton home to serve a house arrest order. Mbeki fled to Johannesburg, where he moved to MK's headquarters at Lilliesleaf Farm in Rivonia. With a laugh, Mbeki recalled the confusion he caused: "Brian didn't know. I didn't tell him I went underground. He had no idea where I was, but I knew he was angry because so little was coming from Port Elizabeth for *New Age.* And then, once I left, nothing at all."[94]

"One lived in constant tension," remembered Bunting. "You never knew what was going to happen next or who was doing what. We were very much on edge."[95] Security Branch detectives raided the newspaper's offices almost daily.[96] Virtually all white as well as black staff members operated under some sort of banning order that restricted them to certain magistrate districts, and forbade them to enter African locations, townships, or hostels. Ruth First's prohibitions sounded like a bad joke: "Over the years I had been served with banning orders that prohibited me from leaving Johannesburg . . . from entering African townships . . . from attending meetings, so that others had to take the notes and photographs, from writing anything for publication, so that I had to sit at my desk with a legal opinion that sub-editing someone else's copy might just slip past the ban. Working in the midst of these ministerial bans and under continuous raids and scrutiny was like going to work each day in a minefield."[97]

Mine fields in South Africa traditionally yield gold or silver, but, for the weekly, only hardship was brought to the surface. Signs of a weakened newspaper abounded. Circulation, before the emergency at around 28,000, dipped to under 20,000.[98] Advertising revenue was less than negligible, and donations, except for the ever-supportive Indian shopkeepers, dried up.[99] "*New Age* is a hungry monster," Carneson noted in December 1961, but not enough food could be found, as the monster needed £1,800 a month in donations, twice what usually arrived.[100] To raise readers' interest, the weekly held a poll on the appropriateness of tribal dress, and Carneson offered £3 for the best caption for a cartoon of a police constable reporting to his superior. By May 1962, Barrack Street had a debt of almost £3,000. In August, Bunting borrowed money and dismissed a large number of administrative staff members, a "drastic and dangerous pruning" that left them with "the barest of bare skeletons."[101] Even with the downsizing, the weekly almost closed at the end of the month. It gave notice to staff and prepared a statement of closure, but the newspaper managed to limp into September. Adding insult to injury, *Die Vaderland* and the *Cape Argus* telephoned Barrack Street to ask if rumors were true, that the weekly had collapsed.[102]

Salvation came from London. In August 1954, Max Joffe and other South African exiles founded the London *New Age* Committee to raise money and support for the weekly in Great Britain. Throughout the 1950s the committee, by issuing *New Age* Christmas cards and hosting parties where Paul Robeson occasionally would sing, posted helpful sums of sterling to Barrack Street. After the emergency, Yusuf Dadoo took over the chair of the committee and used the new influx of South African exiles to his advantage.[103] Often the money raised by the committee was the difference between the newspaper going under or not.

In February 1962, *New Age* celebrated its silver jubilee with a Grand Celebration Dance at Cape Town's Banqueting Hall and a dance at the Four Aces Club in Fordsburg. Rica Hodgson, now "*New Age*'s national finance organiser," wrote a letter to friends of the weekly asking for a twenty-fifth anniversary donation. "It may not be good manners to solicit birthday gifts," she wrote, but "our greatest danger is that we may slip by default." On 22 March, *New Age* issued a special twelve-page issue in commemoration of twenty-five years of publication. Inside, Albert Lutuli said, "I have not always agreed with everything it says, but on questions affecting the non-white peoples in South Africa, *New Age* has been and continues to be the fighting mouthpiece of African aspirations."[104]

Surely, This Country Is Not a Kindergarten

On 21 May 1962 the new minister of justice, Balthazar Johannes Vorster, stood in Parliament. Turning to his new Sabotage Bill, Vorster waved a copy of the twenty-fifth anniversary issue. This should be banned, he said: "The *Guardian* was the mouthpiece and propaganda organ of the communists . . . to this day its editor is still an outspoken and active communist. . . . I make no secret of the fact that one of the newspapers which ought to be forbidden is this paper, *New Age*, which is the propaganda organ of the Communist Party. . . . It is furthering the aims of communism, and it makes no secret of the fact."[105]

The House roared with approval. Ten days before, Vorster had introduced new legislation, a Sabotage Bill that gave the minister the power to outlaw strikes and to ban, place under house arrest, and forbid any person from any specific activity —a "blanket ban." One provision was directed at *New Age:* no new periodical or newspaper could publish without a security deposit of up to £10,000, forfeitable if the newspaper was banned. Vorster slammed shut the loophole that allowed the *Guardian* to reappear in 1952 and 1954 under a new title.[106] Two days after Vorster's newspaper-waving speech, a Nationalist MP, Bertie Coetzee, applauded his moves:

I also wish to congratulate the Minister on putting an end to another childishness in this country, and that is that a newspaper like *New Age* can be banned and appear the following day under another name. That is childishness. Surely this country is not a kindergarten. A newspaper which is a danger to the state gets banned by the Minister, and then makes a fool of the state by simply appearing the following day under another name. I wish to congratulate the Minister for the ingenious way in which he has put a stop to this ridiculous situation.[107]

New Age was nonplused but not surprised. Since the late 1930s, the weekly had been a vexing and vitriolic thorn in Pretoria's side, and it was only a matter of time before another pruning began. In early 1961 the newspaper had reported on several instances when the police had informed *New Age* sellers to stop distributing the newspaper because it had been banned.[108] Now, in May 1962, with the four-inch-high banner headline "THIS IS A POLICE STATE," *New Age* rose to protest its imminent demise.[109] Pages of the weekly detailed each provision of the bill and its effect on the liberation movement. Fred Carneson wrote an open letter to Vorster "to register hereby my formal and emphatic protest," and Bunting wrote an editorial reiterating the weekly's policies:[110]

> *New Age* insists that it has a right to exist. We have a point of view to put forward which is entitled to be heard.
> - We stand for equal rights for all South Africans, an end to apartheid and colour bars, the creation of one integrated South Africa with equal citizenship for all, irrespective of race, creed, or colour.
> - We stand for peace and harmony between the nations of the world and the elimination of the last vestiges of colonialism.
> - We stand for the right of all peoples to be free from exploitation in any shape or form.
>
> These are the basic principles of decent social living, and we have fought for them in the teeth of Nationalist oppression for all the years of our existence. Now we are to be silenced because the Nats, in their march to the jackboot states, can no longer tolerate any opposition.[111]

Jackboots goose-stepped up and down Barrack Street, and Bunting looked to London for help. On 23 May 1962 he sat at his desk and typed a letter to Yusuf Dadoo asking for the "maximum possible protest. . . . The essence of the matter, however, is speed. At the moment we can count our future in weeks unless the protest is so overwhelming as to stay the Minister's hand."[112] Responding quickly, Dadoo launched a protest campaign in London. The London *New Age* Committee wrote a declaration, calling the Sabotage Bill "astonishing," "grim," and "disturbing." Dozens of well-known British writers signed the declaration, including William Plomer, Basil Davidson, Doris Lessing, Kingsley Amis, Iris Murdoch, Muriel Spark, and Robert Bolt.[113] On 7 June 1962, Dadoo sent a copy of the declaration and a list of the signatories to all newspaper editors in the United Kingdom, asking them "to lend the weight of the editorial columns of your valuable paper to condemn the South African government."[114]

Hanging fire, with the Sabotage Bill now law, Vorster waited. With the financial crisis of August 1962, the weekly seemed destined to lead itself to the knacker's yard.[115] Vorster tightened the noose when he banned the Congress of Democrats in September and in October began to house-arrest activists. In mid-November, in a staggering blow to the weekly, Vorster placed Rica Hodgson, Sonia Bunting, Alex La Guma, Jack Tarshish, Michael Harmel, Cecil Williams, Rusty Bernstein, Ahmed Kathrada, and Walter Sisulu under twenty-four-hour house arrest for five years.[116] The minister house-arrested Brian Bunting for thirteen hours a day and forbade him to enter any factory premises—so he could not help put the newspaper to bed at the printers.

All those house-arrested were forbidden to communicate with anyone banned. Since nearly everyone on the *New Age* staff was banned, this meant, as *New Age* wrote, "that inter-office communication will become practically impossible." Bunting was, in addition, specifically forbidden to communicate with Fred Carneson. "Since the two of them work in adjoining offices and are daily in almost constant contact with one another," wrote *New Age* without any understatement, "it will be practically impossible for Mr. Bunting to carry out his functions on *New Age*."[117] Of the twenty people under house arrest up to 15 February 1963, thirteen were staff members or had direct relationships with *New Age*.[118] The house arrests represented a new deterioration of civil rights and frightened many South Africans. Writer and Liberal Party leader Alan Paton told the weekly, "these are vicious, barbaric conditions. No one can say now that this is not an imitation of a Nazi country." And *New Age* noted, in light of the weekly's parlous state: "If the paper goes under, the liberation movement will be like a man blinded, sightless in the desert of apartheid."[119]

On Friday, 30 November 1962, Vorster issued a proclamation prohibiting the printing and publication of *New Age*. For the third time in a decade, the weekly was banned. The banning spurred an enormous amount of publicity, and a number of organizations sent Vorster letters of condemnation. Leaders of the Liberal Party, Progressive Party, South African Congress of Trade Unions, Natal Indian Congress, South African Society of Journalists, and the Anti-Apartheid Movement in London protested *New Age*'s demise.[120] Lutuli and Martin Luther King Jr. issued a joint statement on 10 December 1962, appealing for action against apartheid and referring to the banning.[121] The *Cape Times* editorialized:

> the political opposition of *New Age* becomes communism because Mr. Vorster chooses to call it communism. He does so without hearing argument, without having to produce evidence, without having to give reasons, subject to no appeal to any impartial authority. How many people outside the ranks of the Nationalist Party will be convinced that Mr Vorster is not simply getting rid of inconvenient political opposition by authoritarian methods which have become so popular in the wilder territories of the new Africa? If this is the reaction, Mr. Vorster will have only himself

to blame, that is why civilized countries do not close down news-papers until they have evidence acceptable to a court that they are breaking the law.[122]

Even Patrick Duncan, in *Contact*, wrote bitterly of the banning: "Besides its ideological alignment, which we found distasteful and possibly harmful to the freedom movement in South Africa, *New Age* has over the years been among the staunchest opponents of White Supremacy.... It was a focal point around which a strong body of opposition to apartheid had centred."[123]

Doom pervaded Barrack Street. Carneson told reporters who visited the offices Friday afternoon, "I am going to do my best to provide them [*New Age* staffers] with alternative work. It is not illegal to produce other publications."[124] But with what? *New Age* was surely gone. Real Printing and Publishing Com-pany, which published *New Age*, lodged a suit in court against the government, asserting that Vorster had not followed the regulations stipulated in the Suppression of Communism Act. There was no committee of three, Real argued. The suit was thrown out of court, as the magistrate took at face value the minister of justice's assertion that it was contrary to public in-terest to disclose information on the decision to ban *New Age*.[125] There seemed, in light of the Sabotage Act and the £10,000 de-posit, nothing for the weekly to do but lie down and die.

Sailing Close to the Wind

On Thursday, 6 December 1962, six days after the banning of *New Age*, a four-page newspaper called *Spark* came out of Bar-rack Street. Half a year before, Bunting and Carneson had eyed the Sabotage Act with trepidation. A proscription surely was in the offing but to raise the £10,000 deposit was a non-starter. They decided to start publishing other titles in order

A typical *New Age* front page in June 1961 featured a statement from underground ANC leader Nelson Mandela calling for "a full-scale campaign of non-cooperation with the government."

SPARK

New Series, Vol. 1 No. 6 — PRICE 5c — December 6, 1962

"VERWOERD'S DAYS ARE NUMBERED"

1,500 AT NATAL CONFERENCE

DURBAN

OVER 1,500 delegates from all parts of Natal jam-packed an old disused factory at Clairwood, Durban, last week-end at one of the most successful and representative conferences ever held in this Province.

The Conference, which was called jointly by the Natal Rural Areas Committee and the South African Congress of Trade Unions (Natal), met to discuss labour and rural problems.

The days preceding the Conference saw unprecedented police activity in the City. The offices of the Natal Indian Congress and the South African Congress of Trade Unions were raided and several documents pertaining to the Conference were confiscated.

A day later the office of the Textile Workers' Union was raided and two members of the Union staff—Secretary, Mr. Mannie Isaacs and Organiser, Mr. Melville Fletcher—were arrested and taken before a Magistrate for questioning.

CHARGE WITHDRAWN

Later, after legal representations, the Special Branch agreed to summons the two trade unionists and they were to have appeared last Saturday. But, when they did, the Special Branch withdrew the charge against them.

(Continued on page 13)

OUR PRICE

With this issue the size of "Spark" is increased to 16 pages, including a special four-page feature entitled "Africa and the World" (pages 7 to 10).

In view of the increased expenditure, we regret that the price of the paper will have to be increased to 5 cents (6d.)

Miss Gladys Manzi and Miss Dorothy Nyembe, Secretary and Chairman of the Women's Federation, who attended the Durban conference in traditional costume.

The first issue of *Spark*—the last of a long string of titles in the *Guardian* stable—on 6 December 1962. The front page featured two leaders of the Women's Federation "in traditional costume" at a joint conference of trade unions and rural action committees meeting in Durban "to discuss labour and rural problems" in Natal province.

to have a newspaper legally ready in case of a banning. Just before the Sabotage Act became law, Real Printing and Publishing bought two newspapers, *Morning Star* and *Spark*. In July 1962 an edition of *Spark* and *Morning Star* appeared. Each ran four pages. In August the newspapers appeared again. In accordance with the stipulations in the Sabotage Act, Bunting, as "editor" of *Morning Star* and *Spark*, formed a company, Table View, that issued each newspaper once a month to maintain its registration status. Each month, as Bunting recalled, "we'd shove overmatter, extra bits from *New Age*, into them. Anything that was laying around the office. It was not something we'd pay much attention to."[126] Full-page poems, enlarged photographs, long articles on the evils of tobacco and liquor, and reprints of newspaper cuttings filled the two monthlies.

Morning Star and *Spark* readers, though, did not care about the haphazard look of the monthlies. There were no readers. Only five copies of each issue were published, and Bunting sent them to the required libraries and institutions that, by South African law, had to receive each registered periodical in the Union.[127] No one bought, sold, or even saw the newspapers. The deception was legal, as long as the government did not discover that five instead of 15,000 copies were being printed. Playing along with the charade, Bunting lowered the price of *Spark* and *Morning Star* in October 1962 from three pennies to one, "owing to strong pressure from our readers."[128]

If librarians had been watching carefully, they would have noticed a strange explosion on 6 December 1962 in the hitherto sleepy *Spark*.[129] Four pages quadrupled to sixteen, the newsstand price shot up from that reader-requested penny to sixpence, and the monthly became a weekly. Naturally, *Spark*'s existence was tenuous. With La Guma and the Buntings under house arrest, the burden at Barrack Street fell to Fred Carneson. On 3 December 1962 he wrote a letter to Dadoo in London outlining *Spark*'s problems:

The banning of *New Age*, the house-arrest orders on Brian, Sonia and Rica, together with restrictions on others who have helped us in the past, have combined to create a crisis far worse than anything we have ever experienced in the past. . . . We are prepared to face all this and carry on, sailing ever more dangerously close to the wind, for as long as it is humanely possible, exploiting every legal loop-hole that exists. Our plans, however, will all come to naught—and that before the end of the month—unless we receive immediate and substantial financial assistance from our friends overseas. To give you an idea of how serious the situation is, I need only mention that we were ready to announce the closure of *New Age* in the issue of 29 November. Only strenuous efforts on the part of our depleted staff . . . saved *New Age* from the indignity of having to close down before the Nationalists banned it. Our local resources are now exhausted. Even if we had double the personnel now available we would definitely not be able to raise anything like what we need to carry on. Some of our staff have not been paid for October, and it is a battle to find money even for street-sellers' wages.[130]

Spark soldiered on, picking up where *New Age* left off. The newspaper reported on ANC and Umkhonto we Sizwe activities. Lovedale, the prestigious African high school in the eastern Cape, was on strike, the police were still raiding the townships, and women were still protesting against the passes. Howard Lawrence wrote a column entitled "Bright *Spark*s," which followed the same tone and style as La Guma's "Up My Alley." Martin "Chris" Hani wrote a thoughtful letter to the editor on the lessons of the Paarl riots: "My purpose is to help to arrive at a clear analysis of the situation and not to be cynical. We should understand quite clearly that to seek cheap martyrdom at this stage of the struggle is naive and criminal. We must not evade the challenge which faces us."[131] Desperate for staff, the newspaper advertised for "young people to act as voluntary trainees—reporters and editorial assistants, for several days a week. You'll be especially useful if you can use a camera and have one; if you can type; if you've done journalism before."[132] The Special Branch continued to visit the offices each morning.[133] The saddest occasion was New Year's Eve. At eleven in the evening, the police crashed into the Bunting's home expecting to find the usual party, something that now, with their house arrest orders, would have been illegal. Instead the police found Brian and Sonia reading quietly. One detective even looked under the beds of sleeping children, checking, as it were, for Reds under the beds.[134]

Lowering the boom, on 22 February the minister of justice issued a proclamation prohibiting all banned persons and those who were former members of now-banned organizations from belonging to a group that prepared, compiled, printed, published, or disseminated any printed matter. Anyone remotely associated with the liberation struggle could now not work for *Spark*. A week later Vorster specifically served orders on Ruth First, Bunting, Carneson, Rica Hodgson, and Kodesh, forbidding them from being on the premises where a publication was prepared, compiled, printed, published, or disseminated.[135] These specific orders took effect 1 April 1963.

"There was nothing we could do," recalled Carneson. "We had struggled so hard and had really done a magical thing bringing out *Spark* after they banned *New Age*, but our luck had dried up."[136] Thoughts of making the newspaper a fortnightly or even a monthly were mooted, but who would run the newspaper? There was no one left to replace the house-arrested staff. To start over was impossible. Sonia Bunting suggested publishing from Basutoland and smuggling *Spark* back over the border, but this idea, heatedly discussed, was ultimately discarded because of logistics and because as Bunting said, "it would have to be cyclostyled, and we didn't want to cyclostyle the weekly. It wouldn't have the same effectiveness."[137] Carneson sent an aerogram on 15 March 1963 to Max Joffe in London, telling him that *Spark* was going to close down as a weekly at the end of March and asking him to raise funds to pay the twenty-four remaining staff and administrative workers their March wages and perhaps an extra month's severance salary:

> Our assets (mostly office furniture of ancient vintage) are a drop in the ocean and our circulation debtors are going to freeze onto their sales monies once they know we have closed down. It will be the devil's own job getting it out of them. So, as I say, and as things stand now, it looks as if we have to throw everyone onto the street as if they were employees found rifling the petty cash! We knew that this might well be the position. The threat of it has been hanging over our heads for years. It was a risk we had to take and took with full knowledge of what we were doing. Nevertheless, it is sad that it should happen. Some of the staff have served the paper for almost twenty years, which is a very big slice out of a man's working life. And the wages we have paid have never been sufficient to enable anyone to build up a nest-egg out of them! We are in for a very difficult time. The activists are being put in deliberately through the wringer, as an object lesson for those bold enough to think of following in their footsteps.[138]

Twenty-six years and 1,328 issues after the first issue of the *Cape Guardian* hit the streets of Cape Town in 1937, the final edition of *Spark* appeared on Thursday, 28 March 1963.[139] Reminiscent of General Douglas MacArthur's famous line on leaving the Philippines in 1942, *Spark*'s front-page five-column banner headline proclaimed: "We Say GOODBYE But We'll Be Back." Inside the twelve-page issue were biographies of the "five great journalists" who had dominated the newspaper in its final years: Bunting, First, Mbeki, Carneson, and Naicker. Written by Bunting, except his own profile, which Mbeki penned from underground, the five long pieces told of each journalist's life and work.[140]

Two items in the final edition held a poignancy—considering what was to come. A photograph showed Duma Nokwe addressing a Trafalgar Square rally against South Africa, an indication of the shift of focus in the liberation movement to outside the country. And readers were told to "remember the men and women in jail," a place so many activists were soon to be going, some for life.[141] "Brian actually wanted me to write the final pieces," said Albie Sachs, "but it had quite a large extent to do with the history of the paper and he was the link to the *Guardian*. To a large extent he was the *Guardian*. We forced him to do the writing. . . . and the idea was to go out with a bang, to go out confident and come back one day and look at the issue and say, 'we were successful, we stood firm.'"[142]

Although the newspaper succumbed, although the dark years of the late 1960s followed, it reaped a bountiful harvest in the distant future of the 1990s. All that it had fought for came to fruition. A few months before the historic 1994 elections, Douglas Manqina spoke of the weekly. Manqina had sold *New Age* and *Spark* from 1958 to 1963 in Cape Town. He had been imprisoned on Robben Island for six months before being deported to the Transkei. "When I came back from deportation," said Manqina, now an elderly man with a hushed, deliberate voice, "all those places where I used to sell *New Age*, we now have the strongest ANC branches. We now have many members there. All those places, we have a very big organization now. . . . You see, to me, it appears as the preachers talking to the congregation, as they preach to the people. They say, 'you sow the maize, but it is not for you. That maize must come out from the ground.' We were sowing these people. That seed, we have been sowing it. It came out. *New Age* was the seed that we sowed. Now it has come up and it is very rich."[143]

Notes

1. This chapter is taken, in a slightly different form, from a book manuscript on the history of the *Guardian*, which contains a complete list of acknowledgments. I must, however, thank Les Switzer,

Katherine Guckenberger, and my father, Jim Zug, all of whom read and commented on earlier drafts. Linda and Brooks Zug were kind enough to give me rooms in both forest and on water to work on the manuscript. I am most grateful to the many former *Guardian* editors, reporters, managers, fund-raisers, and sellers who shared their memories of the old newspaper. They made the difference.

2. Memories of this New Year's Eve party came from my interviews with Sadie Forman, May 1994; Ray Alexander, January 1995; Fred and Sarah Carneson, March 1994; Brian and Sonia Bunting, November 1993.

3. Typical of South African mining practices, 223 of the dead miners were from Basutoland and another 206 from Mozambique.

4. Fatima Meer, *Higher than Hope: The Authorized Biography of Nelson Mandela* (London: Penguin, 1988), 147.

5. Kwedie Mhlapi, interview by author, November 1993.

6. Duncan was opposed to the COD because he thought the organization was dominated by communists. South African Congress of Democrats, AD 2187, William Cullen Library, University of the Witwatersrand. See *Contact*, 2 May 1959, for a famous attack on the U.S.S.R.

7. C. J. Driver, *Patrick Duncan: South African and Pan-African* (London: Heinemann, 1980), 173–81; T. Lodge, *Black Politics in South Africa since 1945* (London: Longman, 1983), 217.

8. Lodge, *Black Politics*, 218–19; Joseph Lelyveld, *Move Your Shadow: South Africa, Black and White* (New York: Penguin, 1985), 323.

9. *Contact*, 16 April 1960.

10. *New Age*, 24 March 1960. Bunting might have also been jealous of Duncan's audience with Harold Macmillan at a garden party when the British prime minister visited Cape Town seven weeks before.

11. *New Age*, 9 March 1961.

12. Phillip Kgosana, *Lest We Forget* (Johannesburg: Skotaville, 1988), 22.

13. Patrick Duncan's diary, quoted in Driver, *Patrick Duncan*, 176.

14. Brian Bunting, interview by author, December 1993; Phillip Kgosana, conversation with author, October 1997. See also Carter and Karis Microfilm Documents, reel 11a, 2DA 17, for Tom Karis's notes from an interview with Kgosana, 5; also Meer, *Higher than Hope*, 147. During the week, Kgosana also gave an interview to the

Argus (Lelyveld, *Move Your Shadow*, 324). Bunting and Duncan clashed later in the year over the Lumumba crisis in the Congo. See *Contact*, 3 December 1960, where Duncan wrote: "The latest news from the Congo is good. Colonel Mobutu is quietly building up a real Congolese army. . . . When its power is great enough, and the signs are that that day is now near, it will deal with the man who tried to sell his country to the Russians—Patrice Lumumba." On 22 December 1960, after the coup, *New Age* attacked Duncan. "Evidently believing that any stick, no matter how dirty, is good enough with which to beat his enemy," editorialized Bunting, "Mr. Duncan is spitting in the face of all genuine African patriots. . . . [He] always shows a fine disregard for facts. . . . It is obvious that Mr. Duncan's anticommunist blinkers let no light through."

15. *New York Times*, 31 March 1960.

16. Brian Bunting, interview by author, December 1993. After hearing about the Sharpeville massacre the week before, Ronald Segal and staff members of *New Age* were now witnessing the demonstration at Caledon Square. The revolution was right outside their offices. Ronald Segal, *Into Exile* (London: Jonathan Cape, 1963), 273.

17. Brian Bunting, interview by author, December 1993.

18. Descriptions of the Langa march, especially about the debate over Patrick Duncan's role, can be found in Lelyveld, *Move Your Shadow*, 315–26; *Spectator*, 8 April 1960; *Cape Times*, 31 March 1960; Kwedie Mhlapi, interview by author, November 1993; Edward Roux, *Time Longer than Rope: A History of the Black Man's Struggle for Freedom in South Africa* (Madison.: University of Wisconsin Press, 1964), 410; Janet Robertson, *Liberalism in South Africa, 1948–1963* (Oxford: Clarendon Press, 1971), 216; Anthony Hazlitt Heard, *The Cape of Storms: A Personal History of the Crisis in South Africa* (Fayetteville: University of Arkansas Press, 1990), 96; *Weekly Mail and Guardian*, 27 March 1997. Other demonstrations in South Africa that day were not peaceful. In Worcester, sixty miles from Cape Town, police used tear gas to break up a procession; in Stellenbosch a police baton charge dispersed marchers, who turned violent and burned government buildings. *New York Times*, 31 March 1960.

19. Vigne, *Liberals against Apartheid*, 126.

20. No one was allowed in or out after 8 P.M.

21. M. Blumberg, *White Madam* (London: Victor Gollancz, 1962), 35. On the morning of 30 March, 234 people were arrested.

22. *New Age*, 8 September 1960; see Thomas Karis and Gail M. Gerhart, *Challenge and Violence, 1953–1964*, vol. 3 of *From Protest to Challenge* (Stanford: Hoover Institution, 1977), document 52 ("Congress Fights On" April 1960), 577–79 for a list of detainees that included many *New Age* supporters, sellers, and staff members: Ronnie Press, Trudy Gelb, Hilda and Rusty Bernstein, the Cachalia brothers, Issy Heyman, Jack Simons, Helen Joseph, Paul Joseph, Mary Moodley, Issy Wolfson, Harold Wolpe, Babla Saloojee, Walter Sisulu, Nelson Mandela, Moosie Moola, J. B. Marks, Harry Bloom, Cissie Gool, Jimmy La Guma, Harry Lawrence, Zollie Malindi, Jack Tarshish, Sarah Carneson, Denis Goldberg, Temba Mqota, Raymond Mhalba, Errol Shanley, Dawood Seedat, Harry Gwala, A. Docrat, and Z. K. Matthews.

23. *New Age*, 7 April 1960.

24. Albie Sachs, interview by author, March 1994.

25. *New Age*, 8 September 1960. *Torch*, the Unity Movement newspaper, was also banned under the proclamation. *Contact*, however, was not banned and its circulation jumped to 30,000. See Vigne, *Liberals against Apartheid*, 127.

26. Paul and Adelaide Joseph, interview by author, May 1994; Len Lee-Warden, interview by author, December 1993. A copy of the 7 April 1960 edition ended up in Joseph's possession.

27. Cecil Williams, the playwright, organized the Shakespeare productions, Govan Mbeki danced, and Alex La Guma wrote most of his first novel, *A Walk in the Night*.

28. Karis and Carter, *Challenge and Violence*, 574.

29. Ben Turok, interview by Brian Bunting, November 1973, Bunting Collection, Mayibuye Centre, University of the Western Cape. Kotane was in his late fifties, but thirty years earlier he had lived in Sophiatown in hiding under the name K. Motsoakai. Turok and Harmel grew to harbor great antipathy toward each other. Turok felt Harmel was sloppy, prone to security lapses, and drank too much, while Harmel believed Turok was politically inexperienced.

30. Wolfie Kodesh, interview by author, December 1993. See Chris Vermaak, *Braam Fischer: The Man with Two Faces* (Johannesburg: APB Publishers, 1966), 33.

31. Amy Thornton, interview by author, December 1993.

32. Brian Bunting, interview by author, December 1994.

33. *New Age*, 6 October 1960. See Alex Hepple, *The Press under*

Apartheid (London: International Defense and Aid Fund, 1974), 37; Elaine Potter, *The Press as Opposition: The Political Role of South African Newspapers* (Totowa, N.J.: Rowman and Littlefield, 1975), 118. The magistrate ruled that since the emergency was over, no one could be tried under its regulations. The government appealed to the Supreme Court, which referred the case back to a lower court for another hearing. At the second hearing, Real was acquitted on a technicality. Patrick Duncan was also charged with subversion under emergency regulations, 13,000 copies of *Contact* were impounded, and Duncan was found guilty and fined £500. John Sutherland, editor of the *Evening Post*, was charged with contravening the emergency regulations for publishing a report from two Canadian visitors who found South Africa "a country afraid to talk." He was acquitted.

34. *New Age*, 8 September 1960.

35. Albie Sachs, interview by author, March 1994.

36. *New Age*, 8 September 1960. Fred Carneson, as so often in these final three years, was officially designated editor.

37. *New Age*, 22 September 1960.

38. *New Age*, 8 September 1960.

39. Ruth First, *One Hundred Seventeen Days: An Account of Confinement and Interrogation under the South African Ninety-Day Detention Law* (London: Bloomsbury, 1965), 118.

40. Fred Carneson, interview by author, March 1994.

41. June 26 refers to a liberation movement holiday that began in 1950 with mourning for the May Day 1950 shootings. The 1952 Defiance Campaign and the 1955 Congress of the People were also launched on 26 June. *New Age*, 5 July 1962 (picture of the 26 June celebrations in Dar es Salaam); *New Age*, 26 July 1962 (picture of Walter and Albertina Sisulu on their eighteenth wedding anniversary); *New Age*, 17 January 1963 (article on the opening of an ANC center in Algeria).

42. *New Age*, 24 August 1961.

43. *New Age*, 27 April 1961. For more on Tambo, see *New Age*, 23 November 1961 (article on meeting Jomo Kenyatta). For articles by Yusuf Dadoo, see *New Age*, 11 January 1962 and 29 March 1962 (the latter a long and interesting article on why the United Front failed).

44. *New Age*, 24 August 1961.

45. *New Age*, 23 February 1961; 24 May 1962; 29 September 1960

(for an antipass leaflet); 1 February 1962 (on Transkei "independence"); 8 November 1962 and 1 November 1962—"To date no details on resolutions and conference decisions have reached *New Age*. But reports have filtered in of the vigorous spirit that dominated the proceedings."

46. *New Age*, 1 November 1962; 22 March 1962 (Duma Nokwe article on Urban Black Councils); 30 March 1961 (Nokwe interview on the extension of the ban on the African National Congress).

47. *New Age*, 8 February 1962.

48. *New Age*, 29 March 1962.

49. *New Age*, 16 November 1961 (Lutuli thanks readers), 14 December 1961 (speech printed).

50. *New Age*, 2 November 1961 (Lutuli article); 21 June 1962 (Lutuli's last statement: "it was no coincidence that he had chosen *New Age* to make this statement"); 13 April 1961 (message for Africa Day); 12 October and 2 November 1961 (Lutuli election surveys).

51. *New Age*, 21 December 1961; *Spark*, 1 January 1963.

52. *New Age*, 16 August 1962 (for slogans); 28 December 1961 (for telephone poles).

53. *New Age*, 21 December 1961.

54. *New Age*, 21 December 1961 (telephoned); 8 November 1962 (found its way); 29 September 1960 (ANC antipass leaflet sent to Johannesburg office); 1 February 1962 (by post); 7 June 1962 (slipped under door).

55. Ebrahim Ismail Ebrahim, interview by author, January 1994.

56. Govan Mbeki, interview by author, February 1994.

57. Ibid.

58. Ronnie Kasrils, *Armed and Dangerous: My Undercover Struggle against Apartheid* (Oxford: Heinemann, 1993), 38: In July 1961, Naicker recruited Kasrils into MK, so he obviously was in a leadership position in Natal. As the Special Branch policeman said to Kasrils during a raid later that night—as part of the police's routine to check up on suspected MK men after any disturbances—"You'll read about it in the papers tomorrow."

59. Ebrahim Ismail Ebrahim, interview by author, January 1994; Heidi Holland, *The Struggle: A History of the African National Congress* (New York: George Braziller, 1989), 142.

60. *New Age*, 8 November 1962, headline: "Pylons Dynamited in Natal." Each carried 88,000 volts of electricity—two in Pinetown,

two in Montclair area. For another description of the attack, see Kasrils, *Armed and Dangerous*, 53–54.

61. Mary Benson, *Nelson Mandela* (London: Penguin, 1986), 99.

62. *New Age*, 24 August 1961.

63. *New Age*, 31 August 1961.

64. *New York Times*, 10 January 1999 (for an obituary of Mokhehle).

65. He also devoured books by Mao, Che Guevara, Liddell-Hart, and Reitz's *Commando*. See Benson, *Nelson Mandela*, 107.

66. Nelson Mandela, *Long Walk to Freedom: The Autobiography of Nelson Mandela* (Boston: Little, Brown, 1994), 241.

67. *New Age*, 8 February 1962.

68. Martin Meredith, *Nelson Mandela: A Biography* (London: Hamish Hamilton, 1997), 220.

69. *New Age*, 25 October 1962 (pictures of Winnie Mandela). First and Harmel were among the visitors Mandela received in prison during the trial. Meer, *Higher than Hope*, 204.

70. *New Age*, 29 December 1960.

71. Govan Mbeki, *South Africa: The Peasant's Revolt* (London: Penguin, 1964), 121–27; *New Age*, 6 July 1961. Mpondos were forced to drink large amounts of water and then were kicked in the stomach; 10 May 1962. *New Age* was eventually banned in the Transkei. Oliver Tambo was from Bizana.

72. Mbeki, *Peasant's Revolt*, 123.

73. *New Age*, 10 November 1960.

74. *New Age*, 13 and 20 October 1960.

75. *New Age*, 10 November 1960.

76. *New Age*, 17 November 1960.

77. *New Age*, 23 February 1961 (article by Jones Kgasane); 26 January 1961 (report on Tembuland *New Age* sellers being harassed by the police).

78. *New Age*, 19 October 1961.

79. *New Age*, 5 December 1961.

80. Meer, *Higher than Hope*, 126.

81. *New Age*, 25 January 1962 (Fenner Brockway, MP, raised the question in Parliament).

82. Ibid. (Louw apology); 8 February 1962 (bottles); 1 March 1962 (picture of Ganyile back at his Basutoland hut).

83. Emma Gilbey, *The Lady: The Life and Times of Winnie Man-*

dela (London: Jonathan Cape, 1993), 69. Sisulu's suggestion to join *New Age* apparently gave rise to a great deal of enmity and was connected somehow to his brother's arson attempt at the Mandela home in 1965.

84. *New Age*, 28 June 1962.

85. Harold Strachan and Joseph Jack were also charged in the trial. For an interesting eyewitness account of the trial, see Athol Fugard, *Notebooks 1960–1977* (New York: Knopf, 1984), 48–51.

86. *New Age*, 15 March 1962 (Mbeki arrested and charged under the Explosives Act); 10 May 1962 (Mbeki acquitted); 11 October 1962 (Mbeki arrested); 15 May 1962 (raid on Port Elizabeth branch offices); Govan Mbeki, interview by author, February 1994.

87. Ruth First, *South-West Africa* (London: Penguin, 1964), 11.

88. *New Age*, 18 and 25 October 1961.

89. *New Age*, 25 May 1961.

90. *New Age*, 28 June 1962: "As Alex La Guma is banned from attending gatherings we regret that, in terms of the General Laws Amendment Act, we are no longer permitted to publish any of his writing." A total of 102 people were gagged by the government in August 1962. In the *Cape Times*, next to the announcement of the banning of the 102 people, was a story on Yves St. Laurent's new collection. See Adam Hochschild, *Half the Way Home: A Memoir of Father and Son* (New York: Viking, 1986), 110. As a university student on holiday, Hochschild spent the winter of 1962 in Cape Town working for Patrick Duncan at *Contact*.

91. Meer, *Higher than Hope*, 169. See Political Trials Collection, AD1901, Wits, for State v Joe Gqabi. When asked about leaving the country in 1962 without a passport or permit, Gqabi told the court: "I am a journalist photographer by profession. I realised that since the *New Age* newspaper was banned, the present paper *Spark* had no future in the country. I thought therefore that if I left the country, I would have better prospects in Dar-es-Salaam."

92. *New Age*, 8 December 1960 (Resha article about the lack of advisory board candidates in Johannesburg); 9 February 1961 (Resha articles on the Treason Trial and boxing); 11 May 1961 (last Resha article); 29 June 1961 (Resha appointed ambassador).

93. J. N. Lazerson, *Against the Tide: Whites in the Struggle against Apartheid* (Boulder: Westview, 1994), 232.

94. Govan Mbeki, interview by author, February 1994.

95. Brian Bunting, interview by author, December 1993.

96. *New Age*, 17 May 1962 (Port Elizabeth and Durban offices raided. In Durban three detectives end a half-hour search when they find a telegram addressed to Ronnie Kasrils); 23 August 1962 (in Port Elizabeth); 19 April 1962 (raids after the Roeland Street bombs were found. Police visit the homes of Bunting, Carneson, and La Guma); 20 September 1962 (one more lunchtime raid in Barrack Street).

97. First, *One Hundred Seventeen Days*, 118. First was echoing the famous comment by Horace Flather, editor of the *Star*, who in 1952 said editing in South Africa was "like walking blindfolded through a minefield."

98. Brian Bunting, correspondence with author, April 1991. *New Age*, 13 April 1961: "Our circulation is on the up and up."

99. *New Age*, 10 November 1960 (trip to Natal raised £1,194); 28 September 1961 (raised R1,782).

100. Brian Bunting, interview by author, November 1993.

101. *New Age*, 9 August 1962, 4 January 1962, and 3 May 1962 (on donations); 9 August 1962 (loan).

102. *New Age*, 30 August 1962 (notice); 6 September 1962 (*Die Vaderland* and the *Cape Argus*).

103. Essop Pahad, "A People's Leader: A Political Biography of Dr. Y. M. Dadoo," unpublished manuscript, Bunting Collection, Mayibuye Centre, University of Western Cape, 207.

104. Amy Thornton Collection, box 24, Manuscripts and Archives, University of Cape Town, Hodgson letter dated 7 March 1962.

105. Hansard, 21 May 1962, col 6070–1; Hepple, *Press under Apartheid*, 26–27.

106. Parallels to the 1824 Somerset Affair—in which the governor of the Cape colony, Lord Charles Somerset, attempted to ban the first independent publications in the colony—continued to crop up. In 1824, Somerset had insisted George Greig, as printer and publisher of the *South African Commercial Advertiser*, deposit 10,000 rix-dollars "lest he publish anything untoward." Jennifer Crwys-Williams, *South African Dispatches* (Johannesburg: Ashanti, 1989), 15.

107. Hansard, 21 June 1962, col 6216. *New Age* was noted as "a publication which has not yet been banned."

108. *New Age*, 26 January 1961; see 3 April 1958 about a possible attack on *New Age*.

109. *New Age*, 17 May 1962.

110. *New Age*, 14 June 1962.

111. *New Age*, 31 May 1962. In a letter dated 28 May Bunting wrote: "It is because *New Age* has been the most determined opponent of Apartheid in the ranks of the opposition press that it is to be snuffed out at the pleasure of the Minister of Justice." London *New Age* Committee Collection, Mayibuye Centre, University of the Western Cape.

112. London *New Age* Committee Collection, Mayibuye Centre, University of the Western Cape. Bunting continued: "I need hardly emphasise the seriousness of the situation as far as we are concerned. What I am writing to ask now is that the maximum possible protest should be roused against the proposed banning of *New Age*. . . . It seems to me that this is the sort of issue on which a lot of support could be mobilised abroad, and it would be fine if the Minister could be deluged with protests against his proposal to ban us. . . . An all-out fight is being waged locally. All international support would be welcome."

113. Called "A Declaration of Protest against the South African Government's Attacks on the Freedom of Publication and the Press," the letter was also signed by Ronnie Segal, Max Gluckman, John Osborne, Angus Wilson, John Wain, Bishop Ambrose Reeves, six MPs and two CBEs (an order of British knighthood).

114. The *Times* of London declined, the editors of the *Daily Telegraph* and the *Daily Herald* simply signed the declaration; the *Guardian* and the *Observer* had editorials on the issue. See *New Age*, 7 and 28 June 1962. The issue became so internationalized that Vorster received a letter from a man in Gresham, Oregon, about a possible *New Age* banning.

115. London *New Age* Committee Collection, Mayibuye Centre, University of the Western Cape, Max Joffe letter signed 12 December 1962.

116. *New Age*, 15 November 1962; La Guma was actually house-arrested on 20 December 1962.

117. *New Age*, 15 November 1962.

118. Brian Bunting, *The Rise of the South African Reich* (London: Penguin, 1964), 219.

119. *New Age*, 18 October 1962, 22 November 1962 (sightless in the desert).

120. AAM asked supporters to send copies of British newspapers

to South African friends "to beat Dr. Verwoerd's censorship." London *New Age* Committee Collection. Hepple, *Press under Apartheid*, 26; *Spark*, 5 December 1962 (Dadoo, in a letter to Vorster, called the banning "arbitrary" and "callous"). See *Evening Post* (Port Elizabeth), 30 November 1962.

121. United Nations, *The United Nations and Apartheid, 1948–1994* (New York: United Nations, 1996), 252.

122. *Cape Times*, 3 December 1962.

123. *Spark*, 12 December 1962.

124. *Cape Argus*, 20 November 1962.

125. *Spark*, 14 February 1963.

126. Brian Bunting, interview by author, December 1994; Brian Bunting, interview by Shaun Johnson, January 1984.

127. They were the South African Library in Cape Town, libraries in Pretoria and Bloemfontein, and the British Museum. One assumes that the editors made an extra copy or two to have around the office for the inevitable visits from the Security Branch.

128. *Spark*, 22 October 1962.

129. *Morning Star* continued to come out each month and even survived the death of *Spark*. The last issue was 14 May 1963, published by M. I. Cajee of Macosa House, Commissioner Street, Johannesburg.

130. London *New Age* Committee Collection, Mayibuye Centre, University of the Western Cape.

131. *Spark*, 27 December 1962 and 21 February 1963.

132. *Spark*, 14 February 1963.

133. *Spark*, 7 March 1963 (the police raid all four offices and remove blank *New Age* letterhead stationery).

134. Gillian Slovo, *Every Secret Thing: My Family, My Country* (Boston: Little, Brown, 1997), 54–56. Sonia Bunting, interview by author, December 1994: "We lived high on Lion's Head and it was eighty-four steps up the hill. The CID hated it to climb up."

135. *Spark*, 21 March 1963; Hepple, *Press under Apartheid*, 28. Vorster might have been motivated by more black-on-white violence —most of the killings being attributed to Poqo, the armed guerrilla wing of the PAC. On 2 February 1963 the guerrillas used petrol bombs and guns to murder five whites sleeping in campers near Bashee River Bridge in the Transkei, and six days later a white debt collector was killed in Langa.

136. Fred Carneson, interview by author, March 1994.

137. Brian and Sonia Bunting, interview by author, December 1993. Fred Carneson made an exploratory visit to Maseru in 1962 to scout out the possibilities. Fred Carneson, interview by author, March 1994.

138. Fred Carneson letter to Max Joffe, 15 March 1963, London *New Age* Committee Collection, Mayibuye Centre, University of the Western Cape.

139. See *Cape Times*, 28 March 1963: "Bannings Cause Newspaper to Shut Down."

140. Govan Mbeki, interview by author, February 1994; Albie Sachs, interview by author, March 1994.

141. *Spark*, 28 March 1963.

142. Albie Sachs, interview by author, March 1994.

143. Douglas Manqina, interview by author, December 1993.

4

Representing Blackness

Steve Biko and the Black Consciousness Movement

Mbulelo Vizikhungo Mzamane and
David R. Howarth

The Black Consciousness movement (BC) in South Africa emerged in the years following the Sharpeville, Vanderbijl Park, and Langa massacres and the bannings of the African National Congress (ANC) and Pan-Africanist Congress (PAC) in March–April 1960. Dissidents of the Freedom Charter generation were all but silenced inside South Africa, but resistance reemerged toward the end of the decade. Black Consciousness activists would produce a body of published work in their own political and literary journals, and in a commercial press aimed at the black community. They stressed transforming consciousness, overcoming fear, and building racial pride. It was the beginning of a new phase in the history of the antiapartheid movement.

White Trusteeship

African youth tried but failed to revive the legacy of the ANC and PAC in the early 1960s. Students loyal to the ANC formed the African Students' Association and students loyal to the PAC formed the African Students' Union of South Africa, but South Africa's security police continually harassed members of both groups and they did not last very long.

Many African students began to drift toward the white-dominated National Union of South African Students (NUSAS) between 1963 and 1966, while others joined the University Christian Movement (UCM) for a brief period beginning in 1967. The authorities of the segregated black universities, with the exception of the University of Natal's black medical facility at Wentworth in Durban, refused to allow their students to affiliate to NUSAS, which was composed mainly of whites from the English-speaking universities.[1] The students in NUSAS and the UCM championed the cause of Africans and were seen by some blacks as important spokespersons for the cause. But this situation was felt to be unsatisfactory by more radical activists: they desired to see an end to all forms of white trusteeship and believed NUSAS could not meet their deepest political and cultural aspirations.

When most extraparliamentary opposition groups in South Africa were suppressed in the early 1960s (the Communist Party had been banned in 1950), some dissidents, co-opted essentially from the ranks of the petty bourgeoisie, began to entertain the notion of using government-created institutions like the Bantu Authorities in the African reserves, the Coloured and Indian Representative Councils, and the Urban Bantu Councils to try to subvert apartheid policies. The government also embarked on a new policy of dialogue with the outside world—strained since the Sharpeville crisis, which had led to South Africa's withdrawal from the British Commonwealth in 1961—to gain acceptance for its policies in independent Africa.

B. J. Vorster became prime minister in 1966 after the assassination of H. F. Verwoerd, the main architect of apartheid. Vorster would strive to persuade the world to accept separate development for the African reserves or Bantustans, as they were now called. He invited Prime Minister Leabua Jonathan of Lesotho to pay an official visit to Cape Town in January 1967. Vorster promised to look into the possibility of granting economic and technical assistance to Lesotho in return for guarantees of political stability and vigilance against "international communism." Shortly after Jonathan's visit, a delegation of ministers from Botswana arrived in South Africa to discuss matters of common concern with their South African counterparts. A significant breakthrough to the north was marked by the visit in March 1967 of three ministers from Malawi to negotiate a bilateral preferential trade pact. Malawi subsequently opened an embassy in Pretoria, the first and only African state in the apartheid era to do so, and in 1972 President Hastings Banda of Malawi made an official visit to South Africa. In 1970, South Africa also established informal diplomatic links with Madagascar, Ivory Coast, and Senegal.

These developments were discussed in the African community and in the African commercial press (especially the *World* and *Weekend World*, published in Johannesburg), and rejected as window dressing. African critics saw the National Party policy of winning over poor African states with foreign aid as a ploy to convince outsiders that South Africa was moving away from racial discrimination. The propaganda exercise was aimed at convincing the world that South Africa's projected Bantustans would be treated like Lesotho, Botswana, Malawi, or any other independent state once they were given independence. African critics said the dialogue should be taking place between blacks and whites living in South Africa to determine the government's sincerity in bringing about meaningful change. These views found expression in the polemical writings of Stephen Bantu Biko (1946–1977), the central figure in the Black Consciousness movement, and in the poems of BC poets like Mongane (Wally) Serote ("The Actual Dialogue") and Mafika Pascal Gwala ("Paper Curtains"),[2] who were opposed to the duplicity of the apartheid regime and united in their rejection of government-created institutions.

The Rise of Black Consciousness

Much soul searching took place among black students within NUSAS and the UCM in 1967 and 1968. The outcome of their deliberations was the decision to abandon all forms of dependence on white patronage and establish a united black front outside the framework of apartheid that would consist of all those subordinated by color in South Africa. Their initial purpose was to frustrate government efforts to separate the subordinate black population along racial or ethnic lines.

The students convened a meeting of representatives from the segregated "black" (African, Coloured, Indian) universities in December 1968 to discuss issues that affected their interests as blacks. The meeting was held at Steve Biko's old high school at Mariannhill in Natal. A resolution to form an organization to be known as the South African Students' Organisation (SASO) was adopted. The conference examined the question of whether the interests of black students were being served by multiracial student bodies like the UCM and especially NUSAS. The general consensus was that these organizations did not meet the educational, social, and political needs of black students. The students complained of being numerically swamped in NUSAS to the extent that white liberal views prevailed on every issue. The conference proposed that blacks should break with NUSAS and form their own organization, and they agreed to hold a SASO inaugural conference in July 1969 for this purpose at Turfloop in the northeastern Transvaal, where a segregated, apartheid-era "tribal" college called the University College of the North was located.

A communiqué issued at the Turfloop conference addressed the key issue of the government's divide-and-rule tactics that had led to the establishment of separate racial and ethnic universities: "That there is a need for more effective contact is unquestionable, especially in view of the ever-increasing enrolment at the non-white institutions of higher learning, particularly the university colleges. For all intent and purpose [*sic*], these students have remained isolated, not only physically but also intellectually. . . . There is no way of stopping this except by interfering with the programme of indoctrination and intimidation so effectively applied at all South African universities."[3]

The most pressing issue at this conference was the relationship of SASO to NUSAS. A debate ensued between students who advocated a complete break and those who favored the retention of certain links with NUSAS. The divergence of opinion arose because students at most black campuses had been forbidden to join NUSAS and many still aspired to become members. They felt that if they disassociated themselves from NUSAS they would be siding with the Bantustan universities and the government in their attacks on the oldest national student body in South Africa. They criticized what they saw as the racial character of SASO, which they accused of playing into the hands of apartheid. Thus the first constitution of SASO, adopted at Turfloop, stated the case for multiracial cooperation cautiously while advocating black solidarity.

The term *Non-White*, used in all official government communication, was dropped. The students viewed the designation as a negation of themselves as human beings. It was a description of a "non-something," a description that implied something else was the standard and they were not that standard. As Biko, first president of SASO, explained in 1976, "They felt that a positive view of life, which is commensurate with the build-up of one's dignity and confidence, should be contained in a description which you accept, and they sought to replace the term Non-White with the term Black."[4]

Blacks were defined as those who were discriminated against politically, economically, and socially—a definition that excluded whites. The *SASO Newsletter* of September 1970 explained the strategic considerations at work behind the semantic exercise:

> The term . . . must be seen in the right context. No new category is being created but a re-Christening is taking place. We are merely refusing to be regarded as non-persons and claim the right to be called positively. . . . Adopting a collectively positive outlook leads to the creation of a broader base which may be useful in time. It helps us to recognise that we have a common enemy. . . . One should grant that the division of races in this country is too entrenched and that the Blacks will find it difficult to operate as a combined front. The black umbrella we are creating for ourselves at least helps to make sure the various units should be working in the same direction, being complementary to each other.[5]

In Black Consciousness parlance, as in the poetry it inspired, *Non-White* came to have a derogatory connotation. It referred to blacks who aspired to white values or were deemed to be serving the white power structure. Mafika Gwala, who would serve as the 1973 editor of *Black Viewpoint,* became the foremost literary exponent of this view ("Black Status Seekers"), and Biko also made this point in several articles in BC publications.[6]

By redefining themselves, adherents of Black Consciousness sought to transform expressions like "Black is Beautiful" into more than mere slogans. Biko's elaboration on the significance of this term during the SASO Nine trial in 1976 is reminiscent of Gwala's poetry at the time and of the poetry of Léopold Senghor ("Black Woman") and Okot p'Bitek ("Song of Lawino" and "Song of Ocol"):

When you say "Black is Beautiful" what you are saying to [the black person] is: Man, you are okay as you are; begin to look upon yourself as a human being. Now, in African life . . . the way women prepare themselves for viewing by society . . . the way they dress, the way they make up . . . tends to be a negation of their true state and in a sense a running away from their colour. They use [skin] lightening creams, they use straightening devices for their hair. . . . They sort of believe that their natural state, which is a black state, is not synonymous with beauty. And beauty can only be approximated by them if the skin is made as light as possible and the lips are made as red as possible and their nails are made as pink as possible. . . . "Black is Beautiful" challenges exactly that belief which makes someone negate himself.[7]

Black Consciousness writers taught blacks to assert themselves in order to overcome their inherent fears and self-hatred. Using tools of analysis popularized by Frantz Fanon,[8] they said blacks had developed a state of alienation from themselves. Black Consciousness poetry and theatre, picking up the cue from Biko's writings, injected a tone of defiance to counteract stereotypes that looked down on African culture and debased blacks. They had to liberate themselves from the habit of identifying everything good with whites and looking down on their indigenous culture as inferior.

Barney Nyameko Pityana replaced Biko as SASO president at the July 1970 student council meeting of SASO in Wentworth, Durban, and Biko was elected chairman of SASO Publications. This was a crucial post because the early to mid-1970s witnessed an outpouring of scholarship (on subjects like poetics, aesthetics, culture, politics, economics, and theology) within the movement. This material appeared in Black Consciousness publications like the *SASO Newsletter*, the official organ of SASO; *Creativity and Development*, a collection of papers delivered at a SASO symposium in July 1972; *Essays on Black Theology*, by leading proponents on the subject; and annuals like *Black Review* and *Black Viewpoint*.

SASO Newsletter front page in May/June 1972 depicts a montage of struggle news clippings.

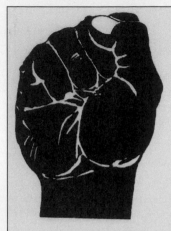

SASO BULLETIN

Vol. 1 - No 1
June 1977
30 Cents

CONTENTS
1. Graduation from Illusions to Disillusion
2. Presidential Address to the 8th GCS.
3. Alienation and the Economy
4. Heroes Day
5. Factors Determining Liberation in S.A.

SASO
86 Beatrice Street,
Durban.

A graphic symbol of Black Power on the front page of *SASO Bulletin*, June 1977.

Disseminating the Message in Black Consciousness Media

SASO divided its overall political strategy into two phases: an initial period of conscientization, followed by a later stage of political confrontation that would probably involve a commitment to armed struggle.[9] Phase One involved four main aspects: Directive Politics, which consisted of direct political criticism of the regime; Infiltration Politics, which meant the penetration and transformation of existing political formations; Orientation Politics, which would endeavor to foster a different and distinctive ethos toward economic, cultural, educational, and religious practices; and Self-Reliance Politics, which would make possible the formation of an independent civil society where blacks took the leading role.[10] Important debates, which were never resolved, took place within the movement about the precise timing and nature of the transition from Phase One to Phase Two, though in 1972 it was generally accepted that the movement take maximum advantage of the emergent political space civil society offered and persist with its "above ground" practices.

"Conscientization" was of critical importance in Phase One. The objective would be met by creating and disseminating the Black Consciousness message through existing media and by constructing alternative avenues of communication. The commercial press, controlled by whites, was the dominant mode of mass communication, and these publications often incurred the wrath of Black Consciousness intellectuals because they did not promote the advancement of BC ideas and practices.[11] The critique of the commercial press was directed at the production and circulation of negative, largely traditional, images and stereotypes of blacks, though criticisms were also aimed at white ownership of the commercial press and wage discrepancies between white and black journalists. To counter these negative tendencies, BC activists designed various strategies to provide new opportunities to reach the black population and to counter white portrayals of blacks.

They sought to penetrate the white-controlled, commercial black press with messages that countered negative portraits of the movement. SASO, for example, actively challenged the representation of blacks through letter-writing campaigns, made persistent efforts to recruit black journalists to their cause —a process greatly accelerated by the formation of the Union of Black Journalists (UBJ) in January 1973—explored the possibility of setting up an alternative black-owned newspaper, an endeavor that ultimately failed, and exerted considerable pressure on amenable black journalists and editors to endorse the cause of Black Consciousness.[12]

One way of challenging the representation of Black Consciousness in the liberal, mainly English-language, white commercial press took the form of expelling reporters of the *Star* and *Rand Daily Mail* from a SASO student council meeting in July 1972 for their continued use of *Non-White* in their reports of Black Consciousness activities.[13] This resulted in the *Rand Daily Mail* decision to adopt the term *black* when covering the activities of SASO and other organizations in the Black Consciousness movement, a decision subsequently copied by other sections of the liberal English and eventually the Afrikaans-language press.[14]

The gradual insinuation of Black Consciousness concerns, and styles of language, into the liberal press is evidenced by Steve Biko's much-heralded relationship with Donald Woods, who was then editor of the East London *Daily Dispatch*.[15] This resulted in the spread of BC ideas to the wider white liberal community and to middle-class Africans who read the *Daily Dispatch*. By the time of the Soweto uprising in 1976, and largely as a result of these events, the *World*, flagship newspaper of the white-owned black press, under the editorship of Percy Qoboza, had moved away from its old apoliticism and come out strongly against existing apartheid institutions from a qualified Black Consciousness perspective.[16]

SASO activists accepted the structural limitations of using commercial newspapers to articulate and expand its views. The BC movement could seek to counter its negative images, but a more reliable strategy was to develop an independent news voice. In this respect, Black Consciousness intellectuals made important use of the *SASO Newsletter*, which was the major means of communicating the Black Consciousness message from 1970 until mid-1973. During the initial period of success, the *SASO Newsletter* appeared four or five times a year and, at its zenith, circulation reached 4,000 copies (though the newsletter was undoubtedly read by many more people).[17] It carried key statements on Black Consciousness ideology, critically examined current social and political issues, and was a forum for ongoing political debate among supporters of the movement. The newsletter was combative and intense, "forcing racial issues to the foreground of the black political agenda, and set[ting] the tone for the emergence of similar communicational channels."[18]

A typical edition would be about twenty pages and consisted of an editorial analyzing contemporary political events (while outlining SASO's particular viewpoint), a letters page allowing readers to comment on ongoing debates, a section reporting events on the various campuses where SASO was represented, and various news stories and briefings on happenings in the rest of Africa. The newsletter also contained elaborations of BC philosophy as well as manifestos and statements of SASO policy. There were sections on the arts, with reviews and criticism of theatre, books, and poetry, and efforts were made to represent indigenous poetry, art, and design, which were often displayed as cover sheets and graphics in the newsletter.

In addition to the newsletter, SASO and other affiliated organizations produced occasional pamphlets in their efforts to recruit membership and enunciate Black Consciousness views.

The formation of the Black Community Programmes (BCP) in 1972 brought greater finances and resources to the Black Consciousness movement and with it the capacity to expand the range of publications. In January 1973 the Christian Institute and the Study Project on Christianity in Apartheid Society (SPROCAS) launched the Ravan publishing company, and Ravan enabled BCP to start its own publication series.[19] This series would include a directory of black organizations researched by BCP entitled *A Handbook of Black Organizations* and a quarterly entitled *Black Viewpoint* (the first edition appearing in September 1972) that printed speeches and articles by the BC leadership.[20] Biko, for example, took on the task of correcting misrepresentations and distortions in the depiction of blacks in the white-dominated press—a point he made clear in his editorial in the first issue, when he referred to the paucity of black contributions in the media: "So many things are said so often to us, about us, and for us, but very seldom by us."[21] *Black Review* was also launched in 1972 initially under the editorship of Ben Khoapa to "present trends in the Black Community in order that leaders can assess these directions in the light of societal conditions predicted for the future, determine which trends should be changed and identify the kinds of interventions necessary to effect such changes."[22] *Black Perspectives*, launched in 1973, was supposed to be a more scholarly publication catering to academics and professionals, but only one issue of the journal came out.[23]

The banning of key Black Consciousness leaders and activists during 1972 and 1973, including both editors of *Black Review* and *Black Viewpoint*, meant that Biko's editorial had to be dropped, and the entire edition of *Black Review*, some 230 pages, withdrawn from distribution. Only four more issues of the *SASO Newsletter*, moreover, were printed after mid-1973.[24] Nevertheless, as Peter Randall records, these efforts reaped enormous benefits for the movement. By mid-1973, despite government pressure, a total of 12,300 copies of these publications had been sold.[25]

As the chair of SASO publications, Biko became the key catalyst in the production of a Black Consciousness literature. Leading poets like Njabulo Ndebele (the 1971–72 Students' Representative Council president at the University of Botswana, Lesotho, and Swaziland), Mafika Gwala, and Mongane Serote became household names through their writing in BC publications. As Serote acknowledged, "At that time many people were responding to literary criticism in the newspapers; their writing was being influenced by the standards created by white newspapers. Then SASO . . . and other black organizations came out with their own magazines, through which we could publish; they gave us a platform from which we could speak directly to the black community."[26]

"I Write What I Like"

Biko's column "I Write What I Like" (which he wrote under the pseudonym Frank Talk) first appeared in the *SASO Newsletter* of August 1970. These essays provide the most precise formulation available on the Black Consciousness movement. Above all, they explain the political importance of the cultural struggle—the philosophy behind Black Consciousness art, literature, music, and drama. More than any previous resistance organization in South Africa, Black Consciousness would privilege cultural form in seeking to raise the political consciousness of the black community.

Biko's first article was entitled "Black Souls in White Skins?" —a borrowing from Frantz Fanon.[27] Although Biko did not evince the same understanding of class issues as, for example, Njabulo Ndebele,[28] he was just as unsparing in his criticism of white liberals—prime targets in the early years of Black

Consciousness—whom he referred to sarcastically as "people who say they have black souls wrapped up in white skins." Biko rejected patronage from whites, who wanted to determine what was good for blacks and to act on their behalf. He also argued that superficial integration in white-dominated structures only served to reinforce the black people's sense of inadequacy by establishing a discourse in which whites did "all the talking and the blacks the listening."[29] He also questioned the earnestness of whites involved in multiracial, antiapartheid organizations by casting doubts about their commitment to the destruction of a system in which they were also beneficiaries.

Biko compared blacks who relied on white liberals to eradicate white privilege to slaves who had surrendered leadership in the antislavery struggle. They had relied on the children of slave masters who had declared themselves on the side of the slaves. Biko argued that meaningful integration would only come about once whites had been stripped of their paternalistic power and blacks of their arsenal of inferiority complexes, a notion seized upon by Serote and reiterated in his poem "The Actual Dialogue."[30]

Biko advocated a grassroots buildup of Black Consciousness. He rejected the notion that whites were more intelligent than blacks and questioned their qualification and competence to set the pace for and determine the direction of black advancement. At a symposium in Cape Town sponsored by the Abe Bailey Institute for Inter-Racial Studies in January 1971, Biko cited Aimé Césaire, a leading writer in the Negritude movement, to his mainly white audience: "No race possesses the monopoly of beauty, intelligence, force, and there is room for all of us at the rendezvous of victory."[31]

The "Black Souls" column expressed suspicion about white liberal politics, arguing that their views and actions actually upheld the social order: "They vacillate between the two worlds, verbalising all the complaints of the blacks beautifully while skilfully extracting what suits them from the exclusive pool of white privilege. But ask them for a moment to give a concrete meaningful programme that they intend adopting, then you will see on whose side they really are."[32] Like fiction writer Nadine Gordimer,[33] he exposed white liberalism as bold at the verbal level but incapable of effecting meaningful change. White liberals gave blacks the impression that they were doing something to transform South African society, but in reality their actions were calculated to contain black hostility and enable whites to retain their political, economic, and cultural dominance.

White liberals identified with the black people's struggle either to salvage what they could for themselves or to assuage their own consciences. Once they had eased their guilt, for example, by engaging in ritualistic protests, they withdrew into their racial cocoons. Superficial integration at parties defined the limits of their actions: "As a testimony to their claim of complete identification with blacks, they call a few 'intelligent and articulate' blacks to 'come round for tea at home,' where all present ask each other the same hackneyed question 'how can we bring about change in South Africa?'"[34]

In the "Black Souls" column, Biko portrays white liberals as people who divert attention from essential to peripheral issues. Because of the stake they have in the system, they have no genuine desire to upset the status quo. Thus they are more closely identified with the oppressor than with the plight of the oppressed. A resolution adopted by the SASO student council in July 1971 focused on the ambivalence and vacillation of white liberals: "The white man must be made aware that one is either part of the solution or part of the problem; that in this context because of the privileges accorded to them by legislation and because of their continual maintenance of an oppressive regime whites had defined themselves as part of the problem."[35]

White liberals like Alan Paton, author and chairman of the multiracial Liberal Party until it was disbanded in 1968 (political parties were not allowed to have racially mixed memberships under the 1968 Prohibition of Political Interference Act), accused Black Consciousness of counteracting white racism with black racism. Biko charged white critics with trying to stifle black self-determination: "When the blacks announce that the time has come for them to do things for themselves and all by themselves all white liberals shout blue murder"—a statement that would be echoed by Gwala in several poems during the early 1970s.[36] White liberals, according to Biko, had set up a racial trap. They wanted to maintain a situation in which their values and interests would dominate forever. Blacks did not possess the power to subjugate others, if racism is defined as "discrimination by a group against another for the purpose of subjugation or maintaining subjugation."[37]

The new emphasis in SASO was on self-reliance. Whites could still carve themselves a place in the struggle but only in supporting roles and if they confined their activities to conscientizing other whites. Blacks wanted to take their destiny into their own hands. Another section of this resolution expressed the view that multiracial integration could only be meaningful if it was based on a partnership between equals: "Before the black people should join the open society they should first close their ranks to form themselves into a solid group, to oppose the definite racism that is meted out by white society, to work out their new direction clearly and bargain from a position of strength."[38] As the wording of this resolution suggests, Black Consciousness in South Africa was finding numerous parallels with Black Power in the United States.

Black Consciousness was equally critical of blacks who embraced white values and aspired to white privilege. Critics at SASO's annual conference in July 1972, for example, attacked the black petty bourgeoisie for their individualism, acquisitiveness, political apathy, and lack of creativity. Biko wrote: "They [the black petty bourgeoisie] have been made to feel inferior for so long that for them it is comforting to drink tea, wine or beer with whites who seem to treat them as equals. This served to boost up their own ego to the extent of making them feel slightly superior to those blacks who do not get similar treatment from whites."[39] The black middle class dissipated their energy in fruitless appeals to the white establishment instead of educating people about their collective predicament. Biko accused them of being as much an impediment to black advancement as their white liberal middle-class mentors, whose gradualist approach they had absorbed without realizing that for liberals gradualism was a trick to retain white privilege indefinitely. They failed to grasp the essential dynamic inherent in white liberalism, "the superior-inferior white-black stratification that makes the white a perpetual teacher and the black a perpetual pupil (and a poor one at that)."[40]

Black Consciousness activists urged black communities not to be slaves to white archetypes. Blacks who faked commitment to the black cause while aspiring to positions of privilege were singled out for attack in Gwala's poem "Black Status Seekers":

> You don dashikis
> then go off on super-per talks
> in praise of the London/New York
> that you've never come to know.
> "When I was in London . . ." you'll say,
> just to seek oneupmanship.
> You avoid ghetto truths
> in your neighbourhood,
> Yet you'll go around
> bragging of the "real rough" place
> that's whirling the blackman
> for a drown.
> Brother, how can you be a wolf
> with a cat's face.[41]

Biko also condemned blacks who, in the company of whites, had acquired what Fanon called a "psychological minus value" and sought to annihilate their own identity as blacks.[42]

The extent to which Black Consciousness ideology had begun to permeate society is also reflected in the poems of Sipho Sydney Sepamla, who revived the literary journal *Classic* as *New Classic* and also took over the editorship of *Sketch*, a theatre magazine. Sepamla demonstrates in poems like "Stop the Lie" the hypocrisy of whites who hold that blacks should be gradually absorbed into the intricacies of government to maintain social and political stability:

> I want you to stop the lie
> don't tell me how much you feed the poor
> because you made hunger
> when you dropped those of my blood into the hole of gold.
> I want you to stop the lie
> don't tell me of the schools you've built
> because you made ignorance
> by creating an education only for my kind.
> I want you to stop the lie
> don't tell me of numbers of clinics and hospitals operating
> because you made disease
> when you paid pittance for all my labour.[43]

Closely related to the problem of counteracting white-prescribed solutions to black predicaments was the problem posed by the false consciousness of white-dominated culture. Biko discouraged the slavish imitation of others as inimical to the cultivation of a critical consciousness among oppressed groups. He saw himself as the personification of the African paradox—detribalized and Westernized, a committed Christian even, but still African.

Black Consciousness sought to arrest the further erosion of African culture by emphasizing communal rather than Western-inspired individual values. As Biko put it in the "Black Souls" column, "A country in Africa, in which the majority of people are African, must inevitably exhibit African values and be truly African in style."[44] He elaborated on this point in his second column in the *SASO Newsletter*, "We Blacks": "The oneness of community for instance is at the heart of our culture. . . . These are characteristics we must not allow ourselves to lose. Their value can only be appreciated by those who have not as yet been made slaves to technology and the machine."[45]

Molefe Pheto, echoing some of Serote's sentiments on the importance of projecting African values and aspirations, explained in his prison memoirs what such cultural nationalism entailed: "Gone were the days when our productions aped white people. Gone were white written plays and poems. . . . The emphasis had become black pride and nationhood through the arts, drawing from our cultural background, a decided return to our cultural origins."[46]

When Ndebele became the editor in 1970 of *Expression*, journal of the English society at the University of Botswana, Lesotho, and Swaziland, he began to express his views on the use of traditional poetic modes. In the manner of Negritude poets but without their glorification of the African past, he suggested in a 1970 *Expression* editorial that African poets should recognize the interdependence between humanity and earth and draw their inspiration from precolonial African myths, beliefs, and moral codes. In July 1976, during the inaugural conference of the ill-fated Institute of Black Studies in Wilgespruit, Roodepoort (a city near Johannesburg), he presented a paper on literary archetypes as found in such traditional forms as the Xhosa *intsomi*, the Zulu *inganekwane*, and the Sotho *tsomo*. He argued that literary studies in Africa should begin with such precolonial literary archetypes.[47]

In the "We Blacks" column of the September 1970 *SASO Newsletter*, Biko urged blacks to look more critically at some of the assumptions by which they lived. Like Fanon, he was drawn to the concept of the colonized mind. "The type of black man we have today has lost his manhood," Biko wrote. "Reduced to an obliging shell, he looks with awe at the white power structure and accepts what he regards as the 'inevitable position.'"[48] Biko attributed black subservience to whites as a form of psychological enslavement. The inferior systems of African, Coloured, and Indian education, he said, had been designed to produce compliant blacks and had contributed to their resignation, dehumanization, and emasculation.

This dimension of psychological empowerment distinguished the new literature, written under the momentum of Black Consciousness, from the protest literature of the previous generation. The protest tradition had hovered dangerously close to identifying evil with whites and turned a blind eye to the sociopolitical ills generated by blacks themselves. The self-inflicted maladies of the black community would become a major theme in the poems and essays produced by writers of the Black Consciousness era.

For Biko and his colleagues, one of the most lamentable byproducts of the colonized mind was the African community's fratricidal violence. Africans often vented their anger and frustration in the wrong direction, on the physically weaker members of their families and on their fellow Africans in the townships. Elaborating on his views, Biko told the court during the trial of the SASO Nine, "When you are in the township it is dangerous to cross often from one street to the next. . . . rape and murder are very, very common aspects of our life in the townships. . . . You see an old man being assaulted by a number of young men for apparently no reason whatsoever except that of course it is the end of the month and possibly he might have some money around him."[49]

Writers of the *Drum* era, like Can Themba, Casey Motsisi, and Alex La Guma, had written about black-on-black violence, but with the exception of La Guma the issue was handled with fatalistic resignation. Sometimes these writers romanticized the violence as *tsotsigeid*—the actions of street-wise, happy-go-lucky youth whom no white or black person can cower. Black Consciousness writers, however, sought to address township violence[50] by prescribing correct conduct and by conscientizing youth as future leaders in the struggle with the "formation" training schools. At the first of these formation schools in 1969, Biko gave a paper on SASO and stressed its objectives in boosting the low morale of blacks, heightening their self-confidence, and rendering community service.

Biko's closest associate, Barney Pityana, explained the importance of shared leadership many years later:

> Black Consciousness has made sure that black South Africa is never without its own leadership. During Biko's time many black people were trained and had experience of leadership, planning, strategising and mobilising, and yet drew closer to the broad masses of people in their suffering and pain and frustrations. Arguably, one can hardly find a notable leader in South Africa today who was in his or her twenties in the early 1970s, who has not been through the Black Consciousness mill. . . . When Black Consciousness emerged, leadership had become remote and ideas seemed to owe more to the guilty conscience of the white liberal establishment than to the concrete experience of the oppressed people themselves. Prior to that there had been leadership of a more traditional, one-man, individualistic kind. Biko spread the net so that leadership could come from many sources.[51]

The repression blacks had experienced since Sharpeville had added to their sense of inadequacy, as Biko saw it in the "We Blacks" column. It had produced "a spineless breed of people" who had become masters at dissimulation. In their own segregated world they condemned whites, but in the presence of whites they brightened in sheepish obedience and spoke in praise of the government: "All in all the black man has become a shell, a shadow of man, completely defeated, drowning in his own misery, a slave, an ox bearing the yoke of oppression with sheepish timidity." Biko urged blacks to see themselves for what they really were. Their hope for emancipation from mental slavery as a prelude to their political liberation rested ultimately on their capacity to diagnose their psychological problems accurately. Explaining the role of Black Consciousness in the liberation of black people, he wrote, "The first step therefore is to make the black man come to himself; to pump back life into his empty shell; to infuse him with pride and dignity, to remind him of his complicity in the crime of allowing himself to be misused and therefore letting evil reign supreme in the country of his birth."[52]

Biko noted that Africans in South Africa probably felt the need to rehabilitate their much-maligned past even more acutely than Africans elsewhere on the continent. Black Consciousness stood for reclaiming the African past and stripping it of every insult from whites bent on discrediting blacks. Biko proposed that research into history by Africans was essential to correct the negative image of biased white historians. Black Consciousness poets and dramatists like Serote, Mtshali, and Sepamla were among the first to respond to Biko's challenge.

There was a renaissance in the history of resistance in much of this work. The theatre of Black Consciousness by such playwrights as Fatima Dike and Basil Somhlahlo dipped into historical themes, the favorite being the story of the Xhosa prophetess Nongqawuse and the Cattle Killing episode of 1856–57. Serote and Sepamla occasionally turned to history, being concerned mainly with early resistance to European penetration. Ndebele and Gwala tried to cultivate (in the manner of earlier writers like H. I. E. Dhlomo and Mazisi Kunene) a historical approach to African poetics.[53]

Gwala responded to the Soweto massacre, for example, with a sense of outrage. In a short bilingual poem entitled "Old Man Nxele's Remorse: 20 June 1976," he wrote:

> Sons
> They are gunning down
> our children in Soweto
> What more
> are we living for?[54]

The prophet Nxele, the archetype of armed resistance in the Cape-Xhosa wars of conquest in the nineteenth century, is the spiritual custodian of his people's warrior tradition, which he wants to instill into the hearts of the young. The Zulu version sounds even more ominous. It recalls the Battle of Isandlwana in 1879 between the British and the Zulu, when the British suffered their worst defeat in the nineteenth century at the hands of a Zulu *impi* (regiment). When an outraged Zulu warrior asks in the last two lines of the poem, "Yini enye pho / esisayiphilela?" ("What else are we still living for?"), he is ready, regardless of consequences, to hurl himself headlong against machine guns.

The poem "Old Man Nxele's Remorse" was published in *Staffrider*, a journal of the new writers' movement that flourished after Soweto. Gwala also employs an historical perspective in another poem called "Tap-Tapping" from the same issue of *Staffrider*. He describes, more explicitly this time, the horrors unleashed on generation after generation of Africans:

> Rough wet winds
> parch my agonized face
> as if salting the wounds of
> Bulhoek
> Sharpeville
> Soweto.[55]

The Bulhoek massacre occurred on May 24, 1921, when 163 Africans belonging to a religious community were killed and 129 others wounded for refusing to comply with a government order evicting them from their homes. Gwala links Isandlwana, Bulhoek, Sharpeville, and Soweto on the long road to freedom.

Some Black Consciousness writers had read works by Nigerian novelist Chinua Achebe and were inspired to follow his example in deploying history for literary purposes. Achebe had said, "I would be quite satisfied if my novels (especially those I set in the past) did no more than teach my readers that their past—with all its imperfections—was not one long night of savagery from which the first Europeans acting on God's behalf delivered them."[56] Some writers had also read the novels of Kenyan writer Ngugi wa Thiong'o, who wished in his work to "restore the African character to his history."[57] Ngugi was probably more of a role model than Achebe because he was less concerned with the past as history. Black Consciousness writers wanted to retrieve the African past in order to forge an accessible myth that would help them to come to terms with their present predicament.

Black theology was also of crucial importance to the BC movement. Biko argued that black liberation theology (imported from America and first propagated in South Africa by the UCM) had to fuse pre-Christian with Christian concepts of worship in a meaningful syncretic way, for Africans had not heard of God for the first time from Christian missionaries.[58] He stressed the need for Africans to oppose religion that kept them docile and in servitude by discouraging them from retaliating against white brutality. Oswald Mbuyiseni Mtshali's poems "The Washerwoman's Prayer" and "An Old Man in a Church," for example, depict the situations Biko deplored and reflect the criticism made against the church by many politicized Africans.[59]

Before Biko relinquished editorship of the *SASO Newsletter*, he turned to the problem posed by black leaders who operated within the framework of apartheid. In a column in the June 1971 issue, entitled "Fragmentation of the Black Resistance," he noted the conversion of former ANC and PAC activists to Bantustan politics. He singled out Chief Buthelezi, once regarded as "the bastion of resistance to the institution of a territorial authority in Zululand," as the most influential figure in convincing his followers to accept Bantustans and the sectional politics they represented. South Africa only needed to convince opponents it was sincere in its policy of decolonization by creating a homeland for each of its nine designated African ethnic groups. All government-created institutions for blacks, Biko asserted, worked to the advantage of the white minority regime. They confronted international critics of apartheid, and in due course they would condition blacks to adapt their "well-considered resistance to fit within the system both in terms of the means and the goals."[60]

The Bantustans-cum-homelands represented a cul-de-sac for all Africans who rejected separate development as a euphemism for apartheid. The independent African as reflected in the Black Consciousness movement was a dramatic contrast to the dependent African as fostered by the architects of apartheid. As Biko testified at the SASO Nine trial in what was to be his last public appearance, "What we want is a total accommodation of our interests in the total country not in some portion of it."[61]

Intellectual Antecedents of Black Consciousness

Black Consciousness writers were influenced by a variety of intellectual trends in the 1960s and 1970s. The ideas of Black Power advocates in the United States, as noted earlier, found a receptive audience among Black Consciousness advocates in South Africa. Student activists in particular had read works by or about Frantz Fanon, Malcolm X, Eldridge Cleaver, and Stokeley Carmichael. They were familiar with African-American writers of the Harlem Renaissance during the 1920s and with the generation that had come of age during the 1950s and 1960s—people like Richard Wright (who is said to have coined the phrase Black Power), Ralph Ellison, LeRoi Jones (Imamu Amiri Baraka), and James Baldwin.

Black Consciousness writers were also familiar with literary trends elsewhere in Africa—notably the Negritude movement and especially the work of Aimé Césaire of Martinique (who is said to have coined the word Negritude) and Léopold Sédar Senghor of Senegal. They read the works of Nigeria's Chinua Achebe and Wole Soyinka, Kenya's Ngugi wa Thiong'o and Uganda's Okot p'Bitek, and they were familiar with the ideas of African socialists and Pan-Africanists like Kwame Nkrumah, Julius Nyerere, Sékou Touré, Amilcar Cabral, Jomo Kenyatta, Oginga Odinga, and Kenneth Kaunda. They had also come across a few works by banned black South African writers like James Matthews, Ezekiel Mphahlele, Peter Abrahams, Alex La Guma, and Keorapetse Kgositsile.[62]

The voices of the Black Consciousness movement in the 1970s sought to combine the principles of the Non-European Unity Movement (NEUM), the ANC, and the Pan-Africanist Congress.[63] The NEUM as early as August 1943 had agreed "to enter into negotiations for a unification of all Non-European peoples in the struggle against segregation, a struggle for full citizenship rights."[64] The ANC's bill of rights manifesto, "Africans' Claims in South Africa," was adopted in December 1943 and its Programme of Action in December 1949 (it was based in part on a policy statement drafted by the ANC Youth League a year earlier). The PAC's position was outlined in detail at its inaugural convention in April 1959.[65]

The dominant themes in Black Consciousness ideology during the 1970s—black assertion and self-determination, noncollaboration with the government and its agents, a rejection of white patronage, and the confinement of white revolutionaries to the task of politicizing other whites—were based in large part on these political and intellectual traditions. As C. R. D. Halisi puts it, "Black Consciousness philosophy incorporates three distinct traditions of political thought, two of which are international in scope: the complex tradition of black South African political thought, theories of anti-colonialism and racial liberation developed in Africa and in the African diaspora, and New Left student radicalism with its straightforward recognition of the legitimacy of black power politics."[66]

Black Consciousness, however, was blind to some aspects of power relations, such as gender. Activists once associated with Biko, for example, held a conference in June 1990 in Harare, Zimbabwe, under the title "The Legacy of Steve Biko" and among other points of discussion was one about male chauvinism in the Black Consciousness movement. Mamphela Ramphele, who had been with Biko at medical school and continued her association with him to the end of his life, pointed out that gender was never raised as a political issue on a par with race in Black Consciousness organizations. Her comments were echoed by Vuyelwa Mashalaba, who had also been with Biko at medical school and had helped define and formulate the earliest policies of the movement.[67]

The SASO leadership had from the outset attempted to represent the interests of *all* "non-white" students regardless of ethnic or racial identification. Biko and his political comrades, as medical students at the University of Natal, had established strong networks with, and commitments to, Indian students such as Saths Cooper, Strini and Lingham Moodley, and Solly Ismail, all of whom eventually became prominent leaders of SASO and the Black Consciousness movement.[68] In its cultural signification, however, *black* was used synonymously with *African*. This cultural chauvinism tended to make those of Asian descent in particular feel somewhat unaccommodated for in the movement.[69]

Another aspect of power relations that was never confronted by Black Consciousness activists was the problem of social class. Communist and socialist discourses were known to SASO intellectuals, and the South African Communist Party was operating outside (and to a very limited extent inside) the country at the time, but the new student movement demonstrated a marked reluctance to articulate these positions—believing them to perpetuate white tutelage and domination. The students claimed, perhaps disingenuously, that socialist traditions were symptomatic of Western or white imperialist hegemony. Thus Biko writes of the "twisted logic" of "Class theory" that Black Consciousness sought to "eradicate."[70] In later phases of the BC movement, activists made an effort to privilege workers, but they did not aspire to construct an explicitly proletarian movement.[71]

Socialist ideas were cast in the form of an indigenous African socialism, sometimes referred to as "African humanism" and "black communalism," and Black Consciousness leaders remained generally skeptical of class discourse. The movement's effort to clarify its economic policies in the mid- to late 1970s essentially involved attempts to revise the idea of black communalism. Efforts were made to steer a tertium quid between the non-Marxist and increasingly prevalent Marxist sentiments in certain quarters of the movement. A so-called Mafeking Manifesto, a thirty-point economic program for a future South Africa, for example, was adopted in May 1976.[72] This document, the first of its kind since the adoption of the Freedom Charter in 1955, proposed the establishment of a "mixed economy," with a significant interventionist role for a future democratic state, and promised to redistribute the country's wealth. The document, however, was submerged in the Soweto uprising in June 1976, and it was never perceived, like the Freedom Charter, as a rallying point for the people.

Race took precedence over both class and gender during the 1970s. Nevertheless, women activists like Mamphela Ramphele, Vuyelwa Mashalaba, and Thenjiwe Mtintso (who worked in the Black Community Programmes, joined the ANC's guerrilla arm,

Umkhonto we Sizwe, and subsequently became the ANC's representative in Uganda) would emerge from the ranks of the Black Consciousness movement to help revitalize the liberation struggle and give radical scholarship in South Africa an appreciation of the linkages between race, class, and gender.

Beyond the University Generation

The diffusion of Black Consciousness beyond the university generation took the form of the establishment of an adult umbrella wing called the Black People's Convention (BPC), which was formally launched at a conference in Pietermaritzburg, Natal, in July 1972.

The BPC served to accommodate the postuniversity generation of SASO members and drew in other black community organizations, like the Interdenominational African Ministers' Association of South Africa (IDAMASA). The Transvaal (and later the national) president of IDAMASA, the Rev. Fr. J. B. M. Mzamane, had been a supporter of SASO since its formation. The leaders of the Association for the Educational and Cultural Development for the African People (ASSECA)—M. T. Moerane (then editor of the *World*) and Dr. William Nkomo— had been founding members of the ANC Youth League. Drake Koko, the first BPC president, was a trade unionist. He headed the Salesmen and Workers' Allied Union and was instrumental in launching an umbrella Black Allied Workers' Union in 1972. Rev. A. Mayatula, who represented the African Independent Churches' Association, was on the first BPC executive committee. Women's organizations like the Young Women's Christian Association were represented by Winnie Kgware (who became BPC president in 1974), Ellen Kuzwayo, and Deborah Mabiletsa.

Operating as an autonomous wing of the Black People's

Convention was the Black Community Programmes, an organization created to carry out specific community development projects. BCP operated under the auspices of the Study Project for Christian Action in Society, a program of the Christian Institute and the South African Council of Churches. The underlying belief in BCP was that blacks needed to diagnose their own problems and participate in administering remedies to these problems.

Considerable emphasis was placed on avoiding a top-down strategy in initiating these community projects. The stress would be on "conscientisation," defined by Biko as "a process whereby individuals or groups within a given social and political situation are made aware of their situation."[73] Conscientization was a concept that embodied the development of all the mental and material resources at the command of the black community. The projects undertaken by the BCP included the erection of clinics and crèches; the establishment of adult literacy and preventive medicine programs; legal counseling; leadership courses and youth programs; and home industries, which were economic projects set up mainly in the impoverished rural areas.

The spread of Black Consciousness to high schools was facilitated by young teachers like Abraham Onkgopotse Tiro, who died in February 1974 in Botswana in a letter bomb explosion. He taught at Morris Isaacson high school, which was in the forefront of the Soweto revolt in 1976. Tiro had been expelled from Turfloop for his attack on Bantu education in his graduation address at the university in April 1972. Mzwandile Maqina's unpublished play *Give Us This Day*, which attacked Bantu education and township administrators and was based on Tiro's life, had a major impact in Soweto when it was presented in 1975. The authorities would not allow the play to be staged in Soweto's public halls so it was staged in churches, where there were sometimes two or three shows a day by popular demand. *Give Us This Day*, like most of the radical theatre and poetry of the 1970s, heightened political consciousness to the point where in retrospect the Soweto uprising seemed almost inevitable.

Inspired by the example of SASO, students in Soweto had launched the South African Students' Movement (SASM) with branches in almost all the African high schools in South Africa. A federation of youth groups called the National Youth Organisation was also formed in Natal, Transvaal, and the Cape Province. These organizations subscribed to Black Consciousness and were behind the revolt of the youth, which began as a protest against Bantu education in Soweto on 16 June 1976.

Meanwhile, the philosophy of Black Consciousness was presented to the world during the seventeen-month trial of the SASO Nine that finally ended in December 1976. Sathasivan Cooper, Muntu Myeza, Mosiuoa Gerald Lekota, Nchaupe Aubrey Mokoape, Nkwenkwe Nkomo, Pandelani Nefolovhodwe, Karobane Sedibe, Strinivasa Moodley, and Zithulele Cindi were given sentences ranging from five to ten years on various charges under the Terrorism Act. Biko's banning order confining him since March 1973 to King William's Town had been relaxed to enable him to travel to Pretoria as a defense witness. The crowded courtroom at the Palace of Justice in Pretoria listened for five days to Biko's testimony, and he used the platform to restate Black Consciousness policy on such issues as white supremacy, Bantustans, Bantu education, and the black people's struggle for liberation. Statements made by the SASO Nine, Biko, and other defense witnesses (like Gessler Muxe Nkondo, a lecturer in English at Turfloop, who gave an exposition of Black Consciousness poetry) were given wide coverage inside and outside South Africa. As Gail Gerhart puts it, "instead of contributing to the suppression of Black Consciousness ideology, the trial, by giving the accused a continuous platform through the press, merely disseminated that ideology even more widely, and held up to youth once again a model of 'rebel courage.'"[74]

By 1976 the disciples of Black Consciousness probably included a majority of the African population of high school age as well as the intellectual élite. Poetry readings in private houses, at student gatherings, and on other social and political occasions, for example, were now common in African townships in the metropolitan areas. The dramatization of poetry and the performance of music and plays by township groups like MDALI, Mihloti, and Dashiki had become a significant factor in spreading the message of Black Consciousness on the Witwatersrand.

The poems and essays of Mongane Wally Serote, Molefe Pheto, Mafika Gwala, Njabulo Ndebele, Mafika Mbuli, Mandlenkosi Langa, and many others reflected the political attitudes and preoccupations of Black Consciousness.[75] Sydney Sipho Sepamla (who remained of two minds about giving unconditional support to Black Consciousness) and writers of the previous generation like James Matthews (an inspiration for many writers during the 1970s), Oswald Mtshali, Don Mattera, and Adam Small reflected the movement's ideological fervor. Mothobi Mutloatse began a popular poetry column in the *Sunday World*, and announcements of poetry readings and theatre performances became regular features in the black commercial press.

The Black Consciousness Movement in Retrospect

Black Consciousness has received an ambiguous response from critics. One established and powerful picture presents the movement as an elite-driven, self-possessed ideology obsessed with cultural and racial exclusivity—an inverse racism, as some have been wont to call it—whose concern with ideological and "spiritual" opposition to the apartheid system did little, if anything, to bring about its end.[76]

In this scenario, the movement was unwilling to link up with the black working classes, and it functioned primarily to promote a form of petty-bourgeois nationalism that masked its real capitalist class interests.[77] While the BCP did set up programs among youth and working-class groups in several urban and rural areas, it had only a limited influence on industrial workers, and its links with African peasant communities were tenuous at best.[78] Black Consciousness is presented as adding nothing new to the existing ideological landscape, and it is placed with other forms of racial separatism as found in the PAC and in the discourse of American Black Power advocates of that era.[79]

Evidence for this image of Black Consciousness can be adduced in both "progressive" popular appraisals of the movement, which include liberal, nationalist, and communist constructions, and in key academic accounts of the movement and its ideology. The view was bolstered by the ruling National Party's apparent indifference, even vague endorsement, of the movement in its early years. SASO's stress on an exclusively "non-white" student organization and its powerful critique of liberalism seemed to tally with apartheid doctrine.[80]

In July 1971, for instance, the Afrikaans daily newspaper *Die Burger,* a mouthpiece of the NP and apartheid ideology, drew attention to the "new spirit" among "non-white" students and stressed the affinities between SASO and the policy of separate development. SASO supporters did not "want to be objects of white politics any longer, *but desire to determine their future themselves as people in their own right.* . . . In South Africa we can be thankful that certain opportunities have been created in advance for the realities of the new ideas. It has been done among other things by the development of Bantu Homelands."[81] In

1973 the German sociologist Heribert Adam characterized this as a form of "repressive tolerance," which allowed blacks to enjoy the illusion of political expression without fundamentally challenging the system as such. The stress of Black Consciousness activists and leaders on "psychological liberation" was "[r]eminiscent of nineteenth century idealistic philosophers, not real liberation from material and spiritual bondage alone, but spiritual freedom, is viewed as being able to achieve the desired state, in spite of continued (actual) subjugation."[82]

Against these interpretations, we have argued that Black Consciousness did make an important contribution to the antiapartheid struggle. The BC movement and its ideology of black awareness and self-assertion resuscitated overt political, social, literary, and religious resistance to the apartheid order in the late 1960s and 1970s by endeavoring to construct a cultural and political frontier in South African society. It was based around a black-nonblack opposition designed to interrupt the project of "grand apartheid."[83] Black Consciousness was not simply a reactionary ideology of racial and cultural exclusivism, because it did make reference to certain universal values in its construction of a black identity. Far from being a pale imitation of other forms of separatist discourse, Black Consciousness represented a novel articulation of ideological elements in South Africa, ideological resonances that still have significance today.

Black Consciousness laid the foundation for the cultural and political regeneration of the African community after Sharpeville that would help to transform the liberation struggle outside as well as inside South Africa. Black Consciousness activists were not composed of a small intellectual elite. The vast majority of black students at the segregated universities, for example, came from working-class and peasant backgrounds. Some, like Ranwedzi Harry Nengwekhulu, former SRC president at Turfloop and SASO national organizer, had paid their own way through university by working as factory laborers, and a few others had worked as miners. They were not insulated from the harsh realities of apartheid, which had marked their entire lives.

The ideological content of their messages was important in challenging the intellectual and moral hegemony of the apartheid state. The practices of the BC movement and its supporters were represented in its own publications, and these played a significant role in gradually transforming white-dominated commercial publications and their representations of black aspirations and forms of protest.

Not just the young and impressionable, but blacks in all walks of life were affected by Black Consciousness, which enabled them to overcome the feeling that "they were sub-humans or negatives of a greater humanity represented by whiteness."[84] The profoundly liberating effect of such a realization is expressed by Serote in the following terms:

> Black Consciousness transformed the word "black" and made it synonymous with the word "freedom." This definition, which imbued the followers of Black Consciousness with spiritual power which is otherwise absent among the apathetic, while transforming objects into initiators, inferior beings into equals among peoples and claiming a country and a right to be in the world, was also an effective manner of raising one of the most crucial issues of the liberating process and freedom—the national question. . . . The Black Consciousness philosophy and its slogans claimed the past for black people, a country and the right of its people to its wealth and land.[85]

The prison sentences meted out to the SASO Nine at the end of 1976, the death in detention of Steve Biko on 12 September 1977, and the banning a week later of eighteen Black Consciousness organizations were a serious but temporary setback for the movement. In retrospect, the outlawing of the Black Consciousness movement in October 1977 signaled a third stage in the movement's ideological trajectory—its fragmentation as a viable discourse in resistance politics. The first stage, more or less complete by 1972, had resulted in the construction of a distinct Black Consciousness ideology, and the second stage had witnessed the penetration of this ideology into more and more spheres of black community life in the years preceding the Soweto uprising.

The Black Consciousness movement was "radicalized" further after 1977 by incorporating explicitly proletarian and socialist elements. This occurred both inside the country with the formation of the Azanian People's Organisation (AZAPO) in May 1978 and in exile with the creation of the Black Consciousness Movement of Azania.[86] Some BC activists and intellectuals were also "converted" to the reemergent discourse of democratic nonracialism as communicated by the reactivated Congress tradition in South Africa.[87] Thus the revolutionary potential of Black Consciousness would be realized in the post-Soweto generation.

Notes

1. As Steve Biko noted in his letter to Student Representative Council presidents and others in February 1970, there were about 27,000 white students affiliated to NUSAS compared to 3,000 blacks. S. Biko, "Letter to SRC Presidents," in *I Write What I Like*, ed. Aelred Stubbs, C. R. (London: Bowerdean Press, 1978), 8–13.

2. M. W. Serote, "The Actual Dialogue," *Yakhal' inkomo* (Johannesburg, 1972): 1; M. P. Gwala, "Paper Curtains," *Jol' iinkomo* (Johannesburg, 1977): 14–15.

3. Cyclostyled handout in Mbulelo Mzamane's personal files, n.d.

4. S. Biko, *The Testimony of Steve Biko: Black Consciousness in South Africa*, ed. Millard Arnold (London: Granada, 1979), 14.

5. *SASO Newsletter*, September 1970, 1.

6. "Literary responses to *apartheid* (2): Interview with Mafika Pascal Gwala," in *SAIWA: A Journal of Communication* 3 (1985): 81–86. See also Biko, *I Write What I Like*.

7. Gwala, "Paper Curtains,"*Jol' iinkomo.* See also L. S. Senghor, *Prose and Poetry,* selected and trans. John Reed and Clive Wake (London: Oxford University Press, 1965); O. p'Bitek, *Song of Lawino* and *Song of Ocol* (Nairobi: East African Publishing House, 1972).

8. Esp. F. Fanon, *Black Skin, White Masks,* trans. Charles Lam Markmann (New York: Grove Press, 1967); and *The Wretched of the Earth,* trans. Constance Farrington (New York: Grove Press, 1968).

9. K. Mokoape, T. Mtintos, and W. Nhlapo, "Towards the Armed Struggle," in *Bounds of Possibility: The Legacy of Steve Biko and Black Consciousness,* ed. B. Pityana, M. Ramphele, M. Mpumlwana, and L. Wilson (Cape Town: David Philip, 1991), 138.

10. "Report by Strini Moodley on SASO Leadership Training Seminar," Pietermaritzburg, December 5–8 1971, in *Nadir and Resurgence, 1964–1979,* ed. T. G. Karis and G. M. Gerhart, vol. 5 of *From Protest to Challenge* (Bloomington: Indiana University Press, 1997), 489–90.

11. For example, M. Mangena, *On Your Own* (Johannesburg: Skotaville, 1989), 29–30.

12. L. Raubenheimer, "From Newsroom to the Community: Struggle in Black Journalism," in *The Alternative Press in South Africa,* ed. K. Tomaselli and P. E. Louw (London: James Curry, 1991), 94–100. See also *Black Review,* 1974; H. Mashabela, *A People on the Boil* (Johannesburg: Skotaville, 1987), 98–99; P. Qoboza, "The Press as I See It," *South African Conference on the Survival of the Press,* L. Switzer and C. Emdon convenors (Rhodes University, Department of Journalism, 1979).

13. "Agenda and Resolutions, SASO's General Students' Council, Hammanskraal, July 2–9, 1972," in Karis and Gerhart, *Nadir and Resurgence,* 510.

14. G. M. Gerhart, *Black Power in South Africa* (Berkeley: University of California Press, 1978), 278.

15. See D. Woods, *Biko* (Harmondsworth: Penguin Books, 1980), 250–54. Donald Woods's initial reaction to Black Consciousness, however, was negative. He describes the emergence of SASO in a *Daily Dispatch* editorial, as "one of the sad manifestations of racist policy at Government level" in which "[t]he result is the emergence of a 'Blacks only' mentality among Blacks." SASO is described as "wrong" and accused of "promoting apartheid [through] encouraging the idea of racial exclusivity" and "doing the Government's work." *Daily Dispatch,* 10 August 1971. The remarkable rapprochement

between Donald Woods and Steve Biko, documented in Woods's sympathetic biography of Biko and eventually made into the motion picture *Cry Freedom*, was a product of the later phases of the Black Consciousness movement.

16. R. Tomaselli and K. Tomaselli, "The Political Economy of the South African Press," in *The Press in South Africa*, ed. K. Tomaselli, R. Tomaselli, and J. Muller (London: James Currey, 1987), 52–57. Woods, however, had only a limited impact on news content in the *Daily Dispatch*, and even his "political deviancy" on the editorial page was permissible under apartheid until the late 1970s. L. Switzer, *Media and Dependency in South Africa* (Athens: Ohio University Press, 1985), 53–54.

17. Karis and Gerhart, *Nadir and Resurgence*, 125. See also S. Biko, *Black Consciousness in South Africa* (New York: Random House, 1978), 127.

18. S. Johnson, "An Historical Overview of the Black Press," in Tomaselli and Louw, *Alternative Press*, 28.

19. Karis and Gerhart, *Nadir and Resurgence*, 125.

20. P. Walshe, *Church versus State in South Africa* (London: C. Hurst, 1983), 153. The first edition of *Black Viewpoint* was edited by Biko, but he was banned in April 1972 along with other prominent members of the Black Consciousness movement. When the first issue was printed, Bennie Khoapa's name was inserted as editor. Subsequent issues were edited by Khoapa.

21. Editorial, *Black Viewpoint*, September 1972.

22. B. A. Khoapa, introduction, *Black Review 1972*, 1–2. Cf. *Black Review 1972*, ed. B. A. Khoapa (Durban, 1973); *Black Review 1973*, ed. M. Gwala (Durban, 1974); *Black Review 1974–75*, ed. T. Mbanjwa (Durban, 1975); *Black Review 1975–76*, ed. A. Rambally (Durban, 1977).

23. *Black Perspectives* (Durban, 1973).

24. Walshe, *Church versus State*, 153.

25. Walshe, *Church versus State*, 153 (citing Peter Randall's *A Taste of Power*).

26. M. W. Serote, "Panel on Contemporary South African Poetry," *Issue* (Austin, Tex.) 6, 1 (1976): 298–305.

27. This column served as the inspiration for Serote's poem, "They Do It," in *Yakhal' inkomo*, 14.

28. Ndebele voiced the suspicions Africans harbored against

whites who professed liberal views on racial matters in the following terms: "The liberal cry against the oppression of the black man is essentially ethical. They do not want a politically free black man, they simply want a happy labour force. They have publicly declared that the happier the blacks, the more they can produce economically. To the liberal, the black person is still a thing, only the thing must be given more oil to function with better efficiency." N. Ndebele, "Black Development," in *Black Viewpoint*, 20.

29. Biko, *I Write What I Like*, 20 ("Black Souls in White Skins?").

30. Serote, "The Actual Dialogue," *Yakhal' inkomo*, 1.

31. Biko, *I Write What I Like*, 61 (as cited in "White Racism and Black Consciousness").

32. Ibid., 21 ("Black Souls in White Skins?").

33. For example, N. Gordimer, *The Black Interpreters: Notes on African Writing* (Johannesburg: Spro-Cas/Ravan, 1973).

34. Biko, *I Write What I Like*, 22 ("Black Souls in White Skins?").

35. "SASO Resolution," cyclostyled handout in Mbulelo Mzamane's personal files, n.d.

36. See M. Gwala, "Election Pincers," *Ophir*, no. 11 (June 1970): 20–22; Gwala, "Paper Curtains," *Jol' iinkomo*, 14–15. Both poems observe the hypocrisy of whites who claim they are for equality but only if it comes gradually.

37. Biko, *I Write What I Like*, 23–24 ("Black Souls in White Skins?"). This idea was borrowed from a book by Stokeley Carmichael and Charles Hamilton. They had defined racism as being "not merely exclusion on the basis of race but exclusion for the purpose of subjugating or maintaining subjugation." *Black Power: The Politics of Liberation in America* (New York: Vintage Books, 1967), 61.

38. *Black Review*, 1972, 40–42.

39. Biko, *I Write What I Like*, 23 ("Black Souls in White Skins?").

40. Ibid., 23–24.

41. Gwala, "Black Status Seekers," *Jol' iinkomo*, 35–36.

42. F. Fanon, *Black Skin, White Masks*, 58.

43. S. Sepamla, "Stop the Lie," in *Selected Poems* (Johannesburg: Ad. Donker, 1984), 131.

44. Biko, *I Write What I Like*, 24 ("Black Souls in White Skins?").

45. Ibid., 30 ("We Blacks").

46. M. Pheto, *And Night Fell: Memoirs of a Political Prisoner in South Africa* (London: Allison and Busby, 1983).

47. For example, N. S. Ndebele, "A Child's Delirium," *Black Poets in South Africa*, ed. Robert Royston (London: Heinemann Educational, 1974), 40–42.

48. Biko, *I Write What I Like*, 28 ("We Blacks").

49. Biko, *Testimony*, 25.

50. Mongane Serote, for example, produced a number of powerful poems on violence in the townships at the time. See especially M. Serote, "What's in This Black Shit?" and "My Brothers in the Street," in *Yakhal' inkomo*, 8, 19.

51. N. B. Pityana, "The Legacy of Steve Biko," in Pityana et al., *Bounds of Possibility*, 255–56.

52. Biko, *I Write What I Like*, 29 ("We Blacks").

53. David Rabkin in his study of the *Drum* era claims black writers lacked a historical consciousness: "Black South African writers have not turned to the past for any image of their national revival. The reason lies not only in the depth of the white penetration but also in the extent of its impingement, through urbanisation and industrialisation, upon the African present. The absence of a modern myth of the black past—even in contemporary 'black consciousness' poetry—is striking indeed." D. Rabkin, "*Drum* Magazine (1951–1961), and the Works of Black South African Writers Associated with It" (Ph.D. diss., University of Sussex, 1975), 232. While this may be true of most *Drum* writers, it was not true of the vast majority of black writers before and after the *Drum* era. One has only to cite Sol Plaatje's *Mhudi*, Peter Abrahams's *Wild Conquest*, and Mazisi Kunene's *Zulu Poems, Emperor Shaka the Great, Anthem of the Decade*, and *The Ancestors and the Sacred Mountains* to suggest that Rabkin is in error on this point. The past was also in the present for writers in indigenous languages such as R. R. R. Dhlomo.

54. M. P. Gwala, "Old Man Nxele's Remorse: 20 June 1976," *Staffrider* 2, 3:55.

55. M. P. Gwala, "Tap-tapping," *Staffrider* 2, 3:55–57.

56. J. Miller, "The Novelist as Teacher: Chinua Achebe's Literature for Children," *Children's Literature: Annual of The Modern Language Association* 9 (1981): 7–18.

57. In Ngugi wa Thiong'o, *Homecoming: Essays on African and Caribbean Literature, Culture and Politics* (London: Heinemann, 1972), 43.

58. Biko was influenced by John Mbiti's *African Religions and Philosophy* (Garden City, N.Y.: Doubleday, 1970).

59. These poems are published in Mtshali's *Sounds of a Cowhide Drum* (Johannesburg: Renoster Books, 1971). Biko first made his call for a more positive role for African Christianity and for a theology of advocacy in a paper entitled "Some African Cultural Concepts" at a conference in 1971 organized by the Ecumenical Lay Training Centre in Edenvale, near Pietermaritzburg (Natal). He gave another paper on this theme entitled "The Church as Seen by a Layman" during a second conference held at Edenvale in May 1972.

60. Biko, "Fragmentation of the Black Resistance," in *I Write What I Like*, 35–37.

61. Biko, *Testimony*, 59.

62. Many had also read works by various activists and scholars writing in the classical marxist tradition, contemporary revolutionaries like Mao Tse-tung, Vo Nguyen Giap, Che Guevara, and Fidel Castro, and radical intellectuals like Jean Paul Sartre, Herbert Marcuse, and Paulo Freire. The intellectual antecedents of Black Consciousness are summarized in Gerhart, *Black Power*, 270–81.

63. C. R. D. Halisi, "Biko and Black Consciousness Philosophy: An Interpretation"; L. Wilson, "Bantu Stephen Biko: A Life," in Pityana et al., *Bounds of Possibility*, 100–110 and 15–77.

64. T. Karis, *Hope and Challenge, 1935–1952*, vol. 2 of T. Karis and G. M. Carter, *From Protest to Challenge: A Documentary History of African Politics in South Africa, 1882–1964* (Stanford: Stanford Institution Press, 1973), document 64 (All-African Convention executive committee manifesto 26 August 1943), 351. Isaac Tabata, probably the NEUM's most prominent African member at the time, wrote *The Awakening of a People* (Nottingham: Spokesman Books, 1950; reprint, 1974), which had some influence on the Black Consciousness movement.

65. Karis, *Hope and Challenge*, document 29b (Africans' Claims in South Africa manifesto, 16 December 1943), 209–233; document 57 (Basic Policy of the Youth League manifesto issued in 1948), 323–31; document 61 (Programme of Action adopted 17 December 1949), 337–39; T. Karis and G. M. Gerhart, eds., *Challenge and Violence, 1953–1964*, vol. 3 of *From Protest to Challenge: A Documentary History of African Politics in South Africa, 1882–1964*, document 39b (Manifesto of the Africanist Movement), 517–24.

66. Halisi, "Biko and Black Consciousness," 100–101.

67. These comments are also based on Mbulelo Mzamane's recol-

lections of the debates at the Biko conference. See M. Ramphele, "The Dynamics of Gender within Black Consciousness Organisations: A Personal View," in Pityana et al., *Bounds of Possibility*, 214–27.

68. Steve Biko, interview by G. Gerhart, 1972, 15. David Howarth was allowed access to these interview notes in preparing for this chapter.

69. Kogila Moodley, "The Continued Impact of Black Consciousness," in B. Pityana et al., *Bounds of Possibility*, 143–52.

70. Biko, *I Write What I Like*, 64.

71. See Karis and Gerhart, *Nadir and Resurgence*, 147–48.

72. "The Mafikeng Manifesto," statement on economic policy debated at a symposium of the Black People's Convention, 31 May 1976, in Karis and Gerhart, *Nadir and Resurgence*, 548–50.

73. Biko, *Testimony*, 117.

74. Gerhart, *Black Power*, 298–99.

75. This literature has been published in numerous anthologies. For example, Gordimer, *Black Interpreters*, esp. section 2 ("New Black Poetry in South Africa"); M. Mutloatse, comp. and ed., *Reconstruction: Ninety Years of Black Historical Literature* (Johannesburg: Ravan, 1981); T. Couzens and Patel, eds., *The Return of the Amasi Bird: Black South African Poetry, 1891–1981* (Johannesburg: Ravan, 1982), esp. part 3 ("From Sharpeville to Soweto"); M. Chapman and A. Dangoe, eds., *Voices from Within: Black Poetry from Southern Africa* (Johannesburg: Ravan, 1982), esp. "Post-Sharpeville (1960–1976)."

76. Liberal commentators like Heribert Adam criticized SASO and Black Consciousness ideology for making "the helpless white liberal now a more frequent target for verbal attack than Afrikaners have ever been." See H. Adam, "The Rise of Black Consciousness in South Africa," *Race* 15 (1973): 158. See also A. Paton, "Black Consciousness," *Reality*, March 1972, 9–10; and R. Turner, "Black Consciousness and White Liberals," *Reality*, July 1972, in Karis and Gerhart, *Nadir and Resurgence*, 427–32. As noted earlier, even Biko's good friend Donald Woods was initially critical of the movment (see note 15). Some black activists, who might have been considered sympathetic to a new, assertive attack on the apartheid system, adopted much the same position as many white liberals. As late as 1985, for instance, the "Political Report of the National Executive Committee" to the African National Congress's second consultative conference noted "the limitations of this movement which saw our struggle as

racial, describing the entire white population of our country as 'part of the problem.'" O. Tambo, *Preparing for Power* (London: Heinemann Educational Books, 1987), 118–19. And, writing shortly after the re-launching of the Natal Indian Congress in 1972, the prominent activist Farouk Meer argued, "There is a genuine danger of black consciousness leading to black racism. The safeguards against this eventuality seem to us to be very tenuous." See F. Meer, "The Natal Indian Congress," *Reality*, March 1972, 5.

77. B. Hirson, *Year of Fire, Year of Ash* (London: Zed Books, 1979), 297. See also A. Brooks and J. Brickhill, *Whirlwind before the Storm* (London: International Defence and Aid Fund for Southern Africa, 1980), 76–80; A. Callinicos, *South Africa between Reform and Revolution* (London: Bookmarks, 1988), 61, 79–80; A. Callinicos and J. Rogers, *Southern Africa after Soweto* (London: Pluto Press, 1977).

78. For example, S. C. Nolutshungu, *Changing South Africa: Political Considerations* (New York: Africana, 1982), 188–93, 202 (note 12).

79. Gail Gerhart, who has provided the most exhaustive and compelling reading of Black Consciousness, stresses the strong parallels between the new ideology and its predecessors: "Almost point for point, SASO had arrived anew at the diagnosis and cure originally devised by Lembede and Mda [of the ANC Youth League] in the 1940s under the rubric of 'Africanism.'" See Gerhart, *Black Power*, 272. This emphasis on continuity is not confined to academic accounts of Black Consciousness ideology. It is a view put forward by certain activists and intellectuals who were themselves part of the movement as it formed in the late 1960s and early 1970s. Barney Pityana, one of the movement's foremost intellectuals, writes, "There was actually nothing new about Black Consciousness" as the "movement was self-consciously part of a long line of people's resistance," all of which "found substance within a Black Consciousness concept." See B. Pityana, introduction to Biko, *I Write What I Like*, 9. A stronger and far less nuanced version of this continuist reading comes from Temba Sono, a controversial former SASO president, who argues that "Black Consciousness emerged first in the United States. *So Black Consciousness as we know it today in South Africa is a Black American invention*. Case settled" (emphasis added). See T. Sono, *Reflections on the Origins of Black Consciousness in South Africa* (Pretoria: Human Sciences Research Council Publications, 1993), 61.

80. Gerhart, *Black Power*, 268.

81. Ibid., 269 (as cited; emphasis added).

82. Adam, "Rise of Black Consciousness," 155.

83. Robert Fatton has argued, "The diffusion of Black Consciousness undermined the hegemony of apartheid to such an extent that the defense of white supremacy came to rest almost exclusively on the use of brute force. . . . In other words, the Black Consciousness Movement has created an alternative hegemony which can only be satisfied by the complete liberation of the black masses." See R. Fatton, *Black Consciousness in South Africa* (New York: State University of New York Press, 1986), 36. While the BC movement certainly constituted a fundamental challenge to the apartheid state, it was never able to construct an alternative hegemony.

84. Pityana et al., *Bounds of Possibility*, 9 (intro.).

85. M. W. Serote, "The Impact of Black Consciousness on Culture and Freedom," paper presented at the Legacy of Bantu Stephen Biko Conference, Harare, Zimbabwe, June 1990.

86. An AZAPO policy document read, "The philosophy and policies of the organisation will be based on the broad provisions of the philosophy of Black Consciousness. We recognize the fact that in our country, *race is a class determinant*. Thus the concentration of economic and political power in the hands of the white race enables it to promote a rigid *class structure*. . . . We envisage a state where all persons shall have the right to ownership of property and complete participation in the political machinery of the country, where capital and profits accruing from labour shall be equally distributed." Cited in J. Frederikse, *The Unbreakable Thread: Non-Racialism in South Africa* (London: Zed Books, 1990), 169–70 (emphasis added).

87. For an overview and analysis of this transition, see A. Marx, *Lessons of Struggle* (Oxford: Oxford University Press, 1992), 73–105.

Part II

ON THE BARRICADES: THE STRUGGLE FOR SOUTH AFRICA

5

The Media of the United Democratic Front, 1983–1991

Jeremy Seekings

The popular movements, organizations, and protests of the 1980s were not the first in South African history. But they— unlike those of the 1910s, 1920s, 1950s, or even 1970s—were to culminate in the negotiated transition to representative democracy. Too weak to achieve a revolutionary seizure of power, popular struggles packed enough punch to force changes on the state, stymie attempts to reform its way toward a semi-democratic outcome, and thus foreclose alternatives to negotiations with the banned African National Congress (ANC). The power of popular struggles in the 1980s lay in the breadth of their support—in both social and geographical terms—and their sustained nature. Both the breadth and the resilience of popular struggles were due, in large part, to the overarching role played by the United Democratic Front (UDF).[1]

The UDF was formed in August 1983 with the initial objective of mustering opposition to constitutional reforms proposed by the ruling National Party (NP). The key reform was a new constitution providing for a tricameral parliament in which Coloured and Indian citizens, as well as white citizens, would be represented in racially segregated chambers. Most Africans in urban areas outside the African reserves-cum-Bantustans would be represented, again along racial lines, at the municipal level only. The UDF's initial objective was to mobilize Coloureds and Indians against the tricameral parliament. And the UDF—together with its affiliates, since the UDF, with its headquarters in Johannesburg, was in principle a front for otherwise autonomous organizations—was very successful: turnout was low in the elections to the new Coloured and Indian chambers in August 1984, and the institutions never achieved significant legitimacy.

In the months prior to the 1984 elections, overt protest began to proliferate in African townships across the country. On the very day the tricameral parliament was inaugurated, the townships of the Vaal Triangle, a heavily industrialized area south of Johannesburg, erupted in what became known as the Vaal Uprising. In the following eighteen months the township revolt spread across much of the country. By mid-1986 about 2,000 had died, most of them Africans, and the system of elected councils in African townships had all but collapsed. Only through a heavy military presence could the government retain any control over many parts of the country. In June 1986 the NP imposed a countrywide state of emergency (a partial state of emergency was declared in July 1985), detained thousands of leading antiapartheid activists, and later restricted severely the UDF and other organizations.

The National Party government attributed the spread of protest and violence to the UDF, and its leadership was charged in court with fomenting discord in support of the banned ANC. The evidence suggests, however, that the NP itself deserves much of the credit for the township revolt. Government policies on issues like urban housing, development and taxation, and schooling, as well as political representation, prompted the discontent that fueled the revolt. By extending unpopular policies across a wide area, the government created the conditions in which revolt would be widespread, even if uncoordinated. Furthermore, in many areas the brutality of the security forces swelled the ranks of the opposition, uniting and radicalizing people against the state even where antiapartheid activists had hitherto failed to establish a strong, active presence.

Taking advantage of partial liberalization in 1983 and 1984 and again in the first half of 1986, the UDF provided much of the organizational framework and strategic vision that sustained public dissent. The UDF forged a countrywide movement out of hitherto disparate fragments, strategies were developed and promoted to sustain pressure on the state at an intense level, and the state's attempts at reform were undermined. From June 1986, under the state of emergency, the UDF helped to ensure that the momentum of protest was never entirely dissipated. From late 1988, amid another period of reform, a resurgent UDF led renewed opposition, at the same time drawing disaffected elites into a broad antiapartheid alliance. Looking back in 1991, ANC veteran Walter Sisulu assessed correctly that the front had "decisively turned the tide against the advances being made by the [National Party] regime."[2]

The UDF played these roles through a variety of mechanisms. For short periods of time it was allowed direct contact with the public through meetings or door-to-door campaigns, but generally the front relied on indirect popular contact. This took two forms. On the one hand, the meetings of UDF structures at different levels—national, regional, subregional, and local—allowed for considerable contact between the UDF and its affiliates and between affiliates themselves. Networks were forged through linked hierarchies of coordinating structures. A series of conferences, some held openly and others clandestinely, helped to promote countrywide cohesion and a more unified strategic direction. On the other hand, the UDF used the press extensively—including the commercial press (whenever it offered the prospect of coverage), alternative publications,[3] and its own press.

This chapter reviews the evolving relationship between the UDF and the press. It begins with an analysis of the UDF and the press in the UDF's early years, from 1983 to 1985, when the young front used mass-produced, short newsletters to help forge an integrated, countrywide political movement.

In this period, the UDF's regional and subregional structures became better established, and the UDF emphasized increasingly the importance of strengthening organization to ensure that political protest—primarily the township revolt in response to the newly created tricameral parliament—could be sustained. Coverage of the UDF in the commercial press was uneven, national alternative newspapers (*Weekly Mail* and *New Nation*) were yet to be launched, and much of the community press became, in practice, mouthpieces for the UDF.

A photo montage of some left-wing publications supportive of the UDF and the wider Charterist movement in the 1980s.

The core UDF leadership was very concerned that the experience of 1976–77, when widespread protests after the Soweto uprising had given way to several years of political inactivity and quiescence, should not be repeated. So the UDF turned to the mobilization and recruitment of disaffected white elites beginning about 1986. This new emphasis grew in importance as repression curtailed the opportunities for direct action and protest, and more whites began to distance themselves from the apartheid state. The UDF used its publications to reach out to an ever-wider range of white South Africans.

The success of this strategy became clear from early 1989, when new space for opposition opened up as the National Party government embarked, under pressure from inside and outside the country, on a process of liberalization. The UDF began to enjoy considerable access to and coverage in the commercial press, and the need to produce its own media diminished. Once the ANC was unbanned, in February 1990, the UDF declined rapidly in importance, although it would not formally disband for another eighteen months.

Building a Countrywide Movement

Prior to the formation of the UDF, opposition politics was highly fragmented along geographic lines. As apartheid had coerced people into defined physical spaces according to racial classification, opposition politics was often fragmented along racial lines. Interregional and interracial contacts had developed, but these nascent networks tended to be based on links between specific individuals. The first major achievement of the UDF was to build an integrated, countrywide interorganizational movement.

Early in 1983 it was agreed that the UDF would operate essentially as a federation for regionally based fronts. UDF regional structures were launched in Natal, the western Cape, and Transvaal prior to the national launch with little publicity either before or at each launch. This caution probably reflected a combination of the sensitivity of political alliance building at this time and prudence in the face of possible state repression. The national launch, however, was intended to be very different. Part of the national launch would be closed to outsiders, but a second part was designed as a public event to attract media attention and assert the presence of the UDF.

UDF News

The UDF relied primarily on its own media to publicize the launch and rally support. The front did this through a newsletter entitled *UDF News*. The first issue was a four-side newsletter, with photographs, in A3 format. Subtitled *National Newsletter of the United Democratic Front*, it explained the reasons for forming the UDF and how it would be organized. The newsletter carried endorsements by the leaders of a range of prominent organizations—presumably intended to indicate political legitimacy and to reassure cautious sympathizers. *UDF News* was a generic term for a collection of regional publications that used the same broad format but tailored content to regional concerns. English predominated, but most of one page was in Afrikaans and most of another in an "African" language. The African language used in the Cape editions was Xhosa; in Natal, it was Zulu; and in the Transvaal, it was Zulu and Sotho.

The number of copies of *UDF News* to be distributed rose sharply as the launch date of Saturday, 20 August 1983, approached. At the beginning of August, UDF records note that it planned to distribute 80,000 copies in the western Cape, including 20,000 in Cape Town's main Coloured residential area of Mitchell's Plain, where the launch was to be held. By 12 August the UDF claimed to have distributed more than 400,000 copies, reaching (they estimated) more than one million readers. At a press conference on 16 August, UDF officials claimed that as many as one million copies had been distributed nationwide, with 350,000 in the western Cape alone.[4]

Many copies were distributed through organizations to their own members, but many others were distributed to the general public. UDF supporters were arrested at several railway stations for handing newsletters to commuters. In Mitchell's Plain, officials estimated that 300 volunteers were needed to get copies to every household. In addition, the three existing UDF regions produced their own pamphlets and regional versions of *UDF News*. The first issue of the western Cape version comprised four sides of A4 format, with the last page in Afrikaans. In addition, more than 15,000 stickers and 5,000 posters were distributed, and a twelve-page brochure in A5 format was produced for participants at the national launch. Public meetings were also held in different parts of Cape Town to rally support for the UDF launch.[5]

The Commercial Press

While the UDF relied primarily on its own media to publicize the national launch, it also sought coverage in the commercial press. Initially, an interim publicity secretary—lawyer Zac Yacoob from Durban—liaised with the press, holding a press conference three weeks before the launch. In the week prior to the launch, the UDF held a further press conference in Cape Town, which was rehearsed beforehand. According to western Cape UDF secretary Trevor Manuel, who served as a UDF spokesman at the press conference, "Two days before the big launch in Cape Town we rehearsed the press conference with journalists and a video crew. When we watched the video, we saw that this could not go on. We laughed for about one hour, and then set out to put our act together. To begin with, we went out to purchase ties."[6]

This kind of relationship with the commercial media was new to many UDF leaders. They had a background in alternative community newspapers, but few had used the commercial press with any success. The adoption of what was essentially a new strategy reflected in part the front's objectives and intended audiences. Rising numbers of Africans read the commercial press, and readership was especially high among the Coloureds and Indians the UDF sought initially to reach.[7] The new strategy also reflected the involvement of individuals with some experience in working with the commercial press.

The newspapers in which the UDF really needed coverage were the newspapers read by Coloureds and Indians. In the Natal Indian community, Durban's *Daily News* had by far the highest daily circulation, and the *Sunday Times*, *Sunday Tribune*, and Natal *Post* had the highest circulation of the Sunday and weekly newspapers. In the Cape Coloured community, the *Argus* led the *Cape Times* and the Afrikaans-language *Die Burger*, although the differences in circulation were minor. The most read Sunday newspaper was the *Rapport*, followed by the *Sunday Times*.

Coverage of the UDF in these newspapers was very uneven. At one extreme, the *Daily News* virtually ignored the launch of the UDF altogether. It was relegated to page five, and the story was not deemed worthy of any editorial comment.[8] In the preceding three weeks, the newspaper only mentioned the UDF three times and never on the front page.[9] The first substantial coverage of the UDF was a feature published a week after the launch.[10] The *Sunday Times* was not much better: the UDF launch was reported, on the following day, on page two of the main newspaper, although the extra edition aimed at Coloured readers elevated the report to page one.[11]

At the other extreme, the UDF's efforts found a broadly receptive audience among all three English-language newspapers in Cape Town. The *Argus,* for example, had good coverage of the UDF in the run-up to the launch. On the previous Wednesday, it reported on the press conference and published a photograph, and welcomed the UDF launch in an editorial for bringing "together voices . . . that need to be heard for the sake of peace and good government."[12] On the Friday, the lead story focused on bogus pamphlets being distributed that announced the launch had been called off, and almost an entire inside page was dedicated to features explaining the UDF.[13]

On the day of the launch itself, the early editions of the *Argus* (an afternoon newspaper) led with reports of people arriving for the launch under a massive headline, "Mass UDF Rally in City." A feature on an inside page announced that the UDF launch marked "the beginning of a new political ball-game in South Africa" with the formation of a real extraparliamentary opposition movement. Later editions of the newspaper reported on the launch itself and included almost a page of photographs from the event.[14] The following Monday there were more reports and photos, and a positive editorial in which the UDF was described as "representative of a spectrum of opinion from moderate to radical."[15]

These reports also reflected the political position taken by many commercial, mainstream newspapers on the issue of the 1983 constitutional reforms, which in turn reflected the political situation at that time in each of the provinces. Some supposedly liberal newspapers lined up in support of the National Party—welcoming the constitutional reforms—and they were not very sympathetic to critics. In the case of the *Daily News,* this meant providing little coverage even to KwaZulu chief minister Mangosuthu Buthelezi, who was strongly opposed to the reforms.[16] On the other hand, the Progressive Federal Party (PFP), the official opposition party in Parliament, together with several business groups and newspapers, was more critical. The reforms might be a step in the right direction, but the step was perilously small and inadequate. The Cape *Argus* was strongly critical of the 1983 constitution, denouncing "group rights" (entrenched in the tricameral parliament system) as a mere "euphemism for apartheid and baasskap."[17]

There were other reasons leading to the UDF receiving generous coverage in newspapers such as the *Argus*. First, the security forces were blamed for covert disinformation activity aimed at the UDF, and the government-controlled South African Broadcasting Corporation (SABC) was lambasted for ignoring the UDF launch entirely. On the day of the launch, the main television news reportedly dedicated twenty minutes to a media conference held by rugby administrators but none to the UDF. This provoked strong criticism.[18] The PFP's media spokesman, Alex Boraine, described the SABC's silence as "deafening," given that "the coming into being of the UDF is the most important development in South Africa since the 1950s."[19]

Second, Chief Buthelezi's opposition to the tricameral parliament served to legitimate other organizations like the UDF voicing similar objections and helped such organizations present themselves as moderate. Moreover, at the outset the UDF and Buthelezi made placatory statements about each other, although in later years the relationship would sour. Third, some sections of the liberal press recognized the need for credible voices for disenfranchised South Africans outside KwaZulu and Natal—and would be especially well disposed to such voices if they professed commitment to nonviolence and nonracism.

One problem the commercial press did have was how to assess the strength of the UDF compared to other alternative political groups. By 1983 it was clear that support for Inkatha and Buthelezi was largely concentrated in the KwaZulu homeland, Natal province, and among Zulu migrant workers outside Natal. But it was unclear how strong the UDF was relative to the rival National Forum, formed about the same time and rooted in more of a Black Consciousness tradition. The commercial press probably gave the UDF slightly more coverage than the National Forum, but it was not until mid-1984 that it became clear that the UDF was by far the more important movement and deserved much greater attention.

After the Launch

The UDF quickly settled into a pattern of media work following the launch. At the national level, the UDF employed activist Patrick "Terror" Lekota as full-time publicity secretary. His role was essentially to liaise with South Africa's commercial press and overseas media. There was no structure at the national level responsible for producing the UDF's own media, and most issues of *UDF News* were produced at the regional level. In practice—since the UDF was based in Johannesburg —Transvaal regional structures often worked closely with national officials.

The UDF had an elected publicity secretary, responsible for liaison with the commercial media in each of the major regions. Two publicity secretaries had past experience in the media—a journalist on the community newspaper *Ukusa* (Lechesa Tsenoli) in Natal and a former leading official (Charles Nqakula) of the Media Workers' Association of South Africa (MWASA) in the Border (eastern Cape) region. Elsewhere, new people were brought in, some of whom proved to be very talented.[20] In each of the major regions the UDF also had a media committee comprised of volunteers who produced regional issues of

UDF News, pamphlets, and other printed material. Media committees worked closely with—and often drew their members from—specialist affiliates or sympathetic organizations such as the national student newspaper *SASPU National* or the Johannesburg-based Media and Resource Services. MARS, for example, ran workshops called "media mindblasts" for the UDF and its affiliates.

From its launch in 1983 to the second half of 1985, the bulk of the UDF's own media production was concentrated at the regional level and was campaign-oriented. The UDF's role can be illustrated by examining the UDF-led campaign against elections to racially segregated local government in African areas in late 1983.[21] On the one hand, the UDF sought to strengthen media produced by UDF township-based affiliates running the campaign at the local level. In the Transvaal, township-based civic organizations initially produced little material, and some reportedly did not even have officials with responsibility for media. With prompting from the UDF, along with technical support and funding, civic and other organizations gradually acquired media skills. They produced pamphlets, for example, that advertised public meetings or explained why people should not vote. These were distributed by hand, at train stations, bus stops, road intersections, and door to door. Posters were also produced.

On the other hand, the UDF regions themselves produced media designed to complement the media produced by affiliates. The UDF sought to root local struggles in a bigger picture. According to a report of the Transvaal Media Committee, "The UDF media took a bird's eye view of all the areas in which the campaign was going on, and even focussed on other sites of struggle elsewhere. This was aimed at knitting together all these struggles into one stream. Insofar as people from smaller isolated townships got to know that they are part of a broad movement opposing the same puppet structures, the UDF media played a tremendously good role."[22]

The UDF adopted a similar approach in its media strategy in another campaign, opposing repression in the Ciskei bantustan. In an article in the *Cape Times*, the western Cape UDF's publicity secretary emphasized that the issue of bantustan repression was linked to other issues. The UDF's call "is more than a call to halt the terror of the Ciskei authorities. It focusses our attention on a life of misery and starvation for the mass of South Africans, on the exclusion of the majority from the constitutional process, on the retention of the pass laws, the Group Areas Act and the Population Registration Act."[23] The UDF's media was explicitly integrative.

The most important campaign coordinated by the UDF in this period was the campaign for a boycott of the elections to the Coloured and Indian chambers of the tricameral parliament in August 1984. The UDF's affiliates—especially in Natal—took primary responsibility for producing UDF media, but the UDF itself sought to communicate through the commercial press. As had been the case when the UDF was launched in 1983, the commercial press was divided in its response. Some newspapers provided ample coverage, while others did not. The *Sunday Times*, for example, continued to be supportive of the government's reforms and hostile to critics such as the UDF. The campaign waged by the UDF and its affiliates was largely ignored by the *Sunday Times*, and politicians who opted for participation in the new tricameral parliament were praised for their "moderation" and "courage"; calls for a boycott were part of a "revolutionary" project, an editorial claimed.[24] When most Coloured and Indian voters chose to boycott the elections, the newspaper was compelled for the first time to take notice of the UDF and accord it some importance.[25]

Funding

Publishing its own material cost the UDF a large share of its income. According to Azhar Cachalia (national treasurer of the UDF from April 1985, and holding this position de facto before then), "A conscious decision was made to spend a major part of the UDF's resources on media, in order to create a public presence for the front."[26] The UDF later said that it had spent "vast amounts" on "posters, banners, stickers, pamphlets, newsletters, publications and placards." These media, the UDF assessed, had played "a crucial role in mobilising the masses and in encouraging participation in the democratic movement."[27]

The surviving financial records of the UDF are fragmentary, but they provide some indication of the UDF's commitment to media production. The regions initially tried to raise their own funds but soon came to rely on handouts from the head office. About 60 per cent (perhaps more) of the UDF's income was distributed as grants to the regions; most of the remaining 40 percent was absorbed by the salaries of national officials and travel expenses, and only about 10 per cent was spent on publicity at the national level. Accounts for the western Cape and Transvaal regions during 1983 and 1984 indicate that printing and publicity expenses represented between 40 and 50 per cent of regional expenses. It is likely that, overall, 30 to 35 per cent of the UDF's expenditure was spent on publicity between 1983 and 1985. This probably amounted to between R100,000 and R200,000 over a period of under two years.

As in other UDF activities, media production raised difficult questions concerning the relationship between the front and its component affiliates. Formally, the UDF played a coordinating role only, and the affiliates maintained full organizational autonomy. But in practice, the UDF controlled much of the financial resources. This antagonized organizations and individuals who felt denied their fair share and risked generating a dependence on "UDF charity" among those who did receive funds. Thus the UDF's coordinating role sometimes meant intervention in the affairs of affiliate organizations.

UDF Update

From the outset the UDF leadership worried about the lack of understanding of key issues within the front and its affiliates. Meeting for the first time the day after the national launch, the new national leadership worried that there was little clarity as to what the UDF was to do and even as to the very "concept of a front."[28] The UDF nearly split at the end of the year amid bitter divisions over tactics.

The need for a common understanding on key issues increased in mid-1984, as the question arose as to what the UDF should do once the new tricameral parliament was operative. The leadership proposed workshops and solicited discussion papers on these questions.[29] These plans, however, were overtaken by events, as the township revolt erupted and spread, and the government detained and then prosecuted UDF leaders on treason charges. Popo Molefe, the UDF's national secretary-general, believed at the time that the front was "trailing behind the masses."[30]

In early 1985 the UDF leadership sought to chart a new strategy, summed up in the slogan adopted as the theme for the UDF's second full national conference in April: "From protest to challenge, from mobilisation to organisation." The UDF's role would be to strengthen organization across the country to ensure that resistance both intensified and became more sustainable. The national leadership argued that "education in our ranks is crucial"; the "quality" of activists and leaders needed to be improved; and action against apartheid needed to be more "disciplined."[31]

This strategic emphasis heightened the need for internal UDF media that provided information and analysis to activists. From the beginning, the UDF had criticized its own media for adopting a shortsighted strategic approach. Pamphlets and newsletters were judged to be overly focused on immediate events (such as election boycotts) rather than on organization building. They were said to emphasize mobilization rather than information and education. They lacked adequate "content" with regard to issues such as nonracialism and the UDF as a front organization. They relied on slogans and abstractions like "we want our rights."[32]

In January 1984 the UDF held a national workshop for its regional media committees, where a need was identified for a new publication with limited circulation to provide news about the UDF to activists in the front and its affiliates. This publication would be called *UDF Update*, but the first issue was not published until eighteen months later. This reflected the UDF's lack of resources at the national level, especially given government repression (with the detention and then prosecution of much of the national leadership) and many other distractions arising from the escalation of political resistance.

The first issue of *Update* eventually appeared in July 1985. Although *Update* proclaimed it would be published monthly, the second issue only came out in December and the third the following April. Two further issues followed in 1986. *Update* had an A4 format, with twelve pages in the first two issues, sixteen pages in the next two issues, and twenty pages in the fifth issue. *Update* was subtitled *UDF Information Bulletin*. Its policy was outlined in the first issue: "*Update* is the UDF's very own information bulletin. It aims to update UDF affiliates, supporters and sympathisers of the events, issues, news and views in the UDF. . . . *Update* brings you factual information on the UDF and the situation in the country. Through *Update* we will come to know more about the UDF and its affiliates. We will build links between regions and in this way we will be able to march forward as a united force."[33]

Update was produced by a small team of activists who reported directly to the acting secretary-general, Valli Moosa.[34] The first issue included reports on UDF-led campaigns against racially segregated local government, the UDF's national conference in April 1985, acts of government repression, and prospective action over the cost of living. Most issues comprised a compilation of reports, primarily from the different regions, emphasizing the countrywide impact the UDF had as a resistance organization.

Soon after the first issue was completed, the government imposed a state of emergency (July 1985) in parts of the country where the township revolt was most acute. This increased further the need to distribute better educational information within the front and its affiliates. In early 1986 the UDF again outlined *Update*'s policy: "The main aim of this publication is to inform affiliates and other organisations both locally and abroad about developments within the front. *Update* assists in overcoming the problem of information flow which has been created by the emergency and other repressive measures. The publication gives a general report on UDF campaigns taking place in the different regions, as well as covering events nationally."[35] Because there had been "a very enthusiastic response," the UDF report continued, it had "been decided that *UDF Update* will be a permanent project of the Front."[36]

Initially, *Update* also served as an educational vehicle. A report on UDF strategy in the first issue, for example, was accompanied by a note suggesting that "this paper could form the basis for group discussion in your region." Four questions were provided "to help you lead the discussion." The lesson was clear: readers should distinguish between "mobilisation" and "organisation," and invest their efforts in organization. In October, *Update* produced a discussion paper entitled "The Tasks of the Democratic Movement During the State of Emergency." In the changing political context, however, the UDF decided that political education required a more specialist vehicle. A new publication, *Isizwe*, was launched for this purpose.

Political Education and Organization Building

The commercial media was now providing considerable coverage of political events in general, and much of its reporting on the UDF was broadly sympathetic. National alternative publications like the *Weekly Mail* and *New Nation* provided openly sympathetic coverage, albeit to a much smaller readership. Murphy Morobe, who assumed the post of acting national publicity secretary when Lekota was arrested and charged with treason in 1985, later said in an interview that "by and large, the UDF had a favourable press."[37] But neither the commercial nor the alternative press met the specific needs of organizations such as the UDF in terms of political education. As the township revolt escalated, the UDF attached more importance to political education. Regional UDF structures in several areas were increasingly involved in political education workshops and the production of discussion papers.

The proposal to publish a journal was driven by the western Cape region of the UDF,[38] and in particular by Jeremy Cronin, a former lecturer in politics at the University of Cape Town who was released in 1983 after spending seven years in jail for political offenses. Together with Raymond Suttner, a law lecturer at the University of the Witwatersrand and member of the UDF regional executive in the Transvaal, he edited a book celebrating the Freedom Charter, and he also engaged in strategic debates with critics of the UDF in the independent trade union movement.[39] From 1985, Cronin occupied the political education portfolio on the UDF's regional executive committee in the western Cape. When much of the national UDF leadership was detained in mid-1985, Cronin evaded detention and became a member of the acting national leadership.[40]

The first issue of *Isizwe* was published in November 1985. Its audience was the same as *Update*'s audience, but no attempt was made to provide news. The UDF later described the need for the journal: "The rapid expansion of the UDF's ranks has created the need for a publication that can assist in introducing greater theoretical clarity amongst activists and members of affiliates. *Isizwe* is aimed mainly at activists however it is also designed to serve as a forum for debate and exchange of views within the front."[41]

Isizwe was produced in Cape Town. There was supposed to be an editorial collective, but the context of political oppression made that impossible. In practice, Cronin worked with a handful of other activists, wrote much of the material himself, and reported back to the national leadership.[42] The production of *Isizwe* was largely separate from the production of *Update* and other UDF media. At the outset, the UDF decided that 2,500 copies of the journal would be printed,[43] but Cronin recalls a print run of 10,000 to 12,000 copies.[44] The first issue comprised forty-eight pages on A5 format, the next three were fifty-two pages, and the fifth was sixty pages. The journal was produced in English only; some activists translated articles into other languages, but readers responded that they wanted the journal to be in English because they wanted to be part of a national movement and debate.[45]

While the format of *Isizwe* was explicitly modeled on that of the ANC's political education journal, *Sechaba*, the journal was produced by the UDF inside the country independently of the ANC in exile. Cronin, like much of the UDF leadership, was actively involved in underground structures of the ANC, but the relationship between the UDF and the ANC was certainly not the subordinate one alleged by the government. As Cronin himself puts it, UDF activists learned early on that you could not ask for ANC confirmation before you did something because the communication channels both to and within the exiled ANC were too slow. The ANC, however, was able to communicate its general approval of the journal and even used sections of *Isizwe* in its own political education work.[46]

The introduction to the first issue reported that "the apartheid government is going all out to crush the UDF" through detentions, trials, and the banning of a leading affiliate, the Congress of South African Students (COSAS). It continued, "In order to steel ourselves against the attacks of the government, and to carry forward our tasks, it is important that we should develop our understanding of the struggle. Let us use theory as another weapon in our march forward. . . . In this first issue of *Isizwe* we look at some important issues for our struggle. The views expressed in these papers are not the official views of the UDF or any section of the front. They are designed to encourage discussion, debate and education within our ranks." The introduction concluded with a slogan: "The UDF lives! Forward to people's power!"[47]

The first article, entitled "The Tasks of the Democratic Movement in the State of Emergency," was the discussion paper previously distributed by *Update*. The article sought to explain the purpose and nature of state strategy and then turned to the consequent tasks of the democratic movement. "In the first place, as always, our job is to isolate the enemy." This should involve not only frustrating the regime's attempts to co-opt Coloureds and Indians but also sharpening the differences between business and the state. Second, the democratic movement should develop "mass-based democratic organisations" without which "we will not attain victory. . . . Without organisation, our struggle will risk becoming chaotic, we will not be able to learn from our victories and from our mistakes. Each day will be a new day. . . . above all, we need to understand that mass-based democratic organisations are not a luxury . . . [but] an absolute necessity for the survival of our struggle."[48] The more mass based the movement, the less vulnerable it would be to repression.

These points were reinforced in an article on "discipline," which took up issues raised at the April 1985 national conference:

> The UDF is a broad front of organisations. In the short period of our existence, we have mobilised tens of thousands of South Africans into our ranks. There has been a massive growth in terms of our numbers. Those drawn into the front have come from many different backgrounds, and sometimes out of different political traditions. It is not surprising that we should find that there is much unevenness in the understanding of our struggle. . . . At the moment there is a limited understanding of many basic issues within our ranks. There is also an unequal development, and differences in the way in which we see issues such as national democratic struggle, working-class leadership, etc. It is essential for our unity, and for our ability to oppose the enemy effectively, that we begin to overcome these problems.[49]

The article emphasized the need for education and training at all levels. The first issue of *Isizwe* also included articles on the Convention Alliance (see below), unemployment, and the UDF's international work. Most articles were accompanied by several "questions for discussion" on the issues covered in the articles. The article on unemployment, for example, was followed by questions on the causes of unemployment and how the unemployed could be organized.[50]

"People's Power"

By the time the second issue of *Isizwe* was published, in March 1986, the UDF had begun to develop a new strategic framework based around the concept of "people's power," which combined the ANC's emphasis on the goal of popular power, the immediate excitement of apparent insurrection, and the UDF leadership's emphasis on organization building. Through organization on the ground—from the level of the street committee upward—areas would be "liberated" from government control and run by the people themselves. The strategic framework of "people's power" helped revive the UDF's leading role in opposition politics.[51]

The media played a central role in developing and promoting this strategic framework. The second issue of *Isizwe* was dedicated to explaining people's power. It appealed first to militancy: "It is true that the fullest consolidation of people's power is still in the future. It is true that control over central state power is the key to many things. . . . Nevertheless, the building of people's power is something that is already beginning to happen in the course of our struggle. It is not for us to sit back and merely dream of the day that the people shall govern. It is our task to realise that goal now."[52]

But *Isizwe* also insisted that "organs of people's power must be democratic and they must be under political discipline." *UDF Update* and other alternative publications reported widely on the spread of street committees and people's courts across South Africa. But it was the articles in *Isizwe* that played the most important part in reorienting activists around the country toward a more principled understanding of the terms and practices of people's power.

Isizwe also served as a vehicle for criticizing alternative strategic and ideological approaches to political opposition. Successive issues included articles on the "errors of populism" and the "errors of workerism" penned by Cronin working with other activists. UDF strategy was described as building a broad popular alliance. Unlike "populism," it did not ignore differences within the broad alliance and did not downplay organization. Unlike the "workerism" championed by sections of the labor movement, *Isizwe* argued, the UDF underrated neither the struggle for political power nor the need to draw into the struggle classes besides the working class. These articles thus sought to recast the political debate from an either-or workerist-populist mold into one that allowed space between each extreme.

Political education was emphasized once again in the Programme of Action adopted by the UDF in May 1986: "With the rapid expansion of our ranks and the unprecedented scale on which the struggle is being waged, the need for political education and cadre development is greater than ever. Political education programmes in each area must be launched. Our journal, *Isizwe*, must be read and studied by all activists."[53]

The purpose of this reading and studying was made apparent in "organisational guidelines" adopted at the same time. Activists were urged, inter alia, to ensure "the active and willing participation of all our people. . . . It is only in this way that the struggle can be intensified." Activists should learn from the lessons of each area, and ensure that operations could continue even amid repression.[54] *Isizwe* itself sought responses from readers: "If there are any issues which comrades would like *Isizwe* to discuss, or if you are unclear or unhappy about what we have said so far, write to *Isizwe* through your organisation or local UDF office."[55]

The Countrywide State of Emergency

The government responded to the threat of "people's power" by imposing, in June 1986, the first countrywide state of emergency. Detentions and restrictions meant that the UDF initially could do little more than conduct, in the words of acting secretary-general Valli Moosa, a "holding operation."[56] *UDF*

News was not produced, and only one issue of *UDF Update* came out (in November 1986). Looking back at the previous year, in May 1987 the UDF acknowledged that repression had hampered media production:

> Apart from *UDF Update*, no national publications were published. This was due to difficulties in communication, printing and distribution. . . . While national propaganda has an important role to play, the most crucial form of propaganda is that which is published at a local level. It thus becomes an urgent task for us to build media and propaganda departments in each and every affiliate. It is only with locally based and decentralised production and distribution of propaganda that we would be able to counter the apartheid propaganda strategy.[57]

Regions and affiliates were said to rely too much on the head office. In addition, commercial and alternative media were constrained by emergency regulations. The definition of prohibited "subversive statements" was widened to include statements promoting and reporting on protest activity. The publication of blank spaces or of text obscured by thick black lines was also prohibited in order to conceal the extent of censorship. Newspapers were issued specific orders preventing them from publishing statements on specific UDF campaigns.

One UDF response was to intensify an existing campaign around the slogan "Unban the ANC." In January 1987 whole-page advertisements calling for the unbanning of the ANC appeared in sixteen newspapers. Three newspapers were prevented from printing and several others refused to print the advert. Valli Moosa later wrote, "The advertisement made a tremendous impact both at a mass level inside the country and internationally. In the face of a plethora of media restrictions and the declaration of the UDF as an affected organisation, the advertisement served to boost the morale of UDF supporters. . . . In this sense it was a psychological victory."[58]

The impact of the action was reflected in the state's response. The commissioner of police issued an order under state of emergency regulations prohibiting any advertising or reports in the media that promoted the image of any banned organization. The president, P. W. Botha, appointed a commission of inquiry to investigate how the advertisements had been financed. It turned out that the funds had been routed through an Indian businessman and Barclays Bank—the bank's involvement reflecting growing elite disaffection from the government.[59]

These restrictions severely curbed coverage of UDF activities, and the front placed even more emphasis on "education and training'" within the organization's regional affiliates. *Isizwe* played a central part in this effort—issues being produced in late 1986 (no. 3), March 1987 (no. 4), and September 1987 (no. 5). In March 1987, *Isizwe* explained the importance of organization in the face of heavy repression: "To continue our struggle we need to broaden our unity, double our vigilance, and, above all, deepen our organisation. It is for this reason that this issue of *Isizwe* puts special stress on organisational topics."[60]

An article examined in detail the question "Why we organise."[61] When the UDF met, clandestinely, in a national conference in mid-1987, representatives noted a major problem facing the front was the gap between political understanding and practice. This underscored the need for more political education. The following issue of *Isizwe* included more analysis of organization building under the title "Build the Front,"[62] and this article was distributed separately as a discussion document (with guidelines on how to proceed when discussing the document).

In February 1988 the government went one step further, effectively banning the UDF. The production and distribution of *Isizwe* became impossible, especially after Cronin's departure into exile. But just as the UDF resurfaced in the form of a new grouping called the Mass Democratic Movement, or

MDM (joining together with close allies in the churches and COSATU), so political education was continued through a new journal, *Phambili*. The first issue of *Phambili* appeared in April 1988 with a second issue (and supplement) in October: "*Phambili* is a journal for political education and discussion. It is aimed at activists of the front and the entire democratic movement. To get the greatest benefit from *Phambili*, organisations should set up discussion groups to read and discuss the articles." Activists were urged also to translate and simplify articles for mass distribution. Distribution, the journal advised, is a "political" task.[63]

Recruiting Disaffected Elites

The general escalation of repression coincided with another strategic shift by the UDF. Having initially been concerned primarily with mustering opposition among Coloureds and Indians to the government's parliamentary reforms and then concerned primarily with organization building among mostly African participants in the township revolts, the UDF began to organize among whites. The media played a central role in the "calls to whites" made by the UDF and its allies.

While the UDF had always emphasized its commitment to nonracism and welcomed whites into its ranks, the initial approach had "focused only [on] bringing whites directly into [the] extra-parliamentary democratic movement."[64] In some cities, separate organizations were formed and affiliated to the UDF, so that white activists could participate in the front—for example, the Johannesburg Democratic Action Committee (JODAC). In other cities, activists formed local UDF structures to participate directly. In Cape Town, for example, activists in predominantly white residential areas organized through UDF area committees. White students were also involved through the National Union of South African Students (NUSAS) and various service organizations, and other whites participated through the Black Sash.

From mid-1985, moreover, an increasing proportion of the white community as a whole began to show serious disaffection with the government and indeed the parliamentary political system. A stream of politicians, businessmen, students, intellectuals, and others visited the ANC in exile. In February 1986, PFP leader van Zyl Slabbert, together with fellow PFP member of parliament Alex Boraine, resigned dramatically from both the party and parliament. The UDF began to seek ways of working with such disaffected white groups.

The UDF's changing approach was reflected in, and to some extent pushed forward by, a UDF publication produced in Cape Town called *Upfront*, which began life in mid-1985 as the newsletter of the Claremont and Observatory UDF area committees. It soon became a vehicle for recruiting people to support these committees, and was later repackaged in magazine format and aimed at a wide range of disaffected whites. As an editorial in late 1985 concluded, "We believe that the development of a body of opinion and action in the white community which rejects minority rule, and stands shoulder to shoulder with black South Africans in the struggle for democracy, is a crucial contribution to the achievement of peace in our land."[65]

This issue, for example, contained articles on a white person's experience attending an African township political funeral (and subsequent police action), the economic crisis, PFP political initiatives, and how whites had and could get involved ("Leaving the Laager").[66]

The involvement of ordinary whites remained a central theme in subsequent issues of *Upfront*. Articles examined the involvement in the democratic movement of people like former Cape provincial cricketer Andre Odendaal, UDF regional executive member Graeme Bloch, and author Menan du Plessis.

By June 1986, *Upfront* provided a clear statement of its broadening role: "We aim to provide the white community with an understanding of issues and developments facing the UDF and its affiliates."[67] One important issue was the difference between the positions adopted by the PFP and the UDF. *Upfront* was very critical of the PFP's proposed national convention, which would serve as a forum for a wide range of political organizations inside South Africa to discuss democratization. The UDF insisted that negotiations could not proceed until a series of preconditions had been met—especially the unbanning of the ANC and the unconditional release of political detainees and prisoners. When the PFP replied that it accepted these preconditions, *Upfront* responded with further criticisms of the PFP position for reserving power during the proposed negotiation process to the present parliament, which the UDF regarded as illegitimate, and for envisaging an elitist process of negotiation and democratization.[68] These differences were perhaps more procedural than substantive, with the UDF favoring initiatives based in extraparliamentary politics.

In April 1986 the UDF launched a more systematic "Call to Whites," initially through its Johannesburg-based affiliate, JODAC. According to the UDF leadership, "More and more whites are losing confidence in the ability of the government to secure a peaceful future for them. This has resulted in many whites looking towards the democratic movement for an alternative. Our task is to spare no effort in welcoming such people and calling upon others to join the democratic movement. Every region should investigate the possibility of initiating this campaign."[69]

The states of emergency, then, raised the importance of organizing among disaffected white South Africans. Besides the principled reasons for organizing in white constituencies, there were now very pressing strategic reasons. As the UDF treasurer put it, "If we are not going to be able to convince enough whites not to turn their guns against their fellow South Africans, if we are not going to be able to turn enough whites against apartheid, the struggle is going to be much longer and much more painful."[70] The UDF's own press was to play a central role in this strategy.

The challenge of organizing among whites required the UDF to be flexible in its tactics: "To take up this challenge we have to embark on a process which begins with where they are at. We need to address their fears and concerns and provide direction and language in a style to which they can relate."[71] The UDF recognized that liberal whites had not really been involved in black boycott politics, which meant it had to adopt tactics that engaged with a parliament regarded by other UDF activists and supporters as "illegitimate." The UDF's press had to tell white sympathizers how they might oppose apartheid and explain to the UDF's existing support base why the front was adopting these positions. *Upfront* dedicated considerable space in early 1987 to the whites-only parliamentary election, distinguishing separate messages to "traditional" NP supporters, PFP supporters, "white UDF supporters and democrats," and "the voteless majority."[72]

With the government renewing a state of emergency every year, more and more white South Africans adopted dissenting political positions. In February 1988 the UDF was effectively banned, but by the end of the year the government was being forced once again to negotiate for political change. Although it was not widely known at the time, talks were in progress between the government, the jailed Nelson Mandela, and the exiled ANC leadership. In early 1989 political detainees embarked on hunger strikes and secured their release. The UDF and its affiliates began to act more assertively—although, in the face of restrictions, rarely in the name of the UDF itself.

In this fast-changing political environment, *Upfront* was relaunched as a magazine with a cover price of R2 (later increased to R3) or a subscription rate of R10 for four issues. *Upfront* as a magazine was initially thirty pages but quickly increased to fifty pages. Given the restrictions on the UDF, *Upfront* played down its origins as a publication of UDF area committees: "*Upfront* is an independent publication aiming at providing informative and analytical articles reflecting the exciting and changing times in South Africa."[73] As the democratic movement gathered momentum, however, *Upfront* became more direct: "*Upfront* is an independent journal which aims to promote critical thought and discussion around current political issues. *Upfront* seeks to provide insights into topical MDM debates and concerns. The journal is aimed at all those who have an interest in mass liberation politics in South Africa."[74] The first issue gave the name of one of the editors. By late 1989—when the second issue was published—*Upfront* felt confident enough to print the names of its entire editorial committee.

The first issue in the new magazine format carried articles on a planned antiapartheid conference that had been banned at the last moment, the imminent municipal elections, meetings between business and UDF/MDM leaders, and the End Conscription Campaign. The role of *Upfront* was set out in comments from ordinary whites involved in the democratic movement: "I had been to a UDF meeting before but this year working as a teacher really brought things up directly. I felt I had to get involved. Things are getting so bad I don't think that any one can sit on the fringe any more." The teacher had hosted a UDF house meeting, which revealed problems with public knowledge and understanding of the UDF: "There is a lot of confusion over the UDF. People tend to see it as a political party. Even among people who had shown an interest in UDF and been to meetings, they don't understand the basics, especially about who makes up the UDF and how discussion goes on at different levels to make decisions."[75]

It is impossible to evaluate precisely what impact a magazine like *Upfront* made on white consciousness. It seems likely, however, that its very existence contributed to an atmosphere in which large numbers of whites could, for the first time, identify with nonracial, extraparliamentary protests. In late 1989 whites participated in burgeoning public demonstrations —such as a march in Cape Town against racial legislation (a march that exhorted participants, in Afrikaans, to Loop Kaapstad Oop, or March Cape Town Open).

Success: Dependence on the Commercial Press, 1989–1991

The resurgence of public opposition in 1989, and especially the broadening of protest to include a wide range of people from the churches and liberal white political and business organizations, as well as the trade unions and UDF affiliates, transformed the UDF's relationships with the media. The mainstream white-controlled commercial press increasingly shrugged off restrictions and reported extensively on protests—especially when the protests led to incidents of government repression.

In August 1989 the UDF—in the name of the MDM— launched a defiance campaign, initially focused on the segregation of beaches, hospitals, and buses, and later extending to protest against new elections for the racially segregated tricameral parliament. The campaign depended on media coverage in seeking to highlight the persistence of racial segregation, to embarrass a government (under the new leadership of F. W. de Klerk) hoping to project a more reasonable image, and to overcome the caution among many UDF supporters instilled by three years of heavy repression.

Protests at the time were designed to maximize national and international media attention. Blacks sought treatment at hospitals officially reserved for whites; they sought access to "whites-only" beaches and traveled on "whites-only" buses. Protests were headed by figures attracting international attention —such as Nobel peace laureate and Anglican Archbishop Desmond Tutu.

Police brutality against nonviolent protesters ensured international as well as local coverage and forced the government to make concessions. Indeed, just as American civil rights campaigners in the 1960s had strategized in anticipation of the political benefits from media reports of police brutality, so it is likely the UDF/MDM leadership were aware that police brutality was great publicity. In Britain television screens and news pages were reported to be filled with "stories of baton-toting police, teargassed Archbishops, and barbed wire on the beaches."[76]

As the elections to the tricameral parliament drew near, the police handled protests with increasing violence—in the full gaze of media attention. On the eve of the election, the media seized on the description by a police officer of Cape Town's riot police as acting "like wild dogs" with a "killer instinct." On the day of the election itself between twenty and thirty people were killed by the police, mostly in Cape Town. This was a public relations disaster for the NP government, which had sought to project a reformist image at home and abroad. Even government-supporting Afrikaans newspapers such as *Die Burger* and *Rapport* criticized police conduct.[77]

The government responded by permitting public demonstrations, banning the use of sjamboks by the police, and ordering riot police to stop beating protesters. In mid-September somewhere between 30,000 and 50,000 people marched through Cape Town in protest against police brutality. Over the next few days, at least a quarter of a million people participated in protest marches across the country. In October the government, which was immersed in negotiations with Mandela and the ANC, released most of the top ANC leadership from jail. It was clear that fundamental political change was imminent. The UDF itself produced very few publications after 1989: it had no need to do so, because the white commercial press provided more and more coverage of the democratic movment.

In February 1990 the ANC was unbanned and Mandela released. The UDF was disbanded formally in August 1991, but from early 1990 it had clearly ceded its political functions and roles to the ANC—to usher in South Africa's new era.

Conclusion

In an interview, Valli Moosa remarked, "Most of the time, the UDF was barking louder than it could bite."[78] Certainly, the UDF's access to the commercial media (especially in 1985–86 and 1988–89), and its own capacity to produce publications (especially at the time of its formation in 1983 and again in 1985–86), allowed it to maintain a loud voice, even when its own organizational capacity was uneven.

The UDF's "barks," however, had very important effects. Publicity helped the UDF forge fragmented networks and organizations into a nationwide movement, to raise morale and thus sustain the movement during repressive periods, to reduce the space in which the government could maneuver, and to recruit new layers of activists into political action and organization. The UDF also used print media, especially its own, as a tool for organization building and for promoting particular strategies, and above all as a vehicle for political education and for the maintenance of links between activists and organizations.

Notes

1. I provide a general history and analysis of the UDF in my book *The UDF: A History of the United Democratic Front in South Africa, 1983–1991* (Cape Town: David Philip, 2000).

2. Walter Sisulu, address to the UDF's national general council, KwaNdebele, 1 March 1991.

3. It is important to emphasize that the experiences of community newspapers like *Grassroots* in Cape Town had important consequences for the UDF, since many influential UDF activists had been involved, directly or indirectly, with the alternative press.

4. Memorandum to exec members from secretariat, handwritten, 4 August 1983; "Press Update," 12 August 1983; *Cape Times* and *Argus*, 17 August 1983.

5. Memorandum.

6. Quoted in Ineke van Kessel, "'Beyond Our Wildest Dreams': The United Democratic Front and the Transformation of South Africa" (Ph.D. diss., University of Leiden, 1995), 112.

7. Daily newspapers were read by 57 percent of the adult Indian population and weekly newspapers by 76 percent; 38 percent of the Coloureds read dailies and 59 percent weeklies. Readership rates were much lower among Africans: Only 13 percent read a daily and 26 percent a weekly newspaper. *All Media and Products Survey (AMPS) '83*, vols. 2–4.

8. "New-Born Opposition Front Plans Talks with UN Chief," *Daily News*, 22 August 1983.

9. The UDF was mentioned in a report on a civic meeting in Durban (*Daily News*, 1 August 1983, 4), a report on squatters (5 August 1983, 5), and in a feature comparing the UDF and National Forum (5 August 1983, 14).

10. Ami Nanackchand, "A Political Happening," *Daily News*, 26 August 1983. The same issue included a column by Graham Linscott, "The Black Press," in which he notes that the UDF had been reported with enthusiasm in the *Sowetan* and *Ilanga*—rather ironic, given the general silence on the part of the *Daily News*.

11. "Massive Rally Launches UDF," *Sunday Times*, 21 August 1983, and extra edition. The UDF was not, however, the lead story even in the extra edition: a story on a schoolboy dying trying to save his brothers in a burning house was deemed more important.

12. "Anti-Conscription Body to be Launched," *Argus*, 17 August 1983; "Uniting against the Botha Plan," editorial, ibid.

13. "UDF Leaflet Hoax in City," *Argus*, 19 August 1983; David Breier, "UDF: Biggest Alliance since the Fifties," and Hugh Robertson, "Who's Who," ibid.

14. "Mass UDF Rally in City," *Argus*, 20 August 1983; "5000 Pack UDF Rally," late extra edition with photos; "Thousands at UDF Launch," late sport final edition with photos.

15. "New Political Factor," editorial, *Argus*, 22 August 1983.

16. The one exception was a feature published in the *Daily News* on 3 August 1983 summarizing Buthelezi's reasons for opposing the reforms.

17. "'Group Rights' Are White Rights," editorial, *Argus*, 16 August 1983. "Baasskap" in Afrikaans literally means "boss-ship"—a term for blatant white racism.

18. See "Fixing the News," editorial, *Argus*, 23 August 1983.

19. Quoted in " 'Biased' SABC Ignored UDF," *Cape Times*, 23 August 1983.

20. See van Kessel, *Beyond Our Wildest Dreams*, 110.

21. Transvaal UDF media committee, "Report on Campaign against Local Authority Elections in 1983," April 1984.

22. Ibid.

23. Baba Ngcokoto, "Unrest in the Ciskei: UDF's View," *Cape Times*, 1 October 1983.

24. "Why It's Worth Casting a Vote," *Sunday Times*, 19 August 1984.

25. The first mention of the UDF in a *Sunday Times* editorial, at least that I can find, was in the week after the elections, on 26 August 1984.

26. Quoted by van Kessel, *Beyond Our Wildest Dreams*, 109.

27. UDF, Secretarial Report, February 1986, 15.

28. UDF, Report on National Launch Conference.

29. See Seekings, *UDF*, chaps. 3 and 5.

30. UDF, Secretarial Report to the National General Council, Azaadville, April 1985.

31. For details, see Seekings, *UDF*, chap. 6.

32. Transvaal UDF media committee, "Campaign against Local Authority," April 1984; UDF, report on Media Workshop, Khotso House (Johannesburg), 5 February 1985.

33. *Update*, July 1985.

34. Kim Morgan, interview by author, 1 July 1992.

35. UDF, Secretarial Report, February 1986, 17.

36. Ibid.

37. Quoted in van Kessel, *Beyond Our Wildest Dreams*, 111.

38. UDF, minutes of National Working Committee (NWC), 8–9 June 1985, Johannesburg, item 5.

39. See J. Cronin, "The Question of Unity in the Struggle," in *South African Labour Bulletin* 11, 3 (1986): 29–37. Cronin actually wrote the article in November 1985 in response to an article by Alec Erwin in *SALB* 11, 1 (1985).

40. Jeremy Cronin, interview by author, 3 August 1998.

41. Secretarial Report, February 1986, 17.

42. Jeremy Cronin, interview by author, 3 August 1998.

43. UDF, minutes of NWC, 8–9 June 1985, Johannesburg, item 5.

44. Jeremy Cronin, interview by author, 3 August 1998.

45. Ibid.

46. Ibid. See also Seekings, *UDF*, esp. chap. 11.

47. *Isizwe*, November 1985.

48. Ibid.

49. Ibid.

50. Ibid.

51. See Seekings, *UDF*, chap. 7.

52. "Building People's Power," *Isizwe*, March 1986.

53. UDF, minutes of NWC, May 1986.

54. Ibid.

55. *Isizwe*, September–October 1986.

56. See Seekings, *UDF*, chap. 8.

57. UDF, secretarial report to NWC, May 1987, 27.

58. Ibid., 22.

59. See South African Institute of Race Relations, *Race Relations Survey 1987/88*, 388–91, 819.

60. *Isizwe*, March 1987.

61. Ibid.

62. *Isizwe*, September 1987.

63. *Phambili*, October 1988.

64. "A Call to Whites," *Upfront*, April 1989.

65. *Upfront*, October 1985.

66. Ibid.

67. *Upfront*, June 1986.

68. See "Botha Is on the Run" (interview with Murphy Morobe) and "PFP: Not the Enemy," *Upfront*, March 1986. See also "Spanning the Divides with a Unifying Goal," *Upfront*, February 1988.

69. UDF Programme of Action, as adopted by the extended National Working Committee on 24 and 25 May 1986, para. 7.

70. Quoted in "A Call to Whites," *Upfront*, April 1989.

71. "UDF Call to Whites," discussion document, n.d. (mid-1987), 2.

72. "Look towards the Majority: UDF Statement on the White Election," *Upfront*, April 1987.

73. *Upfront*, April 1989.

74. *Upfront*, November 1989.

75. *Upfront*, April 1989.

76. "Voiceless—the MDM Is Heard," *Star*, 2 September 1989.

77. See "The Limits of Violence," *Financial Mail*, 15 September 1989.

78. Valli Moosa, interview by van Kessel, quoted in *Beyond Our Wildest Dreams*, 112.

6

East Cape News Agencies

Reporting on a Black Hole

Franz Krüger

The mid-1980s saw a dramatic escalation of political conflict in South Africa, and simultaneously the reemergence of what became known in that decade as the alternative press. This trend toward independent journalism affected the eastern Cape, too, but in this region no attempt was made to start a fully fledged alternative newspaper. Instead, a network of news agencies was established called the East Cape News Agencies (Ecna).

There were four agencies involved in the network: Veritas (based in King William's Town), elnews (based in East London), Albany News Agency (Grahamstown), and Port Elizabeth News (which boasted several other names before settling on Pen). These agencies provided news to alternative weeklies, other alternative periodicals, and growing numbers of mainstream news media. By 1990, Ecna had turned itself from a network into a single organization. While most of the alternative press failed to survive the new political dispensation set in motion during the 1990s, Ecna is still functioning.

It was no accident that a successful regional news service

developed in the eastern Cape. The 1991–92 Ecna annual report described the region's significance:

> The eastern Cape—including the Border, Ciskei and much of Transkei—is a region with a rich and varied political history. From last century's frontier wars to the campaigns of the fifties, and further to the consumer boycotts and street committees of the late eighties, it is an area where political organisation has been as strong as the tradition of resistance. . . . It is a region where some of the oldest institutions of black education are to be found. . . . In the field of media, it has also played a pioneering role, with probably the oldest black newspaper, *Imvo zabaNtsundu*, being founded by John Tengo Jabavu in King William's Town in 1884.

The region has been one of the poorest in South Africa throughout the twentieth century. Unemployment remains high, while migrant labor, influx control, and forced removal policies generated huge populations of rural poor. Apartheid policy created two "independent" homelands, the Transkei and the Ciskei, ruled by a succession of corrupt hoodlums.

This fascinating and complex region was very badly served by the mainstream media. East London had only one daily newspaper, the *Daily Dispatch*, which had become increasingly conservative after the former editor, Donald Woods, fled the country. Under the irascible editorship of George Farr, the newspaper considered its civic duty was to support the apartheid status quo, which meant playing down any news of civil strife. In one notable incident, East London was hit by an almost complete stayaway. The only reference in the following morning's newspaper to this important event was to be found in a blob paragraph tucked away at the end of another story, which merely reported changes in bus schedules and assured readers there had been no incidents.[1] In another instance, the editor declined to print a reader's letter criticizing the government's propaganda arm, the Bureau for Information, on the grounds it could "be ruled that you are undermining confidence in the integrity of the government."[2]

Port Elizabeth was slightly better served. The city had three daily newspapers, the *Eastern Province Herald* and the *Evening Post*, both owned by the English-language media conglomerate Times Media Limited, and *Die Oosterlig*, owned by the Afrikaans-language media conglomerate Nasionale Pers. The two English-language newspapers adopted a slightly more liberal line than the *Dispatch*, but these journalists were also frustrated by their editors' unwillingness to report uncomfortable subjects. Mike Loewe, at the time a staffer on the *Evening Post*, describes the newspaper's coverage of a stayaway on 21 March 1985 by workers in Uitenhage, an industrial area near Port Elizabeth, and the violent reaction of the police that resulted in several deaths. The story missed the first edition because the editor insisted on having a police comment: "and when it [the story] broke, it was under the banner headline which went something close to: 'Stones fell like raindrops.' This was the police version of the killings, and was, I recall, provided by the *Evening Post*'s crime reporter. . . . Judge Donald Kannemeyer later found that only one stone was in fact thrown."[3]

The rest of the country relied on these mainstream, white-owned commercial newspapers for almost all reporting about the eastern Cape. The newspapers were members of the South African Press Association (SAPA) and acted as its correspondents in the region. In addition, the *Dispatch* and the *EP Herald* were members of another news conglomerate, the Morning Group of newspapers, which acted as an additional news exchange. Some newspapers in other regions, notably the Cape *Argus* and the Johannesburg *City Press*, maintained offices in the eastern Cape, but these were scaled back in the mid-eighties. Thus the regional newspapers to a large extent also controlled the news flow out of the region to the rest of the country. This stranglehold on the flow of news was to be a significant factor in Ecna's development and success.

In the electronic media, the region was dominated—as elsewhere—by the SABC. With its main base in Port Elizabeth, the SABC broadcast Radio Xhosa and Radio Algoa across the region. A radio station was one of the trappings of "independence," so the Transkei had its own radio station (Radio Transkei), and the Ciskei later got its station, too. Nevertheless, one other station—Capital Radio—was fiercely independent. It was originally located in the Transkei, so it was subject to control by the Transkei. But the homeland government allowed the station significant freedom to develop an independent news style so long as the homeland itself didn't come under scrutiny. Capital Radio had its biggest following in Natal but was heard on FM in the Transkei and on medium wave in the Border area. By the mid-eighties the station had moved from its original base in Port St. Johns to Johannesburg and then to Durban.

This, then, was the backdrop to the development of the East Cape news agencies. The region was highly politicized, and there were many stories to tell. But it was very poorly served by the local mainstream media.

Regional News Agencies: A Brief History

The oldest of the four Ecna agencies was Veritas, which was set up in 1982 by two journalists, M. J. Fuzile and Charles Nqakula. Its first office was a shop in Zwelitsha, one of King William's Town's African townships and technically a part of the Ciskei homeland. Extensive harassment by Ciskei security police forced the agency into dormancy for some years. In

1985, however, the agency was revived by Fuzile and Phila Ngqumba—Nqakula having fled into exile. The office was moved to King William's Town, beyond the reach of the homeland. Ngqumba, a long-time Veritas staffer, describes the motivation for reestablishing the agency: "It came out of their experience of coverage in the region. The newspapers were neglecting issues that people felt were real issues."[4]

Elnews in East London was the next office to be established. Initially, it functioned under the aegis of Afesis (a Greek word meaning "liberation"), a church-based, nongovernmental organization (NGO) that also ran an advice office, resource center, and various other projects. Its offices were in a house on the edge of Pefferville, a Coloured township adjacent to Duncan Village, an old and very squalid African township. Franz Krüger, at first the only staff member, operated out of a storeroom at the back of the house. The agency began operations on Mayday 1986, and six weeks later a state of emergency was declared. This imposed immediate difficulties on elnews, since the entire Afesis staff immediately had to go into hiding. Krüger had to deal with the administrative details of keeping the larger project alive while monitoring repeated police raids on the main office of Afesis. As he noted in the elnews quarterly report at the time, "This has proved severely disruptive, as the administrative tasks have often had to take precedence over reporting work, which has then had to be left undone." Despite these difficulties, elnews's initial report lists eleven regular clients, and by the beginning of 1987 two more journalists were employed.[5]

The first national state of emergency declared in June 1986 (a partial state of emergency had been imposed in July 1985), however, affected the other agencies far worse. Both Fuzile and Ngqumba were detained almost immediately. They would spend seventeen months in detention—the only journalists in the country detained explicitly for their work as journalists.[6]

In Port Elizabeth, efforts were being made to set up an agency under the name Vukani! Mike Loewe, later to become Ecna editor, describes the early days:

> I bought a manual typewriter from the *Evening Post* with a broken q key and, with R30 in pocket, started freelancing from my flat. . . . I supplied news about the township revolt, security force abuses, the consumer boycotts, detentions, the state of emergency, funerals for police victims in small towns and leaders in hiding. These were telexed to the emerging alternative and independent publications such as *New Nation* and the *Weekly Mail* as well as *City Press* and the foreign press agencies, AFP, AP and Reuters. I also managed to obtain a small retainer fee of R200 from *New York Times* correspondent Alan Cowell. Nobody paid that well and I must admit that I obtained my start-up monies from an article I wrote for *Scope* magazine about a surfer who was savaged by a shark at East London![7]

In September 1985 three of the journalists involved—Loewe, Mbulelo Linda, and Brian Sokutu—were detained. Needless to say, this delayed the Port Elizabeth initiative significantly. Loewe was released with a restriction order prohibiting him from working as a journalist, but this was withdrawn after court action. By the end of 1985 the agency was operating under the name East Cape News Agency. (The name was later changed to Pen to allow the umbrella body to use the name Ecna.) Varying numbers of journalists were involved, including a photographer, although unlike the situation in East London and King William's Town, they initially operated as a collective of freelancers rather than as full-time staff. Meanwhile, in Grahamstown, the Albany News Agency began operating at the beginning of 1987 with one journalist, Peter auf der Heyde.[8]

It was a difficult time for journalists, with intense police harassment. Ecna reports are littered with examples: cars sabotaged, homes raided, and in one instance an Ecna journalist

ANA
Albany News Agency

9 Hayton's Building, 94 High Street (Box 188) Grahamstown -6140. Telephone 0461-29565 Telex (9)24/5502

26 March 1987

Dear....................

The State of Emergency, which is entering its tenth month, has had a severe
effect on the dissemination of news in South Africa. A comprehensive set
of media regulations which have been designed to curtail the information
flow of the mass media, has created a distorted picture of the reality
of everyday life. Furthermore, it has created a national and international
media black-out of events in this country.

It is in this context that an abundance of independent news agencies have
been established to cover news in particular regions. The Eastern Cape
hosts four of these. They are East London News (elnews), Eastern Cape
News Agency (ECNA), Albany News Agency (ANA) and Veritas News Agency.

The Albany News Agency which came into being recently offers a press
cuttings service with an Eastern Cape focus. This service became active
in November 1986. The intention is to collect information on the Eastern
Cape which is published in the regional commercial press as well as in
the national media. A list of over one hundred categories, guiding the
cuttings service, has been compiled.

A full list of the news categories is attached to this letter. A numbering
system has been used to identify the categories. The major categories have
been systematized alphabetically, while the sub-categories have been systematized numerically.

    eg: <u>Major categories:</u>
    A - Areas
    B - Political
    C - Economy and Housing
    D - Other

    eg: <u>Sub-categories:</u>
    A1 - Grahamstown
    A1.1 - Fingo Village (as a sub-category of A1)

The compilation of the weekly press clippings will be numbered as above
and will correlate with the list of categories included here. You will
thus receive sheets of news clippings coded alphabetically and numerically.
The list of categories will be your decoder and guide to the filing of
the press cuttings.

The newspapers used for the press cuttings, as well as the abbreviations
used on the cuttings, are listed below:

Daily Dispatch	(DD)	Weekend Post	(WP)
Eastern Province Herald	(EPH)	Weekly Mail	(WM)
Evening Post	(EP)	New Nation	(NN)
Oosterlig	(OL)	City Press	(CP)
Grocott's Mail	(GM)	Sunday Tribune	(ST)

The service is offered at R200 per year, while a reduced rate of R120
per year is offered to individual subscribers. News cuttings packages are
collated and distributed weekly.

If you are interested in subscribing to the news cuttings service, please
let ANA know as soon as possible.

A letter announcing the press cuttings service offered by the newly
established Albany News Agency in Grahamstown.

found a note in the postbox asking the postmaster to pass letters on to the security police![9]

From the beginning, the four news agencies, in touch with each other, were looking for ways to cooperate. The first joint project was a press clippings service, giving each office a reference tool for background to stories. These efforts took place without Veritas, which remained dormant due to the detention of both staff members.

From February 1987 regular meetings were held to swap experiences and discuss common difficulties. Areas of cooperation rapidly expanded: joint approaches were made to common clients when there were problems with payment, insurance was arranged jointly, and a common approach was formulated to ongoing requests from community-based organizations to use agency facilities. Joint projects were launched or anticipated, like a news brief called *East Cape Update*. Others, like the training program, played an important role in Ecna's operations (see below).

The agencies were operating with considerable uncertainty in terms of organizational structure. They had various constitutions, which effectively constituted these agencies as voluntary associations. They set up committees of community leaders to ensure they remained accountable to a rather vaguely conceived "community." But these committees functioned erratically at best: members were often themselves activists, heavily involved in various organizational activities and subject to clashes with security police. They generally lacked the expertise to oversee journalistic enterprises, and so the agencies were really run by the journalists who worked there. Ecna saw itself as an umbrella body, with the four agencies as members who controlled its operations.

The South African government again imposed a state of emergency on the country in June 1988—with a provision that threatened Ecna's existence as a viable organization. The new regulation required news agencies to register with the government. Initial registration was just a formality, but the minister had complete discretion to withdraw the permit if he thought it necessary "for the safety of the public or the maintenance of public order."[10] The measure was aimed primarily at the Ecna agencies: the only other significant news agency—Concorde, based in Durban—had become dormant when most of its members got involved in setting up an independent weekly in the city, *New African*.

The significance of the new regulation was not widely understood. Minutes of an Ecna meeting held a few days after it became law noted, "the regulations in effect are the beginning of a register for journalists and . . . this is something the commercial press has not picked up on at all."[11] Ecna decided to campaign against the regulations: meetings were held in Johannesburg with a range of affected groups, and an eastern Cape "Save the Press" campaign was launched.[12]

The regulations, however, were withdrawn when it became clear that the definition of a news agency was so loose that white commercial newspapers, public relations officers, and even the government's own Bureau for Information would have to register. With only days to go before the deadline for registration, the government announced the suspension of the measure "for practical considerations." The "problem" of the independent news agencies, however, remained a grave concern, and the government hinted at alternative measures.[13] The announcement meant Ecna did not have to implement a decision to disband rather than register.

During 1989 it became clear that the agencies needed to rejuvenate initial attempts to sponsor cooperative ventures. Although jealous of their independence from each other, they were faced with many problems that could better be dealt with jointly. There were chronic financial crises. Even though Ecna relied on overseas funding for support, the copy often suffered because of a lack of quality subediting, and there were ongoing administrative problems. The minutes record one journalist's view that Ecna should be "a support base for the agencies. She saw Ecna as being valuable to the agencies—that there was a need for a minimum central control body which would coordinate mutual interests so that time is not wasted in duplicating certain tasks. Also as Ecna the agencies have a front to face the onslaught from the state and an important forum to discuss joint strategies."[14]

It was decided to establish a central office for Ecna in Grahamstown and employ a coordinator, later called group editor, and an administrator. In early 1990, Krüger moved to Grahamstown as group editor, and Jean Burgess was employed as administrator. As Burgess gradually gained control over administration for the four news agencies, Krüger provided centralized diaries for the five independent weeklies using the service.[15] The role of the central news desk expanded rapidly, until all but radio copy was being filed with Ecna from Grahamstown. More staff was brought in to ensure that all material was first edited before being sent to clients.

Toward the end of 1990, Ecna felt confident enough about the quality of its service to approach clients with the suggestion that they subscribe to a Standardised News Service (SNS). Until then, Ecna had been paid on a freelance basis. This was unsatisfactory for a range of reasons: "It places a ceiling on the number of papers we can deal with, is administratively difficult and means we are always 'second-guessing' the newspapers instead of applying our own editorial judgment. These problems were difficult enough when the agencies were doing most of their marketing themselves, but when a lot of this became the group editor's responsibility, it became impossible."[16] Subscription rates were initially pitched at between R1,000 a month for a daily newspaper and R300 a month for a "tipoff service," which involved people who sent in tips to SNS.

Foreign correspondents in South Africa might use the service to obtain background information or find leads about important stories. Individual rates, however, were always negotiated and therefore varied greatly.

The SNS was launched early in 1991, and by the end of the year there were twenty-four subscribers. These included the independent weeklies, specialist publications, some mainstream newspapers—particularly from the Argus group—radio stations, a sprinkling of foreign correspondents, and even an embassy.[17] Other clients were still serviced on an ad hoc basis.

The SNS formed the basis for some rapid improvements in revenue. The list of subscribers grew, but improvements were also achieved through some fairly dramatic increases in rates. Annual reports for the East Cape News Agency as a whole noted that revenue from all sources more than doubled from R119,552 in 1991 to R243,784 in 1992, and there was a nearly 50 percent increase in revenue to R345,812 in 1994.[18] A key goal for Ecna was financial independence, but funding from overseas donors continued to be necessary to cover the shortfall.

The scale of the operation at this stage required some new technological innovations. In the beginning, the agencies had relied on telex to file material to newspapers. The first elnews office in East London, for example, had been equipped with a relatively advanced Teletex machine—being equipped with a screen—but it was still very cumbersome. As modem transmission became more widespread, Ecna could drop stories directly into client computer systems, and newspapers did not need to input the story. Nevertheless, faxing remained the method of sending stories to many clients for a long time. Communication between the agencies and the Ecna head office was also an issue: stories needed to be sent electronically to Grahamstown for editing, and an internal bulletin board was set up for this purpose, called Ecnet. However, sending some twenty stories a day to upward of twenty-five clients remained a major chore, since even electronic transmission involved a range of different systems and protocols. It was only later that e-mail became the standard. In recent years, Ecna has made use of SAPA's distribution system to send its material to clients. By the time the new South Africa was born with the April 1994 election, Ecna saw itself as "a unique media organisation developing innovative approaches in a range of areas. . . . Our work is gaining increasing recognition, and we receive periodic inquiries from people in other parts of the country who want to copy the 'Ecna model.' Our challenge now is to strengthen our work sufficiently to put it on a sustainable footing in the long term, while still remaining open to new possibilities."[19] Ecna had established itself in the national media as a key source of news on the eastern Cape, and even the regional media had begun to accept it as legitimate. There was a successful training program and a very active community media development program. A production unit did high-quality design work for both community and commercial clients, although it never became profitable as had been hoped. There was a full-time staff of fifteen and two part-time subeditors.

Self-sufficiency, however, was still elusive. In the postelection period, donor funds outside South Africa began to dry up, leading to the closure of the majority of other independent media projects. Ecna was enough of a commercial success to survive, but it did have to shed staff and give up several projects. The community media initiative hived off as an independent entity, the Development News Agency, and Ecna has returned to its core purpose, journalism. It now focuses primarily on serving the regional newspapers, where it has a strong presence, but still files to outlets in other parts of the country.

Stories and News Values

Allister Sparks, former editor of the *Rand Daily Mail*, has often referred to the eastern Cape as a "black hole" of information. Poor coverage, as noted earlier, was due to the region's peculiar media landscape. From the start, the Ecna agencies saw as their primary purpose to put the region "on the map" for the national media. A general outline of Ecna's work, written in 1990, put it as follows: "[The agencies] see themselves as part of the progressive, or alternative, press in South Africa. . . . They see themselves as committed to democratic media practices, which mean covering issues of importance to the majority of South Africans, and consciously opposing government restrictions on reporting, as well as the selectivity and bias in much of our press."[20]

It was a tall order, particularly since Ecna wasn't able to publish but relied on many of the newspapers it was criticizing to get its material into print. The growth of Ecna, however, coincided with the development of the alternative press. Newspapers like the *Weekly Mail* and *New Nation* were important clients for Ecna, as were some alternative magazines like *Work in Progress*. It was easy to work with people with whom there was a congruence of journalistic approach and a camaraderie that came from being "on the same side" in opposition to the apartheid government. But Ecna needed more income than this sector was able to supply.

From the beginning, news was also supplied to mainstream media. Perhaps fortuitously, the establishment of East London's elnews coincided with the closure—for financial reasons—of the East London office of Cape Town's *Argus* newspaper. This meant there was an established appetite on the *Argus* for stories from the eastern Cape, which elnews could supply.

There was a widespread perception among mainstream editors that the eastern Cape story was not properly covered by the existing eastern Cape press. Even within the parameters of their relatively restricted news values, it was clear they were not hearing from their usual sources about important things happening in the region. So Ecna was able to develop a foothold in the mainstream media.

What did this mean for Ecna's own news values? It meant that a fine line had to be tread between being "progressive" and fitting in with the news values of clients. On the one hand, Ecna saw itself as truly different. On the other hand, there was a need to conform to the expectations of customers. One report by the group editor exhorted staff: "We have to write the kind of stories people will want to run. And this means being imaginative in our approach to stories. . . . Look for the humorous angle, the unusual. And remember that we can't write only from an organisational perspective. We have to take into account more conventional news values as well. It often seems we are writing for activists: we need to write for other people as well."[21]

The issue became particularly acute when a contract was signed with the Argus group of newspapers in 1991. The Argus group was the biggest media group in the country and the contract was worth a lot of money, but there was also a clear danger that Ecna would simply be swallowed by the giant company. A workshop was held to discuss various issues of principle as well as practicalities. Shifts were rearranged to improve Ecna's ability to meet the group's early morning deadlines, new contact lists were drawn up, and arrangements were made to improve the organization's monitoring of other media. But Ecna was determined to maintain its own identity.[22]

The attempt to pursue a progressive agenda within a predominantly conservative media market must ultimately be declared a success. There were countless stories that Ecna was able to cover in a better and more thorough way or that would never have seen the light of day without the agency. Murders of activists like Eric Mntonga, Matthew Goniwe, and Bathandwa Ndondo, details about evictions and other community struggles, and industrial disputes were among the stories Ecna uncovered. The Bisho massacre of 1992 (Bisho, capital of the Ciskei homeland) was seen as an example of the way in which Ecna was able to add value to coverage: "We were in a position to supply important background to the incident. . . . We had been reporting consistently on the ongoing, low-level violence in the Ciskei which was important background to the massacre, but which was generally ignored by other media." And in another example from the same report: "We have been very interested in instances where popular organisations co-operate with state agencies around particular issues. The Port Elizabeth Black Civic Organisation is a case in point: they are administering a multimillion rand feeding scheme for the government. It is a significant dynamic, but our reports have been virtually the only ones to focus on it."[23] In addition, there were many other stories that were not unique, such as the sinking of the *Oceanos* off the eastern Cape coast, the ongoing squabbles of homeland leaders, and priests arrested for stealing condoms.

The difficulties of the alternative press began when prime minister F. W. de Klerk announced his reformist initiative in early 1990. Overseas funding began to dry up, because it was believed the role of these newspapers was being made redundant. Ecna argued against this view:

> Now that the mainstream papers are covering extra-parliamentary news, the argument goes, there is nothing to set the independents apart. Our experience in Ecna has been quite the opposite. Our experience has been that the mainstream media are still far from being in tune with the new South Africa. Most papers now quote the pronouncements of Mandela and the ANC, and that is clearly an advance. But when schools open we get a cute picture of white Sub A kids, while the chaos in black schools is largely ignored; crime coverage remains profoundly racist—the murder of a white

person receives saturation coverage, township crime is just a statistic.[24]

The mainstream media did begin to shift their focus as the political situation changed, and Ecna was able to take advantage of this shift. It was able to tell the story of the eastern Cape in a way that news desks in Johannesburg, Durban, and Cape Town could simply not get anywhere else.

The regional newspapers were much slower in adapting. Initially, they regarded the agencies with deep suspicion. Krüger was told never to enter the building again when he left the *Dispatch* to set up elnews. Stories the agencies ran were hardly ever followed up by the regional newspapers, but this changed over time. The *Weekend Post* took stories almost from the start but paid rather poorly. The breakthrough came ironically from Nasionale Pers, which closed down *Die Oosterlig* in Port Elizabeth and replaced it with a regional edition of Cape Town's *Die Burger* in early 1993. This edition became the first full Ecna subscriber in the region and was followed by the other regional newspapers.[25] Regional, white-owned commercial publications now relied on Ecna stories, and they became the key clients for the news agency in the 1990s.

Ecna also became a regular contact point for foreign correspondents and some diplomats, and thereby contributed to the flow of information out of the region. Particularly during the state of emergency years, when reliable information was hard to come by, there were regular visits by people anxious to receive briefings on the regional situation. The agencies tried to turn this to profit by offering their services as "fixers" to foreign news teams, and some revenue was generated from these sources.

An important theme for Ecna from the beginning was the desire for its own space. In the first meetings the agencies held in 1986, as noted earlier, there was discussion about publishing a news brief called *East Cape Update*, which was aimed at a national and international audience interested in developments in the region. This was not intended to be a newspaper—it was clear the agencies did not have the capacity to publish a weekly like other regions. A huge amount of energy went into the project, but it ultimately failed when the government inserted a clause in the Internal Security Act that empowered the government to require new publications to deposit a registration fee of up to R40,000, which could be forfeit if the publication was banned.[26]

After lengthy discussions, Cape Town–based *South* launched an eastern Cape edition of the newspaper in 1991. The front page and a few inside pages were changed for the region, and there was to be a push to improve distribution and readership. The edition was to be produced in collaboration with Ecna: production and printing would remain in Cape Town but the layout would be done from page plans supplied by Ecna. The arrangement, however, proved unsustainable, and the edition was soon dropped: the logistics were too complex for two small organizations to sustain, insufficient resources were made available, and expected funding support failed to materialize.

Projects, Projects, Projects

From the beginning, the news agencies saw their purpose as being more than journalistic. East London's elnews constitution adopted on 14 June 1988, for example, listed the agency's objectives: first, "to gather and disseminate news on events and developments in the Border region"; second, "to assist disadvantaged communities to bring their concerns to the attention of a broader audience, through the established media and otherwise"; and third, "to undertake training projects to raise the level of media skills in disadvantaged communities."[27]

The basis for a trainee journalist program was laid when a young student, Chris Mabuya, approached elnews in 1986 asking for assistance. Mabuya had been asked by the national student newspaper, *Saspu National,* to be their correspondent in the Border area. Elnews agreed to help him with his stories, and in time he was taken on as a "trainee journalist." Pen, Ana, and later Veritas, followed suit, but initially the training was informal and on the job. Intermittent workshops were conducted in various media-related skills, but the objectives were still pursued in an ad hoc manner.

The course became more formalized beginning in 1991. With funding support, a full-time trainer was employed, and trainees were more carefully selected. They attended classes in Grahamstown for three months. Emphasis was placed on intensive coaching in news-writing skills and practical assignments, but the recruits also were allowed to attend lectures offered by Rhodes University's journalism department. Thereafter, they worked for three months in the Ecna agencies and were then attached to the *Sowetan, City Press,* and *New Nation* for another three months. "Compared to previous years, the course was a vast improvement. The trainees left with a pretty solid grounding in the basics, as well as a lot of practical experience."[28]

The period of classroom study in later years was extended to six months, and more sections were added, including radio, photography, and desktop publishing technology. A specially devised language development component was also seen as essential if people from disadvantaged backgrounds were to be equipped for a journalism career. The success of the training model could be seen in various ways: in one year, for example, 160 applications had to be processed to select four trainees, and other organizations commissioned Ecna to train prospective journalists on their behalf. Media organizations were generally very eager to accept trainees for attachment and often ended up offering them employment. Ecna files show that over the years about 75 percent of trainees went on to work in the media.[29]

The other side of training came to be known as community media development, which was essentially informal and only as needed before the establishment of the Ecna central office in Grahamstown. Ecna became involved in one previously established project soon after the office was organized in 1990.

Student groups for some years had run a newspaper in the city called *Ilizwe Lase Rhini* (Voice of Grahamstown). The onset of the emergency had made it impossible to continue publication, and a decision was taken to change the focus to a community media-training program. Nothing much happened, however, until Ecna arrived and was able to take over the project and its funding. At that stage, it seemed possible to restart the *Voice*, and an edition of the newspaper appeared at the end of the year.[30] Attempts to set up the *Voice* independently of Ecna continued for some years but never fully succeeded. With funding from Standard Bank, for example, special editions of the newspaper were published during the Grahamstown Festival of the Arts, an intensive and enjoyable practical training exercise from which the trainee journalists benefited as much as those involved in the *Voice* itself.[31]

Ecna conducted training workshops on request from a range of organizations, from the ANC to Radio Transkei and the Red Cross. A major focus was support for community newspapers, of which there were several in the eastern Cape. For instance, there was the *Nemato Voice*, set up in Port Alfred by an Ecna trainee. With ongoing support from the agencies, this newspaper was published regularly for more than a year.[32]

Ecna also organized a Media and Democracy Festival in Grahamstown in 1992 in conjunction with Idasa, the Institute for a Democratic Alternative in South Africa. More than 200 delegates attended a program that combined panel discussions and speeches with training sessions in practical skills.[33] Early in 1994, a partnership developed between Ecna and the Independent Development Trust (IDT). Initially, the IDT asked Ecna to arrange a national workshop for community newspapers to consider issues of common concern. As a result, the IDT began to play a role in supporting community newspapers in various innovative ways.[34] Ecna's community media work increasingly focussed on community newspapers, and training was hived off in a separate organization in 1997 under the name Development News Agency.

Community media training occupied an important place in "the struggle" in South Africa, and Ecna's efforts need to be seen in this context. The intention was to improve community members' capacity to express their concerns. Projects came and went, and a lot of work was done, but it is still unclear how much lasting benefit they brought.

There were projects other than those focusing on training. A DTP-based (desktop publishing) production house, for example, was set up under the name the Cutting Edge in the hopes it would provide a service to community groups and generate additional income for Ecna.[35] Although a great deal of work was done, it did not become profitable and eventually had to be closed. In 1993 special funding allowed Ecna to run an investigative journalism project for six months. Several important stories were broken as a result, including a major scam by district surgeons, disclosures that murdered Cradock activist Matthew Goniwe was a key figure in the ANC underground, and the involvement of Ciskei officials in fomenting violence in Port Elizabeth.[36]

Conclusion

Ecna developed out of a peculiar set of circumstances—heightened political conflict coupled with the particularly hostile media landscape prevailing in the region—in the early to mid-1980s. But the growth of alternative titles in other centers provided both a market and an example to the journalists that set up the eastern Cape agencies. They survived the extremely difficult and repressive atmosphere of the late eighties and were able to pool resources and set themselves on a path to growth when the de Klerk government began to liberalize South Africa's political culture in the early nineties. These were years of growth and diversification, with Ecna active in a number of more or less interrelated fields—journalism, production, training, and community media development. Today Ecna concentrates on its journalism.

The media landscape provided Ecna with a growing market in national mainstream media and eventually even the regional news media. This commercial base enabled Ecna to survive, whereas most of the independent weeklies have closed down. As subsidies dried up, Ecna slimmed down, shedding staff and various projects. But it has remained an organization focused on its core competency—reporting the eastern Cape.

Ecna was able to offer a unique and different perspective on regional news, and there's no doubt that in the thousands of stories published with an Ecna tag there were many that would not have otherwise seen the light of day. In that sense, Ecna contributed significantly to a new mediated representation of the eastern Cape. As the mainstream media shifted its news values to accommodate changing political circumstances, this contribution became less dramatic, but East Cape News Agencies has remained a spunky, independent voice in this region of South Africa.

Notes

1. *Daily Dispatch*, 29 March 1985.
2. G. Farr to C. Plasket, 22 July 1986.

3. M. Loewe, statement to the Truth and Reconciliation Commission, 17 May 1996.

4. Phila Ngqumba, interview by author, March 1998.

5. Elnews quarterly report, May to July 1986. Originals of elnews and Ecna reports and meetings can be found in the Ecna offices in Grahamstown.

6. In court papers defending their detention, police gave their reporting as the reason. In all other cases where journalists were detained, as far as is known, either no reasons were given or other pretexts were sought.

7. M. Loewe, statement to the Truth and Reconciliation Commission, 17 May 1996.

8. Elnews, second quarterly report, August–December 1986.

9. Mike Loewe statement to the TRC, 17 May 1996, and various Ecna reports.

10. *Government Gazette* no. 11342, 10 June 1988.

11. Ecna, minutes of meeting, 14 June 1988.

12. F. Krüger, "Word Wars: South African Media under the Emergency" (M.A. thesis, City University, London, 1989), 66–68.

13. *Guardian*, 29 July 1988.

14. Ecna, minutes of meeting, April 1989.

15. Ecna, minutes of meeting, 15 March 1990.

16. Ecna, end-of-year report, 1991.

17. Ecna, annual report, 1991/92.

18. Ecna, annual reports, 1991–1993.

19. Ecna, annual report, 1992/93.

20. Ecna, general outline, 20 February 1990.

21. Ecna, group editor's report to working committee, 14 March 1991.

22. Ecna, minutes of Ecna Group discussions at *Argus* workshop, 3 October 1991.

23. Ecna, end-of-year report, 1992.

24. Ecna, annual report, 1991/92.

25. Ecna, annual report, 1993/94.

26. Ecna, minutes of meeting, 23 April 1988.

27. Elnews constitution.

28. Ecna, annual report, 1991/92.

29. Ecna, annual report, 1993/94.

30. Ecna, end-of-year report, 1990.

31. Ecna, annual report, 1992/93.

32. Ecna, annual report, 1993/94.
33. Ecna, annual report, 1992/93.
34. Group Editor's Report, 6 June 1994.
35. Ecna, annual report, 1992/93.
36. Ecna, annual report, 1993/94.

7

Grassroots

From Washing Lines to Utopia

Ineke van Kessel

The revival of popular protest in the first half of the 1980s, with the emergence of hundreds of new community and youth organizations, was also marked by a proliferation of new mass media. The sophisticated use of media in addressing both internal and international audiences was one of the distinct characteristics of this last generation of resistance against apartheid. *Grassroots*, a publication aimed at a Coloured and African readership in the Cape Peninsula, was a pioneering effort to forge a new genre of local community newspapers.[1] *Grassroots* formed part of the new alternative media that sprang up in the 1980s to contest the prevailing world view of the mainstream, white-controlled commercial newspapers.[2] While communication between mainstream newspapers and their publics is largely a one-way street, community newspapers aspired to interact with their readership and to help shape, rather than only report, events.

The commercial press was seen as upholder of the status quo, while nonprofit community media regarded themselves as part of the movement for political and social change. Launched in 1980, *Grassroots* became a model for local publications. University towns in particular proved fertile ground for the planting of alternative newspapers and pamphlets. Many ventures were short lived, but *Grassroots* lasted a decade before it finally ceased publication in 1990.

Inspiration for the community newspapers was derived from experiments with popular mobilization in Latin America, from Leninist classics, and from the ANC. Faithful to Lenin's prescription for a newspaper as an organizing tool, producing a newspaper was not seen as a goal in itself but as a means to an end. *Grassroots* staff members were known as organizers— "news organizer" rather than "journalist" was the job title for the person in charge of news gathering and editing. The newspaper's ambitions were summed up in the acronym POEM: Popularize, Organize, Educate, and Mobilize.[3]

A tabloid with a five-week cycle of publication, *Grassroots* aimed to "articulate the views and aspirations of communities and workers."[4] The frequency of five weeks rather than a month was a tactic used to avoid falling within the legal definition of a newspaper, and therefore *Grassroots* was not required to register and pay a security deposit of R40,000. In almost every issue, a bold headline exposing a scandalous deed by the government or celebrating a heroic victory by the people was featured under its bright red masthead: "They'll Starve Us to Death," exclaimed a story about a rise in the bread price. "Afdakkies to Stay," assured an article that explained how "the people" had forced the town council to give in to their demand that residents be allowed to build corrugated iron extensions to their houses. On the inside pages, *Grassroots* offered advice on pensions, divorce, unemployment benefits, and the prevention of nappie rash; celebrated Charterist heroes of the 1950s; and detailed the everyday struggles of ordinary people. Prominent themes were housing and rent struggles, labor issues, and the costs of living.

Community issues were the lifeblood of the newspaper, but addressing community issues was not an end in itself. *Grassroots* strategists initially went for low-threshold campaigns, on the assumption that it is easier to involve people in local issues that carry a low risk and a high chance of success than to plunge them into "high politics." A demand for more washing lines in the courtyard was nonconfrontational and could attract support from women who would normally stay aloof from politics. Once the battle for more washing lines had been won, *Grassroots* would introduce the message that people can improve their own situation through organizational efforts. Building confidence in the benefits of collective action was important to counter a history of disempowerment. Among Coloured people in the Cape it was widely believed that while Africans had a history of organized resistance, Coloured people lacked the confidence to stand together: "Kleurlinge kan nie saamstaam nie" (Coloureds cannot stand together).

As an organizing tool, *Grassroots* set itself the long-term goal of engaging local organizations in the struggle against the South African state. Bread-and-butter issues were a means to an end, stepping-stones in a process of mobilization against racial and class oppression. The *Grassroots* staff did not perceive themselves primarily as journalists. Notions like objectivity and separation of news and comment belonged to the realm of the "bourgeois" liberal press, which served the interests of the ruling class. *Grassroots* "organisers" were media workers with an unashamedly propaganda mission. While the commercial press presumably anesthetized its readership with "sex, sin, and soccer," the community media meant to conscientize their readers and to encourage them to promote change through collective action.

Grassroots defined its constituency as "the oppressed and exploited majority," a phrase that refers to the African, Coloured, and Indian population. Although these population groups could all be considered oppressed, they were differentially affected by apartheid legislation. The use of the term *community* suggests a certain homogeneity and cohesiveness. In fact, the "community" that *Grassroots* meant to serve is one of the least homogeneous of South Africa. In terms of organizing and mobilizing people, the composition of the western Cape population posed obvious problems.

The Western Cape: A Fragmented "Community"

In apartheid terms, the western Cape was to be the unofficial "homeland" of the Coloured people. The introduction of the Coloured Labour Preference Policy in the mid-1950s aimed at reducing the size of the African population. Under this policy, which was only abolished in 1984, employers were obliged to give preference to Coloured labor. African workers could only be hired if no Coloureds were available. Africans were therefore relegated to the most poorly paid and unskilled jobs. As Cape Town was destined to be a "white" city, its Coloured and African inhabitants were forcibly resettled on the uninviting sandy plains of the Cape Flats, and the multiracial heart of the city, District Six, was destroyed. The Group Areas Act, designed to purge the white-designated cities of their black inhabitants, caused enormous social and psychological dislocation. The social fabric that held District Six together disintegrated when its inhabitants were scattered over the Cape Flats, where persistent high unemployment went hand in hand with a high crime rate. For the Cape Coloured people, the Group Areas Act was perhaps the most hated piece of apartheid legislation.

One consequence of the Coloured Labour Preference Policy was the lack of opportunities for African advancement. Most African workers were unskilled or semiskilled, and many were migrants. Apart from the three established African townships of Langa, Nyanga, and Gugulethu, no housing was made available to Africans. Coloured people and African township residents with permits enjoyed secure residential rights. But most Africans in the western Cape were "illegals," who settled in sprawling squatter camps, continuously subjected to police raids and deportations to the Transkei and the Ciskei. While organizations in the African townships of the Transvaal could draw on a sizeable reservoir of professionals and an educated working-class leadership, the western Cape had only a limited potential for providing African leadership in trade unions, community organizations, and the umbrella structure of the United Democratic Front. The UDF western Cape was dominated by Coloureds —including many with university backgrounds— and some white intellectuals.

ANC traditions have generally been weak in the western Cape. The Coloured People's Congress, which represented the Coloureds in the Congress Alliance in the 1950s, was small in numbers and weak in organization, in contrast to the much more influential South African Indian Congress. A large part of the Coloured population kept aloof from politics. Social conservatism and the religious orthodoxy of the main Coloured church, the Nederduits Gereformeerde Sendingskerk, were more characteristic of large sections of the Coloured population than political radicalism or working-class consciousness. The Coloured Muslim population of the Cape also tended to be conservative. Radicals in both communities found outlets in the Trotskyite New Unity Movement and other smaller leftists movements. The African townships in the western Cape did have an ANC presence, which was to some extent carried over into sections of the trade union movement such as the African Food and Canning Workers' Union. But when young Coloured activists began "discovering" the ANC in the early 1980s, they were mostly discovering the ANC in exile rather than the ANC tradition that had survived in the townships.

The racial divide was not the only dividing line; the fracture pattern also ran along ideological, religious, linguistic, generational, and socioeconomic lines. Afrikaans is the language of the Coloured working class; Xhosa is most widely spoken in the African townships; English was the language of the anti-apartheid struggle and sections of the intellectual elite. The economy is dominated by light manufacturing, mainly textiles and food processing. Industrial strikes, a common phenomenon around Johannesburg and Durban, were a rare event in the western Cape. Most Coloured workers were organized in white-controlled "sweetheart" trade unions. A few radical black unions had emerged or reemerged in the late 1970s, but these had a mainly African membership.

In order to mount an effective opposition to the apartheid state, these divisions needed to be overcome. *Grassroots* had set itself the task of promoting the building of community-based organizations, raising political awareness and bridging the divide between Coloureds and Africans. What was to be done? Where to start?

Sources of Inspiration: Leninism, Charterism, Populism

The idea of launching a community newspaper in the Cape Town area was first mooted in May 1976, a month before the 16 June Soweto uprising, by a group of Coloured academics, professionals, businessmen, and community leaders who linked up with the Union of Black Journalists.[5] But the wave of repression that followed the Soweto revolt led them to conclude that a large-circulation, independent black newspaper was not a realistic project. Government restrictions, however, could be circumvented by launching a newspaper that was inexpensive, would not require registration, and could be circulated through a ready-made distribution channel provided by community organizations.

The repressive post-1976 years, when overt political activity was virtually impossible, forced activists into more reflective and strategizing sessions. This was also a period of ideological reorientation. The long suppressed tradition of Charterism, associated with the ANC, reemerged and began to supplant Black Consciousness as the dominant ideology of black resistance. Marxist analysis, which had gained prominence in the humanities and social science curricula at "liberal" English-language universities, became an essential part of the activist tool kit. Through activist networks, popular versions of Marxist and Leninist texts filtered first into the trade union movement and next into to the newly emerging community organizations, youth movements, and social service organizations set up to provide legal advice or other assistance. The notion of a newspaper as an organizing tool was derived from Lenin's famous book *What Is to Be Done?* and from an article in Lenin's newspaper, *Iskra*, entitled "Where to Begin."

Here Lenin described how the urban workers and the "common people" in Russia were ready for battle, but the intellectuals were not fulfilling their role: there was a lack of revolutionary organization and guidance. A newspaper was needed to give direction to the waves of protest and to give meaning to the struggles of the people. The newspaper would not only serve to instill a socialist consciousness in the workers but also broaden the horizon of revolutionaries immersed in parochial concerns. A newspaper was needed as a catalyst to link local organizations to the common cause—a revolutionary vanguard to direct workers and infuse them with a socialist consciousness: "The paper is not only a collective propagandist and collective agitator, but also a collective organiser."[6] Left to their own devices, workers would forsake their long-term socialist aspirations for short-term pay increases, and local organizations would not relate their struggles to broader political struggles.[7]

Reading these texts in the late 1970s, western Cape activist Johnny Issel argued that a newspaper could be a useful tool to get an organization started.[8] Workers in the western Cape were manifesting an unprecedented militancy with a wave of strikes and boycotts. Students involved in school boycotts were receptive to Marxist-Leninist recipes prescribing a student-worker alliance. Student-parent committees, formed in response to the school boycotts, took up other issues, such as rent increases. But there was no organization to channel all these struggles into one coordinated attack.[9] In early 1980, Issel, a former student at the University of the Western Cape, became the first full-time organizer at *Grassroots*. Because of a series of banning orders, Issel's public profile was not as prominent as that of some other western Cape activists. But throughout the 1980s he remained a key figure both at *Grassroots* and in the UDF.

The newspaper was launched in 1980 after an intensive process of consultation involving some fifty-four groups.[10] Initial plans to rely solely on volunteers had to be dropped. Without a core of paid staff, it would be impossible to sustain a regular publication. Some money to subsidize the new publication was obtained from local church funds, but most funding came from overseas donors, notably the World Association for Christian Communication (WACC) in London and the ICCO (Interchurch Organisation for Development Co-operation), an NGO run by Protestant churches in the Netherlands. It was expected that a takeoff subsidy would be sufficient to put *Grassroots* on its feet. After 1981, *Grassroots* expected to raise money from local sources.[11]

The funding request fitted well with the priorities of the new projects officer on ICCO's southern Africa desk. He had a network of contacts with the liberation movements of southern Africa, with whom he had worked in church and developmental projects. From a visit by Mac Maharaj, a member of the ANC executive and a prominent member of the South African Communist Party, ICCO learned in 1980 that the ANC backed the promotion of an above-ground, radical press inside South Africa. In a later conversation in 1982, Maharaj remarked that ANC people were involved in *Grassroots*. Most of the people in the *Grassroots* project, however, were unaware of this explicit ANC endorsement.

ICCO was to remain the project's most loyal funder. Initially, ICCO urged *Grassroots* to become self-sufficient but as resistance and repression escalated, funding alternative media became a regular part of antiapartheid funding channeled by NGOs to South Africa.[12] Advertising revenue and newspaper sales were never sufficient to cover the costs of publication. On average, two thirds of the costs were covered by ICCO, while the newspaper's own revenue accounted for one third. The first edition in 1980 had a print run of 5,000, and by 1982 circulation had increased to 20,000. Copies were sold for fifteen cents until 1984, when *Grassroots* apologized to readers for having to raise the cover price to twenty cents.

Western Cape activists deviated from Lenin's recipe in that they chose to set up a local newspaper rather than a nationwide newspaper. Recent experience in community organization had also shown that it was easier to organize people around concrete local issues like rents, bus fares, and labor conflicts. While the founders of *Grassroots* recognized the tactical advantages of mobilizing people around everyday grievances, they never lost sight of the long-term perspective: they were the ideologically trained vanguard called to lift community struggles to a higher political level. The link between local and national struggles was frequently emphasized: "Our local rent, electricity and factory floor struggles must not be an end in themselves. We must link our local problems with the oppression and exploitation of our people in this country and the struggle for change."[13]

Apart from Leninism, another source of inspiration was the ANC. Early issues of *Grassroots* had no overtly political profile —Marxist and ANC perspectives could not be exposed to public scrutiny at the time—but soon the newspaper would play a role in establishing Charterist hegemony in the western Cape. As the ANC "unbanned itself" in the course of the 1980s, ANC slogans and leaders figured more prominently in its columns. For the Marxists on the *Grassroots* project, one central question was the extent to which the Freedom Charter entailed a socialist program. An editorial in 1985 stating that the Freedom Charter was the *minimum* demand of the people caused much internal debate. As *Grassroots* organizer Saleem Badat later put it, "Implicit in this argument is that you see the Freedom Charter as the national democratic revolution. It lays the foundations for the next step, which is socialism. Because that was part of the *Grassroots* project—building working-class unity."[14] But this code language was only intelligible to the ideological vanguard. Debates were limited to the circle of initiates and did not spill over into the newspaper columns.

Leninist vanguardism, emphasizing the role of a political elite, stands in stark contrast to another source of inspiration behind *Grassroots*—the participatory and egalitarian ethos of the 1980s. Everybody ought to be involved in everything. The ideal operation was represented by the Electricity Petition Campaign. A committee was formed in 1981 by some Coloured working-class residents in Mitchell's Plain, who wanted to have the due date of electricity bills changed to the end of the month, when workers were paid. Initially the campaign was spearheaded by this Electricity Petition Committee, but the victory was presented as a "people's victory" with "the people" taking the initiative themselves: "The campaign reached its peak when 200 Mitchell's Plain residents—the people themselves

—marched on [Cape Town's] Civic Centre to present City Council with a memorandum containing their demands and a petition signed by 7,500." The story of "People Power from the Plain," in which "People" is consistently capitalized, explains that this campaign had produced a "new concept of leadership." Should the petition to the city council be handed over by a delegation from Mitchell's Plain? "No! The People would be their own leaders. They would ALL go to Cape Town and hand in copies of the memorandum. . . . Before they boarded the buses it was decided not to have a spokesperson or persons. The People would speak for themselves. Each and every one was fully acquainted with the issues at stake. It didn't matter which individuals eventually spoke. The People were One."[15]

The emphasis on collective leadership and the rejection of specialization that would exclude the uninitiated is typical of this concept of democracy. *Grassroots* is not bothered by the question—To what extent is this manifestation of People Power actually representative of the residents of Mitchell's Plain? The 200 who demonstrated in the city hall are presented as "the people themselves," although they numbered perhaps 0.1 percent of the inhabitants of Mitchell's Plain. And the People were painted as uncompromising heroes, not to be intimidated by officials or security police. When a security policeman was spotted in the gallery during the discussion with the deputy town clerk, they objected to his presence: "Go! Go! Go!, the People thundered. And the security police, in the gallery and in the doorway, left."

The role of *Grassroots* in promoting organization was not limited to the coverage of these events. Half a dozen members of the Electricity Petition Committee came together to write the story and devise a cartoon, which was then submitted to the full committee for approval. The Sunday morning after *Grassroots* came out, Mitchell's Plain volunteers gathered as usual to sell the newspaper door to door. They had been briefed beforehand about the electricity issue so that they could draw people's attention to the story and invite them to a meeting. In this way, some 3,000 copies of *Grassroots* were sold, and 1,000 people attended the meeting.

Running a People's Newspaper

The central principle behind the *Grassroots* operation in the early 1980s was "the paramountcy of democracy"—not only in terms of the news content but also in terms of structure, organization, and the production. An elaborate process of deciding on news content, collecting, and writing stories was aimed at involving as many people as possible. The production and distribution of *Grassroots* was also calculated to enhance participation. This model of direct democracy was less efficient, but for many it was an important learning experience. At *Grassroots*, people learned how to run a democratic organization, "how to take minutes, how to put up your hand if you wanted to speak, how to chair a meeting. Without *Grassroots*, there would not have been such a wide range of organisations."[16]

All aspects of the *Grassroots* project were geared to maximize popular participation. The decision-making body was the General Body of *Grassroots*, which set out the major policy lines at an Annual General Meeting (AGM). It was composed of member organizations such as local community groups (the "civics"), trade unions, women's organizations, youth clubs, and so forth. Apart from determining policy, member organizations also took part in making the newspaper. Out of the General Body, subcommittees were formed for news gathering and production, distribution, fund-raising, and workshops to train people in media skills. In content, format, and methods of

Grassroots was one of the flagships of the left-wing community press.

Grassroots made excellent use of political cartoons to communicate the meaning of resistance.

Learn and Teach
NUMBER 3 1982.

20c
excl G.S.T.

Say goodbye to skin lightening creams
The man who makes time stand still
The boxer who never gives up.

Learn and Teach, Learning Roots, and the *Reader,* launched by the Grassroots project, were informal educational supplements that circulated in many black townships.

LEARNING
Roots
The Student Paper
Vol 2 No. 2 April 1986

ON THE ROAD TO STUDENT POWER!

Spirit of Unity at NECC Conference

DELEGATES from all over the country converged on Durban on March 28 and 29 for the second National Education Conference.

They came in buses and kombi's, from the smallest dorp and town, to discuss ways of resolving the education crisis in South Africa.

After two days of serious discussion, the conference resolved that:
- Students should return to school at the beginning of the new term;
- The Congress of South African Students (COSAS) should be un-banned;
- May Day (May 1) should be celebrated as a national holiday; and
- June 16, 17 and 18 should be a national stayaway.

From the start it was not certain whether the conference would get off the ground. A week before the conference was due to start at the Natal University, the offices of two lecturers were burnt.

Fearing further violence, the university administration refused permission for the conference to be held on the campus.

The organisers of the conference tried to get another venue, but without success. On the eve of the conference, no venue was finalised.

INKATHA ATTACK

As delegates moved into Durban, they were attacked by a large "vigilante" group, believed to be Inkatha members who were bussed into Durban.

The "vigilantes" walked the streets of Durban, armed with spears and knobkierries. During one of these attacks, some of the delegates sustained minor injuries and had to be taken to hospital.

A House-wer, carrying delegates, pulled into the campus grounds with all its windows smashed in. In a confrontation the Saturday morning, two of the "vigilantes" were killed.

A delegation, made up of members of the National Education Crisis Committee and Dr Beyers Naude, general secretary of the South African Council of Churches, went to speak to the police at their head-quarters in Durban. They expressed their concern for the safety of the delegates of the conference.

On the Saturday all 1,400 delegates were gathered on the sportsfield of the University of Natal kombis. The atmosphere was tense as an attack by the "vigi-

lantes" was expected at any time. In spite of the danger, the delegates and organisers felt that the conference should go ahead.

The conference was moved to another venue. By this time the spirit among the delegates was very high and they started singing freedom songs.

The hall that was to be used was only available for the Saturday evening. The conference was started at midnight and delegates sat in discussions until 5 a.m.

The open session of the conference was addressed by Dr Beyers Naude and Zwelakhe Sisulu, the editor of a Johannesburg newspaper. The press and observers were not allowed to attend the closed session where discussions were held and resolutions adopted.

The conference noted that demands made by the first conference in Johannesburg in December were not all met. Cosas remained banned, students and teachers were still detained, SRC's were not recognised, school buildings were unrepaired and troops were still in the townships.

The conference felt that the students had played a major role in challenging the state. The students' demands were just and legitimate.

The conference felt that parents, teachers and members of the community also have a role to play in developing a People's Education. This people's education should reflect the needs and aspirations of all the people of South Africa. This form of education could only be achieved by

broadening the student struggle. All sectors of the community had to be involved.

Students should go back to the schools and re-organise themselves. They should also link up and build strong community organisations.

By building strong organisations they could develop to a stage where the power would be with the people and not the minority government.

The conference also resolved to take up broader community issues, like rents.

At the end of the conference the delegates, tired after meeting through the night, had to make the long journey back home with the task of building People's Education for People's Power.

★ See page 4

Worker and student unity at the launching of the Congress of South African Trade Unions (COSATU) on March 23. The launch was attended by over 5000 people.

December Demands still not met

THE NECC conference was the second national conference on education held in the last few months.

The first conference was called by the Soweto Parents Crisis Committee (SPCC) in December and brought together almost 800 delegates and observers from throughout the country.

At this conference, students, parents, teachers and members of community and other organisations gave the Government until the end of March to meet a number of demands.

It was decided that the second national conference would be held at the end of March so that people could decide what action they must take.

The boycott was suspended for that period and the demands included:
- that troops withdraw from the townships;
- that Cosas is unbanned;
- that the state of emergency be lifted;
- that all students and other detainees be released unconditionally;
- that harassment of teachers st stop;
- that students be allowed to form SRC's and organise at their schools.

Despite promises from the government, only one demand has been partially met. - The state of Emergency has been formally lifted, although it is effectively operating in many areas. The other demands have been ignored by the government.

★★★★★★★

Forward to Education Charter

"WHAT problems do you have at school? What would you like to learn about? What kinds of teachers would you like?"

These are some of the questions that students will be asking for the Education Charter Campaign.

The Campaign, launched by Azaso in 1982, aims to collect education demands from students, parents, teachers and workers, all over South Africa.

Students believe that the campaign has taken on a new significance with the present struggle for a People's Education. They have set June 16, 1986 as a deadline for drawing up the Education Charter, based on demands collected.

The Education Charter will be very important in helping us build a new education for a free South Africa" a student said. "We would like to appeal to all students to start discussing their demands in education."

In Cape Town, a regional committee has been set up, with representatives from ASAC, WECSO, Joint SRC's, Pupils Awareness and Action Group, NUSAS, Azaso and YCS.

The committee will be holding a workshop to discuss the campaign on April 19. Students interested in attending can contact Cameron (ph. 417-1722). All are welcome.

★★★★★★★

Learning Roots

THE

READER

A STEP TO BETTER ENGLISH

NO DUMPING

We love Alex

CLEAN IT!

ALEX HAS BEEN SAVED...

AND THERE IS MORE IN THE READER

The Reader   2 July, 1981   Page 1

The Reader

production, *Grassroots* wanted to distinguish itself from the commercial newspapers, where "decisions are taken at the top and filtered to the bottom. At *Grassroots*, all decisions are taken democratically by all the community people and organisations involved."[17]

At the first news-gathering session, all worker and community organizations were invited to send representatives, so that "the new issue can grow from the very grassroots of the people." A list of stories for the next issue was discussed and approved, and the assignments parceled out among the participants. Three weeks were available to complete the stories, with another meeting in between to check on progress. If organizations were involved, the stories were submitted for their approval. On printing day, about fifty youth volunteers assembled for the folding and collating of the newspaper. Distribution was also seen as an important link in the operation. Civics were the most important outlet: civic activists used *Grassroots* to go house-to-house and to gain entry into houses by starting a discussion about local issues. But from this point, the media activists lost sight of the operation. "While *Grassroots* is reaching the communities, we still do not know whether the paper is being read."[18]

This way of producing a newspaper ensured wide participation, but it was still difficult to give everybody an active part and there was a considerable degree of uniformity in terms of content. "Our stories follow the same formula," noted the news-gathering committee in 1982: "a victory through community action is usually the thrust of the story. . . . we do not address ourselves to problems experienced and mistakes made by organisations. Instead we glorify their actions."[19] By 1983 the AGM was still grappling with the overemphasis on victory. It was resolved that news content be more critical and educative, and stimulate debate. There were also calls for more diversity, to broaden coverage to include sports and culture and other items with popular appeal.

It never happened. In common with many other alternative newspapers, *Grassroots* did not develop an editorial formula to deal with conflicts and crises *within* progressive organizations. Since the commercial press was blasted as divisive, the "People's Press" ought to project an image of "unity of the oppressed." Nonracialism was proclaimed as the accepted norm rather than as a learning process. Throughout the 1980s community organizations in the western Cape struggled with the gap between norm and practice. Civic organizations in the Coloured areas and in the African townships each maintained their own umbrella structures after plans for a merger had failed. Coloured and African youth organizations did merge in the Cape Youth Congress but only after a difficult start marked by bitter confrontations.

Within the Cape Housing Action Committee (CAHAC), the umbrella structure for the Coloured civics, for example, an ideological battle raged between the Charterist majority, which opted for the popular-front politics of the UDF, and left-wing civics, who argued that the interests of the working class could not be ensured in an alliance that included both workers' organizations and "the bosses and their agents."[20] The left-wing critics, claiming to represent the interests of worker-tenants, objected to CAHAC's "middle class" position on home ownership, which held that workers should also have the right to buy their houses. Within the Western Cape Civic Association, the umbrella for civics in the African townships, opposition mounted to the heavy-handed leadership of squatter leader Johnson Nxobongwana, who was regarded as corrupt and in collusion with the police in the battle for control over the Crossroads squatter camp. The readers of *Grassroots* were completely left in the dark about these developments, which were crucial both for community organizations and for the wider arena of liberation politics.

Democracy Turning Democrazy

The newspaper did carry a discussion on the balance between democracy and efficiency, which originated in the civic movement. This debate provides some interesting insights in shifting notions of democracy, evolving from an emphasis on mass participation, with everybody being involved in everything, to a phase where specialization set in and the emphasis shifted to concepts of mandates and accountability.

A good example of the first phase is the story of how the people of Mitchell's Plain delivered their petition demanding a change in the due date for the electricity bill to the town clerk of the Cape Town city council. In this phase, the message driven home is the importance of organization, of standing together to achieve common goals. Conditions can be changed if people are properly organized. Repenting scabs regret that they have broken workers' unity and are welcomed to join the ranks of striking workers. The emphasis is on the importance of winnable goals and standing by your organization. Hence the focus on the battle for washing lines and more flexible rules for the payment of electricity bills. These were modest but achievable goals. Rent struggles proved more difficult to sustain, at least in Coloured areas. While people might be willing to take the risk of having their electricity cut off for a while, they were less likely to risk eviction.

Much space was devoted to explaining the general notions of democratic organization: how the elected officials are at all times responsible to the general membership, voting procedures, a quorum, motions and resolutions, making minutes, and so forth. Democracy meant, above all, popular participation. But when participation became an end in itself, it began to have a paralyzing effect on popular action.

At the *Grassroots* AGM in 1983 it was decided that the newspaper could also present the views of individuals, which were expressed independently of organizations. This led to a debate in the pages of *Grassroots* on the nature of democracy. "Are we all going democrazy?" asked an anonymous contributor to *Grassroots* in May 1983:

> Democracy is running wild within our organisations. It is sweeping like a wind through all our subcommittees, leaving us all exhausted. When we are about to make a decision, it rears its head and reminds us that to be democratic, we have to ensure that more people participate in making that decision. We cannot decide and act upon that decision without further consultation. All members of our organisation must be party to the discussion. . . . But what does it matter? The struggle is still long. We have all the time in the world. Don't we?[21]

Responding to this issue in the next edition, *Grassroots* basically stuck to the notion of general involvement, avoiding a division of labor. The characteristics of democratic organization were contrasted with the way in which a factory is run. Interestingly, the defining feature that makes a factory "undemocratic" is not related to the boss being the owner of the means of production but to the managers, who monopolize knowledge and insight. The managers are the "thinkers," who plan, organize, and control the workers. Otherwise, the work is divided into specialized jobs, which means the workers only get familiar with their particular role in the production process: "People at the top of the factory have important information. They do not share it with the workers. In any organisation to make the right decisions all the information is needed." By contrast, in democratic organizations "all members are workers and managers. Everyone has a say in planning, organising and controlling what happens. All share in the *thinking* and doing. Everyone in the organisation makes the rules. . . . People learn as much as possible about running the whole organisation. People who have special information share it with others. People are helped to get the skills so that they can do the whole job."[22]

The focus on "the People" and "the Community" is illustrative of a populist approach in which class divisions are obscured in order to underline the joint effort for the common good. This "unity of the oppressed" is a constant theme in UDF discourse. But *Grassroots* staff were somewhat uneasy with this concept of a "community" newspaper. They not only aspired to promote popular struggles, they also made conscious efforts at building a workers' consciousness.

In a reappraisal of editorial policy in 1983—the year the UDF was launched—it was decided the time had come to adopt a more outspoken political profile. *Grassroots* organizer Leila Patel felt that the issue-oriented formula of the newspaper was getting out of touch with the now more politicized mood of "the People." The political content of the lessons of struggle needed to come out more clearly, "linking present struggles around rent, higher wages and so more directly to Apartheid and capitalism."[23] In the mind of the newspaper's core activists, the alternative media were important weapons in the battle for hegemony between two competing worldviews: the dominant view versus the People's view. "Dominant media is there to maintain the status quo and alternative media is linked to the struggle for a free and democratic South Africa." While the state and capital used the mass media to instill a false consciousness in people, the alternative media made them aware that their troubles were caused not by fate but by apartheid and capitalism. The government, the bosses, and the mainstream media conspired in their propaganda, based on "lies and distortion," to make people accept the status quo. Counterpropaganda by people's organizations, on the other hand, was based on the truth and aimed to expose the injustices of the system.[24]

From Coloured Identity to Workers' Consciousness

Two elements occupied a central place in attempts by *Grassroots* to construct a counterhegemony—nonracialism in the tradition of the ANC and socialism. In addressing its readers, *Grassroots* used both a popular and a class appeal. Building working-class unity required instilling a workers' consciousness that would also serve to overcome the division between African and Coloured workers. If workers would identify with their position as workers in a capitalist economy, then the divisive legacy of apartheid could be overcome.

A graphic example of how *Grassroots* tried to guide its readers from Coloured consciousness to workers' consciousness is a comic strip featuring Mrs. Williams, a middle-aged clothing worker from Manenberg, as the heroine. Mrs. Williams is first introduced in the August 1984 issue, where she is watching Labour Party leader Allen Hendrickse giving his election talk on television. She is marveling how wonderful it is that "we Coloureds are getting the vote at last," until a UDF activist knocks on the door. The visitor explains that the new constitution, which extended voting rights to Coloureds and Indians but excluded the African majority, will only benefit a handful of sell-outs, while more hardship and oppression are in store for the majority of the people. Rents and prices will go up to pay for the newly privileged Coloured and Indian members of Parliament; the Group Areas Act will remain intact; Coloured sons will be conscripted into the army to be sent to the border in order to defend apartheid; Africans will become more vulnerable to deportation to the homelands. At the end of part one, Mrs. Williams has decided not to vote in the tricameral elections.

Half a year later we find Mrs. Williams at her workplace, where the boss is giving her hell because she is fifteen minutes late. She is late because she stopped on the way to buy a *Grassroots* "with this 'Freedom Charter' thing in it." During the coffee break, an elderly African cleaner explains the origins of and the ideas behind the Freedom Charter. From a marginal nonperson, the old man suddenly becomes a fountain of wisdom, which he derives from his participation in the campaign in the 1950s to draw up the Freedom Charter. Bright pictures of the workers' paradise of Cuba appear in the strip while the old man relates that employment is not a privilege but a right: "in countries where workers make the laws, everybody has a job." At the end of the story, while the boss again yells at her for exceeding the break, Mrs. Williams has truly imbibed a proletarian consciousness. She is pondering a bright future, when "we'll make the laws one day, we'll control the factories. And your days of rudeness and bossing will be over."[25] This is a rather sudden conversion from Coloured compliance to worker militancy: it is doubtful whether a real-life Mrs. Williams from Manenberg could identify with the comic strip heroine.

The history of *Grassroots* itself provides a clear illustration of the problems encountered in attempts at bridging the divide between Coloureds and Africans. *Grassroots* had originated as a "Coloured" initiative without the active involvement of Africans from the townships. It never became solidly rooted in the townships, where it was perceived as a "Coloured paper." With assistance from *Grassroots*, some African UDF activists produced a newsletter in Xhosa, but this irregular publication, *Township News*, also did not have much impact. Some progress was made when *Grassroots* employed an African "township organiser," but both women hired to fill this position found it very difficult to involve township people in the production of *Grassroots*. Apart from the newspaper's image problem as a "Coloured" newspaper, media were apparently not a priority for African activists who relied more on word of mouth to organize meetings, boycotts, or demonstrations. Township activists did not believe that the newspaper was of much benefit to them.

Conversely, *Grassroots* lost touch with much of its Coloured constituency when the newspaper became overtly political and more militant. After the launch of the UDF in 1983, *Grassroots* gradually became a mouthpiece of the front. Organizations that had not affiliated to the UDF fell out of favor and were totally ignored in the newspaper. From the very beginning of *Grassroots*, coverage of local organizations had been limited to those in the Charterist fold. Organizations in the Black Consciousness tradition and the ultraleft movements peculiar to the western Cape had not been involved in the *Grassroots* project and were therefore completely disregarded in the newspaper's columns.

Grassroots was also a tool in the persistent factionalism, caused by ideological differences and personality clashes, that plagued the Charterist movement in the western Cape. *Grassroots* was perceived as "Johnny Issel's paper": if one did not belong to the Isselite faction, one had no access to the newspaper. Thus Women's Front, a UDF affiliate based in the African townships, was completely ignored by *Grassroots*, which only featured the rival, more sophisticated United Women's Organisation. From 1983 the cold shoulder was extended to progressive unions like the General Workers' Union, which had decided against affiliation to the UDF. Coverage of labor struggles was now largely limited to UDF affiliates, such as CLOWU (Clothing Workers' Union) and RAWU (Retail and Allied Workers' Union), even though these were not the leading organizations in the sphere of trade unions. The newspaper thus deviated from its original mission to serve as a platform for antiapartheid resistance in a wider sense, as was frankly admitted by the chair of the *Grassroots* board: "It was always the policy of *Grassroots* Publications to serve as a broad forum—to give expression to progressive political views prevailing in the oppressed community. It is clear that this policy was not implemented in practice."[26]

From 1985 the UDF leadership began to exercise direct control over editorial policy. Members of the UDF executive told the *Grassroots* staff what campaigns were planned and what coverage was required. At the time, this seemed a natural development. While *Grassroots* had initially promoted the growth of community organization, it could now serve as an organizing tool to help build the United Democratic Front. Community issues receded into the background as media were enlisted in the struggle for political power. With hindsight, however, several *Grassroots* activists identified this takeover by national politics as the fatal moment in the development of the community newspaper.[27] As popular mobilization escalated into a state of insurrection, *Grassroots* became increasingly irrelevant. It was of little use in the street battles fought by militant youth, and it was far too "political" for the taste of the average Coloured reader. In Coloured areas, *Grassroots* came to be seen as an "African paper."[28]

In trying to guide its readership from Coloured consciousness to both nonracialism and a workers' consciousness, no concessions were made to accommodate Coloured identity. While Afrikaans is the language of the Coloured working class, *Grassroots* activists preferred to use English as the unifying language of the struggle. However, in its language policy, *Grassroots* was not as puritanical as in its politics. The newspaper did include stories in Afrikaans and Xhosa, but this did not really solve the language problem. The newspaper's rural editions were largely published in Afrikaans, as was *Saamstaan*, a community newspaper in Oudtshoorn that was launched with the help of *Grassroots*. Although these were not large-circulation newspapers, the fact that some of the titles of the resistance press opted for the use of Afrikaans, usually branded as "the language of the oppressor," was symbolic. Coloured activists reappropriated Afrikaans as a medium in which to articulate an alternative worldview, thus denying white Afrikaners the exclusive ownership of *Die Taal*. While *Grassroots* proved fairly flexible on the language issue, which was discussed at length over the years, in other respects media activists refused to take account of the popular culture of their target readership.

Many at the time would have been adamant that there was no such thing as Coloured identity. While the struggle against the apartheid state was being waged, no cracks could be allowed in the facade of nonracialism. Only in the more open political climate of the early 1990s could ethnicity be recognized as a relevant issue on the agenda of progressive organizations and publications.

In this respect, *Grassroots* mirrored the UDF western Cape at large: it offered a political home for Coloured people but at the price of denying or effacing their cultural baggage. Interviewed in 1991, Jonathan de Vries, publicity secretary on the UDF's regional executive in the western Cape, made a critical assessment of this one-dimensional view of people and politics. "We were all Marxists, then. We were building the workers' revolution: we were going to perform the socialist transformation of South Africa. People were important only insofar as they were useful in this process. There was an enormous lack of humility. People were a means to an end."[29] Looking back, de Vries acknowledged that for working-class people it was difficult to be involved in the UDF. Many never came to meetings, because they were not fluent in English. They could not follow the latest political or ideological argument; they were not well versed in the activist jargon. Their days were filled with work, with considerable time spent on travel between home and work, on housework, looking after the children, and so on. "So the UDF became a playground for young people, many with a university education, many having cars so that they were mobile; they became the operators of the UDF."

In spite of this criticism, his overall judgment of the UDF remained positive. One of its most important achievements in the western Cape was that Coloureds were given a political home, "which they did not have before; it gave them a sense of belonging." But he was also acutely aware of the price that had to be paid for becoming part of mainstream resistance. In this political home, there was no place for Coloureds as such but only for "Blacks." To be accepted as "Black," Coloured identity had to be given up. Years later, de Vries still became emotional about the negation of Coloured identity, about the taboo that meant one could at best talk about "so-called coloureds" but not about "Coloureds."

> I am not a very coloured Coloured. I have moved away from my background, I have travelled abroad, I make music with whites and Africans. But from this now somewhat more detached perspective, I do believe that there is "Coloured identity," and that the UDF should have tried to accommodate that identity, rather than denying it. But the liberation culture was an African culture; the songs were either military songs or church hymns. There was no incorporation of Coloured identity in the UDF. That could not even be discussed.

De Vries regretted that the UDF and *Grassroots* had not tapped the creativity of ordinary people but had rather sought to mold them into a unitary culture that would facilitate the imposition of a new hegemony. Coloured culture, he believed, requires a kind of carnival atmosphere. The military style alienated ordinary people.

Coloured identity, of course, is not shaped by carnivals only. Church and religion are other important ingredients. But the young Marxists at the helm of the UDF and *Grassroots* were not inclined to cater to the religious sentiments of their basically conservative, churchgoing constituency. They were building a secular movement: the youth were seen as taking the lead in breaking the stranglehold of the church. Although he had secured a job with a western Cape church project in social work on the Cape Flats, Johnny Issel saw the churches as an obstacle rather than an ally: "The Youth . . . who have been bearing the frustrations within their denominational and ecumenical church youth groups very patiently for a long time broke with these and set out to build secular movements which would articulate, in no uncertain terms, there [*sic*] bottled-up political grievances."[30] Religious arguments and dignitaries were seen by the secular Marxists of *Grassroots* as most suited to mobilize the not-so-sophisticated Coloured people in the rural areas. The newspaper's rural editions and *Saamstaan* did indeed feature church leaders.

The Utopian Phase

Grassroots was instrumental in building a network of activists in the western Cape, thus laying the foundations for the UDF in this region. Nearly everybody who became involved in the UDF had at one time or another worked for *Grassroots*. While the newspaper was important in forging a "community of activists," the activists themselves tended to become intoxicated by an activist discourse that was distant from the discourse of ordinary people.

> When we became activists, with our workshops in Marxism-Leninism and Gramsci, we lost touch with ordinary people; they would only get confused. Debates were for activists. The activist subculture was too remote from ordinary middle class and working people. We became a subculture. We all looked like Che

Guevaras. . . . We were into reggae, not disco. We called each other comrades, we embraced African comrades. And we took for granted that non-racialism, socialism and so on were accepted by "the people."[31]

Paradoxically, while popular interest declined, the utopian vision of popular participation reached new heights. At the peak of the insurrectionary phase, in 1985 and 1986, *Grassroots* and the UDF propagated the concept of People's Power as the embodiment of democracy. Civic organizations were now portrayed as organs of People's Power, the embryonic form of future local government, not as community organizations lobbying for lower rents and a more convenient date to pay electricity fees. The participatory ideal behind the slogans of People's Power was that people would take control of their own lives: "they were going to run the schools, the factories, the towns, everything."[32]

People's Power had to manifest itself in all spheres of life, including the media: "The task of the People's Press is to challenge the power of the ruling class media, to minimize its influence and eventually to take over state media and commercial newspapers, and use their institutions to serve the interests of the people."[33] The ambition of media activists was no longer limited to providing an alternative worldview to the prevailing orthodoxy in the mainstream press. They were now going to supplant these bastions of the old order and establish a new hegemony. By now, *Grassroots* made it quite clear that this promised land could only materialize in a socialist order.

The Soviet Union, Cuba, Mozambique, Nicaragua, and Libya were paraded as models of people's power. The *Grassroots* ideal of popular democracy was quite remote from the traditional ideals of liberal democracy, with its emphasis on fundamental individual rights such as freedom of speech. Not pluralism but participation was considered the paramount principle of democracy.

While propagating workers' control over the economy, *Grassroots* had in reality become quite distant from the progressive trade union movement in the Cape. Before the launch of the UDF, the unions had participated in the newspaper and their victories featured prominently in its pages. But the unions kept their distance from "populist movements" such as the UDF, wary of being hijacked into campaigns over which they had no control. When leading progressive unions such as the General Workers' Union and the Food and Canning Workers' Union decided against affiliating with the UDF, they fell out of favor with *Grassroots*. The union's priority was to build strong unions controlled by the workers, and to work toward a national trade union federation. Union leaders were skeptical of radical student activists whose agenda was insurrection and revolution. Radical adventurism would put the hard-won gains of the young unions at risk. The largely African membership, acutely aware of their vulnerable position in the western Cape, was suspicious of student activists, who showed little understanding of the problems that shaped the lives of migrants and squatters.

Activists tended to mistake activists' consciousness for popular consciousness. While they aspired to build a working-class culture as part of the counterhegemonic project, more often than not they constructed a particular youth culture that posed as class culture. One graphic example of activist youth culture being equated with "People's culture" can be found in one of the 1985 issues of *Grassroots* that dealt with People's Power. Here, graffiti and break dancing are portrayed as "a form of culture originated by the people themselves, understood by them and appreciated by them."[34] In other stories, the Soviet Union is held up as a model of "People's culture." This sounds oddly out of tune with a basically conservative Coloured working-class constituency. Some people on the *Grassroots* project, like news organizer Ryland Fisher, who had a background in journalism, favored a more popular formula in order to keep in touch with the readers. But these proposals were overruled by more puritanical activists. As Essa Moosa, chair of the *Grassroots* board, recalled, "It was difficult to reconcile the political aims with sports stories and horse racing. . . . Activists would criticise the 'gutter stories.' The activists won the day; in the end they were the only people reading the paper."[35]

During the period of heightened politicization in 1985–86, *Grassroots* lost touch with ordinary Coloured people of the Cape Flats. The generation gap widened. Militant youth had now taken over the struggle. The unemployed manned the barricades, while student leadership attempted to provide ideological guidance. Parents in Coloured areas often sided with their children in their unequal battles with the police. Mothers became infuriated when they saw police beating up their children and opened their doors for youth on the run. But it did not follow that they were turning in great numbers toward the ANC, let alone the Communist Party. As repression became harsher and resistance increasingly violent, many simply became scared and preferred to stay out of politics.

Grassroots's coverage of events in these years reflected the concerns of the UDF's largest constituency: the focus was on student struggles in high schools and tertiary institutions. *Grassroots* came out strongly in support of school and exam boycotts. "You know why I am not going to write?" it quoted a boycotting student. "Because my friends were killed by the police and I cannot go on writing exams with a guilty conscience. I personally would feel like a traitor."[36] The argument that "all the organisations of the people" agreed that writing exams would be immoral under these conditions was unlikely to convince parents who had often gone to great lengths to give their children better educational opportunities than they themselves had enjoyed.

The ANC became increasingly prominent on the pages of

Grassroots. Popularizing the ANC was the natural thing to do for young Coloured activists who wanted to demonstrate their loyalty to their newfound political home. But *Grassroots* was losing touch with the community it was supposedly serving. News organizer Ryland Fisher reflected later that the activist frame of mind had become quite remote from the popular mood among ordinary Coloured people. "That heavy high profile political stuff put many people off. It became more an activist paper than a community paper. . . . You have to keep in mind the character of the western Cape; you have to start from people's consciousness. Activists assumed that ordinary people supported the ANC, violence, non-racialism, and all that."[37]

The Decline of Popular Participation

Like everything associated with the UDF, *Grassroots* became a target of police raids. In 1985, *Grassroots* offices were raided twice by the security police. Staff members were repeatedly detained. In October 1985 the building that housed *Grassroots* and various other progressive organizations was gutted by fire. The following year, an unknown gunman shot Veliswa Mhlawuli, *Grassroots* organizer for the African townships. She was severely injured and lost the use of her right eye.

Nevertheless, staff managed to continue publication. The usual total of eleven issues was produced in 1985. The print run was doubled from 20,000 to 40,000. Selling the newspaper had become too difficult and risky, and the previous group of volunteer distributors had moved on to more militant activities. So from the mid-1980s *Grassroots* was distributed free. The overseas funders no longer insisted on financial self-sustainability. Producing the newspaper had become a goal in itself, an act of defiance in the midst of escalating repression. But the *Grassroots* staff could no longer rely on a network of organizations to help produce and distribute the newspaper. The year 1985–86 was judged at the time to be the most difficult year in the newspaper's history. Member organizations had to be reminded that building "the People's Press was not only the responsibility of the already overburdened staff."[38]

With the declaration of a national state of emergency in June 1986 (a partial state of emergency was imposed in July 1985), *Grassroots* could no longer continue as an above-ground operation. Staff members had to go into hiding, but by August 1986, *Grassroots* was on the streets again. Coordination and communication with the UDF leadership, however, became increasingly difficult. *Grassroots* workers were now largely on their own.

Activists at the beginning of the 1980s tended to interpret the newspaper's failure to politicize ordinary people as "false consciousness" instilled in them by the dominant forces in society. But with participation in the *Grassroots* project declining sharply toward the end of the 1980s, activists began questioning their own performance: "We need to question what is wrong with our ability to organise on a mass level and challenge our whole style of work. We need to channel our activists into organisations where the masses have always been based so that they can organise more effectively. Political activists have to keep in touch where the unpoliticised masses are at and not simply reject and be rejected by them."[39]

While student activists mobilized political protest in the western Cape to unprecedented heights in the 1980s, the wave of militancy eventually ran out of steam and crumbled under the weight of repression. The students had built many organizations, but the foundations were fragile. Students often graduated from community organizations to national politics, for example, or took up professional positions and left a vacuum behind.

Participation in *Grassroots* also declined because activists were drawn into various other kinds of UDF activity. In its early phase, the newspaper indeed functioned as a catalyst, but after 1983 the UDF provided more scope for political involvement. Both community organizations and *Grassroots* suffered from a brain drain into the UDF's umbrella structures. To some extent, *Grassroots* had fallen victim to its own success: the staff had assisted UDF member organizations in setting up their own newsletters, pamphlets, posters, and media workshops. By mid-1984 newsletters were being produced by fifteen civic associations, thirty branches of the Cape Youth Organisation, and nineteen branches of the United Women's Organisation.[40]

Another factor that inhibited participation was foreign funding: "We became dependent, taking funds for granted. Before, we used to do our own fund-raising for *Grassroots*. We had a big annual fair where all kinds of organisations could have activities."[41] Compared to many other alternative publications, *Grassroots* was fortunate in having a loyal funder who kept the financial lifeline going throughout the decade. One explanation for the newspaper's survival was the availability of funds to maintain a core of salaried staff. Running *Grassroots* with volunteers did not prove to be a viable option, but this decision may have contributed to a decline in popular support. As *Grassroots* was not financially dependent on its readership, activists could afford to take off toward utopia, leaving Mrs. Williams of Manenberg behind.

Under the state of emergency, most civic associations virtually collapsed. Youth organizations could more easily adapt to an underground existence, but they had lost interest in *Grassroots*. In view of the demise of these building blocks of People's Power, *Grassroots* reverted to its original goal of building community organizations while continuing to popularize the ANC. But the newspaper no longer managed to muster community involvement. "We had become a prisoner of the activists," acknowledged Fahdiel Manuel, the newspaper's last news organizer.[42] "Basically, we were producing papers because the funders wanted to see a paper being produced."

In its campaign against radical elements in the media, the government instituted new restrictions, including temporary closure and the threat of cutting off foreign funding. *Grassroots* and its sister magazine, *New Era*, which aspired to develop more profound theoretical insights, were closed down for three months in 1989.

Staffers at *Grassroots* recognized that the newspaper's overt political profile had alienated the more conservative readership in Coloured areas. So after the ANC was unbanned in early 1990, they began to explore new ways to revamp the newspaper. *Grassroots* suspended publication in August 1990, and a feasibility study suggested there was a potential market for the newspaper as a free sheet focusing on community issues and run on advertising revenue. Advertisers showed an interest, provided the new *Grassroots* would not be overly political and would have a regular cycle of publication.[43]

The staff, which now argued for professional journalism and commercial management, found that other activists were not as flexible in adjusting to the new realities of the 1990s. Distrust of privatization and commercialization dominated the ill-attended annual meeting in October 1991, which was called to discuss the newspaper's future. Going commercial and relying on professionalism was indeed a far cry from *Grassroots'* original mission, which called for it to be eventually taken over by the community organizations.[44] Efforts to transform the "struggle paper" into a commercial free sheet never took off, and in 1992 *Grassroots* ceased publication altogether.

The Legacy of Grassroots

Grassroots shared the fate of most of the alternative newspapers, which did not manage to evolve a new formula to survive in the new conditions. With overseas, antiapartheid funding drying up, most publications did not succeed in finding other ways to maintain production. Readers in the 1990s wanted a more varied diet—a diet that included entertainment and news other than political news. As the alternative newspapers closed down, new glossy popular magazines targeted at a black readership appeared on the newsstands.

On balance, did *Grassroots* meet its objectives? Did it indeed function as an organizing tool, building local organizations? Had the divide between Coloureds and Africans been narrowed? Had Coloured people found a new home in the ANC fold? Was the ruling hegemony effectively challenged?

The relationship between the press and political organization was not as clear cut as the Leninist recipe had promised. In the first stage of organization building, *Grassroots* proved a useful tool, providing activists with a foot in the door to engage residents in a discussion. But once organizations got on their feet, *Grassroots* was increasingly felt as a burden. Many organizations developed their own media—as *Grassroots* encouraged them to do by providing training workshops—and many activists accumulated an increasing number of positions and duties. As noted at the many *Grassroots* assessment and evaluation meetings, the newspaper was as strong as the organizations were. When the organizations collapsed in the second half of the 1980s, *Grassroots* operated in a vacuum. Cut off from its community links, the newspaper became the tool of a limited and increasingly introverted circle of militants.

The defining characteristic of democracy in *Grassroots*'s terms was popular participation, not pluralism. The overriding concern for unity made it problematic that the newspaper could really accommodate diversity and discussion. Ideally, stimulating debate was part of the newspaper's educative function. In practice, conformity prevailed in order not to be "divisive."

In *Grassroots*, as in many community organizations, the tone was set by intellectuals, leaving ordinary working people with a feeling of being excluded. Throughout the decade, letters to the editor complained about too much intellectual talk at *Grassroots* meetings: "'n onnodige rondgooi van groot woorde. . . . Dit is meer soos 'n University lecture as 'n grassroots meeting. Hoekom praat hulle nie dat 'n mens kan verstaan nie?" (an unnecessary throwing around of big words. . . . It is more like a University lecture than a grassroots meeting. Why don't they speak in a way that people can understand?).[45]

The potential for realizing permanent mass participation in the political process proved an illusion. Short-term excitement did not result in sustained involvement. The new South Africa was not going to be built on People's Power, as activists had believed in the mid-1980s. Civics were revealed as weak structures that were not equipped to evolve into organs of local government. With hindsight, several key *Grassroots* activists shared the verdict of their critics—notably in the trade unions—that community organizations were basically organizations of activists. Issues that captured the imagination of activists were not necessarily the most pressing issues in the communities.

Nevertheless, *Grassroots* and the community organizations did provide an important learning experience for many people, student activists as well as a number of others with a working-class background. People learned to stand up for themselves, to speak up, to conduct meetings, to take things into their own hands.

The unbanning of the ANC had a demobilizing effect, pointedly underlining the limitations of the participatory ethos. When the ANC leadership returned home, ordinary folks thought that the struggle was over and now they could sit back while the leaders sorted out the problems. "Being involved in the struggle is not a natural thing for human beings," as *Grassroots* godfather Johnny Issel concluded.[46] Civic leader Willie Simmers in Mitchell's Plain expressed a similar sentiment: "In

Coloured areas, people wait for the 'New South Africa' to come along. They don't realise that they have to build it."[47]

How did *Grassroots*, and the UDF western Cape as a whole, fare in their attempt at bridging the divide between Africans and Coloureds by forging a common identity, either as "the oppressed" or as "workers"?

The UDF was more successful in vertical integration than in horizontal integration. Local activists became effectively linked to national organizations and nationwide campaigns. But contacts between African, Coloured, and white affiliates in the western Cape region remained limited. This is not to say that nothing was achieved. For example, working for *Grassroots* brought Coloured activists for the first time into the African townships. Folding *Grassroots* provided a meeting point for African and Coloured youth: here Coloured youngsters were initiated in the liberation culture of *toyi-toyi* dancing and freedom songs. But overall, the UDF western Cape had been dominated by Coloureds. When the ANC was set up in the western Cape, Africans seized upon it as "their" organization.

The first ANC executive elected at the regional conference in 1990 was strongly dominated by Africans. The role of whites in the ANC proved less contentious than the old African-Coloured divide. When Nelson Mandela addressed the next regional conference, in 1991, he berated local ANC members for having voted an executive into office which was heavily dominated by Africans. This would create the wrong impression that the ANC was an organization for Africans only. In spite of Mandela's efforts to make the regional ANC executive more representative of the western Cape's population, Congress here fared worse than anticipated in the 1994 elections. With the help of Coloured voters, the National Party achieved its one and only election victory in the provincial elections in the western Cape.

Grassroots, along with other media, certainly contributed to popularizing the ANC in the Coloured areas. While the ANC had been unmentionable at the beginning of the decade, toward the end of the 1980s ANC symbols and slogans had become commonplace. By "unbanning itself" before the legal lifting of the ban, the ANC could boast popular legitimacy. But *Grassroots* was not effective as an organizing tool across the racial divide, and probably it could not have been. A large part of the African population, notably those in the squatter camps, were illiterate and beyond the reach of newspapers. Africans in the townships were generally poorly educated, and educational standards lagged behind those in the Coloured schools. To be effective as an organizing tool, a newspaper needs to address a more or less homogeneous constituency.

Not only did the racial divide prove to be a barrier but so also were the generational, educational, linguistic, and socioeconomic divides. Forging a "community of the oppressed" proved an unrealistic ambition. *Grassroots* did, however, play a key role in forging a community of young, educated activists, which subsequently became the backbone of the UDF western Cape.

Did *Grassroots*, as part of the arsenal of alternative newspapers, challenge the dominant ideologies and help construct a new hegemony? Especially in its early years, *Grassroots*'s attempts to give "a voice to the voiceless" was an important innovation in the alternative press. But by choosing to remain an orthodox "struggle paper," *Grassroots* preserved its ideological purity only to miss the opportunity to develop a more popular appeal. The ideologues kept a firm grip on the newspaper, preventing activists with a more practical mind and greater journalistic skill from implementing the stated objective—"to start from where the people are." Whether it is false consciousness or human nature, after a long working day many ordinary folk preferred to be distracted by the capitalist seductions of the TV series *Dallas* than be educated about the workers' paradise in Mozambique.

Part of the legacy of *Grassroots*, such as the utopian concepts of People's Power and the blind adoration of socialist models outside South Africa, belong to the past, to the political culture of the 1980s. In style and content, *Grassroots* was so much the product of a particular youth culture that it could hardly have made a lasting imprint on the worldview of a broad section of people in the western Cape. Other elements of the inheritance, however, have survived the demise of the alternative press. In a more pragmatic form, ideals of popular participation have outlasted the utopian images of People's Power and continue to inspire a new breed of community media: the community radio stations of the 1990s.

Notes

1. This chapter is based on a case study from my Ph.D. dissertation, "'Beyond Our Wildest Dreams': The United Democratic Front and the Transformation of South Africa." A book version has been published in 2000 by the University of Virginia Press in cooperation with the University of Natal Press. Sources used for this case study include the newspaper itself, extensive correspondence, minutes, annual reports, and other material held by the main funder of *Grassroots*, ICCO in the Netherlands, interviews with activists who worked for *Grassroots* as staff members or volunteers, and interviews with activists in various community organizations in and around Cape Town. The interviews were conducted in 1991. I am grateful to *Grassroots* and ICCO for their generous cooperation and hospitality.

2. Keyan Tomaselli and P. Eric Louw, eds., *The Alternative Press in South Africa* (London: James Currey; Bellville: Anthropos, 1991).

3. Don Pinnock, "Popularise, Educate, and Mobilise: Culture and Communication in the 1980s," in Tomaselli and Louw, *Alternative Press*, 133–54.

4. *Grassroots* internal assessment paper, cited by Shaun Johnson, "Resistance in Print I: *Grassroots* and Alternative Publishing, 1980–1984," in Tomaselli and Louw, *Alternative Press*, 193.

5. In 1990 an editorial board was formed that included seven people who had been involved from the start of the project: Jakes

Gerwel, lecturer at the University of the Western Cape and chairman of the Community Action Trust, who subsequently became the vice-chancellor of UWC and a prominent member of the ANC; the reverend Moses Moletsane, a priest in the African township of Langa; Dr. Ramsey Karelse, a psychiatrist; Essa Moosa, an attorney; James Matthews, former executive member of the Union of Black Journalists (UBJ), writer, and poet; Qayoum Sayed, printer and publisher; Rashid Seria, journalist and ex-UBJ. In addition, three new people were included on the board: Dr. Allan Boesak, chaplain at UWC; Aneez Salie, journalist and chairman of the Writers Association of South Africa (WASA), the successor organization to the UBJ; Moegsien Williams, journalist, secretary of the WASA executive, and later to become editor of *South*. The editorial board also acted as a board of trustees. Once the newspaper was on its feet, the board resigned to make place for a central committee in which the participating organizations were represented.

6. W. I. Lenin, "Where to Begin," *Collected Works* (Moscow: Progress Publishers, 1977), 5:22.

7. W. I. Lenin, "What Is to Be Done? Burning Questions of Our Movement," in *Collected Works*, 5:375.

8. Johnny Issel, interview by author, 16 October 1991; Johnny Issel, "Setting up *Grassroots:* Background, Aims, and Process," paper presented at the conference A Century of the Resistance Press in South Africa, University of the Western Cape, 6–7 June 1991.

9. The buoyant mood of the time is well captured in Devan Pillay, "Trade Unions and Alliance Politics in Cape Town, 1979–1985" (Ph.D. diss., University of Essex, 1989); see also Wilmot G. James and Mary Simons, eds., *The Angry Divide: Social and Economic History of the Western Cape* (Cape Town: David Philip, 1989).

10. Issel interview.

11. ICCO project notes, February 1981.

12. *Grassroots* was not the only publication funded from the Netherlands. ICCO also provided financial support to the *SASPU Newsletter* and *Ukusa* and later to *South. Saamstaan,* the rural offshoot of *Grassroots,* was funded by the Vastenaktie, a Catholic NGO in the Netherlands. Toward the end of the decade, the European Community set up a fairly substantial program of financial support for the alternative press in South Africa, which benefited newspapers like *New Nation, Vrye Weekblad* and *South*.

13. Kathy Lowe, *Opening Eyes and Ears: New Connections for Christian Communication* (Geneva: World Council of Churches, 1983), 94.

14. Saleem Badat, *Grassroots* organizer 1983–86, interview by author, 2 October 1991.

15. *Grassroots*, June 1981.

16. Rehana Rossouw, *Grassroots* volunteer worker, interview by author, 11 October 1991.

17. *Grassroots*, March 1982.

18. Ibid.

19. *Grassroots* Newsgathering Committee report for AGM, March 1982.

20. Statement by the Manenberg Civic Association, Parkwood Tenants Association, and BBSK Residents' Association, n.d. [1983].

21. *Grassroots*, May 1983.

22. *Grassroots*, June 1983; emphasis in original.

23. Leila Patel, "The Way Forward," *Grassroots* AGM, 1983.

24. Ibid.

25. *Grassroots*, August 1984 and February 1985.

26. Chairperson's address, *Grassroots* AGM, 27 April 1985.

27. Fahdiel Manuel, *Grassroots* organizer 1988–91, interview by author, Amsterdam, 15 July 1991; Rossouw interview.

28. Willie Simmers, civic activist in Mitchell's Plain, interview by author, 8 October 1991.

29. Jonathan de Vries, publicity secretary Regional Executive UDF Western Cape 1983–1985, interview by author, Johannesburg, 12 November 1991.

30. Issel, "Setting up Grassroots."

31. Rossouw interview.

32. Badat interview.

33. Saleem Badat, "Building the People's Press Is Also Building People's Power," *Grassroots* AGM 1986.

34. *Grassroots*, March 1985.

35. Essa Moosa, chairman of *Grassroots* board, interview by author, 22 October 1991.

36. *Grassroots*, November 1985.

37. Ryland Fisher, *Grassroots* news and production organizer 1984–87, interview by author, 2 October 1991.

38. *Grassroots* report, April 1985–March 1986.

39. Report of *Grassroots* annual general meeting 1988.

40. WACC evaluation report, October 1984.

41. Rossouw interview.

42. Fahdiel Manuel interview, 22 October 1991.

43. A readership survey conducted in 1988 for *South* came up with similar results. In Coloured areas like Mitchell's Plain, "politics" was low on the list of reader preferences. See P. Eric Louw, "Resistance in Print II: Developments in the Cape, 1985–1989: *Saamstaan, Grassroots,* and *South,*" in Tomaselli and Louw, *Alternative Press,* 210.

44. *Grassroots* internal assessment paper.

45. *Grassroots,* October 1982.

46. Issel interview.

47. Simmers interview.

8

"You Have the Right to Know"

South, 1987–1994

Mohamed Adhikari

South was an independent weekly newspaper launched in the western Cape during the most turbulent period in the history of apartheid South Africa. From late 1984 popular revolt and mass insurrection in black townships greeted the imposition of the tricameral parliamentary system on South Africa. As the crisis deepened and organized resistance escalated, the National Party government responded with brutal repression.

Successive states of emergency were proclaimed each year from July 1985 to clamp down on the extraparliamentary opposition. The emergency regulations armed the government with a number of authoritarian measures to block the free flow of information on politically sensitive issues and to muzzle dissenting voices, making the latter half of the 1980s the bleakest years in the annals of press freedom in South Africa.[1]

The founders of *South* recognized that this was an extremely difficult environment in which to launch any newspaper, let alone one with a radical antiapartheid agenda. The first issue of *South* pointed out, "We could not have come at a worse

327

time—with the Emergency, press curbs, economic recession and the closure of some newspapers." *South* nevertheless promised, "We'll keep the news flowing. . . . We are legally bound by the press curbs but we intend through creative and imaginative journalism to pursue the truth and uncover the facts."[2]

A Gap in the Media Market? The Origins of South

During the 1980s the newspaper market of the western Cape was monopolized by big business. Afrikaans-language newspapers such as *Die Burger* and *Rapport* supported the National Party while English-language newspapers such as the *Argus*, *Cape Times*, and *Sunday Times* practiced a high degree of self-censorship by complying with government curbs on the media and reporting only antiapartheid news safe enough not to attract retribution from the state.[3] The left criticized the English liberal press for its conservatism and for shirking its social responsibility. It was accused of shutting its eyes to the crisis facing South African society and instead anesthetizing readers with a diet of "sunshine journalism." Though critical of apartheid policies, the English liberal press was nevertheless seen as essentially supportive of the status quo of white privilege because its reporting generally ignored news of interest to blacks, employed very few black journalists, none of whom held senior positions, and was often hostile toward the resistance movement.[4]

South was the first left-wing commercial newspaper[5] to be published in the western Cape since the *Guardian* and *Torch* had been snuffed out in the repression of the early 1960s that followed the Sharpeville shootings. After a decade and a half of calm, the revolt of 1976 and the civil disturbances of 1980 and 1985–86 created what appeared to be a viable niche for a left-wing political newspaper in the media market of the western Cape. As the populist campaign of the United Democratic Front (UDF) gathered momentum in the mid-1980s, the western Cape generated enough antiapartheid news to justify a regional newspaper. As the number of community and youth organizations mushroomed in black residential areas in the region, so the demand for news about unrest and for radical political commentary seemed to grow. A glaring absence of news from black townships and rural areas appeared to be another weakness of the mainstream media that could be exploited.[6]

The possibility of establishing a mass-circulation weekly newspaper, one that would articulate the grievances and aspirations of the black working class of the western Cape and that would actively campaign for socioeconomic and political change in the country, was contemplated by journalists active in the antiapartheid movement from the latter part of the 1970s onward. Media activists, however, had doubts about the viability of a popular weekly newspaper of this sort because of a lack of capital with which to launch the venture, worries that the target market was too small to sustain it, and logistical problems with printing and distribution. The failure of other alternative newspapers such as *Voice*, *Eye*, and *Ukusa* seemed to confirm these fears. The banning of radical newspapers like the *Bulletin*, *World*, and *Pro Veritate* as well as the banning and detention of prominent black journalists served as further deterrents.[7]

The situation changed significantly with the formation of the UDF in August 1983 and the subsequent upsurge in popular protest. Localized, episodic protest gave way to sustained, organized, mass resistance from the mid-1980s onward. By this time the antiapartheid struggle in the western Cape had developed to a point where political activists increasingly regarded a mass circulation political newspaper to be necessary for propelling the democratic movement forward. It was felt that the democratic movement lacked an effective medium to communicate with its mass informal following and promote its vision of an alternative society. There was also a need to counter the biased and watered-down reporting of "struggle news" by the establishment press.[8]

Community publications such as *Grassroots* and *Saamstaan*, which had played an important role in resuscitating the protest movement in the western Cape, were of limited value by the mid-1980s. Their slow publishing cycle of five weeks and the restricted volume of news they could carry made them unsuitable for a populist political agenda. They focused narrowly on community issues and their penetration beyond the relatively circumscribed network of antiapartheid activists and areas of active political engagement was limited. Media activists also hoped that the establishment of a left-wing commercial newspaper would free them from dependence on donor funding.[9]

While the deteriorating political climate created the opportunity to publish an independent radical newspaper in the western Cape, it was the frustration of a handful of black journalists who worked for white-owned, mass-circulation newspapers in the region that provided the impetus for launching *South*. Black journalists in the western Cape had to contend with what they perceived to be an alienating work environment: they were employed by mainstream newspapers that reflected the concerns of the ruling white minority and promoted media strategies supportive of the status quo.[10] A prominent media activist commented, "The columns of these papers rarely highlight what is happening in the areas where we work, where we live, the businesses we run, the sport we play, the education of our children—except when these news items can be presented in a sensational or divisive manner or to ridicule our people."[11] These journalists also resented the racist practices of liberal English newspapers—such as carrying racially discriminatory advertising, publishing separate editions or special supplements aimed at black readers, and supporting segregated sport. Their opposition to economic and other sanctions against the South African state and the negative reporting about extraparliamentary opposition groups reinforced the perception that the English liberal press was "written by white journalists for a white public."[12]

Black journalists also had to put up with continued suppression of their reportage on politically sensitive issues such as civil unrest, trade union activity, police brutality, and black political opinion. An *Argus* editorial representative at the time noted, "Reporters were never directly told that they had to follow a certain line or could not report on certain things . . . [but] stories would be cut, buried downpage or simply spiked."[13] A more sinister example of news suppression was provided by an *Argus* reporter: "On the day when police announced a clamp-down on the coverage of unrest, my editor ordered two major feature articles—one on the views of black political organisations on the attempts of Afrikaans-speaking students to speak with the ANC, the other on clashes between white vigilante groups and black youths in a Cape Town working class suburb—be removed from the paper. They were replaced with a picture of Table Mountain and an article on penguins."[14]

The mid-1980s, then, were enormously frustrating times for black journalists, particularly those active in the anti-apartheid movement. Some found an outlet for their frustration in various forms of media and political activism.

The initiative for establishing *South* came from two such media activists, Rashid Seria, who became the first editor of the newspaper, and Moegsien Williams, who succeeded him in November 1988. Seria had eighteen years of experience as a journalist on newspapers such as the *Evening Post* in Port Elizabeth, the *Cape Times* and *Cape Herald* in Cape Town, and was working as a subeditor for the *Argus*. He had been instrumental in the establishment of the Cape Town branch of the Union of Black Journalists in 1976 and was a founding member of the Media Workers' Association of South Africa (MWASA), formed in 1980. He also served as treasurer to the United Democratic Front in the western Cape in 1983 and 1984. Williams had eight years of experience as a reporter with the *Argus* and the South African Broadcasting Corporation and was working as senior media officer for the University of the Western Cape before moving to *South*. He was active in the UDF and was an executive member of MWASA. Seria and Williams were also founders of *Grassroots* and were involved in the running of *Saamstaan*, a largely Afrikaans-language community newspaper based in Oudtshoorn.[15]

Seria, who for years had been mulling over the idea of establishing a left-wing commercial newspaper for the western Cape, saw a gap in the market when unrest flared up in the mid-1980s. With the resurgence of popular protest, the market appeared ripe for a new newspaper. After his release from an eighty-day spell in detention toward the end of 1985, Seria conducted a feasibility study with the help of Williams, the results of which were summarized in a document used to consult with key political leaders and progressive journalists about the possibility of starting a mass-circulation weekly.[16] Although these consultations took place throughout the country, Seria and Williams concentrated their efforts on the southwestern and eastern Cape as well as the Midlands and Karoo regions. As the name *South* suggests, they wanted to set up a newspaper that would be distributed throughout the southern half of the country. Encouraged by positive responses to their proposal as well as the success of the recently launched *New*

Nation and the *Weekly Mail,* Seria approached western Cape activist leader Allan Boesak to secure funding to start up *South*. Boesak used his personal contacts to obtain R450,000 for the project from the Interchurch Organization for Development Co-operation (ICCO), a nongovernmental organization sponsored by Dutch Protestant churches.[17]

A public company, South Press Services Limited, was constituted for the purposes of operating the newspaper. The majority of shares in South Press Services—those representing the capital donated by ICCO—were placed with the Ukwaziswa Trust, which consisted of prominent political and community leaders.[18] The trust was set up not only to administer the funding of the newspaper and to demonstrate to donors that *South* had solid political backing, but also to give the democratic movement a stake in the project and to make the newspaper accountable to the community, albeit symbolically. In addition, it was envisaged that the trust would provide the newspaper with a measure of protection should the government attempt to freeze the assets of South Press Services. A small amount of capital was also raised by making shares available to sympathetic individuals and organizations.[19] While *South* handled its own advertising, the printing and distribution was contracted out to the Argus company, since South Press Services did not have the resources to perform these functions.

The appearance of the first issue of *South*, on 19 March 1987, ranks as an important milestone in the history of protest journalism in the western Cape. *South* was unique because it was the only left-wing commercial newspaper in the region in the last decades of the apartheid era. *South* lifted media activism to a higher plane, moreover, by disseminating news about the democratic struggle in the western Cape more widely and more efficiently than other contemporary, left-wing community publications.

The cover of *South*'s 1988 annual report, which contains a representative sample of front pages appearing during the first year of publication.

Walking a Tightrope: South in the 1980s

In his first annual report on *South*—delivered at a public meeting attended by more than 300 people—Rashid Seria declared, "It is a tightrope that we walk. We are hammered on all sides."[20] Seria was referring to the buffeting the newspaper was receiving both from the government and left-wing activists and political groups. The government wanted to bully *South* into compliant reporting, while various constituencies within the antiapartheid movement expected the newspaper to perform a variety of functions that suited their particular political agendas. Having to operate in a hostile environment under exceptionally difficult circumstances, *South* all its life was engaged in a struggle for survival and in more senses than one found itself walking a tightrope.

The main objective of *South* in the words of its founders was "to articulate the needs and aspirations of the oppressed and exploited in the Cape and in so doing serve the interests of the working class people."[21] Its more immediate political goal was to provide the extraparliamentary protest movement, particularly the United Democratic Front—a loose federation of opposition groups inside South Africa launched in August 1983 and aligned with the banned African National Congress—with a voice and to keep the public abreast of news the apartheid government wanted to suppress. *South* also sought to challenge the monopolistic control of the media by the government and a few large corporations.[22]

The newspaper focused on news relating broadly to extraparliamentary politics and the injustices of apartheid in the western Cape. News emanating from progressive political bodies and the activities of community organizations formed part of its staple fare. *South* covered protest action ranging from boycotts, strikes, and mass marches to running street battles between youths and police and the bombing of apartheid targets such as police stations.

South ran feature articles and exposés on topics such as police brutality, township revolt, government corruption, and problems in education, housing, and social welfare. Issues of particular concern were workers' struggles, forced removals, the plight of detainees and the suffering of impoverished rural black communities in areas such as Worcester, Robertson, Ashton, De Doorns, and Swellendam. *South* monitored abuses of human rights and supported a wide range of left-wing political campaigns—including the Living Wage, Release Mandela, Unlock Apartheid Jails, Free the Children, Hands off the Press, and End the State of Emergency campaigns. The newspaper seldom reported news from outside the western Cape and carried virtually no international coverage. It did not attempt to provide conventional news coverage except for some social, community, and religious news. *South's* sports reporting was restricted to events and codes sanctioned by the South African Council of Sport (SACOS), which dominated internal resistance to segregated sport during the 1970s and 1980s.

South fiercely proclaimed that it was "the independent voice of the people of the Cape" and "free from vested interests and financial manipulation from any quarter."[23] The newspaper also asserted a nonsectarian political stance, claiming, "We will not be dictated to by any political party or organization."[24] Nevertheless, *South* was effectively the mouthpiece of the United Democratic Front in the western Cape and thus firmly within the camp of the ANC. This should come as no surprise as the newspaper was founded by UDF activists. Both the board of South Press Services, Ltd., and the Ukwaziswa Trust consisted of UDF stalwarts and the political philosophy of the newspaper was openly "Charterist." Moegsien Williams makes it clear he was under no illusion that "the raison d'être of *South* was to promote the ANC in the western Cape."[25] But

South was less partisan than one might have expected, partly because it saw its role as one of fostering unity within the broader antiapartheid movement. *South* avoided a formal relationship with the UDF and jealously guarded its editorial autonomy. It reported mainly on the UDF in part because the UDF dominated extraparliamentary protest in the western Cape.

South's relationship with the UDF was not without tension or antagonism. The newspaper regularly came under pressure from activists to report news in a particular way. Requests that certain issues be reported in a "responsible manner" were none too subtle attempts at influencing reporting or imposing a degree of censorship. Sometimes activists would go so far as to assert that *South* belonged to "the struggle" or to "the community" and that editors did not have the freedom to publish whatever they pleased. There were also occasions when activists tried to suppress specific stories—such as when a very senior clergyman tried to prevail upon *South* not to report on allegations of sodomy directed at one of the ministers under his jurisdiction. The evidence suggests that the editorial integrity of the newspaper was maintained in the face of such pressure.[26]

Another source of tension within the activist community was the feeling that *South* at times revealed sensitive information about strategy or individuals the government and its security police could use against the democratic movement. In the climate of anxiety and mistrust bred by the repression of the late 1980s, there were worries that alternative newspapers could be infiltrated by the security police and that reporters could be used to gather information about the underground movement. *South* reporters, for example, were barred from the funeral of an activist—a major event attended by a huge crowd of mourners—in the Coloured township of Bonteheuwel as a result of these tensions.[27]

From its fifth issue, *South* adopted the motto "You have the right to know" to signal its intention of challenging curbs on press freedom by reporting antiapartheid news that the mainstream newspapers did not dare publish.[28] Printing news that the National Party government was intent on suppressing called for courage and a caliber of brinkmanship that would continually test the limits of government tolerance. It was not always clear whether the apartheid state of the late 1980s had the political will to implement fully the curbs on the press it had arrogated for itself under the emergency regulations. Thus *South* walked a tightrope in deciding the limits to which it could test censorship laws without being banned.

Despite its determination to break with the compliant reporting of institutionalized journalism, Seria readily admits that *South*, like other left-wing newspapers, exercised a degree of self-censorship.[29] The survival of the newspaper depended on judicious evaluation of all political reporting. Indeed, for the first two years of its existence *South* employed two lawyers to scrutinize every issue for possible infringements of the law.[30] There were times, however, when the editor threw caution to the wind because he felt that political developments warranted defiance of the law.

At other times, risks were taken because the banning of the newspaper seemed imminent and it did not make sense for *South* to pull its punches. On one occasion, *South* drew international attention when the newspaper, in the face of categorical denials by the minister of police, produced proof that two boys held in detention were a mere fourteen years of age.[31] On another occasion, the celebration of Nelson Mandela's seventieth birthday in July 1988, Seria decided to print a poster of Mandela, an offense in terms of the Prisons Act of 1959. The Argus company, however, refused to print the poster and the center-page spread of this issue was left blank.[32] With the government increasingly on the defensive, by the latter half of

1989, Moegsien Williams felt he could afford to take a "publish and be damned" attitude and even dispensed with the precaution of having lawyers vet the newspaper.[33]

It was this "publish and be damned" stance that gave *South* its biggest scoop. In December 1989, *South* was the first newspaper to break the news that Mandela had been in talks with government officials since 1986. *South* reported that Mandela had drawn up a draft discussion document detailing his position and setting preconditions for engaging in negotiations for a political settlement. Williams explains that he sat on the document for three months before deciding to ignore the prohibition against publication placed on it by opposition political leaders, and Mandela himself, for fear of jeopardizing the talks.[34]

A key issue facing the management of *South* from the outset was exactly where to locate the newspaper within the market and how to position it politically. Seria and Williams thought of themselves as "populists" because they wanted to use popular content to reach as extensive a readership as possible. Besides making business sense this would allow them to communicate their political message widely and help to mobilize the masses against apartheid. Their position flowed from the conviction that the priority of *South* should be to serve the needs of the working classes rather than a particular political program.[35]

The populist approach initially came in for much criticism from sectors of the activist community, whose expectations of radical political content and of *South* serving particular political agendas had not been met. They argued that *South* needed to focus on the task of overthrowing apartheid. These critics, some of whom served on the trust and the board of directors, contended that "sensationalist" reporting on crime, coverage of horse racing, fashion, and rock music, and pictures of the Mardi Gras diminished the newspaper and did nothing to undermine apartheid. Others argued that the expectation of attracting a mass readership was unrealistic. Since *South* was unlikely ever to be commercially viable, it should be pressed into political service rather than pursue romantic notions of serving the masses.[36]

At the other end of the spectrum were those who criticized *South* for putting too much emphasis on politics and lacking subtlety in communicating its political message to a mass readership. Recalling his frustration at the newspaper "shoving politics down people's throats," Derek Carelse, art director at *South*, 1987–88, commented, "Every page was just politics, politics, politics. They did not know what interested the man in the street or how to touch people."[37]

The editorial staff of *South* was in an unenviable position because many of the demands made on the newspaper by activists were contradictory and ran contrary to journalistic ideals and sensibilities about what constituted sound professional practice. At the first annual report-back meeting, Seria wryly commented, "Some want it [*South*] to be a propaganda sheet, others want it to be a *Grassroots*-type tool; others want it to be another serious political magazine; still others want it to be a *Cape Herald*–type sex-and-crime sheet."[38]

After a drawn out debate, not without acrimony between the editorial staff and members of the board and the trust, the need to boost flagging circulation figures and maximize revenues prevailed and the populists won the argument. The initial news agenda of focusing mainly on politics resulted in disappointingly low circulation—this approach appealed only to a relatively confined segment of highly politicized and better-educated readers. A survey conducted in 1987 confirmed that the newspaper's projected working-class constituency preferred popular fare to political content.[39] Editorial staff continuously grappled with the thankless task of developing a content mix that would fulfill their professional ideals, satisfy the expectations of the activist community, and appeal to the newspaper's working-class target market. Throughout its existence, however, the imperative of economic survival drove *South* to become increasingly populist in its approach.

The founders of *South* aimed to set up two projects to complement the newspaper. The first project, which never came to fruition, was to establish an alternative news agency to feed news about the western Cape to both local and international publications. Plans for combining with Press Trust in Natal, Veritas in the Eastern Cape, and *New Nation* and the *Weekly Mail* in the Transvaal to form the first national alternative news agency were shelved when the emergency regulations promulgated in June 1988 required news agencies to be registered.[40] Given the fractiousness within the alternative media stable, Williams doubts that such a project would have been able to get off the ground.[41]

The second project, to establish a program to train aspiring black journalists, met with significant success despite teething problems and operating erratically at times. A conspicuous shortage of trained black journalists and their token presence in the mainstream press prompted *South* management to implement the Vukani journalist training program at the beginning of 1987. The lack of trained staff was particularly acute for the alternative newspapers, where pay was low and working conditions demanding. *South* was presented with an opportunity when mainstream newspapers began cutting back on their in-house training programs to save costs. Besides allowing *South* to grow its own wood, as it were, having a training and development component to the newspaper project made it more attractive to funders.[42]

Between ten and fifteen cadets were enrolled each year for the twelve-month course, which was meant to consist of six months of classroom teaching and six months of practical training in the newsroom. Given the pressures under which *South* operated, it is not surprising that trainees, who earned a small monthly stipend, spent more time in the newsroom than in the classroom. Some cadets were employed by *South* after graduating while others were placed with alternative newspapers such as *Grassroots* and *Muslim Views*, and commercial newspapers like the *Star*, the *Sunday Times*, and the *Cape Times*.[43]

Being severely undercapitalized, *South* was run on a shoestring budget, its resources stretched to the limit. The premises were inadequate, equipment rudimentary, and the newspaper chronically short staffed. Despite salaries being approximately half the going market rate, exceptionally long hours were demanded of these journalists. Senior editorial staff earned a meager R1,500 to R2,000 a month, whereas more junior staffers earned in the region of R1,000 a month. Rehana Rossouw, who was working for the *Argus* at the time and joined *South* in 1989, relates that she had little option but to decline the initial offer in 1987 to work for the newspaper as she could not afford the two-thirds drop in salary this would have entailed.[44]

The lack of training and experience of junior staff also put greater pressure on senior staffers, who had to supervise their work, rewrite stories, and provide on-the-job training. Both Seria and Williams were to regret the naive belief that they would be able to "take a bunch of raw youngsters and turn them into great journalists in a matter of a few months."[45] Meeting the Thursday morning deadline for delivery of the newspaper to the printers was a perennial struggle. Staff were usually forced to work through the night on Wednesdays to meet the deadline. There were occasions when some members of the core production team of five or six individuals lived on the premises from Monday through Thursday to put the newspaper together.[46]

Intent on implementing the egalitarian values that informed the antiapartheid struggle, *South* management tried to run the newspaper along democratic lines and eliminate as far as possible the usual hierarchies of the workplace. On the one hand, there were high expectations among an intensely politicized staff regarding progressive employment practices and the quality of the newspaper they wanted produce. On the other hand, the pressure of getting the newspaper out on time every week and the financial stringency forced on management made for an extremely volatile working environment, especially during the first two years. There was always tension between colleagues and long, acrimonious meetings were regularly held to thrash out differences.[47] The core production and management team also endured considerable hardship to keep the newspaper alive. Both Seria and Williams attribute their resignations to the extreme pressures of the job, which took its toll on their health, their families, and their finances.[48]

Despite this stress, one of the great strengths of *South* lay in its ability to draw on a team of people who were committed to the antiapartheid struggle and who were prepared to make sacrifices for the newspaper. Working for *South* required commitment to journalism as a vocation and to media activism as an avenue for promoting social change. It required resourcefulness and provided exposure to a range of skills not usually available in conventional journalism. It is for these reasons that so many of the young, inexperienced staff that *South* attracted displayed a flair for the profession and went on to become journalists of repute.

The greatest threat faced by *South* during the 1980s was harassment from the state both direct and indirect. It is clear that the National Party government under P. W. Botha orchestrated a campaign to force the alternative press to tone down its news reports. The government preferred coercing alternative newspapers into compliance rather than shutting them down because it wanted to create an illusion for the outside world that press freedom existed in South Africa. The apartheid regime could not afford to be seen to be silencing the press. Government attitudes toward the alternative press were also tempered by the perception that newspapers like *South* were preaching to the converted and had minimal influence on the white electorate. The hard line against the alternative press had the added advantage of intimidating mainstream newspapers into toeing the line.[49]

The government's main strategy in persecuting the alternative press was to have Stoffel Botha,[50] minister of home affairs and communication, use his powers under the emergency regulations to harass these newspapers. Botha's first action against *South* was to ban three issues from 23 July to 6 August 1987 as undesirable on the grounds that they were helping to create a revolutionary climate and cultivating a positive image of the ANC and its guerrilla fighters. *South* won an important political and moral victory when it succeeded in having the Publications Appeal Board lift the banning orders.[51] Then in November 1987, *South* was issued with an official warning: a section of the emergency regulations accused the newspaper of publishing subversive propaganda and promoting the public images of the ANC and Pan-Africanist Congress. The emergency regulations empowered the minister to subject any newspaper to prepublication censorship by appointing an internal censor or banning it for a period of up to three months after a third such warning had been issued.[52]

At the end of March 1988, *South* received a second warning notice followed by a third warning notice in May that led to a three-month banning order. *South* was the second newspaper, after *New Nation*, to be banned in this way. Anticipating the banning order, *South* planned a special edition ahead of schedule for 9 May 1988, but it had to withdraw most of the 20,000 copies already printed when the banning order came through on the same day.[53] Nevertheless, the newspaper resumed publication after only five weeks because the emergency regulations expired on 10 June.[54] It would appear that the government used the banning order as an intimidatory tactic rather than as an attempt to close *South* permanently. Not only was the banning order imposed a month before the emergency was due to expire, but Stoffel Botha did not use his power to impose a further two-month banning order when the ongoing state of emergency (imposed every year throughout the country since June 1986) was immediately renewed in June 1988. A full three-month banning order might well have resulted in the permanent closure of *South*. The burden of continuing to pay salaries, rentals, and other overhead costs while being deprived of advertising and sales revenue would have required a major injection of new capital to keep the newspaper afloat.[55]

State harassment of this sort was extremely damaging to the newspaper as it took up much of management's time, involved it in costly litigation, and added greatly to the insecurity of the staff. Moegsien Williams estimates that as many as twenty-four court actions were brought against *South* by the government during the 1980s, and it faced seven separate charges simultaneously under the emergency regulations in early 1989. Ensnaring the newspaper in a web of legal regulation and wearing it down in a courtroom war of attrition seemed to be a deliberate strategy of Stoffel Botha, a lawyer by training.[56]

Because the newspaper was being run by seasoned activists, the publication of *South* was in part an act of defiance. Government harassment only served to strengthen their resolve to keep the newspaper alive. This defiance is captured in an open letter addressed to Stoffel Botha by the directors and trustees of South Press Services in response to his first warning notice: "Let us put it plainly. The deepest problem causing the violence in our country lies not with the press but with apartheid. . . . we are proud of our paper. We are committed to the truth. We are committed to the struggle and true peace and justice. We are committed to the people of South Africa.

This, we submit, is a noble cause and this cause will ultimately triumph."[57]

South was also subjected to a range of informal harassment tactics that involved ad hoc victimization by security police and shadowy operators within the state's security apparatus. Given the climate of violence during the emergency period, during which the security forces were allowed great latitude in dealing with dissidents, *South* was fair game for intimidation. *South*'s premises were often under surveillance and it was not unusual for the newspaper to find, for example, that its postal subscriptions had been tampered with or its trash cans inspected by "unidentified white men clearly not in the employ of the city council's refuse department," as Seria once put it.[58] Security police would regularly visit the newspaper's offices. Sometimes they would arrive in squads to search the premises. At other times they would drop by on more casual visits and intimidate staff by issuing threats, questioning those present, and nosing around to find incriminating evidence. On occasion security police visited the homes of staff when they were not there and harassed their families. Threatening phone calls were received and journalists were regularly followed and sometimes detained. In some instances journalists found their locks jammed with glue, their tires cut along the inside rim, or their wheel nuts loosened.[59]

The security police also succeeded in placing at least one informer on the staff of *South*. Gregory Flatt, employed occasionally as a photographer and darkroom assistant by *South* from September 1987 until his unmasking two years later, earned a salary of R500 a month as a police spy. For example, Flatt not only spied on *South* by copying computer files, he also used his cover to take incriminating photographs and video footage at political rallies and meetings.[60]

The attentions of security police often disrupted tight work schedules, and the knowledge that they were at personal risk caused a great deal of disquiet among staff. Although no one on *South*'s staff suffered serious injury, these terror tactics could not be dismissed. Journalists at other alternative newspapers paid dearly for their defiance of the apartheid order, and several publications, including *Grassroots*, suffered arson attacks on their offices.[61]

South's inability to sustain a circulation that would make it commercially viable, however, proved to be the ultimate undoing of the newspaper. Seria had initially considered a print run of 30,000 and hoped to increase circulation to 50,000 within a year and 70,000 within two years of publication—at which point, it was calculated, the newspaper would be financially independent. Recalling the success of the *Cape Herald*, a newspaper in the *Argus* stable targeting the Coloured community that achieved a circulation as high as 80,000 in the late 1960s and early 1970s, Seria's feasibility study fantasized that circulation could be built up to 120,000 copies a week within a few years.[62]

These heady projections proved to be wildly optimistic. Initially *South* managed to sell in the region of 15,000 copies. Circulation dropped steadily in the ensuing months to around 7,000.[63] Sales would occasionally spike upward when a flare-up in unrest or some extraordinary political development created greater demand for the newspaper. Figures between 7,000 and 10,000 became the norm for the 1980s. The highest circulation during the 1980s—just over 16,000—was achieved immediately after *South*'s banning order was lifted and the newspaper received a great deal of publicity.[64] In his first annual report, a sobered Seria admitted that he had overestimated the demand for a left-wing political newspaper in the western Cape.[65]

Low circulation and the highly competitive business environment of newspaper publishing condemned *South* to a continuous battle to raise advertising revenue. The newspaper had the added misfortune of having to live through the most protracted economic recession in South Africa's recent history.

That recession, which lasted from the beginning of 1989 to the first quarter of 1993, spanned the greater part of the newspaper's existence. Since *South* could not afford to employ more than one advertising representative, senior editorial staff periodically had to pitch in and help raise advertising revenue.[66] While the support of black business was crucial to the survival of the newspaper, *South* could count on the patronage of only a small number of progressive businessmen. The black business community tended to be rather conservative and were further deterred by *South*'s radicalism, while many did not consider the newspaper an attractive medium for advertising.[67] *South* also relied heavily on advertising from nongovernmental organizations, advertising features popularizing various political campaigns, and from a few large companies, notably Shell, willing to place ads in the newspaper as part of their social commitment to the local community.[68] Soliciting advertising on this basis rather than on business interest proved to be more difficult than initially anticipated.[69] That *South*'s circulation figures were not audited by the Audit Bureau of Circulation further deterred potential advertisers.

To make matters worse *South*'s relationship with the Argus company was an uneasy one. *South* was critical of the *Argus* newspaper, but it was dependent on the Argus company for printing and distribution. The only other press group capable of performing these functions, Nasionale Pers, had strong ties with the National Party. Rashid Seria reports that when he and Jakes Gerwel, who had brokered the meeting, discussed his feasibility study with Ton Vosloo, chairman of Nasionale Pers and well known for his "verligte" (liberal) views, Vosloo expressed personal sympathy but declined any involvement.[70]

The Argus company stipulated onerous conditions for entering into the agreement with South Press Services, demanding indemnities, refusing to grant credit, and insisting that *South* appoint its own staff to oversee the distribution. Seria believes that the *Argus* not only provided poor service but deliberately made life difficult for *South*. This was to be expected as the Argus group would have wanted to distance itself from the radicalism of *South* and was not likely to smooth the path for a competitor. From his current vantage point as editor of the *Argus*, Moegsien Williams comments that the poor service was probably not intentional but a reflection of inefficiencies within the Argus company. Seria, nonetheless, feels that their work with MWASA had deeply antagonized top management at the *Argus*—though there were many people at the *Argus* who had great sympathy for *South*'s cause.[71]

The Emperor's New Clothes: Coloured Identity at South

While its criticism of the mainstream press, as the accompanying cartoon suggests, was justified, *South* was also guilty of praising the naked emperor's clothes in its treatment of Coloured identity. The newspaper adopted the left-wing orthodoxy of the 1980s of rejecting Coloured identity and denying that it really existed except as a fiction created by white supremacists to divide and rule the black majority. In response to the overt racism of apartheid, the democratic movement embraced nonracism as a cornerstone of its philosophy. In terms of these values, any recognition of Coloured identity was regarded as a concession to apartheid thinking. Though blatantly at odds with reality, the denial of Coloured identity within the democratic movement was an understandable emotional response to apartheid ideology in left-wing circles in the last decade of apartheid rule.[72]

In its day-to-day affairs, *South* was run on a scrupulously nonracial basis. There was a deliberate attempt on the part of all involved to banish any recognition of race. The etiquette of political correctness of the time demanded nothing less. The

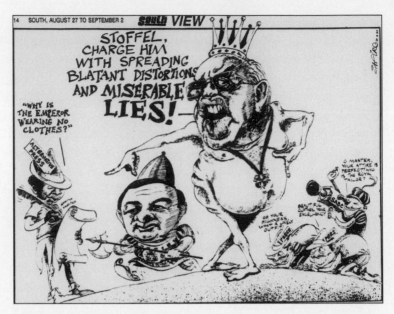

South used cartoons to criticize the mainstream media for abdicating their social responsibilities.

only concession to racial thinking was the preference given to the training and employment of promising African journalists.[73] It was the newspaper's policy to promote unity among the oppressed by using the term *black* for all those who were not designated white by the apartheid regime and to refrain from derogatory or divisive racial terminology. *South* studiously avoided using the word *coloured* throughout the 1980s. Coloured people were usually either subsumed under the generic term *black* or some wider categorization such as "the people," "the community" or "the oppressed."

Racial identities, however, were usually obvious from the context of the discussion. When the word *coloured* was used, it was usually to show up the unjust and arbitrary racial distinctions imposed by apartheid laws or to expose the racist thinking of the dominant white minority. The word was usually placed in quotation marks to signify its superficiality and to distance the newspaper from the values implicit in its use. Prefacing the word *coloured* with *so-called* was another strategy of dissociation from the racial implications of using the word. Sensitivity to the label *coloured* within the democratic movement in the western Cape is further demonstrated by *South* not placing other racial labels such as *white, Indian,* and *African* in quotation marks.[74]

The only time *South* addressed the issue of Coloured identity in the 1980s—and then only obliquely—was in an article entitled "Quisling or Realist?" based on an interview with Richard van der Ross, educator, politician, and former rector of the University of the Western Cape, when the freedom of Cape Town was about to be conferred upon him. Van der Ross, who represents moderate, middle-class political opinion within the Coloured community, made it clear that he embraced Coloured identity fully. In what appears to be a barb directed at the politically correct left, van der Ross asserted, "I have no hangups about being called coloured. Don't put the word coloured in inverted commas. As for those who speak of so-called coloured people, I've never understood what that means."[75]

Despite its nonracist, even antiracist, stance, *South* nevertheless consciously targeted the Coloured working class. This contradiction did not escape anyone associated with the newspaper. The matter was thoroughly debated and despite some misgivings *South* retained a largely racial focus. The targeting of a Coloured readership was justified on several counts. First, it made business sense because this was an area in which the founders of *South* had experience and was the one market segment that did not have a dedicated newspaper after the demise of the *Cape Herald* in 1986. Indeed, Derek Carelse claims that *South* deliberately copied the "look" of the *Cape Herald.*[76] Second, writing for a working-class African readership posed insurmountable problems of language, skills, and resources. And *South* did not wish to compete with Johannesburg's *New Nation* and *City Press*, which were being distributed in Cape Town. Perhaps most important was the recognition that working-class Coloureds tended to be racially exclusive and politically reactionary. The editors of *South* thus adopted the spreading of the message of nonracism to the Coloured community as part of its mission. With this went the hope that *South* would secure political support for the UDF and ANC within this constituency.[77]

Seria and Williams were encouraged to pursue this strategy because deep-rooted, exclusivist tendencies within the Coloured community were widely perceived to be breaking down in the 1980s. Continued unrest in both urban and rural areas of the western Cape from the mid-1980s—and the encouragement given to Coloured youth to join the ANC's guerrilla army, Umkhonto we Sizwe—convinced them that the Coloured community was shedding its insularity and was prepared to make common cause with Africans against apartheid.[78] While some observers may have perceived *South*'s antiracist position of denying the existence of Coloured identity as little more than a knee-jerk reaction to apartheid, the editors promoted this fiction as a pragmatic strategy necessary to the building of a nonracial society.[79]

There was much optimism at the time that *South* was indeed helping to foster a nonracial ethos in the western Cape. Moegsien Williams's favorite metaphor was to liken *South* to the footbridge spanning the railway line separating the Coloured housing estate of Manenberg from the African township of Nyanga. With the resurgence of Coloured exclusivity and growing tensions between Coloureds and Africans in the 1990s, Williams admits to having been naive in thinking that ingrained racial antipathies could so easily be overcome. He feels that it would have been much more productive to have faced up to the reality of racism within the Coloured community than to have swept it under the carpet as *South*, and the democratic movement as a whole, did in the 1980s.[80]

As the political climate changed in the early 1990s, it became more acceptable to use racial terms and ethnic labels in public discourse. The salience of Coloured identity could no longer be denied as organizations across the political spectrum started appealing to Coloured identity for support in the western Cape.[81] Even Nelson Mandela urged the ANC to recognize "coloured ethnicity" as a political reality.

South started shedding the facade of pretending that racial identity did not have an independent existence among black people from the latter half of 1991. The newspaper began to confront issues of Coloured exclusivism and racism toward other groups, particularly Africans.[82] These issues were especially topical in the run-up to the 1994 elections and the postmortem on the failure of the ANC to win the western Cape provincial election. The reality of racial tensions in the region was brought home forcefully to the newspaper when *South* staffers themselves fell victim to African antipathy toward Coloured people. In August 1993 angry protesters from the Pan-Africanist Student Organization turned on *South* journalists covering a march to demand the release of suspects arrested for the St. James Church massacre. When photographer Yunus Mohamed was felled by a brick thrown from the crowd, a protester was heard to shout "One settler down!" and reporter Ayesha Ismael was sworn at and taunted with being a "coloured settler."[83] Perhaps an appropriate chant for the marchers at this point would have been, "One coloured settler, one brick."

Although *South* throughout its existence steadfastly maintained a nonracist stance, it was unable to escape being seen by many as a Coloured newspaper. A double irony is that while it claimed to be nonracial and to be addressing the working class as a whole, *South* was perceived by workers to be a Coloured newspaper that actively targeted the Coloured component of the working class. *South* made no real attempt to reach the African working class and was virtually unknown to African readers except for a circumscribed circle of leading activists and members of the intelligentsia. The denial by a *South* editorial that "we don't fit the ethnic stereotypes. We're not a coloured newspaper—nor white nor black nor anything else" confirmed its sensitivity in this regard.[84] It is no coincidence that this denial came precisely at a time when *South* was reorganized to make the newspaper more commercially viable and became even more narrowly focused on the Coloured community.

The contradiction between maintaining a nonracial facade and targeting a Coloured readership is reflected in ambiguities over Coloured identity in the content of the newspaper. Although *South*'s political reporting was nonracial, its reporting on sports, social, church, and human interest news focused almost exclusively on the Coloured community.[85] The newspaper concentrated on news in Mitchells Plain, a sprawling, almost exclusively working-class set of Coloured housing estates of more than 400,000 people. A curious feature of *South*'s nonpolitical reporting in the 1980s, though, was its extensive coverage of the music scene in Cape Town's African townships. This anomaly is explained by the interest of *South*'s arts and entertainment reporters in jazz, and the best jazz at the time being played in the African townships. *South*'s music reporting was outstanding and it won the inaugural Carling Circle of Jazz Media Award for 1988.[86]

Contemplating the charade of nonracism in the democratic movement during the 1980s, *South* columnist Sylvia Vollenhoven commented, "I heard so much talk of nonracialism and saw so little evidence. . . . Through it all there has always been a part of me that felt like the child in the crowd who saw no new clothes, only a fat, foolish, naked emperor."[87]

"News for New Times": The Failed Transition to the 1990s

On 2 February 1990, F. W. de Klerk's epochal opening address to parliament launched South Africa on a four-year course of transition to democratic rule. The state of emergency was lifted, outlawed political organizations were unbanned, political prisoners were freed, and a wide range of political parties and organizations entered into negotiation to chart the transition to representative government. Despite continuing social unrest and political turmoil, it was clear that circumstances had changed fundamentally.

The management of *South* realized that if the newspaper was to survive, it would have to shift with the times and reposition itself in the media market. *South* needed to change from being an organ of struggle, dependent on donor money and justifying its existence on moral and political grounds, to a commercially viable concern. As the prospects for democracy improved, it became obvious that *South* could no longer be driven mainly by an antiapartheid agenda. Political change would also make donor money increasingly difficult to procure as funding shifted from financing political activism to redressing the legacy of apartheid.[88] Thus *South* embarked on a series of changes in the early 1990s to broaden its appeal—culminating in a revamped newspaper in February 1992 that bore the slogan "News for new times" to signal its fresh outlook.

A repositioning of *South* was already in evidence before de Klerk's watershed speech. The newspaper had depleted the seed money provided by ICCO and was forced to ask for more aid in early 1989. The newspaper had been operating with large deficits in the previous two years—incurring losses of R310,000 and R367,000 for the financial years ending February 1988 and February 1989, respectively.[89]

The first substantive move in the commercialization of *South* came in March 1989 under the editorship of Moegsien

Williams, who had taken over from Seria four months earlier. As part of the move to attract a wider readership, *South* introduced an entertainment insert called *Southside*, and the sport and society columns were beefed up. In an attempt to enhance the newspaper's attraction to younger readers, *South* introduced a hit parade, film reviews, and an advice column. It also started addressing issues around consumerism, law, health, and gender inequality in ways accessible to a popular readership. In late 1990, *South*'s layout was overhauled to give it a more commercial look, and the newspaper also started carrying some international news. From early 1991, *South* introduced a classified advertising section, regular columns on exercise and career advice, as well as trivia questions and puzzles to broaden its appeal. Meanwhile, the departure of Moegsien Williams, who accepted a post with the *Sowetan* from August 1991, resulted in the appointment of Guy Berger as editor. This set the stage for further change. Berger had a degree in journalism and a doctorate in politics from Rhodes University, and he was an ex–political prisoner who had lived in exile as a journalist in Britain since 1985.[90]

These changes, however, did little to improve the commercial viability of the newspaper. Circulation remained low and *South* continued to lose money. Losses escalated to more than R50,000 a month in the early 1990s, as salaries were increased without commensurate increases in profits.[91] The smalls advertising section remained stunted and advertising revenue from NGOs and the popularizing of political campaigns started drying up. Attempts were made to promote the newspaper with door-to-door selling campaigns. *South* also sponsored sports events and targeted groups such as black schoolteachers, staff and students at the University of the Western Cape and the Peninsula Technikon with mailing drives. There was little response to this publicity.

As the incidence of local unrest died down during the early

1990s and public attention shifted to the drama of negotiation for a political settlement, *South* started losing its traditional audience. Reader interest shifted from the western Cape to the violence on the Witwatersrand and in Natal. *South's* regional focus was a liability at a time when the key questions of the day related to national issues—such as whether a so-called third force in South Africa's shadowy security networks was operating to destabilize the country and whether the political center would be able to hold against extremists of both the right and left in the quest for a political compromise. The *Weekly Mail* and other national weeklies became more attractive weekend reading for *South's* primary constituency.

As the emergency regulations were lifted and the more tolerant atmosphere of the de Klerk government took hold, the establishment press started encroaching on the terrain of the alternative press, rendering the political reporting of newspapers like *South* less distinctive.[92] As early as July 1991, Gabu Tugwana, editor of *New Nation,* complained that "mainstream newspapers have moved more like opportunists or hawks. . . . our market has been sort of eaten."[93]

South's role as the voice of the democratic movement was greatly diminished as restrictions against the alternative press were lifted and opposition groups were allowed to operate without interference. *South's* intimate relationship with the western Cape UDF was broken when the unbanning of the ANC changed the nature of extraparliamentary opposition politics virtually overnight. Rehana Rossouw explained the impact of this transformation on the newspaper: "We virtually had carte blanche on their [western Cape UDF] news, and could attend any of their strategy and policy meetings. We also received copies of strategy and policy documents long before anyone else. It probably spoilt us somewhat, and [in the 1990s] we found ourselves out in the cold when South Africa became an international story and the 'in' we had was passed on to the *New York Times* and the *Guardian*."[94] Hopes in 1990 that *South* would somehow "ride the wave of the ANC" did not materialize.[95]

On the contrary, the relationship between *South* and the democratic movement, according to Rossouw, soured rapidly once free political activity was allowed and *South* started asking awkward questions. Antagonisms began building up with the release of Nelson Mandela in February 1990. Questions Rossouw asked about the inefficiency of arrangements around Mandela's appearance at the Grand Parade upon his release led to an abrupt termination of the interview and complaints lodged with the editor. The rapidity with which *South* became sidelined is demonstrated by the ANC "forgetting" to invite *South* to its press conference the day before the Groote Schuur talks of 1 May 1990. Rossouw laments that after 1990 "there were times that the journalists became extremely frustrated, disillusioned and frankly, completely mystified at this change of attitude to us."[96] *South*, with its limited reach, had become subordinate to national and even international agendas now being pursued by the democratic movement.

South's continued probing of problems within the democratic movement did little to endear it to the activist community, particularly those who had something to hide either as a result of inefficiency or corruption. The following year, for example, Rossouw wrote a three-part series on foreign funding that resulted in a "delegation" of activists arriving at *South*'s offices "close to midnight on the night before publication" demanding that the articles either be dropped or be vetted by them. Rossouw claims to have gathered much information on prominent activists who had siphoned off donor funding. Although it was not *South*'s intention to expose culprits but rather to discuss problems and issues of policy around foreign funding, there were individuals nervous enough to demand that the story be spiked.[97] The following year a story Rossouw was researching on the "lack of intelligence displayed by ANC intelligence" resulted in a similar "delegation" to *South*'s offices.[98]

South achieved its highest circulation ever—about 23,000—with the issue covering the release of Nelson Mandela, but sales had slumped again to between 6,000 and 7,000 by mid-1991. It was clear that desperate measures were needed to avert closure of the newspaper.[99] The management of *South* finally conceded that there was no longer a real market for a left-wing political newspaper in the western Cape. It was decided to reposition *South* as a popular, commercial newspaper and shed its image as an "ANC rag."[100]

The new *South*, relaunched on 27 February 1992, was expanded from twenty-four to forty pages with a more trendy commercial format and more color pictures. The sports and entertainment sections were once more revamped and a business section, cartoon strips, and an astrology column were introduced. The most significant change, however, was that *South* now tried to marry serious political reporting with sex and crime stories in an attempt to satisfy its traditional Coloured readership and appeal to Coloured working-class readers. Stories on drug abuse in schools, gang warfare, the lifestyles of gang leaders, family murders, child rape, sexual harassment in the workplace, and breast implants now jostled for space with the usual fare about worker militancy, apartheid exploitation, and popular protest.

The relaunch, however, was not a great success. Circulation remained low, fluctuating between 4,000 and 7,000 much of the time.[101] The attempt to distance the newspaper from the ANC did not last long as *South* soon "slipped back into struggle mode."[102] Ongoing problems of poor-quality printing, poor marketing and distribution, and perceptions by potential advertisers of *South* as being "too radical" continued to plague the newspaper.[103]

In a cost-saving maneuver that reflected the greater political

The first edition of the new *South*, relaunched on 27 February 1992, was expanded from twenty-four to forty pages. In response to the changing political climate of the 1990s, *South* tried to marry serious political reporting with racier sex and crime stories.

and ideological fluidity of the early 1990s, *South* in March 1993 entered into a contract with Nasionale Pers (Naspers) for the printing and distribution of the newspaper. Naspers offered *South* significantly lower rates in return for the political credibility it hoped such a partnership would bring. The more advanced technology-information systems of Naspers also meant that *South* could submit its pages for printing electronically. This not only helped to ease the pressure by extending the deadline for submission but also saved thousands of rand per issue by eliminating the need to produce negatives.[104]

South, however, continued to lose money.[105] The board of directors, under pressure from funders, decided to co-opt progressive businessmen onto the board of South Press Services at the annual general meeting in August 1993. It was in part a recognition that political activists who had hitherto dominated the management of *South* did not have the expertise to run the newspaper profitably.[106] Ebrahim Bhorat, a prominent businessman and property developer, was appointed chief executive officer. Other well-known businessmen, such as Sam Montsi, Fred Robertson, and Yusuf Pahad, were also appointed to the board.[107] In an attempt to tighten financial management, deputy editor Rafiq Rohan was promoted to editor in January 1994, and Guy Berger took over as business manager.[108]

In a major bid for commercial viability, the new board also launched a free sheet, *Southeaster*, on 18 February 1994. The free sheet was meant to subsidize the political and ideological project of *South* and also to campaign for the ANC in the upcoming elections.[109] Management, in addition, needed to counter the growing presence of free sheets in Cape Town's black residential areas, as they were eroding *South*'s viability. By providing local sporting and community news free of charge, these "knock 'n drop" weeklies, funded entirely by advertising revenue, reduced the incentive for potential readers to buy *South*. More important, they seriously undermined *South*'s ability to attract advertising revenue. With their high circulation and wide distribution, these free sheets provided advertisers targeting lower-income households with an advertising medium that *South* could not match.

Since there was no extra funding available, existing resources and staff had to be used to produce *Southeaster*. In essence, *South's* community news section was expanded and parceled separately as a supplement to the newspaper but also distributed independently as a free sheet. *Southeaster*, which claimed an initial circulation of 100,000, went into direct competition with the Argus company's suite of regional free sheets, matching their advertising rates and circulation in Coloured residential areas on the Cape Flats. Besides its editorial superiority, *Southeaster* had a competitive advantage over the Argus free sheets: *Southeaster* offered advertisers a single rate for the area it covered, whereas the same coverage would have required the placing of as many as six separate ads in each of the Argus regional sheets. By undercutting the Argus free sheets in this way *Southeaster* succeeded in attracting growing support from advertisers.[110]

As the year progressed, it became increasingly clear that *South* was becoming less and less viable but *Southeaster* was potentially profitable. In October 1994, *Southeaster* expanded its circulation to 150,000 by moving into new areas, including parts of Cape Town's African townships. A rural edition was also in the planning. *South's* circulation, however, suffered a drastic decline in the latter half of 1994 largely because a substantial part of the newspaper was being distributed free in the form of *Southeaster* and readers were losing interest in political news after the April election. *South's* losses were also escalating as advertisers switched to the free sheet. *South* had shrunk from its usual sixteen-page format to eight pages by the end of 1994, while *Southeaster* had grown from twelve to twenty-eight pages.[111]

Despite the promise of future profitability, *Southeaster* created serious short-term financial problems for South Press Services. Start-up expenses together with the relatively high costs of producing and distributing the newspaper resulted in an acute cash flow problem for the company. *Southeaster*, which initially consumed R30,000 a week for printing and distribution alone, was a severe drain on the resources of South Press Services because it took time to build up a stream of advertising revenue.[112] By the end of 1994, *Southeaster* was still some way from breaking even.[113]

The situation was greatly exacerbated by the failure of management to replace Guy Berger with a business manager when he left at the end of May 1994 to become head of the Department of Journalism and Media Studies at Rhodes University. The gap between expenditure and income widened dramatically as no one was monitoring cash flow within the company, and much advertising and sales revenue went uncollected. By the time South Press Services went into liquidation, for example, there was an estimated R500,000 in uncollected revenue.[114] When management became aware of the problem in the fourth quarter of 1994, South Press Services was running at a deficit of R80,000 a month and owed the printers R400,000.[115] The company had also assumed that R150,000 from the Independent Media Diversity Trust would be paid to *South* in the latter half of 1994, but management realized only in November that the money had already been paid to *South* and most of it had already been spent on *Southeaster*.[116]

In a desperate bid to avert liquidation, the board of directors in November 1994 resolved to try and sell South Press Services to New Africa Publications (NAP), the publishing arm of the African-owned conglomerate New Africa Investments, Ltd. (NAIL). Nthato Motlana, chairman of NAIL, had expressed an interest in purchasing South Press Services as a springboard for NAIL's media interests into the western

Cape.[117] NAIL intended using *South*'s infrastructure to produce a Cape edition of the Johannesburg daily *Sowetan*, which would be targeted at African townships, while *Southeaster* would continue to service the Coloured community. The initiative to sell South Press Services to NAP was facilitated by a strong feeling among trustees, board members, and funders that, with apartheid dead and an ANC government in power, *South* had served its purpose.[118]

Negotiations with NAP were initially very cordial and went smoothly. By the end of November NAP had agreed to generous takeover terms. However, by the time the contract was due to be signed in mid-December NAP had done a complete about-face and had withdrawn its offer to purchase, citing disagreements over the retrenchment of staff and four pending defamation suits totaling approximately R1 million in claims against the newspaper.[119]

There was strong suspicion within the *South* camp that the Argus company had worked behind the scenes to scupper the deal because of the threat *Southeaster* posed to its free-sheet operation. Both Rehana Rossouw and Ebrahim Bhorat stated in interviews that at a meeting on 22 December 1994, when the deal was finally aborted, NAP representatives, who had apparently just come from a meeting with Argus management at Newspaper House, repeatedly claimed that "the boys down the road" were unhappy with their attempt to purchase South Press Services because *Southeaster* was winning market share from Argus free sheets. Rossouw and Bhorat believed the Argus company had the power to twist NAIL's arm on the issue because Argus owned 48 percent of the *Sowetan*, which NAIL was keen to purchase.

When talks with NAIL finally collapsed on 22 December 1994, South Press Services had little option but to go into liquidation. The last issue of *South* was published that same day: the newspaper had managed to survive nearly eight years during the last, decisive phase of the apartheid era. In retrospect, it seems clear that embarking on the *Southeaster* project was a strategic error. South Press Services did not have the capital or the management resources to nurture the publication to profitability. In the words of Guy Berger, "I don't think that anyone had any idea at the time, just how the child would grow to drain, and ultimately consume, the parent."[120]

Given a broader perspective, *South*'s demise came about because South Press Services was in no position to go into direct competition with the establishment press, which had massive technical and financial resources at its disposal, and it was unable to find a niche large enough to sustain the newspaper. One of the ironies of *South* is that despite the noble intention of trying to "serve the interests of the working class," the newspaper was largely bought by the politicized and better-educated sector of the Coloured middle class as well as white left and liberal sympathizers who wanted to keep abreast of struggle news in the western Cape. This readership was not big enough to make *South* financially viable.

The most fundamental problem facing *South* was that working-class Coloureds presented an exceptionally difficult market. First, the purchase of newspapers was very low on the list of priorities of most Coloured working-class families. As Seria diplomatically put it, "we are dealing with a community where . . . the awareness of the importance of [print] media in a changing society has not permeated all levels."[121] The editorial guidelines laid down by the trustees and directors were more blunt, and condescending: "We recognize that we have an educational role as a newspaper with regard to educating the community in their understanding of what a newspaper is."[122]

By the time *South* came into existence, television, introduced into South Africa in the mid-1970s, had effectively displaced print media as a source of news and entertainment among working-class Coloureds. There can be little doubt that they preferred watching television to reading newspapers. They would much rather direct discretionary spending to acquiring television sets and videocassette recorders and renting blood-and-guts action films from the video shops that mushroomed on the Cape Flats from the early 1980s. Television had a serious impact on circulation figures and advertising revenue of newspapers throughout the 1980s.[123] Between 1975 and 1987 newspapers' share of the total amount spent on advertising in South Africa shrank from 46.1 percent to 26.6 percent.[124] *South*'s first annual report singled out the introduction of the subscription television service M-Net in 1986 as a significant damper on newspaper sales.[125]

When working-class Coloureds did buy newspapers, *South* was not likely to have been their first choice. People who purchased the Cape Town dailies as well as those who only bought newspapers over the weekend were much more likely to choose publications such as the *Week-end Argus* and the *Sunday Times*, which were perceived to offer better value for money. There was little hope that working-class people would switch from these well-entrenched brands to *South* for weekend reading.[126] Being largely Afrikaans speaking, working-class Coloureds were also more likely to buy newspapers such as *Die Burger* or *Rapport*—despite their political affiliation to the ruling National Party and their racist practice of having special supplements specifically for Coloured readers. Many Coloureds, it would seem, regarded these supplements in a positive light, feeling that it gave them and their community the recognition they deserved.

The existence of a general culture of nonreading within the working-class Coloured community, a consequence of poverty and poor education, was recognized by *South*.[127] A lack of interest in newspapers was reflected in the readership survey it commissioned. The survey conducted in 1987 claimed that 57 percent of the people living in Mitchell's Plain, the largest of the dormitory suburbs into which working-class Coloureds had been shunted as a result of removals under the Group Areas Act, had never heard of *South*.[128] This was the case despite *South* specifically targeting Mitchell's Plain with periodic door-to-door selling campaigns, special supplements, and the distribution of complimentary copies. The survey also confirmed that there was widespread resistance to political content in newspapers within this social group.[129]

South management put this down to the repressive political climate of National Party rule. While this atmosphere clearly was a factor, they greatly underestimated the extent to which working-class Coloureds resisted the radical politics of the UDF and of *South*. As Sylvia Vollenhoven put it, "The politics of a relatively calm Mitchell's Plain is not the politics of a burning Spine Road."[130] Although Coloured workers were aggrieved at being victims of apartheid, they did not necessarily subscribe to the radical politics of the UDF. This became evident when the majority of working-class Coloureds flocked to the National Party banner in the April 1994 elections.

Conclusion

The *South* newspaper project must ultimately be regarded a failure because the newspaper ceased publication. This judgment, however, needs to be tempered by the realization that it was a triumph just to produce a newspaper regularly—given the repressive political climate and the difficulties involved in financing alternative publications. Although a commercial failure, the newspaper can lay claim to journalistic and political successes.

South to a large degree succeeded in its political purpose of helping to undermine apartheid and providing the extra-parliamentary political movement with a voice. It also fulfilled its journalistic objective of providing struggle news and alternative political analysis to the broad spectrum of supporters of the antiapartheid movement in the western Cape. In this respect, *South* had an impact disproportionate to the size of its circulation, especially during the 1980s, because it was read by a relatively influential constituency of activists and opinion makers within the democratic movement and in antiapartheid activities outside protest politics—in labor, education, sports, religious life, professional and cultural bodies, and even parts of the civil service. *South*'s independent and critical voice not only reflected the views of this readership but also played a role in shaping their perceptions. And, together with the rest of the alternative press, the newspaper played a part in laying the foundations for press freedom in postapartheid South Africa.

Perhaps the most enduring legacy of *South*, however, is the cadre of journalists it has bequeathed to the South African media. There is a sense in which *South* achieved soft vengeance against the rival English dailies, for subsequently Moegsien Williams became editor of the *Argus* and Ryland Fisher editor of the *Cape Times*. Nazeem Howa, one of the founding members and a key contributor during the first two years, became deputy editor of the *Star* and Rehana Rossouw is deputy editor of the *Mail and Guardian*. Other respected names in South African journalism that served an apprenticeship at *South* are Chiara Carter, Sahm Venter, Shannon Neill, Shannon Sherry, Kurt Swart, Jonathan Shapiro, Chip Haddon, Rayhana Rassool, Ayesha Allie, Heather Robertson, Thoraya Pandy, Vuyo Bavuma, Edyth Bulbring, Ayesha Ismail, Karen Rutter, Anton Fisher, "Babs" Omar, Philip Kakaza, Vicky Stark, Edwina Booysen, Joseph Aranes, Henry Ludski, and Chris Gutuza.

South was very much a product of the antiapartheid struggle and it is not entirely surprising that it did not survive the apartheid era. *South* never succeeded in creating a space for itself outside the struggle. Moegsien Williams refers to *South* as having been "schizophrenic."[131] And indeed, it was engaged in a continuous juggling act—to balance the demands of the marketplace with that of the political arena; to reconcile a studied nonracism while targeting a Coloured readership; to square the reality of its middle-class readership with the unrequited desire to attract working-class patronage. *South* was sustained by the belief that it served the working classes, but when South Press Services finally did produce a publication that appealed to the working classes, *Southeaster* helped drag the company and *South* into liquidation.

Notes

I thank Rashid Seria and David Bleazard for allowing me access to personal documents. All interviews cited in this chapter were conducted by the author. The *South* Newspaper Collection consists of photocopies of documents in the possession of either Rashid Seria or David Bleazard, deposited by the author in UCT's Manuscripts and Archives Division.

1. For a detailed discussion of the media curbs introduced by the various states of emergency, see G. Jackson, *Breaking Story: The South African Press* (Boulder: Westview Press, 1993), 128–57; and R. Abel, *Politics by Other Means: Law in the Struggle against Apartheid, 1980–1994* (New York: Routledge, 1995), 259–310.

2. *South*, 19 March 1987.

3. K. Tomaselli and P. Louw, "The Struggle for Legitimacy: State Pressures on the Media, 1950–1991," in *The Alternative Press in South Africa*, ed. K. Tomaselli and P. Louw (Bellville: Anthropos, 1991), 81, 89; Abel, *Politics by Other Means*, 259; Jackson, *Breaking Story*, 10, 152, 160–61. Of these newspapers, the *Cape Times* was the most courageous. Its publication in November 1985 of an interview with Oliver Tambo by editor Tony Heard is the most celebrated of the few instances in which the establishment press openly defied the government.

4. For example, *South*, 18 February 1988; South Press Services,

Free the Press (Cape Town: South Press Services, 1988); Jackson, *Breaking Story*, 12.

5. *Grassroots* and other community newspapers in the western Cape at the time were more in the nature of newsletters than newspapers, and were not commercial publications.

6. South Newspaper Collection (SNC), University of Cape Town Manuscripts and Archives Division, R. Seria, Weekly newspaper project feasibility report, 1986, introduction, 1–2 [hereafter, Feasibility report]; P. Louw, "Resistance in Print II: Developments in the Cape: *Saamstaan, Grassroots*, and *South*," in Tomaselli and Louw, *Alternative Press*, 210; Rashid Seria, interview by author, 16 January 1998; Moegsien Williams, interview by author, 15 July 1998.

7. SNC, Seria, Feasibility report, introduction, 1; L. Raubenheimer, "From Newsroom to the Community: Struggle in Black Journalism," in Tomaselli and Louw, *Alternative Press*, 97–98, 122–23.

8. Moegsien Williams, interview, 15 July 1988; South Press Services, *Free the Press*, 7; SNC, Seria, Feasibility report, 4; K. Tomaselli and P. Louw, "Developments in the Conventional and Alternative Presses, 1980–1989," in Tomaselli and Louw, *Alternative Press*, 8.

9. SNC, Seria, Feasibility report, summary, 1, 6; addendum on consultations, 2–3; S. Johnson, "Resistance in Print I: *Grassroots* and Alternative Publishing," in Tomaselli and Louw, *Alternative Press*, 199.

10. SNC, Seria, Feasibility report, 2–3.

11. SNC, M. Brey and R. Seria, "Memorandum for the Private Placing of Shares in South Press Services Limited" (Cape Town, n.d.), 4. See also A. Akhalwaya, "The Role of the Alternative Press," *Nieman Reports* 42 (1988): 14–18.

12. South Press Services, *Free the Press*, 6.

13. SNC, Seria, Feasibility report, annexure 3 ("News Suppression and Manipulation of South Africa's Liberal English Newspapers as Experienced by Black Reporters"), 3.

14. Ibid., 1.

15. Rashid Seria, interview, 16 January 1998; Moegsien Williams, interview, 15 July 1998; SNC, Brey and Seria, "Private Placing of Shares," 8.

16. The document referred to is SNC, Seria, Feasibility report. Rashid Seria, interview, 16 January 1998, 11 October 1998; Moegsien Williams, interview, 15 July 1998.

17. Rashid Seria, interview, 16 January 1998; Moegsien Williams, interview, 15 July 1998. A number of documents relating to the consultation process are in the possession of Rashid Seria. These documents will be referred to as the Seria Private Collection (SPC).

18. The initial directors of South Press Services were Hamza Esack, Huxley Joshua, Essa Moosa, and Rashid Seria. The trustees of the Ukwaziswa Trust were Di Bishop, Allan Boesak, Jakes Gerwel, Nomatyala Hangana, Essa Moosa, Malusi Mpumlwana, and Charles Villavicencio. Ukwaziswa means "let it be known" in Xhosa.

19. SNC, Brey and Seria, "Private Placing of Shares." Fewer than 50,000 of the 350,000 shares on offer were taken up.

20. SNC, annual report, 1988, 2; *South,* 18 February 1988.

21. SNC, Seria, Feasibility report, summary, 3.

22. Ibid.; SNC, G. Berger, memorandum to *South* directors, 4 September 1993. Moegsien Williams, interview, 15 July 1998.

23. This message was carried in *South*'s appearances panel.

24. *South,* 19 March 1987.

25. Moegsien Williams, interview, 15 July 1998.

26. SNC, minutes of meeting of trustees of South Press Services, 30 July 1987; minutes of meeting of trustees and board of directors of South Press Services, 1 October 1987; Rashid Seria, interview, 16 January 1998; Moegsien Williams, interview, 15 July 1998; Derek Carelse, interview, 13 October 1998; Rehana Rossouw, e-mail communication with author, 20 July 1998.

27. Rashid Seria, interview, 11 October 1998, 10 March 1999.

28. *South,* 2 April 1987.

29. Rashid Seria, interview, 16 January 1998.

30. Clive Thompson, Dennis Davis, and Norman Arendse were among the lawyers who scrutinized *South.*

31. *South,* 15 October 1987.

32. Rashid Seria, interview, 16 January 1998; SNC, annual report, 1989, 3; SNC, Report of the chairperson of the board of directors of South Press Services, 18 August 1988; *South,* 21 July 1988.

33. Moegsien Williams, interview, 15 July 1998.

34. *South,* 14 December 1988; Moegsien Williams, interview, 15 July 1998.

35. SNC, R. Seria, three-month assessment report, n. d. (June 1987?), 2–3; SNC, annual report, 1988, 7.

36. SNC, annual report, 1988, 24; *South,* 20 August 1988; SNC, minutes of meeting of trustees of South Press Services, 30 July 1987;

minutes of meeting of trustees and board of directors of South Press Services, 1 October 1987.

37. Derek Carelse, interview, 13 October 1998.

38. *South*, 18 December 1987.

39. SPC, U. Ferndale, "*South* Survey: The Reading Habits of the Western Cape Community," October 1987; SNC, R. Seria, *South* newspaper project: funding proposal, 1989/90 and 1990/91 (Cape Town, 1989), 17.

40. SPC, Ukwaziswa Trust, South Press Services News Agency, n.d. (1988?); *South*, 25 August 1988; Louw and Tomaselli, "Struggle for Legitimacy," 79, 85–86; Jackson, *Breaking Story*, 132–33.

41. Moegsien Williams, interview, 15 July 1998.

42. SNC, Seria, feasibility report, 10; SNC, minutes of meeting of the trustees and board of directors of South Press Services, 30 July 1987; Moegsien Williams, interview, 15 July 1998; Rehana Rossouw, telephone interview, 12 October 1998.

43. SNC, "Vukani Journalist Training Project Report" (Cape Town, 1988), 2; SNC, annual report, 1988, 14; *South*, 25 August 1988.

44. SNC, Seria, funding proposal 13; SNC, minutes of meeting of trustees and board of directors of South Press Services, 1 October 1987; Rehana Rossouw, e-mail communication with author, 20 July 1998;

45. Rashid Seria, interview, 11 October 1998; Moegsien Williams, interview, 15 July 1998. The quotation comes from Williams.

46. Rashid Seria, interview, 11 October 1998; Moegsien Williams, interview, 15 July 1998; Derek Carelse, interview, 13 October 1998.

47. Rashid Seria, interview, 16 January 1998, 11 October 1998; Moegsien Williams, interview, 15 July 1998; Derek Carelse, interview, 13 October 1998; SNC, annual report, 1988, 14; SNC, minutes of meeting of the trustees and board of directors of South Press Services, 30 July 1987.

48. Rashid Seria, interview, 11 October 1998; Moegsien Williams, interview, 15 July 1998; Derek Carelse, interview, 13 October 1998.

49. K. Tomaselli and P. Louw, "The South African Progressive Press under Emergency, 1986–1989," in Tomaselli and Louw, *Alternative Press*, 186; SPC, R. Seria to W. Minnaard, ICCO, Netherlands, 19 May 1988.

50. The dour, reserved Stoffel Botha was known as dom (stupid) Stoffel in antiapartheid circles, in contrast to his more adroit and en-

gaging colleague Stoffel van der Merwe, minister of information, referred to as slim (smart) Stoffel. Anton Harber, editor of the *Mail and Guardian,* coined the term "to *stoffel,*" meaning "to snuff out," to ridicule dom Stoffel's month-long banning of this newspaper. *Mail and Guardian,* 24 April 1998.

51. *South,* 10 December 1987.

52. For a detailed discussion of state harassment of the alternative press during this period see Abel, *Politics by Other Means,* 259–72. The SPC contains two files of correspondence between South Press Services, the ministry of home affairs and communication, and various law firms regarding state action against *South.*

53. About 25 percent of this edition was sold in the few hours it was on sale. SNC, Report of the chairperson, August 1988; C. Merrett, *A Culture of Censorship: Secrecy and Intellectual Repression in South Africa* (Cape Town: David Philip, 1995), 143.

54. *South,* 7 April 1988, 14 April 1988, 4 May 1988, 15 June 1988, 25 August 1988.

55. It was estimated that a three-month banning order would have cost South Press Services in excess of R100,000. SNC, Seria, funding proposal, 20.

56. Moegsien Williams, interview, 15 July 1998; Rashid Seria, interview, 16 January 1998, 11 October 1998; SNC, Report of the chairperson, August 1988; *Mail and Guardian,* 24 April 1998.

57. *South,* 26 November 1987. Moegsien Williams confirms that for him, defiance of the government played a very important part in publishing *South.* Williams, interview, 15 July 1998:

58. SNC, annual report, 1988, 23.

59. Rashid Seria, interview, 16 January 1998, 11 October 1998; Moegsien Williams, interview, 15 July 1998; Derek Carelse, interview, 13 October 1998; SNC, Annual report, 1988, 23; *Cape Times,* 17 September 1997.

60. *South,* 14 September 1989; *Weekly Mail,* 15 September 1989.

61. *South,* 16 March 1989; 26 October 1989; *Cape Times,* 14 July 1998; Abel, *Politics by Other Means,* 264, 300. *Grassroots* journalist Veliswa Mhlawuli, for example, lost her right eye in an attempted assassination, *Saamstaan* photographer Patrick Nyuka was shot by police for refusing to hand over his camera, and *New Nation* editor Zwelakhe Sisulu spent two years in detention.

62. SNC, Seria, Feasibility report, summary, 6, 11; What Seria failed to recognize was that the *Cape Herald* achieved these sales

toward the end of the long boom of the 1960s and at a time when newspapers did not face competition from electronic media.

63. SNC, minutes of meeting of the trustees and board of directors of South Press Services, 30 July 1987.

64. *South*, 15 June 1988; Rashid Seria, interview, 16 January 1998.

65. SNC, Annual report, 1988, 8; *South*, 9 February 1988. According to Williams, this became apparent within the first few weeks of publication. Moegsien Williams, interview, 15 July 1998.

66. SNC, annual report, 1988, 11.

67. Rashid Seria, interview, 11 October 1998; SNC, advertising report, 7 May 1994.

68. SNC, Report of the chairperson, 18 August 1988, reproduced in *South*, 25 August 1988.

69. *South*, 9 February 1988; SNC, annual report, 1988, 11.

70. Rashid Seria, interview, 16 January 1998.

71. Both Seria and Williams used their contacts at the *Argus*, having worked many years for the company, to access information and technical facilities. Moegsien Williams, interview, 15 July 1998; Rashid Seria, interview, 16 January 1998, 11 October 1998; Derek Carelse, interview, 13 October 1998.

72. For an expression of these views see "Drop All Racial Tags" (letter to editor), *South*, 14 January 1988. A similar stance was taken up in academic discourse. See I. Goldin, *Making Race: The Politics and Economics of Coloured Identity in South Africa* (Cape Town: Maskew Miller Longman, 1987); and R. du Pré, *Separate But Unequal: The "Coloured" People of South Africa—A Political History* (Johannesburg: Jonathan Ball, 1994).

73. Moegsien Williams, interview, 15 July 1998; Rashid Seria, interview, 16 January 1998, 11 October 1998.

74. See, for example, *South*, 25 June 1986, 6 August 1987, 24 September 1987, 4 February 1988, 21 July 1988, 26 February 1989, 30 March 1989, 25 April 1990, 18 April 1991.

75. *South*, 7 July 1988.

76. Derek Carelse, interview, 13 October 1998.

77. Moegsien Williams, interview, 15 July 1998; Rashid Seria, interview, 11 October 1998.

78. Moegsien Williams, interview, 15 July 1998.

79. Ibid.; Rashid Seria, interview, 11 October 1998.

80. Moegsien Williams, interview, 15 July 1998.

81. Ibis Books and Editorial Services, *An Illustrated Dictionary of South African History* (Sandton: Ibis Books, 1994), 79.

82. See, for example, *South*, 7 November 1991, 2 May 1992, 23 May 1992, 14 November 1992, 20 February 1993, 9 December 1994.

83. *South*, 14 August 1993.

84. *South*, 27 February 1992.

85. A greater attempt was made to report news from the African townships in the 1990s. *South's* nonpolitical news, however, remained overwhelmingly Coloured.

86. Moegsien Williams, interview, 15 July 1998; Derek Carelse, interview, 13 October 1998; Rashid Seria, interview, 11 October 1998; *South*, 17 November 1988.

87. *South*, 13 June 1991.

88. *South* was acutely aware of the looming funding crisis. See the series of articles on foreign funding in *South*, 7–21 March 1991.

89. SNC, Seria, funding proposal, 29.

90. *South*, 1 August 1991.

91. SNC, memo to *South* board of directors finance sub-committee, 15 November 1993; Rashid Seria, interview, 16 January 1998.

92. C. Giffard, A. de Beer, and E. Steyn, "New Media for the New South Africa," in *Press Freedom and Communication in Africa*, ed. F. Eribo and W. Jong-Ebot (Trenton: Africa World Press, 1997), 85.

93. Abel, *Politics by Other Means*, 302.

94. Rehana Rossouw, e-mail communication with author, 20 July 1998.

95. SNC, minutes of *South* bosberaad with directors and hods, 7 May 1994.

96. Rehana Rossouw, e-mail communication with author, 20 July 1998.

97. The articles were published in *South*, 7–21 March 1991. Rehana Rossouw, e-mail communication with author, 20 July 1998.

98. Rehana Rossouw, e-mail communication with author, 20 July 1998. Rossouw is highly complimentary about the support she received from Moegsien Williams during these confrontations as well as the editorial integrity he displayed.

99. Moegsien Williams, interview, 15 July 1998; SNC, Seria, funding proposal, 7.

100. SNC, minutes of *South* bosberaad with directors and hods, 7 May 1994.

101. SNC, sales revenue report, n.d. (November 1993?) contains a weekly breakdown of sales for 1993. See also SNC, minutes of *South* bosberaad with directors and hods, 7 May 1994.

102. SNC, minutes of *South* bosberaad with directors and hods, 7 May 1994.

103. SNC, advertising report, 7 May 1994.

104. Rehana Rossouw, e-mail communication with author, 20 July 1998.

105. Losses in the region of R400,000 were projected for 1993. See SNC, G. Berger and H. Veldsman, staff bonus 1993: a proposal by executive directors, 12 October 1993.

106. Rehana Rossouw, telephone interview, 12 October 1998.

107. For a full list of the new board of directors see SNC, minutes of sixth annual general meeting of South Press Services, 16 August 1993.

108. *South*, 21 January 1994.

109. David Bleazard (secretary to the board of directors of South Press Services for 1993–94), interview, 27 January 1999. The idea of launching a free sheet had been contemplated almost from the beginning. See *South*, 25 August 1988; SNC, Seria, funding proposal, 2.

110. Rehana Rossouw, telephone interview, 12 October 1998.

111. Ibid.; Ebrahim Bhorat, interview, 26 October 1998; *Southeaster*, 14 October 1998.

112. SNC, *"Southeaster:* The Way Forward," n.d. (May 1994?); SNC, minutes of *South* bosberaad with directors and hods, 7 May 1994.

113. SNC, Minutes of meeting of board and trustees of South Press Services, 21 October 1994.

114. SNC, Berger to Minnaard (fax), 12 January 1995.

115. Ibid.; SNC, minutes of board meeting, South Press Services, 12 October 1994.

116. SNC, Berger to Minnaard, 12 January 1995; minutes of extraordinary meeting of trustees and directors, 30 March 1995.

117. SNC, minutes of board meeting, South Press Services, 16 February 1994; minutes of meeting of board and trustees, South Press Services, 2 November 1994; minutes of meeting of board and trustees, South Press Services, 16 November 1994.

118. Ebrahim Bhorat, interview, 26 October 1998.

119. Ibid.; Rehana Rossouw, telephone interview, 12 October 1998; SNC, Berger to Minnaard, 12 January 1995.

120. SNC, Berger to Minnaard, 12 January 1995.

121. *South*, 18 February 1988.

122. SNC, annual report, 1988, 8.

123. The *Cape Herald* had been a victim of this shift, its circulation dropping below 20,000 by the mid-1980s.

124. M. Leahy and P. Voice, *SARAD Media Year Book, 1989* (Johannesburg: WTH Publications, 1989), 59; Jackson, *Breaking Story*, 7.

125. SNC, annual report, 1988. See also *South*, 1 September 1988; SNC, annual report, 1989, 3.

126. Brey and Seria, "Private Placing of Shares," 6.

127. *South*, 16 January 1992.

128. SPC, Ferndale, "*South* Survey," section 3.

129. SPC, Ferndale, "*South* Survey," section 4; SPC, R. Seria, editor's report for trustees and directors, 20 August 1987; *South*, 9 February 1988.

130. *South*, 13 June 1991. Spine Road, one of the main thoroughfares in Mitchell's Plain, was a favored place for activists to erect barricades and where numerous clashes between youths and police took place.

131. Moegsien Williams, interview, 15 July 1998.

9

Ambiguities in Alternative Discourse

New Nation and the *Sowetan* in the 1980s

Keyan G. Tomaselli

The final edition of *New Nation* appeared on 30 May 1997. Battered by falling readership, little financial support, and the absence of experienced editorial staff, this alternative newspaper barely survived the installation of the democratic dispensation it had fought so hard to bring about. The well-capitalized *Sowetan*, on the other hand, was a mainstream, commercial newspaper that maintained market share and thrived in the new era ushered in by the 1994 elections. The *Sowetan* was owned by the Argus company—the biggest newspaper conglomerate in southern Africa. Whereas the *Sowetan* was targeted specifically at urban-based, relatively affluent African readers, *New Nation* had a multiracial, mainly urban-based, trade union readership.

This study compares *New Nation* and the *Sowetan* in the mid-1980s, when both newspapers were subjected to continued government harassment as oppositional publications challenging the apartheid order.[1] The term *alternative* is defined here as a serial publication supportive of the broader democratic tendency of the period, organized mainly via the United

Democratic Front (UDF) and the Mass Democratic Movement (MDM), which was formed after the UDF and affiliated organizations were effectively banned in February 1988. These media were also organically connected to community-based religious, civic, student, and women's groups and trade unions. Communities as discussed here are people within specific regions and neighborhoods who organized themselves into a coherent whole through civic organizations united by a commonly perceived oppression.[2]

New Nation *and the Alternative Press*

New Nation was a response to the resolution of an Inter-Diocesan Pastoral Consultation held under the auspices of the Southern African Catholic Bishops' Conference (SACBC) in August 1980. The resolution called for the creation of a "national Catholic" newspaper designed to enter into "the life, struggles, needs and burning aspirations of the majority of South Africa's people."[3]

Like other mission churches, South Africa's Catholic Church —which by the 1980s had a predominantly African membership —was being challenged by independent African churches, whose memberships were growing dramatically. These churches were perceived as more "African" and less tainted by apartheid. The SACBC needed a mechanism to shed its "white colonial" image. A survey of parish priests and parishioners in the Pretoria-Witwatersrand-Vaal (PWV) area by the Ecumenical Research Unit in 1983 indicated support for a national Catholic newspaper that would cover issues related to the church and spiritual matters, social reform, home and family, church and state issues, and issues related to the socioeconomic environment. The study concluded that respondents wanted an "alternative" weekly newspaper.[4]

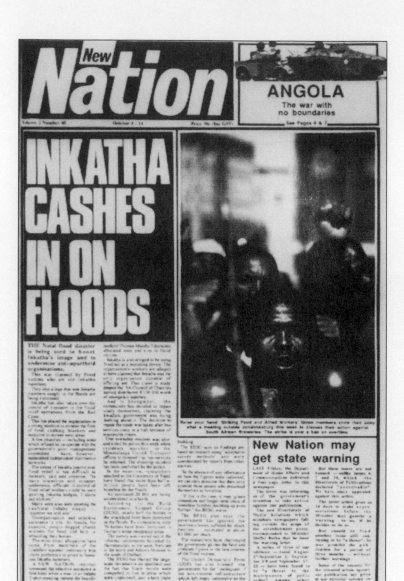

The front page of *New Nation*, 8–14 October 1987 edition, featuring the newspaper's one article on devastating floods in Natal. *New Nation*'s coverage of this event differed dramatically from coverage of the same event in the *Sowetan*, the mainstream commercial African daily.

An African worker in Johannesburg reading a May 1987 issue of the *Sowetan.* The poster headlines the imprisoned Nelson Mandela winning a *Sowetan* poll as the most popular political figure in South Africa.

The launching of *New Nation* on 16 January 1986 filled a specific vacuum in the arena of alternative publishing: "The role of the alternative press has evolved through an on-going assessment of concrete conditions and the required political interventions at any point. . . . It is important to note that this has been the practice of local community newspapers, organisational newsletters and media for specific constituencies. However since we do not have a regular national newspaper aimed at a mass base, this role has not been defined."[5]

The potential role of a national Catholic newspaper was similar to that of contemporary national student newspapers in seeking to develop "the national character of our struggle by linking regional issues with national issues and by drawing out the lessons of particular experiences."[6] *New Nation* filled a specific media niche—a newspaper aimed at a national Christian and largely working-class readership.[7] *New Nation* closely paralleled corporate journalistic practices in terms of management, advertising, and distribution, but a democratic editorial approach involved all staff in decision making. However, *New Nation* found it impossible to adopt the *Grassroots* democratic style of news production. The weekly production cycle made a fully democratic model impractical.[8]

Although *New Nation* supported a socialist economic perspective, the newspaper needed commercial advertisers because absolute dependence on the SACBC made it vulnerable to funding cuts. Nevertheless, certain companies like Shell— believed at the time to be supporting the state—were denied advertising space even for the company's human rights media campaigns.

As a national newspaper, *New Nation* could not really serve individuals and organizations at the community level, but news stringers linked to activist leaders and communities in their respective areas were placed throughout the country. The newspaper tried to represent all South Africa's major geographic regions, but the PWV triangle—the industrial center—tended to dominate news content. *New Nation, South* (western Cape), and *New African* (Durban) had established a cooperative news-swapping system by the end of the 1980s. *New Nation* remained central to this network because it was headquartered in Johannesburg.

New Nation held itself accountable to the MDM and regularly consulted MDM leadership on policy. The newspaper attempted to maintain an ongoing dialogue with various activist communities in the PWV area. The policy of community engagement, however, was severely damaged by the nationwide states of emergency (1986–90), which effectively curtailed opportunities for such interaction and consultation.

New Nation had an estimated circulation of 66,000 and a

total readership of 260,000 in November 1986; 50 percent of sales were in the PWV area, which constituted about 50 percent of the sales of left-wing weeklies at the time. A reader survey suggested that 47 percent of *New Nation* readers in 1987 were between 20 and 29 years of age, 23 percent between 30 and 39, and the majority were men; about 44 percent had a Standard 9 or 10 (high school) education, 30 percent Standard 8 or less, and 25 percent a higher education diploma or university degree. Catholics made up 23 percent of the readers, while 12 percent were Anglican, 21 percent were other mainstream Protestant, and 44 percent belonged to other denominations or had no religious affiliation. About 25 percent of the readers surveyed were students and 25 percent workers. Professionals constituted 37 percent, and the rest (about 13 percent) were unemployed. More than 81 percent identified a Charterist organization as their political preference, but only 1 percent supported Black Consciousness (BC) organizations.[9]

Fifty percent earned an average of R305 a month; the bottom quarter earned R100 a month and the top quarter, more than R400 a month. *New Nation*'s readers approximated South Africa's population as a whole in terms of racial identity—13.5 percent white, 7.5 percent Coloured, 2.4 percent of Asian origin, and 76.6 percent African. The overwhelming majority of readers (87.1 percent) fell below the top two income categories (R500 or more a month) and were unlikely to be of interest to advertisers of consumer goods.[10]

The Sowetan *as a Commercial Newspaper*

African personal incomes increased rapidly in the 1970s and 1980s and there was a corresponding increase in the consumer potential of the African population.[11] In 1979, the McCann-Erikson advertising agency noted that Africans accounted for

75 percent of the country's soft-drink consumption, 60 percent of beer, 54 percent of tobacco, 50 percent of detergents, 40 percent of clothing and footwear, and 40 percent of expenditure on food.[12]

In March 1980 the Argus company inaugurated a free sheet called the *Sowetan*. In the same month, South African Associated Newspapers (SAAN) launched a competitor entitled the *Soweto News*. Both free sheets were distributed weekly to all Soweto homes. These publications were linked to the need expressed by advertisers to tap Soweto's market potential. As pointed out by Nigel Twidale, then general manager of SAAN, "In the past, advertisers complained about the lack of media penetration into Soweto, the most affluent black [African] community in South Africa. The blacks [Africans] who commute to the cities have access to the *Rand Daily Mail* and the *Post*, but most of the township's one million inhabitants have no access to these publications. The freesheets are aimed at anyone occupying a house in Soweto."[13]

The *Sowetan* was relaunched as a commercial daily in February 1981. Distributed mainly in the PWV area, it had a circulation of 160,000. According to a 1987 survey, *Sowetan* readers were almost all Africans and belonged to the top two income groups—above R1,000, and R999–R500. Of these readers, 70 percent were male, 66.5 percent were employed, and 45 percent owned a motor car. Readership was 23 percent in the 16-to-24 age group, 33 percent in the 25-to-43 age group, 27 percent in the 35-to-49 age group, and 10 percent in the over-50 age group. The newspaper was seen by the survey respondents as being too biased toward Black Consciousness, and to a lesser extent, the UDF. *New Nation's* news perspective was believed to be less independent than the white-targeted *Star!*[14]

Product advertising was used by capital as an ingredient in an overall strategy to promote the emergence of a middle class of black consumers.[15] Table 9.1 shows a mini-analysis of consumer advertising in a selection of 1987 issues of the *Sowetan*, distinguishing between advertisements for essential and non-essential commodities. Nonessential commodities included items like television sets, cars, imported designer-label clothes; services like those offered by tax and financial advisors and real estate agents; and forms of entertainment (like cinemas, hotels, and theatres) requiring disposable income. Nonessential commodities comprised almost 70 percent of the advertising space.

Other ingredients in the strategy to promote a middle class of black consumers were indicated by the 1978 Riekert Commission of Inquiry into labor law and practices,[16] and the granting of ninety-nine-year leasehold rights to "qualified" black residents in urban centers. Organizations like the Urban Foundation, created by white corporate business groups in the latter half of the 1970s, were designed to promote a black urban labor aristocracy. This class was expected to be amenable to

Table 9.1
Consumer Advertising in the *Sowetan*

Edition (date)	Essential Items (% total ad space)	Nonessential Items (% total ad space)
22 January 1987	37.4	62.6
26 January 1987	14.9	85.1
9 March 1987	5.2	94.8
10 March 1987	9.8	90.2
4 May 1987	42.7	57.3
15 May 1987	47.9	52.1
26 June 1987	18.3	81.7
1 July 1987	65.7	34.3
17 September 1987	20.4	79.6
23 September 1987	3.5	96.5
6 November 1987	72.6	27.4
Average	30.8	69.2

collaboration with white capital and provide the skills and markets needed by an expanding manufacturing sector.[17]

While most white-owned publications aimed at blacks were concerned with "sensational crime, violence and sex,"[18] a few also functioned as voices of opposition to the policies of apartheid. These became subject to government harassment and even closure. Such was the case with *World* and *Weekend World*, banned in October 1977, and *Post* and *Weekend Post*, which could not be reregistered as newspapers because the government informed the owner (the Argus company) that they would be banned.[19]

The *Sowetan* was also subjected to harassment during the first seven years of its existence. Journalists were continually pressured by the police, copies of the newspaper were seized on two occasions shortly after the declaration of the first countrywide state of emergency in June 1986,[20] and in December 1987 the government refused to renew the passport of the *Sowetan's* news editor, Thami Mazwai.[21] In the same month, *Sowetan* and *Weekly Mail* were prohibited from publishing statements from organizations advocating or supporting a Christmas against the Emergency campaign. Following the introduction of new media regulations in August 1987, the *Sowetan* was one of the newspapers to receive a letter of warning from the minister of home affairs.[22]

White-owned newspapers for blacks, like the *Sowetan*, were racially oriented in terms of politics. The *Sowetan* contrasted sharply with *New Nation*, for example, in its coverage of extraparliamentary politics. *New Nation* focused mainly on the activities of the Congress of South African Unions (COSATU), UDF/MDM affiliates, the church, and other organizations adhering to the principle of nonracialism. Almost no coverage was given to the activities of Black Consciousness organizations and trade unions such as the Azanian People's Organization (AZAPO), the Azanian Students' Movement (AZASM), the Pan Africanist Congress (PAC), and the National Council of Trade Unions (NACTU). The UDF-COSATU emphasis is explained by editor Zwelakhe Sisulu: "there's only one political organisation which is growing, and that's the non-racial, democratic movement. And it's growing throughout South Africa, as well as in the Bantustans. The other organisations are trying very hard but they're not succeeding. It is also no coincidence that the workers' movement supports the non-racial, democratic viewpoint."[23]

While the *Sowetan* covered the activities of both UDF/MDM affiliates and BC organizations, its editorials clearly revealed a BC position. An editorial on the May 1987 "whites only" election described the vote as a "political regression" and concluded, "We blacks will suffer the brunt of radical right-wing policies being thrust down the government's throat."[24] An editorial in June 1987, anticipating a clampdown on BC organizations, commented, "The Black Consciousness Movement, which was spearheaded by excellent black heroes like Steve Biko, is far from being a spent force."[25]

An unlikely empathy existed between some white liberals and the BC movement—the best-known example being the relationship between Donald Woods and Steve Biko. This was because liberals also understood the repression of blacks in terms of race rather than class. *Argus* and other newspapers assumed racial classifications to the point where these defined everything from statistics to newsroom practices. *Sowetan* staff tended to absorb this mindset as a practice under the allocative control of the mining houses,[26] which ultimately owned the newspaper.

One example of race-over-class reporting was an editorial on a strike by workers of the state-owned South African Transport Services (SATS). The *Sowetan* interpreted the way SATS handled a strike, and the inconveniences suffered by commuters, as SATS "taking an even wider swipe at black people."[27]

This ignored the wider context (racial capitalism) of both the injustices suffered by SATS workers and the fact that the majority of workers commuted by rail.

The *Sowetan*'s stress on racial as opposed to class oppression appeased both readers and advertisers. Its more affluent readership may have identified more readily with the issue of racial exploitation. While the *Sowetan* was clearly antiapartheid, its position with regard to big business and the capitalist system as a whole was one of support. This was evident in its coverage of organizations like the Black Management Forum, the Small Business Development Corporation, the Chamber of Commerce, and the Urban Foundation.

Journalism and News Practices

The two newspapers obviously had to comment and report on events and issues they considered of common interest to their reading communities. The Contemporary Cultural Studies Unit (CCSU) at the University of Natal (Durban) was asked to examine how *New Nation* and the *Sowetan* covered various news and interest categories during 1987.[28] The purpose of this commissioned report was to determine the extent to which the content (both editorial and advertising) of the two newspapers overlapped.

A sample of each newspaper was constructed for all of 1987.[29] The percentage of editorial space making up each of the following news categories was determined: political, labor, community, religious, culture/entertainment, education, women, sport, political advertisements, consumer advertisements, editorial content, letters to the editor, general news, and business news.

Given the pervasiveness of successive states of emergency during the late 1980s, and the high profile of security agencies enforcing these edicts, "political news" encompassed items related to the South African Defence Force (SADF), police action, group areas evictions, forced removals, detentions, legislation, Parliament, foreign affairs, and all other events with direct political implications that did not fit into the other categories. "General-interest news" was taken to include human interest, crime, and other news stories. "Political advertisements" were nonconsumer advertisements: they included ads both in support of and opposed to government policy, ads calling for the release of political prisoners, ads appealing for clemency, and ads popularizing organizations. Table 9.2 compares the news content of each sampled edition of *New Nation* with the corresponding editions of the *Sowetan.*

Clearly *New Nation,* as opposed to the *Sowetan,* did not carry enough consumer advertising to be commercially viable. Two factors limited the extent to which *New Nation* might have been able to improve its sale of advertising. First, advertisers were generally reluctant to advertise in newspapers such as *New Nation,* whose content reflected "serious" journalism aimed at a working-class readership.[30] Second, *New Nation's* mandated editorial policy of reflecting the "struggles, needs and burning aspirations of the majority of South Africa's people" limited the type of advertising it could accept.[31] Political advertising took as much as 14.8 percent of *New Nation's* news-advertising content (in March 1987), while only on one occasion (July 1987) did the proportion of political advertising exceed 1 percent of *Sowetan's* news-advertising content.

As Table 9.3 suggests, *New Nation* carried twice as much political news, three times as much community news, five times as much labor news, and nine times as much religious news as the *Sowetan.* Foreign political and religious news was also featured in *New Nation,* which was consistent with the interests of its readers, who read the newspaper for its labor, South African, and international news.[32]

Table 9.2
News Content of *New Nation* and *Sowetan* Samples

Percent of Total Newspaper

News Category	January NN	January S	March NN	March S	May NN	May S	July NN	July S	September NN	September S	November NN	November S
Politics	10.5	7.4	14.8	8.2	18.5	6.8	17.8	4.7	10.7	6.6	21.9	7.1
Labor	8.8	1.6	7.5	1.8	7.2	0.6	13.8	2.6	11.9	1.7	10.3	2.2
Community	17.8	2.8	4.6	1.4	11.5	7.3	7.9	0.4	4.8	1.7	2.0	2.8
Religion	5.3	0.3	4.2	0.0	4.5	0.2	4.2	2.1	4.3	0.1	5.0	0.3
Entertainment	12.5	8.4	11.8	5.2	11.6	7.0	11.7	7.1	12.0	10.0	13.8	6.0
Education	9.4	1.1	11.4	2.3	8.9	0.4	10.1	0.8	9.4	0.4	11.8	0.4
Women/Gender	0.0	0.5	0.6	0.8	0.0	2.0	0.0	0.1	4.2	0.5	0.0	4.1
Sport	13.4	12.5	13.7	17.0	15.7	17.0	15.1	14.3	27.2	16.9	22.2	15.4
Political Ads	0.3	0.1	14.8	0.5	0.0	0.5	0.4	1.4	0.0	0.8	2.2	0.1
Consumer Ads	18.2	52.5	13.3	47.7	18.5	48.7	14.8	54.8	11.2	46.7	5.7	53.2
Editorial	1.2	1.3	1.1	1.7	0.9	0.7	0.9	1.2	0.9	1.5	1.2	0.5
Letters to Editor	2.6	2.5	2.2	2.6	2.7	1.6	2.9	2.1	3.1	2.7	3.9	1.7
General	0.0	8.6	0.0	8.3	0.0	5.9	0.0	7.3	0.3	8.8	0.0	4.2
Business	0.0	0.6	0.0	1.2	0.0	1.6	0.4	1.0	0.0	1.7	0.0	1.9

Note: Since *New Nation* was a weekly and the *Sowetan* a daily, each percentage in the *Sowetan* columns represents the proportion of each news category across the five editions of that paper (e.g., 7.4 percent in row 1, column 2 means that five consecutive January editions of the *Sowetan* put together contain 7.4 percent political news). Due to rounding off numbers for each story unit, total percentages may not always equal 100 percent.

Table 9.3
Average News Content (Percent per Category)
of *New Nation* and the *Sowetan*

	Percent of Total Newspaper	
News Category	*New Nation*	*Sowetan*
Politics	15.7	6.8
Labor	9.9	1.8
Community	8.1	2.7
Religion	4.6	0.5
Entertainment/Arts	12.2	7.3
Education	10.2	0.9
Women/Gender	0.8	1.3
Sport	17.9	15.5
Political Ads	3.0	0.6
Consumer Ads	13.6	50.6
Editorial	1.0	1.2
Letters to Editor	2.9	2.2
General	0.1	7.2
Business	0.1	1.3

The *Sowetan* contained a much higher proportion of general news than *New Nation,* which is consistent with both *New Nation's* perceived role as a political, issue-oriented newspaper and its style of news gathering. *New Nation* differed from the *Sowetan* in two areas in terms of general-interest news: in place of the actions of individuals in crime and human interest stories, *New Nation* preferred reports that emphasized the activities of community, student, religious and political organizations, and trade unions; and in place of conventional news sources, most of *New Nation's* news came from trade unions and community organizations.

Comparing News Values

News values come into focus when comparing the ways the two newspapers reported specific events. Two of several newsworthy events noted by the CCSU research team are highlighted below. The first example shows how each newspaper dealt with a major flood that occurred in the Natal province in September and October 1987. The second example shows how the two newspapers differed in using sources during a workers' strike at the national OK retail chain in January 1987.

The Bizarre versus Injustice

One aspect of commercial news value concerns "bizarre," odd, and extraordinary events.[33] For example, one of the *Sowetan*'s reports on the flood, headlined "Decomposing Bodies Brought Up" (2 October 1987), focused on the exposure of coffins in a subsequent mud slide. The article also reported the destruction of the Lindelani shack settlement near KwaMashu, one of Durban's major African townships. While the issue of the settlement—whose destruction left 350 people homeless and thirteen dead—was clearly a serious one, the article concentrated largely on the issue of the coffins. In contrast, *New Nation* focused on the injustices perpetuated in the wake of the flood and on why only specific areas suffered.

The *Sowetan*'s emphasis on events as opposed to processes was demonstrated in its descriptive rather than analytical approach. It documented the disaster for four days—both at the flood's height and for a few days thereafter, using syndicated material from Argus-style commercial newspapers based in Durban. The 30 September edition, headlined "Natal Flood Toll Goes Up," provided estimates of people drowned and homes damaged, described the impact of the flood on the water supply and communication links, and outlined the nature of rescue and relief work being undertaken. The 1 October edition, headlined "Natal Counting Flood's Damage," provided an update of the damage done, the most recent estimates of lives lost, and quoted a statement by the health minister. The 2 October edition provided a brief update on the front page, and a second article in the same edition, the "Decomposing Bodies" story, reporting the destruction of the settlement, the exposure of coffins, and the relief work being carried out. The flood story in the *Sowetan's* 5 October edition did go a little beyond description in attempting to explain how the flood had created conditions for the spread of disease, crime, and hunger by making existing problems even worse (citing the shortage of drinking water, the high mortality rate among children, and the poorly developed health services in rural areas).

New Nation carried only one article on the flood, headlined "Inkatha Cashes In on Floods" (8–14 October 1987). It highlighted the plight of flood victims who were not members Inkatha, the ruling KwaZulu homeland party. The story provided details of the unfair distribution of flood aid in the areas where Inkatha had taken control of relief operations. It exposed Inkatha's use of flood aid as a recruiting device. Selective assistance was no doubt critical for those resident in areas where Inkatha controlled the distribution of flood aid, but the commercial press paid little attention to this issue (it was ignored by the *Sowetan*). While presenting estimates of the damage caused, *New Nation* also explained why specific areas were particularly badly affected. Referring to a study carried out by the Built Environment Support Group,[34] the newspaper noted that large-scale devastation could be related to the apartheid system because Africans were compelled to live in unplanned areas with no assistance in home building. *New Nation's* coverage of the flood thus reveals a concern to move beyond description to an evaluation of the structural causes of how people may have been affected by events.

"Shop Where South Africa Shops, OK"

An article in the *Sowetan* (13 January 1987) on the nationwide OK workers' strike is illustrative of the newspaper's ambivalence with regard to labor issues.[35] The article, headlined "OK Reacts to 'Starvation Wages' Claim," reported on the response of the OK management to union allegations. It quoted the company's personnel director, who cited his own wage statistics in an attempt to counter the union's claims, and another story followed with a union organizer's comment on the figures. There was also an update on the number of workers on strike and the outlets affected, quoting the representative of the Commercial, Catering and Allied Workers Union of South Africa (CCAWUSA) on the management's treatment of striking workers.

Although the *Sowetan* article showed support for the workers —most space was devoted to an account of the OK strike from the workers' point of view—this support was undermined by a photograph of the smiling managing director above the article, whose image had made regular appearances in OK advertisements in the press and on television. This invoked the business-friendly perception of OK's chief executive as the friendly store manager who has the interests of the public at heart. Similarly, the words "starvation wages" in the headline appeared in quotes, distancing the article from any sympathy with the strikers in their dissatisfaction over wages.

New Nation's coverage of the same strike in the 15–21 January 1987 edition revealed explicit support for the strikers. The front page pictured a picketing worker holding a sign, framed to draw attention to the slogans "OK Cares for Profit Not People—Support 10,000 Workers on Strike" and "Fight for a Living Wage." The composition of the image thus emphasized the worker's message rather than the worker. The headline of the article, "OK Strike Gains Momentum," represented the union organizer's description of the progress of the strike.

In each case, *New Nation* followed the kind of advocacy journalism encouraged by Michael Traber, William Biernatzki, and others, who operate within the social development approach encouraged by the Second Vatican Council (Vatican II) and adopted by the SACBC as funders of the newspaper.[36] As a weekly, *New Nation* provided its staffers the opportunity to interrogate issues from a wider perspective, and they could interview a broader range of activists from marginalized African communities. As a daily, the *Sowetan* followed conventional commercial reporting procedures that emphasized deadlines and news retrieved from a variety of sources—often managed news from the wire services.

New Nation, *the Catholic Right, and the South African State*

New Nation survived three related assaults on its integrity during the late 1980s.[37] First, the government tried to silence the publication. Three issues were banned in February and August 1987, its editor was detained without trial in December 1987, and the newspaper itself was banned for three months, from March to June 1987. While other alternative publications were subjected to this kind of harassment, the government acted with particular harshness in the case of *New Nation*. The newspaper was accused of "systematic or repetitive publishing of matter in a way, which . . . is calculated to have the effect . . . of stirring up the public image or esteem of an organization which is an unlawful organization."[38] In his letter of notification to *New Nation*, the minister of the interior, who was responsible for banning publications, informed the editor that the decision had been made on the basis of reading three issues of the newspaper.[39]

Second, while *New Nation*'s editor, Zwelakhe Sisulu, had been held in detention for nearly two years, advertisers were intimidated by state agencies and warned against "sponsoring a newspaper promoting revolution."[40] Third, a right-wing Catholic lay movement based in Brazil and Argentina called Tradition, Family, Property (TFP) became influential in conservative Catholic circles in South Africa, and adherents mounted a high-profile, if somewhat hysterical, theological campaign to discredit the SACBC.[41] This led to a somewhat unlikely alliance between the South African state with its conservative, Afrikaner Calvinist rhetoric, and this fringe, imported Catholic lobby group.

TFP penetrated South African religious discourse through white Portuguese refugees fleeing Angola and Mozambique after those Portuguese colonies were granted independence in 1975. Many had relatives in South Africa, which was home to a large Madeiran Portuguese community. The influx of these refugees presented an initial problem, because the overwhelming majority were Roman Catholic. In Afrikaner Calvinist ideology there was no room for the "Roomse gevaar" (Roman danger), which was on a par with blackness and communism. TFP, however, was rabidly anticommunist, and it soon became evident that these Portuguese immigrants would be staunch supporters of apartheid policies. Given the South African government's ongoing obsession with communism and matters of race, and the long diplomatic association between Pretoria and Lisbon, it is not surprising that the new immigrants received a warm welcome.

In the 1980s, TFP mobilized South Africa's conservative elements of Catholicism in support of the apartheid regime.

Among its targets were the SACBC and *New Nation*. The government, of course, encouraged and supported TFP in its attacks. A TFP booklet, which purported to offer content analysis and "proof" of the communist leanings of both *New Nation* and the SACBC, was aimed "at whipping up opposition . . . so that pressure would be put on the SACBC to withdraw its patronage of the paper. . . . The Apostolic delegate at the time, Archbishop De Paoli, now a Nuncio in Japan, certainly received correspondence from the TFP asking the Vatican to intervene. . . . [The booklet] was snapped up by those who were opposed to the stand taken by the SACBC."[42]

By focusing on *New Nation*, TFP gave further impetus to the state's attack on the alternative press in general. The TFP "study" booklet was recommended and cited by none other than the minister of home affairs in a response to an inquiry on his reasons for issuing a "warning" to the *Weekly Mail*. He claimed that these newspapers were engaging in "subversive communication."[43]

The CCSU analysis revealed that the main thrust of both the state's and the TFP's attack on *New Nation* was based on the argument that *New Nation* was being mobilized as a surrogate to serve the interests of Soviet imperialism.[44] This argument was based on the assumption that the struggle against the National Party government was a manifestation of "the ANC/SA Communist Party revolutionary alliance,"[45] that the alternative press incited violent revolution, and that a conspiracy existed between those publications and the forces of communist imperialism.

Conclusion

The *Sowetan* was bought by New Africa Investments, Ltd., in 1993, headed at that time by Dr. Nthato Motlana, a businessman who was also the Mandela family's personal physician. While much of the *Sowetan*'s editorial staff remained within the orbit of the evolving Black Consciousness movement, the newspaper became in effect an organ of the ANC. *New Nation* was bought by the *Sowetan* in 1995 but only survived for two years. The new editor of *New Nation*, Gabu Tugwane, was instructed to tone down the newspaper's socialist content. As *Sowetan* editor, Aggry Klaaste noted, "Because *Sowetan* was considered to be anti-ANC, our new owners were under pressure from the ANC to ensure that they reformed the paper. We were also dragooned into buying *New Nation* because of its obvious connections with the people it supported during the liberation struggle."[46]

New Nation had served a plurality of social and cultural interests which united under a specific political agenda—a nonracist, nonsexist, one-person-one-vote constitutional democracy. This agenda opposed the capitalist impetus of colonialism by calling for a socialist economy aimed at increasing the wealth of all its members.

New Nation survived as an anti-apartheid newspaper, and it was supported by the SACBC as an alternative to the commercialism of market-oriented alternative newspapers like the *Sowetan*. Progressive journalists, however, had paid relatively little attention to administrative and financial matters, which were now undermining the viability of their editorial concerns.

The success of the *Sowetan* and the demise of *New Nation* both spring from their respective capacities to apply management practices adequate to their financial objectives. The *Sowetan* managed its affairs by submitting to the demands of whatever market player obtained the greatest return for its investment. *New Nation* was never in a position to survive under such an arrangement, especially when the SACBC ceased funding the newspaper and sold it to Motlana's group. Like

New Nation, most publications associated with the alternative press had folded by the end of the 1990s.

Notes

My thanks to Arnold Shepperson for his assistance on this chapter, which draws on previous research projects led by Ansuya Chetty.

1. Tomaselli and Louw divided the 1980s press into eleven categories: (1) Afrikaans-language publications associated with the National Party (NP) and supportive of the party's "reformed" apartheid, such as *Beeld* and *Rapport;* (2) conservative, English-language publications associated with the NP and supportive of the party's "reformed" apartheid, such as the *Citizen;* (3) English-language, anti-apartheid publications linked to monopoly mining-finance capital, such as the *Star* and *Business Day;* (4) regional and free sheet publications usually linked to English and Afrikaans press groups that offered "apolitical" local-interest news, such as *Highway Mail, Mid-Month Mirror,* and *Ezase Mlazi;* (5) social-democratic independent publications like *Vrye Weekblad* and the *Weekly Mail;* (6) progressive-alternative community publications like *Saamstaan* and *Grassroots;* (7) left-commercial publications like *South* and *New Nation;* (8) neo-fascist, apartheid publications that broke away from the NP, such as *Die Patriot* (linked to the Conservative Party), *Die Afrikaner* (linked to the Herstigte or "Reformed" Nationale Party), and *Die Stem* (linked to the Afrikaner Weerstandsbeweging, or Afrikaner Resistance Movement); (9) publications tied to apartheid homeland governments, such as *Ilanga;* (10) student publications like *SASPU National;* (11) white-owned, commercial publications targeted for the African market, such as *City Press* and the *Sowetan.* K. G. Tomaselli and P. E. Louw, eds. *The Alternative Press in South Africa* (London: James Currey, 1991), 5–6.

2. Tomaselli and Louw, *Alternative Press,* 8–9, 12; K. G. Tomaselli, "Race, Class, and the South African Progressive Press," *International Journal for Intercultural Relations,* 10 (1986): 53–74. For similar definitions of *alternative,* see S. Johnson, *An Alternative Catholic Newspaper for South Africa: A Feasibility Study* (Pretoria: Ecumenical Research Unit, 1982), para. 2.1: "In essence . . . an alternative publication must

have claim to independence, in the sense that it is not directly or indirectly controlled by ruling vested interest groups such as the state or the commercial monopoly press groups in South Africa. Secondly, it must have as its central purpose the provision of some kind of alternative: political, social, economic, cultural or ideological to the South African status quo." My use of the term fulfills Michael Traber's requirement that such media provide voices for ordinary individuals, avoid the views of the powerful, and seek to replace event-driven reporting with explanations of context. M. Traber, "Alternative Journalism, Alternative Media," *Communication Resource*, no. 7 (1985): 3.

3. Johnson, *Alternative Catholic Newspaper*, para. 1.1.

4. J. Fubbs and J. Warden, *Survey Report: An Alternative Catholic Newspaper for South Africa* (Pretoria: Ecumenical Research Unit, 1983), 32.

5. L. Patel, "How Small Media Can Organise Communities," *Media Development* 32 (1985): 14.

6. Ibid.

7. Ansuya Chetty, P. Eric Louw, and Keyan G. Tomaselli, "The *Sowetan* and *New Nation*, 1 January 1987 to 31 December 1987: A Content Analysis and Comparison" (report commissioned by *New Nation*, Durban, 1988, CCSU mimeo).

8. See P. E. Louw and K. G. Tomaselli, "The Popular 'Bottom-up' Approach to Community Development: The Example of the Grassroots Newspaper's Catalyst Role in the Western Cape," in *Development in South Africa*, ed. R. J. W. van der Kooy (Pretoria: Prodder, 1989/90), 85–93. *New Nation* started as a Friday fortnightly but switched to a weekly in 1987. It adopted a Sunday format in August 1993, but circulation plummeted to 15,000. The newspaper quickly reverted to a Friday issue. See also B. Mpofu, "Corporate Monopoly in the South African Print Media: Implications for the Alternative Press with Particular Reference to *New Nation*" (M.A. thesis, University of Natal, Durban, 1995); www.und.ac.za/und/ccms/articles/mpofu.

9. Mark Orkin, New Nation *Reader Survey* (Johannesburg: Community Agency for Social Enquiry, 1987). Our use of racial categories is in no way a reflection of *New Nation*'s conception of its readers. In keeping with *New Nation*'s nonracial approach, the newspaper did not distinguish between readers in terms of racial designations.

10. Ibid.

11. M. Gray, "Coercion, Control, and Censorship," *Media Development* 23 (1985): 26.

12. *Work in Progress*, August 1979, 57.

13. Quoted in *Financial Mail*, 6 June 1980.

14. "Sowetan Survey, 1987" (mimeo).

15. See K. G. Tomaselli, R. E. Tomaselli, and J. Muller, eds., *The Press in South Africa* (London: James Currey, 1987), 42–46; Alexander Holt, "An Analysis of Racial Stereotyping and Content in SABC-TV Commercials in the Context of Reform, 1978–1992," (Ph.D. diss., University of Natal, Durban, 1998).

16. Republic of South Africa, *Report of the Commission of Inquiry into Legislation Affecting the Utilisation of Manpower* (Pretoria: Government Printer, 1979).

17. For example, *Work in Progress*, August 1979, 56. See also R. H. Davies, "Capital Restructuring and Modification of Racial Division of Labour in South Africa," *Journal of Southern African Studies* 15, 2 (1979).

18. K. G. Tomaselli, R. E. Tomaselli, and J. Muller, eds., *Narrating the Crisis: Hegemony and the South African Press* (Johannesburg: Richard Lyon, 1987), 47. The following description was on the cover of the first issue of the magazine *Pace:* "Fashion and Fast Living, Pretty Girls and Politics, Music and Laughter, Sport and Adventure, Violence and Beauty, Love and Sex." Cited in *Work in Progress*, 1979, 64.

19. Tomaselli, Tomaselli, and Muller, *Narrating the Crisis*, 49.

20. *Star*, 9 August 1986.

21. *Citizen*, 17 December 1986.

22. Dated 1 December 1987, reproduced in Zwelakhe Sisulu, *An Editor in Prison* (London: Article 19, 1988), 31.

23. Quoted in Chetty, Louw, and Tomaselli, *"Sowetan* and *New Nation."*

24. *Sowetan*, 8 May 1987.

25. *Sowetan*, 26 June 1987.

26. On "allocative control," see Graham Murdock, "Large Corporations and the Control of Communications Industries," in *Culture, Society, and the Media*, ed. M. Gurevitch, T. Bennett, J. Curran, and J. Woollacott (London: Routledge, 1986), 118–50.

27. *Sowetan*, 14 May 1987. Black urban workers were almost totally dependent on SATS for rail transport between dormitory towns and the white industrial areas where they worked.

28. Chetty, Louw, and Tomaselli, *"Sowetan* and *New Nation."*

29. The sample used in the statistical analysis was a subset of all the editions of both newspapers from 1 January 1987 to 31 December 1987. The study compared each edition of *New Nation* to the corresponding editions of the *Sowetan* with regard to the events and issues covered, the position of each newspaper on a variety of issues as expressed in editorials and news reports, and the style of journalism.

30. P. Eric Louw, "The Libertarian Theory of the Press: How Appropriate in the South African Context?" *Communicatio* 10, 1 (1984): 31–37.

31. Johnson, *Alternative Catholic Newspaper*, para. 1.1.

32. Orkin, *Reader Survey. New Nation's* readers in this survey were most interested in South African news (80 percent) and international news (76 percent).

33. See Traber, "Alternative Journalism," 2. Traber lists timelessness, prominence, proximity, conflict, and the bizarre as among the conventional news values of the mass media. "Timelessness" designates an event that has taken place within a discrete interval and is complete as an event. As such, the event qualifies for inclusion in terms of the production schedule of newspapers and will thus take precedence over longer-term processes and trends that do not occur at publishable intervals. As regards "prominence," the more important or powerful a person, event, or place is, the more likely he, she, or it will appear in the news. "Proximity" refers to how close the event is to the newspaper's office. Events occurring further afield are less likely to merit reporting, unless they have sufficient dramatic impact to force the attention of the media. "Conflict" reflects the tendency of news media to capitalize on events with elements of conflict or disagreement, while the "bizarre" reflects the tendency of news media to capitalize on odd and extraordinary events.

34. The Built Environment Support Group (BESG) is a research and resource unit based in the School of Architecture and Allied Disciplines at the University of Natal in Durban. BESG drew on a multidisciplinary coalition of researchers to develop alternative housing construction, servicing, and development aid to people displaced into the cities, and people fleeing the low-level civil war then taking place in Natal's rural areas.

35. The title of this section was the OK's advertising slogan at the time.

36. See Traber, "Alternative Journalism"; and the work of the

Centre for the Study of Communication and Culture, such as William E. Biernatzki, "Religious News Agencies," *Media Development* 27, 1 (1981); Biernatzki, "Addendum on International Religious News Flows," *Communication Research Trends* 10, 4 (1990); Keval J. Kumar, "Media Education: Growth and Controversy," *Communication Research Trends* 6, 4 (1985); and Robert A. White, "Mass Media and the Culture of Contemporary Catholicism: The Significance of the Second Vatican Council" (Centre for the Study of Communication and Culture, London, 1986, mimeo). White's mimeo expands an earlier article, "The New Communications Emerging in the Church," *Way Supplement* 57 (1986).

37. This section is drawn from an extensive report written for *New Nation* by CCSU (which later became the Centre for Cultural and Media Studies, CCMS). The report, by researchers Ansuya Chetty, Keyan Tomaselli, Ruth Tomaselli, P. Eric Louw, Vukani Cele, and Reshma Ramsingh, was entitled, "*New Nation:* Unmasking Tradition, Family, Property's Media Manoeuvre" (Centre for Cultural and Media Studies, Durban, 1988). Hereafter CCSU, "Unmasking TFP"; www.und.ac.za/und/ccms/articles/ftp.

38. Republic of South Africa, Proclamation R99, 1986.

39. Republic of South Africa, Proclamation R123, 1986.

40. *Article 19,* p. 14.

41. See, for example, Young South Africans for a Christian Civilization, *The "New Nation" and Liberation Theology* (Johannesburg: Young South Africans for a Christian Civilization, 1987).

42. Brother Jude Pieterse, Marist Provinciale, to author, Johannesburg, 21 May 1999. Pieterse also stated, "I recall as well having boxes of petitions delivered to the Secretariat with a demand that [TFP] see me . . . in a detailed examination of the petitions. . . . I noticed that several were signed by the same people, some even objecting to the petition and supporting the SACBC. . . . When TFP arrived for a meeting I was able to give the carpet under their feet a good tug."

43. Department of Home Affairs to K. G. Tomaselli, 9 August 1988.

44. CCSU, "Unmasking TFP," 17.

45. Department of Home Affairs to Tomaselli.

46. Quoted in Mpofu, "Corporate Monopoly," 79.

10

Breaking the Mold
of Political Subservience

Vrye Weekblad and the Afrikaans Alternative Press

George Claassen

The birth of *Vrye Weekblad* on 4 November 1988 came during the worst decade of government repression of media in South Africa since the era of Lord Charles Somerset as governor of British colonial Cape Province in the 1820s. For the Afrikaans press, it was "like taking a deep breath after loosening a restrictive corset."[1]

The debilitating corset was fastened by the rulers of successive National Party governments after 1948, when the party took power and began to construct an institutionalized system of apartheid between designated racial groups. It was also fastened by the mainstream, establishment press and the South African Broadcasting Corporation, which toed the line of these minority white rulers. With a loyal Afrikaans press consisting of dailies like *Die Burger* (Cape Town), *Oosterlig* (Port Elizabeth), *Die Volksblad* (Bloemfontein), *Die Vaderland* and *Die Transvaler* (both Johannesburg), and younger publications like *Oggendblad*, *Hoofstad* (both Pretoria), and *Beeld* (Johannesburg), as well as Sunday newspapers like *Die Beeld* and *Dagbreek en Sondagnuus,* and their successor *Rapport,* the National Party ruled with intrepid bravado against world opinion.

The apartheid state had temporarily blunted resistance by the early 1960s, as the major opposition groups had been banned and their leaders were either in prison or in exile. Apartheid ideology underwent a few cosmetic changes at the end of the sixties under prime minister B. J. (John) Vorster (such as allowing sporting contact between different racial groups and acquiescing to governments from Africa appointing black ambassadors to South Africa), but the country erupted in violence after thousands of African students rioted in the streets of Soweto in June 1976. When the government under prime minister Pieter Willem Botha changed South Africa's constitution in 1983 to include Coloureds and Indians in Parliament but not the African majority, the country again erupted in violence. This led to the declaration of a partial state of emergency in July 1985.

For the first time, dissident Afrikaans voices began appearing in the Afrikaans press. Today it is fairly widely accepted that the Johannesburg-based Afrikaans newspapers *Die Beeld* and *Beeld,* under relatively enlightened editors like Schalk Pienaar, H. J. Grosskopf, Ton Vosloo, and Willem Wepener, as well as *Die Volksblad, Die Vaderland,* and *Die Transvaler,* under relatively enlightened editors like Hennie van Deventer, Harald Pakendorf, and Willem de Klerk, played a more important role in changing the face of apartheid than the Afrikaans establishment press have generally been credited.[2] James McClurg, the highly regarded ombudsman of the Argus group (then the largest media conglomerate in southern Africa), noted shortly after the African National Congress (ANC) and other political organizations were unbanned in February 1990, "When historians turn their eye on this era, will they reserve a chapter for the contribution of the *verligte* [enlightened] Afrikaans press towards change in South Africa? If not, an injustice will have been done."[3]

Many Afrikaner readers, especially among the generation born after 1948, however, were skeptical of the established press as a vehicle for changing the belief system generated by apartheid. They wanted an Afrikaans newspaper independent of the National Party's shackles. The birth of *Vrye Weekblad* answered their prayers.

Right-wing reactions to National Party policies also generated a variety of right-wing alternative Afrikaans newspapers such as *Veg, Ster, Die Afrikaner, Patriot, Die Stem,* and *Boerant.* While these publications should not be ignored in a comprehensive analysis of the Afrikaans alternative press in South Africa, this chapter focuses on four antiapartheid Afrikaans newspapers—*Die Suid-Afrikaan, Vrye Weekblad, Saamstaan,* and *Namaqua Nuus*—that participated in the struggle for a democratic, nonracial South Africa.

The National Party and the Afrikaans Establishment Press

A pen sketch of the history of the Afrikaans press throws light on the close link between the National Party and the mainstream Afrikaans press, which opened up space for these alternative publications. The Afrikaans-language press had its roots in the Dutch press of the eighteenth-century Cape. *Di Patriot* was established as the first Afrikaans newspaper in 1876, and it crusaded for decades to get Afrikaans recognized as a language in South Africa. Although *Di Patriot* ceased publication in 1904, the newspaper played a paramount role in establishing Afrikaans as a written language—twenty-one years later Afrikaans replaced Dutch as one of the two official languages of South Africa.

Die Voorloper, an Afrikaans weekly that appeared between 1912 and 1914, was a precursor to *Vrye Weekblad* in its opposition to the government of the day. *Die Voorloper* was established by the Afrikaanse Koerant Maatskappy (Afrikaans Newspaper Company), which was created by idealistic Afrikaans writers like J. H. H. de Waal and F. W. Reitz, former president of the Orange Free State. The newspaper supported Boer War general (and later prime minister) J. B. M. Hertzog's protest against the pro-British government of Louis Botha, the Union of South Africa's first prime minister.

Nasionale Pers was established in March 1915, and it played a very important role in bringing the National Party to power in 1924 under the leadership of Hertzog.[4] He had established the National Party in Bloemfontein in January 1914, and Nasionale Pers published the first edition of *De Burger* in Cape Town in July 1915, strongly supporting Hertzog against his Boer War colleagues Louis Botha and Jan Smuts.

The Afrikaans press backed the newly formed National Party. The appointment of Daniël F. Malan as the first editor of *De Burger* (the name was changed to *Die Burger* in January 1922) would start a trend in the Afrikaans newspaper world that would continue until the late 1970s: the birth of a symbiotic relationship between Afrikaans publishing houses and the National Party. Malan, a minister in the Dutch Reformed Church, would later become leader of the "Purified" National Party when Hertzog and General Smuts in 1934 decided to fuse the National Party with the South African Party—the object being to unite South Africa's main parliamentary parties to fight the Great Depression.

Die Burger no longer supported Hertzog and campaigned vigorously against the Smuts-Hertzog United Party government. Malan led his new National Party to victory in the 1948 general election, defeating the United Party. The strong support of *Die Burger* and its Bloemfontein-based sister daily,

Die Volksblad, played an important role in Malan coming to power.[5]

Malan was not the only former editor of an Afrikaans newspaper who became leader of the National Party. Hendrik F. Verwoerd was appointed editor of the new Johannesburg daily *Die Transvaler* when it was established by Voortrekkerpers in September 1937 "with the exclusive task of propagating Afrikaner nationalism and Afrikaner culture."[6] Verwoerd, later known as the architect of grand apartheid, was included in Malan's cabinet as minister of native affairs in 1950, and he became prime minister in 1958.[7] C. R. Swart, a leader in the National Party who was appointed the first state president (the post at the time was largely ceremonial) after South Africa became a republic in 1961, wrote a column entitled "Brief uit Bloemfontein" (Letter from Bloemfontein) under the pseudonym Rondloper (vagabond) for *Die Volksblad* in the 1920s and was interim editor of the newspaper for a few months in the 1930s.[8] Andries P. Treurnicht, who became the leader of the National Party in the Transvaal, was the first editor of *Hoofstad* (Capital city), the afternoon daily in Pretoria, when it was established in April 1968.[9]

The birth of various right-wing alternative newspapers and magazines in Afrikaans dates from the late 1960s. They were a direct result of the schism in the National Party brought about by changes in apartheid policy fostered by John Vorster, who succeeded Verwoerd after he was assassinated in 1966, and his successors, P. W. Botha and Frederik Willem de Klerk.

These publications wanted to continue the strict policy of Verwoerdian apartheid: they insisted the state had to play a vital role in organizing society, and they emphasized a dominant place for Afrikaans in officialdom and government affairs. They also refused to toe the self-regulating line of the South African press under the jurisdiction of the Newspaper Press Union (NPU), because they did not belong to the NPU. Their strong criticism hurt the Botha government—especially after the breakaway of Transvaal leader Andries Treurnicht, his cabinet colleague Ferdie Hartzenberg, and fourteen other NP members of Parliament in February 1982 to form the Conservative Party in protest against Botha's constitutional reforms.

The influence of these right-wing publications on the political orientation of Afrikaners, as well as the government's ultrasensitive reaction to criticism of its policies from mainstream English-language newspapers, led the Botha government to impose stricter controls on the media. The Commission of Inquiry into the Mass Media, under the chairmanship of Justice M. T. Steyn, was appointed in June 1980. The commission's report, which in essence proposed new censorship regulations to control journalists and newspapers, was presented to Parliament in February 1982. The Botha government sought to implement some of the Steyn Commission's recommendations, but the outcry of the press, the leadership of the NPU, and its members (including the Afrikaans members) eventually led to a compromise.

Newspapers belonging to the NPU had established a voluntary South African Press Council as early as 1962 in "an attempt to forestall direct government control of the press." Twenty years later, in June 1982, the minister of home affairs, Chris Heunis, tried to introduce a new press law to ensure that the NPU's voluntary council became a statutory body compulsory for *all* newspapers, including right-wing Afrikaans newspapers outside the NPU, so they would be forced to join the NPU and adhere to the council's rules. This plan was also abandoned after strong opposition, but a compromise was approved by Parliament in July 1982—the Registration of Newspapers Amendment Act (no. 84 of 1982). The registration of newspapers could be canceled—which meant they could not be published—if publishers refused to "subject themselves" to the NPU's council "for disciplinary purposes." Most newspaper editors and proprietors vigorously opposed this legislation and decided to set up another "voluntary" council "that would refuse to serve as a basis for government decisions on whether or not the registration of a paper should be withdrawn."

In September 1983 the NPU agreed to replace the old council with a new one, the South African Media Council, that would include broadcast as well as print media. The Media Council would have the power "to reprimand and fine newspapers," but it was still a voluntary body.[10] Although the original legislation was directed primarily at the two main right-wing alternative newspapers—*Patriot* (launched in May 1982) and *Die Afrikaner* (launched in January 1970)—they never submitted to the Media Council's authority and remained a thorn in the side of the government.

The growing anarchy in the country's African townships—especially after the new constitution and tricameral parliament (consisting of whites, Coloureds, and Indians) was implemented in 1984—led to the first countrywide state of emergency in June 1986. The Botha government would sidestep the NPU, which "refused to bring the Media Council into line with government thinking." In its quest to "crush the 'so-called alternative press,'"[11] a directorate of media relations was created in September 1987. The new agency was linked to the directorate of publications, the department of law and order, the department of defence, and the bureau of information—all of which would be under the authority of the department of home affairs. By the late 1980s, then, there were five separate government bodies responsible for policing South Africa's press.

Die Suid-Afrikaan

Die Suid-Afrikaan and *Vrye Weekblad* were launched during the height of political unrest between Botha's 1983 constitution and de Klerk's February 1990 speech in Parliament unbanning the ANC and other political organizations. The relationship between the governing National Party and the Afrikaans press had "an inhibiting influence on reporting," according to Cornelia Faure, which "frustrated some Afrikaans journalists tremendously. They wanted to write in their own language for their own people about the realities of South Africa."[12]

The first edition of *Die Suid-Afrikaan* appeared in the spring of 1984 with the following motto below the masthead: "'n Selfstandige meningsblad" (An independent opinion magazine). It was published in Stellenbosch by Voorbrand Publikasies under the editorship of Hermann Giliomee, a professor in political studies at the University of Cape Town. Giliomee and other editorial colleagues mentioned in the first edition, including André P. Brink, Jakes Gerwel, and André du Toit, were all leading Afrikaans verligtes.[13]

Giliomee was the sole shareholder in Voorbrand Publikasies, and he was the publisher. From the eighth edition of *Die Suid-Afrikaan* (Winter 1986), the editorship became a troika of Giliomee, André du Toit, and Riaan de Villiers, who was responsible for production. The editorial advisory board reads like a who's who of white and black, mostly Afrikaner, verligtes —all critical of the government's apartheid policies and all propagating reform. They included Richard van der Ross, Tjaart van der Walt, Johan Degenaar, Jacko Maree, Jan Mettler, Samuel Ngcongwane, Lawrence Schlemmer, Laurens van der Post, Rykie van Reenen, and Francis Wilson.[14]

Die Suid-Afrikaan, published in magazine format, would focus on the politics, the economy, and the intellectual life of South Africa. The editorial of the first edition clearly emphasized the publication's independence. The editorial took pains to explain that the magazine would "not be published by a press group. The editors would be responsible for the magazine's content and inclination. . . . Our magazine has no party political links. . . . We choose an open society, equality and a peaceful settlement in South Africa."[15] Its readers, for example, were called Afrikane (literally, people "from Africa")—a term that embraced persons of all colors (including white)—instead of Afrikaners (Africans), which referred to one ethnic group with a prescribed color and ideology. This was a significant linguistic innovation, because many conservative white Afrikaners refused to allow Coloured Afrikaners—now the majority in the Afrikaans-speaking community—to be called Afrikaners.

In a manifesto under the headline, "'n Nuwe bedeling?" (A new dispensation?), Giliomee wrote about the problems the country faced with the new constitution excluding Africans from the franchise: "Unification in 1910 directly led to the establishment of the ANC. After that the paths grew further apart, until the coming of the Republic in 1961 was followed by the banning of the ANC. The new Constitution of 1983 gave rise to the establishment of the UDF.[16] Would it be too much to expect that the new dispensation will also eventually give way to black aspirations?"[17] These were the strongest words coming from an Afrikaans publication since Ton Vosloo, then editor of *Beeld*, warned the government in 1981: "the day will come that a South African government will sit with the ANC around the negotiating table."[18]

Die Suid-Afrikaan published articles in English, although most were in Afrikaans. In the only English article in the first issue Charles Simkins asked whether the government could achieve educational equality. Other articles (in Afrikaans) were about black reactions to white constitutions (André Odendaal), the pattern of white-Coloured relations (Richard van der Ross), Afrikaner attitudes on desegregation in housing (Lawrence Schlemmer), the possibility of opening up Stellenbosch University to all races (André du Toit), and the political allegiances of Coloureds (Willem van Vuuren). There were also articles in this issue by prize-winning Afrikaans authors Hennie Aucamp, Karel Schoeman, and André P. Brink.

Die Suid-Afrikaan's incisive journalism set an example for the mainstream Afrikaans press, because it was not afraid to address contentious issues and confront the government. "Although we never felt the same political pressure that *Vrye Weekblad* later went through," Giliomee remembered, "we knew that the government did not like what we were writing. [But w]e had no problems getting the magazine registered."[19]

The role *Die Suid-Afrikaan* played to encourage Afrikaners toward a negotiated political settlement was emphasized in 1987, when a group of South Africans went to Dakar in Senegal to meet a delegation of ANC exiles. South Africa's African townships were burning and the state of emergency allowed little leeway for alternative media to break the mold of demonization that was placed on the ANC and other banned organizations by the government and the mainstream Afrikaans press. The Dakar meeting was arranged by the Institute for a Democratic Alternative in South Africa (IDASA), in close alliance with France's Liberté Institut and the African Jurists' Association.

The Dakar talks were attended by Giliomee, du Toit, and de Villiers, and their direct involvement in the discussions (du Toit delivered the first paper) led to *Die Suid-Afrikaan* devoting the September 1987 edition to in-depth reports on the meeting. The front-page photo taken at the opening ceremony showed ANC foreign spokesman Thabo Mbeki, Frederik van Zyl Slabbert, a codirector of IDASA who was regarded as the leader of the internal South African delegation, and dissident Afrikaans poet and painter Breyten Breytenbach.[20] It was taken by Max du Preez, who would start his own alternative newspaper a little more than a year later. Chris Louw, who joined the editorial staff with this edition, wrote an article on the South African press and became the magazine's first full-time journalist.

Giliomee explained the aim of *Die Suid-Afrikaan*'s involvement in the Dakar talks under the headline, "The ANC, the Afrikaners and the Story of the Baboon":

> What we wanted to do as delegates to Dakar, was to bring about a certain measure of rationality in the propaganda war which has taken the place of serious politics in South Africa. The indigenous delegation wanted to show, by sitting with the ANC at the conference table, that the country was *not* in the grip of a war that was being forced upon us from outside. We wanted to say that the battle was *not* one between the forces of "evil" and those of the "good"; it's an internal struggle with its roots in the country's history—a struggle that must be solved inside the country. . . . Dakar was an effort to break through the propaganda struggle in which both the government and the ANC branded each other as diabolical, holding each other solely responsible for the suffering and death of the past thirty-four months.

Summing up his feeling of the conference, Giliomee wrote, "the greatest surprise was the measure in which the ANC and the NP were mirror images of each other."[21]

Louw's article under the headline, "ANC Safari Uncovered," analyzed the hysteria that developed in the South African press after the *Citizen* broke the story of the intended Dakar conference. Louw pointed out that opposition against the Dakar meeting stemmed mainly from the Afrikaans mainstream press and the English-language *Citizen*, which belonged to Perskor and was established by the National Party in 1975 to serve as a propaganda vehicle for the government.[22]

Louw also noted that three prominent progovernment newspapers (*Die Burger, Beeld*, and the *Citizen*) devoted more space to attacking the Dakar talks than the antigovernment *Star* did in defending the talks. He quoted examples from *Beeld*, which published ten front-page stories on the Dakar conference in three weeks (sample headline: "ANC's Cunning Plan with Dakar"). The *Citizen* attacked the Dakar delegation vociferously in an editorial: "We say that Slabbert and Co. not only betrayed all law abiding citizens of the country by their mad desire to talk to terrorists, but they betrayed the moderate blacks in particular" (17 July 1987). The political columnist Dawie (usually a column written by the editor of *Die Burger,* who was Wiets Beukes at that stage), also attacked the South African delegation: they "wanted to give the whole extraparliamentary movement, and the role of the ANC in it, a strong boost and wanted to establish it as a practical alternative."[23]

The Dakar talks continued to be the center of attention in *Die Suid-Afrikaan's* columns well into 1988. The newspaper published a series of letters in February 1988 between, for example, Giliomee, Breyten Breytenbach, and Pallo Jordan, one of the few members of the ANC's executive council who was not placed on a proscribed list by the government (which meant he could be quoted in print). Giliomee believed that nationalism could not be denied, Breytenbach emphasized that some verligte Afrikaners' thinking was still clouded by "white paint," and Jordan asked, "Why won't Afrikaners rely on democracy?"[24]

According to Giliomee, the magazine barely survived the first three years through subscriptions and advertisements. *Die Suid-Afrikaan's* involvement in the Dakar talks made it possible to get assistance from the German government and the German daily *Die Zeit,* and this established the pattern of overseas funding. Giliomee became managing editor in April 1989, with Chris Louw and Welma Odendaal as production editors, but he gradually withdrew from the editorial side. André du Toit took over as managing editor in June 1990. The editorial office was moved from Stellenbosch to Bree Street in Cape Town in September 1987.

Die Suid-Afrikaan at this stage was being produced by academics working part time on the newspaper—Giliomee, du

Toit, and especially Hein Willemse, who was then a lecturer in Afrikaans at the University of the Western Cape—and two full-time journalists—Louw and Welma Odendaal. Louw was appointed managing editor from the October/November 1992 edition with a student journalist, Sandile Dikeni, filling a part-time position from April 1991. Dikeni would eventually become the last editor before *Die Suid-Afrikaan*'s closure.

The struggle for survival led to some internal strife between Giliomee and du Toit. According to Louw, "personality clashes with du Toit eventually led to Giliomee giving more attention to management matters and du Toit to the editorial side of things." Louw claimed Giliomee was not prepared to use more foreign donor money, but the magazine could not really survive without overseas funding.[25] Giliomee left the magazine as editor after the July 1990 edition, although he edited a special edition on urbanization in November 1990. The publishing of *Die Suid-Afrikaan* was transferred from Voorbrand Publikasies (which he still owned) to a new company called the DSA Trust, but Giliomee continued writing an intermittent column under the pseudonym Willem Adriaan.[26]

With du Toit now the publisher and managing editor, *Die Suid-Afrikaan* began concentrating on special focus editions. "It was a financial strategy," emphasized du Toit. "The niche of the magazine was that it should have an Afrikaans profile, but not exclusively Afrikaans."[27] Full-time journalist Chris Louw left the magazine in 1993, and he was replaced by award-winning Afrikaans poet Antjie Krog. The magazine was still published mainly in Afrikaans, but independent special-focus editions, renamed *DSA in Depth*, were produced only in English.

Die Suid-Afrikaan was totally redesigned under du Toit and Krog (who was named executive editor), when *DSA in Depth* first appeared in August/September 1993. The magazine's masthead was changed to *DSA*, with *Die Suid-Afrikaan* below it. The designer was Jennifer Sorrell, award-winning editor and designer of *ADA Magazine,* one of the leading layout and design publications in South Africa.

The price of the magazine, R1.50 (VAT excluded) for the first issue (Spring 1984), would soar to R10 for the last issue, eleven years later. While the German subsidy had dried up by 1993, Krog was initially optimistic that enough advertising would be obtained to keep the magazine afloat. She noted in the November/December 1993 issue:

> Are we on the right track? The red subscription forms and persons renewing their subscriptions are streaming in. . . . What remains surprising is the hype surrounding the advertisements. . . . "The people who know" do not read the magazine, they page through it and count the advertisements! And the fact that *DSA* now carries more than ten full-page color advertisements, says more than I could have dreamt in my wildest dreams. It says advertisers think we are on the right track. It also says the previous edition, and this one, are breaking even—*DSA* is therefore on its way to an independent future! . . . Because foreign donations have dried up for all the independent magazines, they can only exist if they get enough advertisers.[28]

Revenue from advertising, however, could not be sustained —as Table 10.1 suggests.

Die Suid-Afrikaan published its first special-focus edition, "Black Business Advancement," in April 1992. Other special focus editions were "The Economic and Political Prospects of the Southern African Region" (48 pp., October 1992), "Preparing for Democracy" (48 pp., February 1993), and "Affirmative Action in Action" (48 pp., April 1993, with Wolfgang Thomas as guest editor).

Nico Dekker, executive editor of *DSA in Depth,* explained the reason for establishing a separate edition of the magazine: "The need for 'solid' information on crucial issues behind the process of transformation, based on thorough research by recognizable independent analysts, led to the first copy of *DSA in*

Table 10.1
DSA Advertising, August/September 1993 to
December/January 1996

Date	Total Pages	Color Full-Page Ads	Black-and-White Full-Page Ads
Aug/Sep 1993	64	12	3
Nov/Dec 1993	64	12	2
Jan/Feb 1994	64	5	3
Mar/Apr 1994	64	5	2
Dec/Jan 1994/95	64	3	3
Mar/Apr 1995	48	3	1.5
Sep/Oct 1995	48	3.5	1.5
Dec/Jan 1995/96	48	4	0

Depth. . . . Against this background we decided to wean the supplement from the main magazine and give it a more independent character."[29] *DSA in Depth* was not for sale in shops, but it carried advertisements from industry (Escom, Shell, Mondi, Anglo-American). All subscribers to *Die Suid-Afrikaan* received the independent supplement as a free bonus.

The theme of *DSA in Depth*'s first edition (48 pp., August/ September 1993) was "Reconstructing the State." The guest editor was van Zyl Slabbert, then director of policy and planning at IDASA. In February 1994, *DSA in Depth* published "Reconstructing Education" (72 pp.). The guest editor was Franklin Sonn, at that stage rector of the Peninsula Technikon. It was coproduced with financial aid from Absa Bank, Escom, and IDASA. *DSA in Depth* generally carried more advertising than *Die Suid-Afrikaan*, but it was not enough to make the continued existence of the two magazines viable.

Die Suid-Afrikaan reached its tenth year of publication in October 1994, but André du Toit knew closure was imminent when he wrote a retrospective column lamenting about complaints from some readers that the magazine was carrying too many serious articles:

> the chance that this jubilee edition may be the last of DSA, is just as real as with that first number, ten years ago. . . . Should fifty editions not have been enough to establish a publication's identity and to ensure its right to existence? Apparently not. . . . The hard truth is that publications of intellectual and cultural quality, with an independent and critical impact, have always struggled in the South African environment. . . . Anti-intellectualism is a deep-rooted South African tradition. Today it is not necessarily theological and church dogmas that are enforced, but the dogma of the free market philosophy: especially in the press a short-sighted chase after profits becomes the rule.[30]

Du Toit also responded to those readers who felt the newspaper had not campaigned for the preservation of Afrikaans as a privileged language in the new South Africa:[31] "We believe that we have done our small part since 1994 [the ANC's triumph in the 1994 election] to free Afrikaans from the then accepted label of 'language of the oppressor,' but we also emphasized from the beginning that the publication would 'in no way be part of a language campaign.'" Even the name of the newspaper, *Die Suid-Afrikaan*, was "not 'correct' Afrikaans." The correct term should have been "Die Suid-Afrikaner," which was the Afrikaans term for South African. Using the term *"Die Suid-Afrikaan"* established a link with *De Zuid-Afrikaan*, a Dutch newspaper-cum-magazine published in the Cape in the 1830s. As du Toit put it, "The deliberate use of 'incorrect' Afrikaans with English and with even more indigenous African languages in recent editions has led to significant reaction."[32]

The quality of *DSA*'s articles and reviews on the arts was enhanced with Krog's appointment as executive editor. Krog, the daughter of Afrikaans popular novelist Dot Serfontein, was one of the leading Afrikaans writers in the 1970s. She was a member of one of the groups who went to Lusaka, Zambia, in the 1980s to discuss the country's future with the banned ANC. A winner of the prestigious, albeit controversial, Hertzog prize for literature, Krog was an outspoken opponent of apartheid. By using a modern, mixed Afrikaans, she often mocked in her columns the Afrikaans spoken by purists campaigning for a new Afrikaans-language movement.

The magazine, however, was clearly in trouble when Krog handed the executive editorship over to Sandile Dikeni in the March/April 1995 issue: "Today we are the only, it's bloody true, the only magazine left from the alternative stable—nonaligned. The survival this year will take place under the supervision of the Independent Media Development [she meant Diversity] Trust who has carefully worked out a plan to make DSA last for 1995."[33] This edition changed to an A4 format, slightly smaller than the editions designed by Sorrell, and the standard sixty-four pages was reduced to forty-eight.

An English article by Dikeni in this edition questioned the reasons for the demise of the alternative press after de Klerk's unbanning of the ANC and other opposition groups in February 1990. "Did they jump or were they pushed?" While alternative publications were ignored by the mainstream media in the eighties, Dikeni noted that "many of the big boys were prepared to 'listen' to the alternative press" after de Klerk's reforms. He attacked the press conglomerates for only assisting the Independent Media Diversity Trust with R829,000 of R1.2 million in donations in 1994.[34]

Die Suid-Afrikaan was never afraid to address contentious matters. An example of this provocative stance was an interview by Riaan de Villiers with Zwelakhe Sisulu in the Autumn 1986 issue. Sisulu, editor of the alternative *New Nation*, warned readers of *Die Suid-Afrikaan* that it was "terribly naive to think that the ANC was in Lusaka. The ANC exists in South Africa. For the government to think that the ANC was still banned, is really absurd."[35] Soon afterward Sisulu, the son of Walter Sisulu, who had spent many years as a prisoner on Robben Island with Mandela, was jailed himself for nineteen months in solitary confinement without trial.[36]

DSA died a quiet death as an independent magazine. Dikene left to join the mainstream media, and Krog was beginning to carve out a niche as a radio reporter on the beat of the Truth and Reconciliation Commission.[37] Louw became director of news programs at Radio Sonder Grense, the Afrikaans service of the SABC. Giliomee remained a leading South African political commentator, publishing books, regular columns, and articles in a wide variety of magazines and newspapers.[38] And du Toit was still his university colleague, the only one to remain with *DSA* to the end.

The last edition—December 1995/January 1996—appeared with Rustum Kozain as guest editor. His editorial was called "Brief uit Kaapstad" (Letter from Cape Town) and was written in Afrikaans and English. Below it was an "important announcement" in Afrikaans:

> Dear reader, This is probably the last regular edition of *Die Suid-Afrikaan*, unless Father Christmas surprises us with an RDP package.[39] The editorial staff plans a special jubilee edition for the new year as a retrospective look at *DSA* through the years. Therefore, be on the lookout for this souvenir, which you can save along with your last remaining editions of defunct independent publications. We want to thank you for your support. Subscription fees can be reclaimed at the address mentioned below.[40]

The jubilee edition never appeared.

Die Suid-Afrikaan led the way in creating a think tank of liberal theorists among Afrikaners of all colors and ethnic groups. It stimulated debate about South Africa's political and social problems as no other Afrikaans publication ever did. The intellectual level of its writing—free of academic jargon—was reminiscent of magazines like the *New Yorker, New Republic* and *Spectator.* Its influence on the thinking of Afrikaner nationalist politicians was underestimated at the time, but its role in discussions with the ANC at meetings outside South Africa[41] and its approach to various issues of relevance to South Africans (especially in its supplements and special editions) radically expanded the parameters of political discussion and debate in the Afrikaans community.

Vrye Weekblad

Vrye Weekblad's birth in part was a protest against the tendency in mainsteam Afrikaans newspapers to hire editors loyal to the National Party, who used journalism as "simply a springboard to political advancement."[42] Its founder, Max du Preez, walked the route of many noted Afrikaans journalists by starting his career at a Nasionale Pers publication. Studying at the University of Stellenbosch after growing up in the Free State town of Kroonstad, du Preez cut his teeth at *Die Burger* in 1973 with Piet Cillié as editor. He moved to *Beeld*, the newly established Nasionale Pers daily in Johannesburg, in 1974 and was later transferred to the Windhoek office of Nasionale Pers.

The South African Defence Force in what was then South-West Africa was getting deeper into the civil war raging in Angola. Du Preez's disillusion with the National Party government and Afrikaner establishment had begun: "Journalism changed me. I was right in the heart of the ruling elite. . . . I saw the corruption of the NP up close. I couldn't believe it. The kinds of parties I'd go to . . . the moral degradation, the dishonesty."

This experience led du Preez to break his ties with the mainstream Afrikaans press, but he found little solace in the mainstream English press. To "get some freedom," he said, "I ran away from the Afrikaans press" only "to encounter another den of obsequiousness" (first as political editor for the *Finan-*

cial Mail and later as political correspondent for the *Sunday Times* and *Business Day*).[43] Du Preez was present at the Dakar talks with the ANC, and he remembered: "[The] hysterical way in which the mainstream Afrikaans press and even some English newspapers reacted planted the seeds to begin an independent Afrikaans paper, something that would change the view of Afrikaners that we were all a group of *dom donders* [stupid wretches], blindly supporting the National Party, not being able to think for ourselves."[44]

The first announcement that a new Afrikaans newspaper would be established came in October 1988. The news dominating South African newspapers at that stage was the continuing unrest in the country, necklacing in the townships, bomb explosions in white areas, the state of emergency, and attempts to repress media reports on the violence. In an interview with Shaun Johnson of the *Weekly Mail* three weeks before the launch of *Vrye Weekblad*, du Preez said it would be the first fully Afrikaans newspaper committed to a "non-racial, democratic, united South Africa." He told Johnson he was "not detribalised, and don't see any reason to be. . . . But at the same time, I see no conflict between being an ethnic Afrikaner, writing Afrikaans, loving Afrikaans, being Afrikaans in my environment—and not being a Nat, a racist, or in favour of white leadership. . . . The new newspaper . . . will have the side-effect of changing the image of Afrikaans as the 'language of the oppressor.'" Du Preez said *Vrye Weekblad* would start with a team of six journalists: "[All six] are wholly disillusioned with the party-political straitjacket in which the mainstream Afrikaans press operates . . . and believe even the use of the language is stilted and inhibited ('the language of the church, not the streets')."[45]

Vrye Weekblad did break new ground when it deviated from the path of traditional Afrikaans newspapers in its use of language, often using a colloquial mix heard more in informal discussions than in standard and written Afrikaans. *Vrye Week-blad* differed from *Die Suid-Afrikaan* in writing style—being more adventurous, far more abrasive, and even reckless. And as a weekly newspaper, *Vrye Weekblad* was also more concerned with hard news. "There is tremendous need for reliable information in the Afrikaner community," as du Preez put it. "They don't trust their leaders anymore . . . they need the whole spectrum of news from Tambo to Terre'Blanche."[46]

It was not an ideal climate for a new, rebellious Afrikaans newspaper. The minister of home affairs, Stoffel Botha, had acted against other alternative newspapers in the preceding months: *South* was shut down from May to June and *New Nation* from March to June 1988. The *Weekly Mail* was closed for November 1988, the same month in which *Vrye Weekblad* appeared on 4 November 1988. At least seven other alternative publications had been under government scrutiny since October 1987: *Al-Qalam, Grassroots, New Era, Out of Step* (published by the End Conscription Campaign), *Saamstaan, South,* the *Weekly Mail,* and *Work in Progress* were all officially warned that they might be closed.[47]

Vrye Weekblad was published by Wending Publikasies. Its directors included leading Afrikaans antiapartheid figures like Frederik van Zyl Slabbert, now director of IDASA and a board member of *Die Suid-Afrikaan,* Sampie Terreblanche, rebel economist at the University of Stellenbosch, Christo Nel, a business consultant, and P. G. Bison, a businessman. Du Preez set out the newspaper's credo in the first edition:

> At the moment all the big Afrikaans newspapers are allies of the National Party while the only other primary news source, the SABC, is controlled by the state. This relationship between governing party and the media must by necessity have an inhibiting influence on news reporting. . . . We say: to hell with the Total Onslaught that was so manipulated to keep South Africans in the dark. Afrikaans speakers are not children and they are not stupid.

We have a right to know what is happening in our country and what our government and fellow citizens do and think. . . . *Vrye Weekblad* wants to give our readers as much information as possible —but it is still the time of emergency regulations and serious restrictions. . . . And why is our name *Vrye Weekblad?* Prof. Braam Viljoen was the baptiser. Because we are free from ideologies; free from propaganda and slogans; free from insular inhibitions; free from manipulation by state presidents, ministers, Broeders, generals, and big capitalists—free to say to the modern Afrikaans speaker: read and decide for yourself.[48]

Vrye Weekblad's first edition had a provocative style that was absent from the mainstream Afrikaans press. Beneath the masthead, the newspaper boldly declared its independence: "Die nuwe stem vir 'n nuwe Suid-Afrika" (The new voice for a new South Africa). The phrase "new South Africa" would be the National Party's slogan when F. W. de Klerk began his reform initiatives a year later.

The headline of the first front-page story was "Mandela: 'n Nuwe era" (Mandela: a new era). "For the first time readers could read in Afrikaans about the man Nelson Mandela without him being branded as someone violent, a terrorist, and a godless communist."[49] The reports dealt with rumors that Mandela would be released and speculated about his status as a mediator in a new political dispensation for South Africa. They were written by du Preez and Jacques Pauw, the two journalists who would play the most important role in establishing *Vrye Weekblad's* reputation as a fearless crusader. The main photo next to the Mandela report pictured South African Communist Party leader Joe Slovo—a banned person who could not be quoted in South Africa—with Sampie Terreblanche and Wynand Malan, two Afrikaners who had left the National Party and joined the newly founded Democratic Party (DP). This picture was later used on election posters and in advertisements by the NP against the DP, and *Vrye*

Weekblad successfully obtained an interdict in the Supreme Court to prevent the Nationalists from further use of the photo.

The first edition set the trend with a comprehensive arts page that would later become a supplement called *VryDag* (Friday). This foray into the arts was broadened in October 1989, when the first of a series of book supplements (*Vrye Weekblad Boeke*) made its appearance. The supplement included a comprehensive interview by two young Afrikaans writers on *Vrye Weekblad*'s staff, Koos Prinsloo and Ryk Hattingh, with the doyen of Afrikaans literary figures, author Etienne Leroux.

Two weeks after *Vrye Weekblad*'s birth, the government began a campaign of censorship against the newspaper. In a front-page story in the 25 November 1989 edition, *Vrye Weekblad* reported about a faxed letter it had received on 11 November from the minister of justice, Kobie Coetsee, who warned the newspaper officially that it could "be used as a means to express the views of illegal organizations as stipulated by the Internal Security Act of 1982."[50]

The Internal Security Act empowered the justice minister to require a R40,000 deposit from the publisher of a newspaper or magazine if it was believed the publications might be banned in future. Normally, only a nominal deposit of R10 was required.[51] The government used the Internal Security Act to intimidate newspapers they regarded as hostile by setting a high registration fee—as happened with several alternative publications. If they were banned, the government could confiscate the deposit money.[52]

This was the first time since a partial state of emergency was proclaimed in June 1985 that a newspaper was warned in terms of the Security Act—the same act used to close down the *Guardian* in 1952 and *World* and *Weekend World* in 1977. The warning *Vrye Weekblad* received also came in the form of media regulations announced on 11 June and 28 August 1988, which gave the justice minister permission to ban editions of a newspaper if he believed they endangered the state and the maintenance of law and order. As one anticensorship group put it: the justice minister could simply "use his discretion to prevent registration of newspapers, or to make registration as difficult and costly as possible."[53]

Coetsee cited several reasons—drawn from the first issue of *Vrye Weekblad*—why the newspaper should be warned. *Vrye Weekblad* responded to each point and concluded that "no grounds exist that we should be treated differently from commercial newspapers like the *Citizen* and *Beeld*."[54] *Vrye Weekblad's* representations were to no avail: a registration fee of R30,000 —the highest ever for a South African newspaper—was demanded. *Vrye Weekblad* already had an overdraft of R10,000 after three editions, and it could not pay the salaries of the editorial staff on time. Readers, however, rallied to support the newspaper and sent in more than R60,000.[55]

Vrye Weekblad was not intimidated by Coetsee's actions, as the following statement suggests: "It is clear to us that the government is exceptionally sensitive that an Afrikaans newspaper is at last willing to write honestly about matters such as the government's maladministration . . . the ineffective government, the debilitating discord in the cabinet, and the results of the government's racial policy. . . . We cannot be blamed if we see the government's action as a low-intensity war against *Vrye Weekblad*."[56]

Nevertheless, intimidation took another turn before the end of 1988, when the Botha government sued the newspaper for R100,000 for libel. A report with the headline "Pik, PW en die Mafia-baas" (Pik, P. W., and the Mafia boss) alleged that P. W. Botha and his foreign minister, Pik Botha, had dinner with a notorious mafia leader, Vito Palazzolo.[57] The editor refused to apologize or to pay the amount. He noted the report was based on a sworn statement that a Pretoria accountant, Clifford Frederick Bentley, made to the police in January 1988.[58] After

P. W. Botha's retirement in 1989, the libel case was withdrawn, but not before *Vrye Weekblad* taunted the National Party leader, nicknamed the Groot Krokodil (Big Crocodile) by the media, with a front-page report asking, "Waar's die Krokodil se dagvaarding?" (Where's the Crocodile's summons?)[59]

Vrye Weekblad's reputation was really secured in 1989. Du Preez had already referred to the newspaper registration fee as a government-sponsored "low-intensity war" against the alternative press. When *Vrye Weekblad* quoted Joe Slovo, the banned secretary-general of the South African Communist Party, in the 11 November 1988 issue, du Preez was charged and found guilty in Johannesburg regional court of contravening a section of the Internal Security Act that prohibited the media from quoting a banned person—even though the magistrate admitted the report was objective and did not endanger state security. While fifteen stories quoting Slovo directly had already been printed in mainstream and alternative newspapers (like *Beeld*, *Rapport*, the *Sunday Times*, *Leadership*, the *Financial Mail*, and *Die Suid-Afrikaan*), none had been charged with contravening the act. Du Preez was found guilty in June 1989, and *Vrye Weekblad* wrote a front-page story on 23 June under the headline "Vendetta!!"

Du Preez was sentenced to six months in prison, suspended for five years. Wending Publikasies, publisher of *Vrye Weekblad*, was fined R1,000, also suspended for five years.[60] Only hours after the sentence was announced, the security police notified *Vrye Weekblad* that it was under investigation for contravening various provisions in the Internal Security Act. The newspaper accused the government of harassment: "The security police said the newspaper has 'undermined national conscription.' However, the relevant stories, all older than four months, contain mostly reports of the court case of a conscientious objector. . . . Since *Vrye Weekblad* was first published on 4 November last year, the state has tried on various fronts to cast suspicion on us, to break us financially, and to brand us as a security risk. . . . Why is the government so afraid of *Vrye Weekblad?*[61] *Vrye Weekblad* proclaimed in an editorial that it would not "lie down."[62]

The die was cast. As Cornelia Faure has suggested in a comprehensive study of *Vrye Weekblad* between 1988 and 1993,[63] the newspaper helped set the news agenda of the alternative press—questioning and criticizing the National Party government, exposing the existence of politically motivated death squads in the South African security police,[64] documenting planned terrorism by right-wing groups,[65] and reporting the existence of a secret "Third Force" creating havoc in the peace process.[66] *Vrye Weekblad* revealed corrupt speculation with community housing[67] and probed mismanagement and the squandering of money in SABC's educational programs.[68] Journalists uncovered links between a Stellenbosch academic and his research institute with the security police[69] and secret propaganda movies being made by commercial movie studios for the defense force and security police.[70] Questions were also raised about the existence of the Azanian People's Liberation Army's deadly "workshops."[71]

If *Vrye Weekblad* is remembered for one edition, it would be the 17 November 1989 exclusive—five pages of reports on security police death squads. Readers were exposed to these horrors by Dirk Coetzee, commander of the Vlakplaas unit of the security police. The possibility of death squads in the police was first published a month before by the *Weekly Mail*, when a death row prisoner, mass murderer Almond Nofomela, confessed the night before he was to be executed that he was a member of a police death squad that killed the activist lawyer Griffith Mxenge. Although the *Weekly Mail* continued with the story the next week, police and government officials denied any knowledge of death squads and alleged that Nofomela was just trying to get a stay of execution (which was granted to him).

With his picture virtually filling *Vrye Weekblad*'s front page, Dirk Coetzee was introduced to readers in bold, large text next to the photo with the following caption: "Meet Captain Dirk Johannes Coetzee, commander of a death squad of the South African Police. He tells exclusively the full gruesome tale of political assassinations, poisoned drinks, foreign bomb explosions, and letter bombs. . . . "[72] All the stories were written by Jacques Pauw, the most notable being a report under the headline "Ek was in die hart van die hoer" (I was in the heart of the whore), a title he later used in a book on the death squads. On the same day, *Weekly Mail* reported that Coetzee had fled to London. "Before leaving this week, Coetzee told his story to Afrikaans newspaper *Vrye Weekblad*. When it appears in the newspaper today, it is likely to cause a major diplomatic row and shake the police force."[73]

In his editorial, du Preez wrote:

[The testimony of] cold-blooded murders and bomb explosions in other countries should stigmatize the South African government as a terrorist government in the class of Libya. . . . It is like an ulcer in our nation's bosom. We must open it now so that it can heal. In any other civilized country the government would have resigned immediately after such a scandal. Here this is not the case. But the absolute minimum which each civilized South African now expects from the government, is that a full-fledged commission of investigation immediately be appointed and that all involved are forced to testify and to be questioned in public.[74]

Vrye Weekblad initiated the investigation into this story, competing with *Weekly Mail* to be first with the latest twist to the tale of the hit squads. On 24 November 1989, Pauw exposed Coetzee's successor, Captain Eugene de Kock, who would only admit to the existence of the death squads during his trial in 1997 (where he received a long prison sentence).

Du Preez in an editorial urged the government to clean the Augean stables ("Maak skoon!") and referred to the low-profile reaction of the mainstream newspapers: "There are other newspapers that we hope would be ashamed of the way in which they dealt with this matter. . . . *Beeld* and *Die Burger* again published inter alia on their front pages the provable nonsense of a self-confessed criminal about the Coetzees and their marriage."[75]

Du Preez's point was valid. On the first day of the story, *Die Burger* ignored *Vrye Weekblad*'s scoop, even though the daily could have mentioned it in later editions. *Die Burger* did cover the death squads in various short reports between 20 and 25 November 1989, but they were mostly denials by the police that the squads existed. Only when the story resurfaced in Washington, D.C.—when the *Washington Post* published an interview with state president F. W. de Klerk, in which de Klerk said he wanted to get to the truth—did *Die Burger* and other mainstream Afrikaans newspapers suddenly give the scandal the prominent attention it deserved. This time, ten days after Coetzee's allegations were first published, *Die Burger* used it as the main story on page one. The name of *Vrye Weekblad* was only mentioned once in all these reports. Du Preez became known as Mad Max among senior editors of Nasionale Pers newspapers.[76]

The following week *Vrye Weekblad* again led with another facet of the story on the death squads. With the headline "Lothar se doepa" (Lothar's potion), the newspaper quoted Coetzee's allegations that the head of the police's forensic unit, General Lothar Neethling, had provided poison to murder two ANC suspects.[77] Neethling's libel case against *Vrye Weekblad* would eventually do more to harm the newspaper than the government in all its efforts could do. The trial started in November 1990, nearly a year after *Vrye Weekblad* broke the story.

Vrye Weekblad received a favorable verdict early in 1991,[78] but the Appeal Court in Bloemfontein ruled for Neethling in December 1993. As Cornelia Faure put it: "The Appeal Court could not determine beyond any reasonable doubt who (Neethling or Coetzee) was lying and who talked the truth. It is ironic that it is so difficult for a criminal to persuade a judge that he did commit crimes. . . . The Appeal Court's decision was a serious setback for press freedom. The role and function of the press as watchdog was ignored."[79] Coetzee told *Vrye Weekblad*, "What the judge in effect said, is that a person cannot believe Jeffrey Dahmer's admissions of guilt about his murders because he is a self-confessed murderer."[80]

The case was referred back to the Witwatersrand local division of the Supreme Court for damages, and Neethling was awarded R90,000. This led to *Vrye Weekblad*'s closure. Although support from the public could have enabled the newspaper to continue, du Preez told Anton Harber, coeditor of the *Weekly Mail*, it was time to go: "We could have carried on for a few months and burnt up some more money. But when we discussed it, I thought about the British Anti-Apartheid Movement. They didn't know when to go. We don't want to make the same mistake. . . . Many people have phoned me and said it's terrible and we can't possibly close now. Individuals have offered a total of R1.5 million to keep us going. I personally have taken calls from three people each offering R200,000."[81]

The case of Neethling versus du Preez was given a new perspective in 1998, when the Appeal Court ruled (*Nasionale Media Ltd v Bogoshi*) that the media have the "right, and indeed a vital function" to inform the public about every "aspect of public, political, social and economic activity and thus to contribute to the formation of public opinion." It was a "watershed decision in the revival of the common-law emphasis on freedom of expression, in particular of the print and electronic media."[82] If the Neethling case were heard today, *Vrye Weekblad* would probably have won on appeal, according to Max Loubser, professor in private law at Stellenbosch University: "the publication of libelous allegations about a matter of great public interest can be regarded as reasonable, even if there is doubt about the truth of the allegations."[83]

Further vindication for *Vrye Weekblad* on the issue of publishing Coetzee's allegations came from the Truth and Reconciliation Commission in Cape Town in June 1998. One of the top scientists at the government's secret chemical-biological facility, Roodeplaat Laboratories, "said straight out: every word *Vrye Weekblad* had written about Neethling was true."[84] After testifying at the TRC's media hearings in September 1997, du Preez brought charges at Johannesburg's Brixton police station against Neethling "for conspiracy to murder, perjury and fraud."[85] The damning evidence from numerous witnesses at the TRC hearings (including the head of military intelligence) on biological warfare, conducted by the former intelligence services, again confirmed du Preez's case.[86]

As with *Die Suid-Afrikaan,* money was always a problem during the five years of *Vrye Weekblad*'s existence. The assistance of foreign donors made it vulnerable to criticism from government circles and conservative, mainstream newspapers that did not like *Vrye Weekblad*'s investigative style of journalism.

Reacting to a strident attack in a 1989 editorial by the *Citizen* over *Vrye Weekblad*'s dependence on foreign donors,[87] for example, du Preez explained the newspaper's financial position under the headline, "Hier is die hele storie" (Here is the whole story). Earlier that week, Afrikaans authors André P. Brink and Breyten Breytenbach implored potential donors at a conference in Paris to assist *Vrye Weekblad.* The French government and the European Union indicated within a day that they would help to ensure *Vrye Weekblad*'s continued publication, and they offered the money as a guarantee to the newspaper's printers and distributors:

> *Vrye Weekblad* is the property of the journalists working for it. It was founded with much idealism and the minimum of capital and still is anything but financially strong. . . . We treat donors in the same way as advertisers: no matter how big their assistance is, there never can be any question of influence on the editorial policy

of the paper. Our policy and political principles were spelled out in detail in the first edition. No political party, pressure group, donor, or advertiser will make us deviate from that. . . . We regard the *Citizen*'s commentary about the matter as absurd and presumptuous. And on top of that, it comes from a newspaper which was started in a devious way with taxpayers' money![88]

Du Preez believed that *Vrye Weekblad* lost revenue during its first year when pressure was put on potential advertisers by the government, especially after Justice Minister Coetsee failed to stop the newspaper from publishing by setting an exorbitantly high registration fee.[89] Thus the newspaper was forced to seek aid from foreign donors. The Canadian government, for example, donated R73,000 to *Vrye Weekblad* for its computer system.[90] During the trial in which du Preez was convicted for quoting Joe Slovo illegally, the newspaper "received donated legal services that its editor valued at about R60,000, over and above funding from the International Federation of Journalists to cover other legal costs."[91] The costs involved in defending six charges against *Vrye Weekblad* for undermining the system of military conscription were covered from this donor money. The European Union donated approximately R750,000 to *Vrye Weekblad* until 1991, when foreign donor funds began drying up for all alternative newspapers.[92]

Lack of advertising was also a major factor in *Vrye Weekblad*'s demise. The newspaper seldom carried more than four or five full-page advertisements. Circulation—in the region of 20,000 a week during the Dirk Coetzee expositions, but on average only about 10,000 a week—was not enough to cover the costs of production. Even though *Vrye Weekblad* received assistance from the Independent Media Diversity Trust when it was established in 1991, the newspaper had serious financial problems by 1993.

Negotiations between du Preez, the management of *Die Suid-Afrikaan*, and *Insig*, the Afrikaans monthly opinion magazine of Nasionale Pers, all functioning at a loss, foundered at the end of 1993. Du Preez turned down an offer to be editor of a new newsmagazine that would combine the three publications. Although the proposal was good and the magazine would have been independent, the "idea broke down because Naspers said it should be a monthly, and du Preez said it was weekly or nothing. 'We would be putting our masthead on something we didn't like,' he said."[93]

Vrye Weekblad's impact on the Afrikaans-speaking community came at a critical point in South African history. Sampie Terreblanche, one of the directors, emphasized *Vrye Weekblad*'s influence: "*Vrye Weekblad* gave Afrikaners hope. It gave them an intellectual debate outside the borders of the mainstream Afrikaans press."[94]

Vrye Weekblad's book pages and supplements, moreover, were the best in Afrikaans publishing at the time. The occasional appearance of *Two Tone*, a jazz magazine, as a supplement in the newspaper, introduced its mainly white, Afrikaans-speaking readers to black culture in South Africa. *Vrye Weekblad* initiated an arts festival in Johannesburg in 1991, for example, where artists from Europe and Africa were united on one stage. *Vrye Weekblad* also broke new ground in its layout and design. Anton Sassenberg, "a lean, unemployed painter with a bald head and weird clothes. . . . influenced layout in South Africa more than all the American experts who were brought at millions of dollars to South Africa to redesign newspapers."[95] Sassenberg later went to *De Kat*, another small Afrikaans magazine, where his layouts received numerous awards.

Nowhere was *Vrye Weekblad*'s innovation more obvious than in the way it broke tradition in the use of the Afrikaans language. Du Preez explained: "There was a gap between the Afrikaans spoken by its users and the Afrikaans in the newspapers. The gap was so big that it was unnatural and it did Afrikaans no good. From the beginning we said: but this is not *our* Afrikaans."[96] *Vrye Weekblad* received a lot of criticism from academics and others fighting for the survival of Afrikaans, but the newspaper used a living language that reflected the way people actually talked in South Africa and Namibia. *Vrye Weekblad* was portraying not an Afrikaans for whites only but an Afrikaans for the whole of the southern African population who could speak the language.

Vrye Weekblad started a debate about Afrikaans by publishing letters about Afrikaans from political activist Patrick "Terror" Lekota, who had written them from jail to his daughter.[97] The newspaper also showed how "old black [African] people still spoke an archaic but beautiful Afrikaans."[98] *Vrye Weekblad* opened up the sounds and faces of Afrikaans to its readers— the Afrikaans of the Cape Flats, the Afrikaans of Namibia, the Afrikaans that had long been marginalized because it did not belong to the official Afrikaans of the rulers. The effort was made in spite of the fact that *Vrye Weekblad*'s readership, according to du Preez, was "embarrassingly elite," with "four out of every five readers" having a university education and half having more than one degree.[99]

This vibrant Afrikaans was also reflected in the creative way newspaper posters were written. *Vrye Weekblad*'s yellow posters became compulsory reading for people on their way to work all over its main distribution area in Pretoria and the Witwatersrand: "The best public reading matter ever. It livened up discussions around the table—to think out a *Vrye Weekblad* poster! Sometimes, naturally, scatological! Or rather, call it jocular."[100] *Vrye Weekblad* started a monthly award called the Tarentaal (guinea fowl) award early in 1994 to honor the best advertising copywriter in Afrikaans. The prize was taken over by *De Kat* after *Vrye Weekblad* ceased publication.[101]

Max du Preez, the founder of *Vrye Weekblad* and its first and only editor, received South African journalism's top Pringle Award for his contribution to "the struggle for press freedom against autocratic interference in South Africa."[102] Some of the best Afrikaans journalists and literary figures in the country wrote for *Vrye Weekblad,* including Ina van der Linde, Pearlie Joubert, Elsabé Wessels, Hans Pienaar, Hennie Serfontein, Christelle Terreblanche, Sampie Terreblanche, Andrea Vinassa, Ivor Powell, Beverley Mitchell, Christi van der Westhuizen, Wally Mbhele, Johannes Bruwer, Esma Anderson, Martie Meiring, Jacques Pauw, Charles Leonard, Fanie Olivier, Gerrit Olivier, Vernon February, Soli Philander, André P. Brink, Marlene van Niekerk, Jeanne Goosen, Koos Prinsloo, and Ryk Hattingh.

The last edition of *Vrye Weekblad* as a newspaper appeared at the end of May 1993. Although a new, eighty-six-page fortnightly news magazine (with du Preez as editor) called *Vrye Weekblad die Nuustydskrif* was launched on 24 June 1993, it lasted less than eight months.[103] Using a pun based on words penned by the early Afrikaans poet Jan F. E. Celliers, *Vrye Weekblad* announced its own death in the last edition: "'Be quiet, brothers, a newspaper is passing by.' . . . You are holding the last edition of *Vrye Weekblad* in your hands. The last page of a formidable chapter in South African journalism and politics. The end of an era, but not a tragic end—a proud one. It was a battle well fought. Walk with us over five years and drink a toast on our funeral festival."[104]

Vrye Weekblad ceased publication as a newsmagazine on 2 February 1994, exactly four years after the de Klerk government reforms in February 1990 that set the wheels in motion for a new South Africa.

Saamstaan *and* Namaqua Nuus

Newspapers that focused on working-class and grassroots community matters—like *Saamstaan* and *Namaqua Nuus*—were even more vulnerable to government censorship and intimidation

The first edition of *Vrye Weekblad* (left) appeared on 4 November 1988. The penultimate edition of *Vrye Weekblad* (right), now a news-magazine, appeared on 13–26 January 1994. *Vrye Weekblad*'s style of journalism is reflected in the credo, "onafhanklik, onverbonde, onverskrokk" (independent, unattached, fearless).

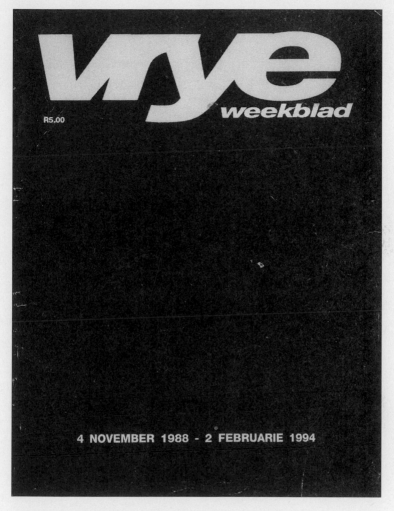

The last edition of *Vrye Weekblad*, 2 February 1994.

Vrye Weekblad's yellow posters, placed every Friday at distribution sites in Johannesburg and Pretoria, where most readers lived, used an imaginative and creative Afrikaans never seen before in the Afrikaans press.

Die Suid-Afrikaan in its last edition, as *DSA*, in December 1995/January 1996.

than *Die Suid-Afrikaan* and *Vrye Weekblad*. Their position was so precarious that the publication of each issue was a struggle for survival. These newspapers have been called "progressive-alternative" publications in an effort to distinguish them from other alternative publications—to suggest that they were "organically linked" to community or workers groups, more partisan in their representations of news and more likely to be banned.[105]

Two Afrikaans newspapers in this mold were *Saamstaan* and *Namaqua Nuus*—both run by people in the community who did not have professional journalism experience.[106] *Saamstaan* was established to create a voice for communities in the Southern Cape after the introduction of the tricameral parliament in 1983. Coloured and Indian groups in towns like Oudtshoorn, George, Plettenberg Bay, Mossel Bay, and Beaufort West joined ranks with Africans excluded from the new parliament. Associated as many were with the United Democratic Front, these communities decided to stand together in their protest against the exclusion of Africans from the new constitutional dispensation. "Laat ons saam staan" (Let us stand together) became their rallying cry, which was carried over to the name of their newspaper. Below the masthead of *Saamstaan*, the words "Ons eie nuusblad" (Our own newspaper) were printed in the first issue (February/March 1984).

On the front page of the four-page first edition was a message from the Roman Catholic bishop of Oudtshoorn, Edward Adams: "This paper is to urge the community to stand together so that they can tackle and solve their problems, big or small, in a united way. It wants to assist them in becoming aware of their rights and duties."[107] The editorial on page one appeared under the headline, "Ons is geregtig op beter huise" (We have the right to better housing), but *Saamstaan*'s main campaign was the fight against the elections for the Coloured House of Representatives and the Indian House of Delegates, which was to be held in August 1984. *Saamstaan* in its August/ September 1984 issue contained a supplement compiled by the United Democratic Front, which urged voters to stay away from the polls. A person voting would be supporting a "kombuis-parlement" (kitchen parliament), referring to the slave-master position Coloureds and Indians would have in parliament in relation to the white chamber. In bold capital letters the newspaper declared, "Ons gaan nie stem nie" (We are not going to vote).[108]

Saamstaan was set up initially in Swellendam by *Grassroots*, another "progressive-alternative" newspaper, but it soon moved to Oudtshoorn. Priced initially at ten cents, *Saamstaan* quickly established itself as a voice of the local, mostly poor, working-class community, and subsequent editions were free until after 1990. Amid increasing protest against the new constitution, *Saamstaan* rapidly expanded its distribution area to the whole of the Little Karoo, along the south coast of the Cape and in the Overberg, and in most of the Great Karoo towns, even as far north as the area around Upington. The publisher was Saamstaan Publikasies in Bridgetown, Oudtshoorn. *Saamstaan*'s circulation soared, and by the end of 1984 between 60,000 and 80,000 copies were being distributed for free. From December 1984 the newspaper started appearing regularly as a monthly —most stories were in Afrikaans with a few in English and Xhosa. The May 1985 edition proclaimed "Oorlog" (War) on its front page. Townships across South Africa were erupting in violent protests, and *Saamstaan*'s front-page reports (in Afrikaans and Xhosa) reflected the unrest in Bongelethu, the African township outside Oudtshoorn.

The office of *Saamstaan* in Oudtshoorn was partially gutted in a paraffin bomb attack in May 1985—harassment by the security police had begun. In subsequent attacks, Reggie Oliphant, director of *Saamstaan*'s board, was nearly killed by a person driving at night without headlights, and journalist Patrick

Nyuka was shot by a municipal constable while covering a story. Three arson attacks were made on the newsroom, one with reporter Mbulelo Grootboom present (he doused the flames). After the partial state of emergency had been declared in July 1985, *Saamstaan* was formally warned by the minister of home affairs that it could be closed down, but instead police harassment continued. The typesetters, Bowles Typesetting, who printed the newspaper in Cape Town, were told by the security police that they could only print sports reports. A print run of 8,000 newspapers disappeared after it was picked up by "unknown men"—the evidence pointed to the security police —at a distribution point. People interviewed for the first edition were visited by the security police to determine the names of the journalists who conducted the interviews.[109]

The first editor-organizers were Mansoor Jaffer, who was released for six and a half months from his position at *Grassroots*, and Humphrey Josephs, who was generally responsible for the newspaper in 1985 and 1986. Josephs and his successor, Derick Jackson, who took over as editor-organizer in February 1986, were both arrested under the Internal Security Act. Josephs was released after a year in jail without trial, and Jackson spent three months in jail. "Every time we were released, we again started the newspaper," Jackson said. "Even the cashier was arrested."[110] Jackson remained the managing editor-organizer until the newspaper finally closed at the end of 1994.

Saamstaan was established with foreign donor funds— initially from the Dutch group Cebemo and later from Sweden's Afrika Gruppe, which provided funds for training journalists. As Eric Louw put it:

> Because of the vast distances separating *Saamstaan* committees, an Annual General Meeting (AGM) replaced the monthly meetings of the *Grassroots* General Body. *Saamstaan* thus functioned without a strong hands-on democratic forum to oversee its operations. This located policy making almost entirely with the execu-

tive. However, as *Saamstaan* relied on the village committees for distribution, failure to sustain their support would have resulted in closure of the paper. *Saamstaan* workers thus continually traveled throughout the area to collect news and views.[111]

The activist stance of *Saamstaan's* journalists, however, changed after 1990. "We wanted to target Coloureds by informing them of their rights," Derick Jackson remembered. "After 1990 the cause of the struggle faded and donor money started drying up."[112]

The Media Training Development Trust began training journalists from the community in the late eighties to work for *Grassroots, Saamstaan,* and *Namaqua Nuus,* and Chris Gutuza at *Saamstaan* played an important mentoring role in this effort. Gutuza was also involved in the establishment of *Namaqua Nuus* in September 1988. While *Namaqua Nuus* was organized like *Grassroots* and *Saamstaan,* Gutuza emphasized that *Namaqua Nuus* was far less militant in rhetorical style. Journalists concentrated more on hard local news for towns in its distribution area.

Namaqua News was actually one of the projects *Die Suid-Afrikaan* launched under the banner of the DSA Trust. It was made possible after a successful fund-raising campaign by Chris Louw, who obtained funds from the Swiss embassy to support the project. *Namaqua Nuus* was a monthly community newspaper, primarily in Afrikaans, aimed at readers in rural communities in the northwestern Cape–Namaqualand region. It was distributed from Clanwilliam in the western Cape to the Orange river in the north, from Hondeklip Bay on the western Cape coast to Pofadder in the northwestern Cape. It was also a free newspaper with a monthly print run of 30,000 copies. *Namaqua Nuus* started carrying advertisements from early in 1989—it received support from businesses and had a classified section. According to Gutuza, advertising content varied from 15 to 30 percent of total news and advertising copy.[113]

Namaqua Nuus, like *Saamstaan*, was subsidized by various foreign donors—of which the U. S. Agency for International Development, the Swiss Development Corporation, the Swedish Afrika Gruppe, and the Dutch Cebemo group were the most prominent. "We wanted to become independent, especially after 1990 when donor fatigue set in, but could not succeed," Gutuza said. "*Saamstaan* was far more an activist newspaper, while *Namaqua Nuus* concentrated on serving the community with the type of hard news you would get in regular newspapers, news about schools, crime, community affairs."[114]

Namaqua Nuus never attracted the attention of the authorities like *Saamstaan* because it was not as militant. "At *Namaqua Nuus* reporters could talk to the police and get comments from them on news events," Gutuza said. "This was out of the question at *Saamstaan*, where the police were often seen as the enemy, as part of the system against which the newspaper was fighting."[115] Gutuza, Welma Odendaal from *DSA*, and Rob Meintjes, an experienced journalist from the mainstream press, were all active after 1990 in training young people to take over and steer these newspapers in a professional way—if and when donor funds dried up. One such student was Makhaya Mani, who first worked for *Saamstaan* and *Namaqua Nuus* as part of his training program. He eventually became editor of *Saamstaan* under the managing editorship of Derick Jackson.

Conclusion

Democracy at last came to South Africa in 1994, but it was twelve months of bloodletting for the few remaining Afrikaans alternative publications. *Namaqua Nuus* and *Saamstaan* outlasted their intellectual mother, *Grassroots*, which closed during the defiance campaign of 1989. And they both covered South Africa's first democratic elections in April 1994. But *Namaqua*

Nuus appeared for the last time in October 1994—six years and one month after its birth. Two months later, in December 1994, *Saamstaan* also closed down. Neither newspaper could survive the new era without external aid.

Perhaps the most fitting memorial to the Afrikaans alternative press is the view of Martie Meiring, for many years a leading Afrikaans journalist at *Die Burger* and *Beeld,* who summarized the impact *Vrye Weekblad* had on the Afrikaans community:

> *Vrye Weekblad* gave you something of Mickey Spillane, a bit of Damon Runyon, a touch of Tom Wolfe—and that all in Afrikaans! . . . Later, when I became a member of the editorial staff and got to know the inner workings of the near anarchic environment, it was specifically the creative energy that impressed. Cynical, scrapping, agreeable, quarrelsome, and excited; boredom was not something which you felt in the office or experienced when you read the newspaper. And I still think: *Vrye Weekblad* truly, good and solidly, cracked the oppressive corset of guilt, apartheid and painful, formal rectitude we as Afrikaners had worn.[116]

Not so for the right-wing alternative press. Viewing democratic South Africa as a new cause of resistance, *Die Afrikaner, Patriot, Boerant,* and their allies seemed likely to survive into the twenty-first century.

Notes

1. Martie Meiring, "Die kleinjong is gebore" (The young boy is born), *Vrye Weekblad,* 2 February 1994, 41 (Afrikaans). All publications in Afrikaans in this chapter are noted. English translations, where relevant, are supplied by the author.

2. A few Afrikaans publications—notably *Die Beeld* and *Beeld*—criticized some apartheid policies in the 1960s and 1970s, but they remained loyal to the National Party. *Die Burger,* under the editorship of Piet Cillié between 1954 and 1977—he coined the phrase

"klein" (petty) apartheid—also clashed at times with the government of Hendrik Verwoerd during the 1960s. (Cillié was later appointed head of South Africa's first graduate department of journalism at the University of Stellenbosch.) Real opposition in Afrikaner press circles against grand apartheid, however, stems from the 1980s, and it came from newspapers in the Transvaal and Orange Free State. Ton Vosloo, editor of *Beeld*, and Hennie van Deventer, editor of *Die Volksblad*, for example, were critical of the government's ban on the ANC and other opposition groups. Willem Wepener, one of Vosloo's successors at *Beeld*, attacked the government for enforcing apartheid legislation like the Group Areas Act and argued for the release of Nelson Mandela (e.g., *Beeld*, 17 August, 18 July 1988). This led to a strong attack on Wepener and Afrikaans newspapers in general by P. W. Botha at the National Party's Natal congress in 1988. Editors Harald Pakendorf of *Die Vaderland* and Willem de Klerk of *Die Transvaler* were dismissed by Perskor (the press group that owned these newspapers) because of their growing opposition to apartheid. H. J. Grosskopf, another editor of *Beeld*, attacked news censorship at the *Star*'s centenary conference: "Our Defence Act in effect bans all reporting on military matters except in specific cases sanctioned by the military establishment. . . . The more power a government has, the easier it can enforce its will to keep something secret. Lesser mortals can then only wonder whether it is indeed national security or only the ruling party's political interests that would be endangered" (*Star*, 9 October 1987, 15).

The underrated influence of mainstream Afrikaans newspapers to change white attitudes about apartheid can perhaps best be seen by the influence of *Die Volksblad* under Hennie van Deventer's editorship. He began criticizing the National Party in September 1980 for not allowing Asians to stay or live in the Orange Free State. After numerous editorials and private conversations, the legislation preventing this population group from settling in the province was revoked. Van Deventer described in his memoirs how he was intimidated and threatened by right-wingers because he used *Die Volksblad* to advocate an end to grand apartheid. In the 1989 general election, for example, the right-wing Conservative Party won half the seats in the Orange Free State—a National Party stronghold for more than forty years. *Die Volksblad*'s reform campaign paid off when whites in the province, against all expectations, voted overwhelmingly in the whites-only referendum three years later for F. W. de

Klerk's proposed power sharing with black South Africans. H. van Deventer, *Kroniek van 'n koerantman: 'n Persoonlike perspektief op die jare ná 80* (Cape Town: Tarlehoet BK, 1998).

3. *Cape Times*, 9 February 1990, 8. See also William A. Hachten and C. Anthony Giffard, *Total Onslaught: The South African Press under Attack* (Johannesburg: Macmillan, 1984); Willem Wepener, "The Role of the Afrikaans Press," in *Survival of the Press*, L. Switzer and C. Emdon, convenors (Grahamstown: Department of Journalism, Rhodes University, 1979); Johan de Villiers, "The South African Community and Its Newspapers: A Socio-Historical Study" (Ph.D. diss., University of the Orange Free State, 1976); M. M. Breytenbach, "The Manipulation of Public Opinion by State Censorship of the Media in South Africa, 1974–1994" (Ph.D. diss., University of Stellenbosch, 1997); E. Schwella, "Die rol van die nuusbladpers in die handhawing van openbare verantwoordelikheid ten opsigte van die Suid-Afrikaanse uitvoerende gesag" (The role of the newspaper press in maintaining public responsibility with regard to South African executive powers) (Ph.D. diss., University of Stellenbosch, 1988).

4. See C. F. J. Muller, *Sonop in die suide: Geboorte en groei van die Nasionale Pers 1915–1948* (Sunrise in the south: Birth and growth of Nasionale Pers 1915–1948) (Cape Town: Nasionale Boekhandel, 1990); C. M. van den Heever: *Generaal J. B. M. Hertzog*, 2d ed. (Johannesburg: A. P. Boekhandel, 1944).

5. Pedro Diederichs, "Newspapers: The Fourth Estate—A Cornerstone of Democracy," in A. De Beer (ed.), *Mass Media toward the Millennium: The South African Handbook of Mass Communication*, 2d ed. (Pretoria: J. L. van Schaik, 1998), 80–81.

6. Ibid., 81.

7. B. J. Liebenberg, "From the Statute of Westminster to the Republic of South Africa, 1931–1961," in *Five Hundred Years: A History of South Africa*, C. F. J. Muller, ed. (Pretoria: Academica, 1968), 384.

8. Muller, *Sonop in die suide.*, 287.

9. Dirk Richard, enlightened editor of *Die Vaderland* in the seventies, writes that Treurnicht was a miniature version of editor Verwoerd, his raison d'être being to maintain the Afrikaner's position of power. D. Richard, *Moedswillig die uwe: Perspersoonlikhede in die noorde* (Yours mischievously: Press personalities in the north) (Johannesburg: Perskor, 1985), 137 (Afrikaans). *Hoofstad* was owned by Perskor, which was one of the two major Afrikaans press chains in South Africa—the other being Nasionale Pers. Perskor represented the

more conservative faction of the National Party, and there was intense competition between the two press groups. The main Perskor dailies in Johannesburg were *Die Transvaler* and *Die Vaderland* and in Pretoria the smaller *Hoofstad* and *Oggendblad. Die Transvaler* was moved to Pretoria in 1983—the competition with the Nasionale Pers newspaper *Beeld* in Johannesburg was too intense—to replace *Hoofstad* and *Oggendblad.* The weekend newspaper *Rapport* was owned jointly by the two Afrikaans press groups.

10. The name was changed back to the South African Press Council in 1995, when a separate body, the Broadcasting Complaints Commission of South Africa (BCCSA), was set up to make a distinction between print and broadcast media. The Press Council was replaced in 1997 by an ombudsman appointed by the Print Media Association. The BCCSA still deals with complaints related to broadcasting matters. Hachten and Giffard, *Total Onslaught,* 50, 81–86, 197–98; Diederichs, "Newspapers," 108–9.

11. Keyan Tomaselli and P. Eric Louw, "The South African Progressive Press under Emergency, 1986–1989," in *The Alternative Press in South Africa,* ed. K. Tomaselli and P. Louw (Bellville: Anthropos; London: James Currey, 1991), 178.

12. Cornelia Faure, "Ondersoekende joernalistiek en sosiale verandering: 'n Ontleding en evaluering van die agendastellingsrol van *Vrye Weekblad,* 1988–1993" (Investigative journalism and social change: An analysis and evaluation of the agenda-setting role of *Vrye Weekblad,* 1988–1993) (Ph.D. diss., University of South Africa, 1995), 118 (Afrikaans).

13. Brink was one of the most outspoken Afrikaans authors, often the victim of the government's censorship policies. Du Toit at the time was a lecturer in political philosophy at Stellenbosch University. Like Giliomee, he later moved to the University of Cape Town. Jakes Gerwel, rector of the University of the Western Cape, was another contributor to the first edition. He became director-general of the office of the president after Nelson Mandela won the 1994 elections.

14. *Die Suid-Afrikaan,* Spring 1984, 2 (Afrikaans).

15. Ibid., 1. The word that embraces Afrikaans speakers of all colors is now *Afrikaanses.*

16. The United Democratic Front (UDF) was launched on 20 August 1983, after the introduction of the 1983 Constitution, in protest

against the exclusion of Africans from Parliament. It quickly became the unofficial and internal wing of the ANC, and most members joined Congress after it was unbanned in February 1990.

17. *Die Suid-Afrikaan,* Spring 1984, 5 (Afrikaans).

18. *Beeld,* 9 January 1981, 10 (Afrikaans).

19. Hermann Giliomee, telephone interview by author, 15 October 1997.

20. Breytenbach, a strong critic of apartheid, had lived in self-imposed exile in France since the 1960s. He was sentenced to prison on charges of planning to overthrow the government after he entered the country in 1975 under a false name.

21. *Die Suid-Afrikaan,* September 1987, 9–10 (Afrikaans; emphasis in original).

22. The *Citizen* was secretly funded with R32 million of taxpayers' money to "provide something the government had never had before: editorial support in an English-language newspaper." Hachten and Giffard, *Total Onslaught,* 7.

23. *Die Suid-Afrikaan,* September 1987, 27, 29 (Afrikaans).

24. *Die Suid-Afrikaan,* February 1988, 24–25, 29 (Afrikaans). Jordan would hold a post in Nelson Mandela's first cabinet after the 1994 election.

25. Chris Louw, telephone interview by author, 15 October 1997.

26. Hermann Giliomee, telephone interview by author, 9 March 1999.

27. André du Toit, telephone interview by author, 15 October 1997.

28. *DSA,* November/December 1993, 3 (Afrikaans).

29. *DSA in Depth,* August/September 1993, 4 (Afrikaans).

30. *DSA,* October 1994, 10 (Afrikaans).

31. After the ANC took power in April 1994, Afrikaans lost its status as one of only two official languages. The 1994 Constitution determined that Afrikaans and English would in future be joined by Venda, Zulu, Tsonga, Tswana, Xhosa, North Sotho, South Sotho, Swazi, and Ndebele as official languages for the country. This led to serious campaigns by Afrikaans pressure groups to prevent a downscaling of the use of Afrikaans in the civil service and the private sector.

32. *DSA,* October 1994, 10 (Afrikaans). *De Zuid-Afrikaan* included English as well as Dutch articles, and it was one of the first publications to protest against the anglicization of the Cape. The British

took over the Cape initially in 1795 but left for three years in 1803. The Cape became a permanent British colonial possession in 1806, after more than 150 years of Dutch rule.

33. *DSA*, March/April 1995, 4 (Afrikaans). The Independent Media Diversity Trust was established in 1991 by the Newspaper Press Union and the European Union to "help struggling alternative media and to foster media diversity—and some publications loosely described as independent media." *Freedom of Expression Institute Update*, May 1995.

34. *DSA*, March/April 1995, 21. Dikeni identified three conglomerates—Naspers, Argus, and Times Media—but he left out Perskor. Naspers was the old name for Nasionale Pers—the name was changed when Nasionale Pers was finally listed on the Johannesburg Stock Exchange in 1997. Naspers is the largest Afrikaans-language, and Argus the largest English-language, newspaper conglomerate in southern Africa. The Argus group changed its name to Independent Newspaper Holdings when press tycoon Tony O'Reilly bought some of the company's holdings in 1994. The "ailing" English-language South African Associated Newspapers (SAAN) group, founded in 1965, was replaced by the Times Media group in 1987. Times Media absorbed the surviving SAAN publications (*Sunday Times, Business Day, Eastern Province Herald, Evening Post, Cape Times*) at the time. Diederichs, "Newspapers," 95.

35. *Die Suid-Afrikaan*, Autumn 1986, 15.

36. *Volksblad* editor Hennie van Deventer apparently played a key role behind the scenes in getting Zwelahke Sisulu released so he could attend the fifty-year celebration of the Nieman Foundation at Harvard University in the U.S. Van Deventer, *Kroniek van 'n koerantman*, 114–15.

37. In 1998 she wrote a book on her experiences as a TRC reporter. Antjie Krog, *Country of My Skull* (Johannesburg: Random House, 1998).

38. For example, H. Giliomee and Charles Simkins, *The Awkward Embrace: One-Party Domination and Democracy* (Cape Town: Tafelberg Publishers, 1999).

39. The RDP was the Reconstruction and Development Programme introduced by the ANC government shortly after it won the 1994 elections.

40. *DSA*, December 1995/January 1996, 3 (Afrikaans).

41. The two key meetings that journalists from *Die Suid-Afrikaan*

attended were at Dakar, Senegal, in July 1987 and Leverkusen, West Germany, in October 1988.

42. Hachten and Giffard, *Total Onslaught*, 179.

43. Hein Marais, "Still Crazy after All These Years," *Leadership* 17, 4 (1998): 36–42.

44. Max du Preez, personal communication, 25 March 1998.

45. Shaun Johnson, "In an Ersatz-Gothic Lair, Four *Rebelle* with a Cause," *Weekly Mail*, 14–20 October 1988, 8.

46. Ibid, 9. Oliver Tambo, exiled leader of the ANC, and Eugene Terre'Blanche, leader of the neo-Nazi Afrikaner Weerstandsbeweging (AWB; Afrikaner Resistance Movement).

47. Gordon S. Jackson, *Breaking Story: The South African Press* (Boulder: Westview, 1993), 149.

48. *Vrye Weekblad*, 2 February 1994, 7 (Afrikaans). Broeders is an abbreviation for members of the Afrikaner Broederbond, a sinister clandestine organization ruling the National Party from within. Membership was by invitation only and women, non-Afrikaners, and nonwhites were not allowed. The Afrikaner Broederbond was the power behind the throne in Afrikaner politics, finance, the public sector, the Afrikaans churches, and even many private companies.

49. *Vrye Weekblad*, 2 February 1994, 6.

50. *Vrye Weekblad*, 25 November 1989, 1.

51. Jackson, *Breaking Story*, 108.

52. The justice minister's decisions were quite arbitrary. *New African*, an alternative newspaper in Durban, had to pay a R20,000 deposit—as did the *Sowetan* and *New Nation*. The *Weekly Mail* paid R5,000 and *South* only R10. The *Namibian* of Windhoek also had to pay R20,000, but it won on appeal.

53. *Anti-Censorship Action Group Newsletter*, March 1989, 2.

54. *Vrye Weekblad* pointed out that the main story about Mandela's imminent release, for example, was nothing new, as *Beeld* and "other commercial newspapers in South Africa" had already published stories urging Mandela's release. The comment about Mandela as a mediator, moreover, was proof of the newspaper's balanced perspective. *Vrye Weekblad* noted that a variety of public figures had been quoted in this report—Ntatho Motlana (civic leader in Soweto), Helen Suzman (Progressive Federal Party), Chris de Jager (Conservative Party), Aggrey Klaaste (editor of the *Sowetan*), Jan Momberg (Independent Party), Beyers Naudé (listed Afrikaner dissident church minister), Allan Hendrickse (leader of the Coloured Labour Party),

Chris Beyers (Afrikaner Weerstandsbeweging), an ANC spokesperson, a spokesperson for the South African Council of Churches, and Oscar Dhlomo (secretary-general of Inkatha). *Vrye Weekblad* noted that a story claiming the ANC would not abandon the option of violence as a means of fighting apartheid was based on the official view reaffirmed by the ANC during discussions with the South African delegation at Leverkusen in West Germany. *Vrye Weekblad*, 25 November 1988, 6 (Afrikaans).

55. Max du Preez, lecture given to the Department of Journalism, University of Stellenbosch, 25 March 1998. See also Chris Louw, "Afrikaanse koerante in 'n noodtoestand" (Afrikaans papers in a state of emergency), *Die Suid-Afrikaan*, February 1989, 21 (Afrikaans).

56. *Vrye Weekblad*, 2 December 1988, 2.

57. *Vrye Weekblad*, 11 November 1988, 5.

58. *Vrye Weekblad*, 16 December 1988, 1.

59. *Vrye Weekblad*, 19 May 1989, 1.

60. *Vrye Weekblad*, 23 June 1989, 1. Jacques Pauw wrote a story in the 12 May 1989 issue citing *Vrye Weekblad*'s legal representative, Eberhard Bertelsmann, on the absurdity of the ban: "A prohibition on a discussion of the viewpoints of listed persons can lead to such an absurd situation that if Oliver Tambo of the ANC comes with a peace offer tomorrow, nobody would know it because no one may publish it." *Vrye Weekblad*, 12 May 1989, 5.

61. *Vrye Weekblad*, 23 June 1989, 1.

62. *Vrye Weekblad*, 23 June 1989, 2.

63. C. Faure, "Ondersoekende joernalistiek en sosiale verandering"; Faure, "Ondersoekende joernalistiek in *Vrye Weekblad:* 'n Agent vir sosiale verandering?" (Investigative journalism in *Vrye Weekblad:* An agent for social change?), *Communicatio* 23, 2 (1997): 2–14 (Afrikaans).

64. *Vrye Weekblad*, 17 November 1989, 1.

65. *Vrye Weekblad*, 22 June 1990, 1.

66. *Vrye Weekblad*, 30 October 1992, 1.

67. *Vrye Weekblad*, 18 November 1988, 3.

68. *Vrye Weekblad*, 11 August 1989, 1.

69. *Vrye Weekblad*, 2 February 1990, 1. The story led to du Preez again being charged—this time under the Protection of Information Act. Again he received a suspended sentence after a trial held in camera (*Vrye Weekblad*, 2 February 1994, 13).

70. *Vrye Weekblad*, 2 August 1991, 4.

71. *Vrye Weekblad*, 19 February 1993, 1.

72. *Vrye Weekblad*, 17 November 1989, 1 (Afrikaans).

73. *Weekly Mail*, 17–23 November 1989, 1.

74. *Vrye Weekblad*, 17 November 1989, 20.

75. *Vrye Weekblad*, 24 November 1989, 20.

76. An example of the derogative way in which Nasionale Pers journalists treated du Preez was a column written by senior writer Johan van Wyk in *Die Volksblad* and *Beeld* (*Beeld*, 26 March 1994, 8). With the headline, "'Mad Max' and His Cronies on Compulsory Leave," van Wyk attacked du Preez, Jacques Pauw, and Dirk Coetzee for appearing on the television program *Agenda* and repeating their allegations against the police generals. Van Wyk made a habit of calling du Preez "Mad Max," using the name in columns on the editorial page of *Beeld* (e.g., 21 May 1994, 18 June 1994, 8 April 1995, 22 April 1995).

77. *Vrye Weekblad*, 1 December 1989, 1.

78. "The court held that in certain exceptional circumstances of burning public interest, even though allegations made may not be able to be proved true, there might well be a duty upon an editor, where the allegations appear to be *prima facie* correct and capable of proof, to publish such allegations." Citing a Freedom of Expression Institute (FXI) document on *General Lothar Paul Neethling v Max du Preez*. A subcommittee of the FXI, the Media Defence Fund, paid *Vrye Weekblad*'s expenses to fight the case.

79. Faure, "Ondersoekende joernalistiek in *Vrye Weekblad*," 12.

80. *Vrye Weekblad*, 9 December 1993, 5.

81. A. Harber, "Quitting—While It'll Still Be Missed," *Weekly Mail*, 21–27 January 1994, 8.

82. Jonathan Burchell, *Personality Rights and Freedom of Expression: The Modern Actio Injuriarum* (Cape Town: Juta, 1998), 223–24.

83. Max Loubser, "Laster en die media: Belangrike nuwe uitspraak" (Libel and the media: Important new judgment), *Die Burger*, 22 October 1998, 15 (Afrikaans).

84. *Sunday Independent*, 14 June 1998, 4. The South African government conducted its program of chemical and biological warfare (CBW) during the eighties and early nineties at the Roodeplaat Laboratories. The leader of the CBW program, Wouter Basson (called Dr. Death), would be charged on twenty-four cases of fraud and

conspiring to commit murder in 1999 (*Cape Times*, 12 March 1999, 1). Basson and Neethling were linked during testimony at the Truth and Reconciliation Commission hearings in Cape Town in 1998.

85. *Cape Times*, 19 September 1997, 3.

86. Max du Preez, telephone interview by author, 8 March 1999.

87. *Citizen*, 5 December 1989, 8: "We suggest the best thing for *Vrye Weekblad* is to decline the money."

88. *Vrye Weekblad*, 8 December 1989, 18 (Afrikaans). See also note 22, above.

89. Max du Preez, lecture given to the Department of Journalism, University of Stellenbosch, 25 March 1998.

90. Jackson, *Breaking Story*, 59.

91. Ibid., 127.

92. "Briefing Paper by the editors of alternative newspapers," September 1989 [given to journalists at a news conference]; Faure, "Ondersoekende joernalistiek in sosiale verandering," 133 (Afrikaans). According to Mark Beare, *Vrye Weekblad's* financial manager, the European Union also donated some money (he declined to specify the exact amount) in 1993.

93. Harber, "Quitting," 8.

94. Terreblanche wrote a political column called "Tuynhuys Monitor" that offered an ongoing critique of the de Klerk government.

95. *Vrye Weekblad*, 2 February 1994, 60.

96. Ibid., 74 (emphasis in original).

97. *Vrye Weekblad*, 29 September 1989, 10.

98. *Vrye Weekblad*, 2 February 1994, 75.

99. Cited in Jackson, *Breaking Story*, 58.

100. Meiring, "Kleinjong is gebore."

101. *Vrye Weekblad*, 2 February 1994, 86.

102. See G. J. Pienaar, *Inleiding tot die kommunikasiegeskiedenis* (Introduction to the History of Communication) (Potchefstroom: Potchefstroom University for Christian Higher Education, n.d.), 115 (Afrikaans). The Pringle Award is named after Thomas Pringle, a pioneer of the press in South Africa. Pringle, John Fairbairn, and a Cape clergyman of Dutch origin, Abraham Faure, published South Africa's first independent commercial newspaper—*The South African Journal* and *Het Nederduitsch Zuid-Afrikaansch Tydschrift*—a bilingual monthly in English and Dutch, in March 1824. After a prolonged

struggle with British colonial authorities, they finally secured legislation guaranteeing a free press in British South Africa. Ordinance no. 60 (8 May 1829) has been called the "Magna Carta of Freedom of the Press in South Africa." Diederichs, "Newspapers," 73.

103. Meiring, "Kleinjong is gebore."

104. The original words used by Celliers opened his poem, "Generaal de Wet," honoring one of the heroes of the Boers in the Anglo-Boer War, General Christiaan de Wet: "Stil, broers, daar gaan 'n man verby . . . " ("Be quiet, brother, a man is passing by . . . "). It was first published in *Die Lewenstuin en Ander Nuwe Gedigte* (Pretoria: J. L. van Schaik, 1925).

105. See P. Eric Louw, "The Emergence of a Progressive-Alternative Press in South Africa with Specific Reference to *Grassroots*," *Communicatio* 15, 2 (1989): 27. Keyan Tomaselli suggests: the "more likely a paper was to be read by members of the working class the more likelihood it had of being banned: censorship was class-based." K. Tomaselli, "The Progressive Press: Extending the Struggle, 1980–1986," in Tomaselli and Louw, *Alternative Press*, 172.

106. Editors of other alternative newspapers generally had at least some professional experience working in the mainstream press. As trained journalists, they would "not allow their reporters to get away with distortions," according to Ameen Akhalwaya, editor of the *Indicator*. "They have too much at stake to risk losing their credibility and self-respect." Cited in Jackson, *Breaking Story*, 56.

107. *Saamstaan*, February/March 1984, 1 (Afrikaans).

108. *Saamstaan*, August/September 1984, 1 (Afrikaans).

109. Mansoor Jaffer, telephone interview by author, 19 March 1999.

110. Derick Jackson, telephone interview by author, 8 December 1998.

111. P. Eric Louw, "Resistance in Print II: Developments in the Cape, 1985–1989: *Saamstaan, Grassroots,* and *South,*" in Tomaselli and Louw, *Alternative Press*, 207.

112. Derick Jackson, telephone interview by author, 8 December 1998.

113. Chris Gutuza, telephone interview by author, 9 March 1999.

114. Ibid.

115. Ibid.

116. Meiring, "Kleinjong is gebore."

11

The *Weekly Mail*, 1985–1994

Christopher Merrett and Christopher Saunders

The *Weekly Mail* was the flagship of the alternative press in the late 1980s and early 1990s. In this chapter we consider the reasons for its establishment, the kind of newspaper it was, its relations with the government, and the way those relations changed over time, as South Africa moved from harsh apartheid repression to a new democratic order. We suggest that the newspaper played a small but not insignificant role in the birth of a new democratic order in South Africa.

The *Weekly Mail* was born in one of the darkest periods in South African history, when the apartheid era was entering its terminal phase. Prime Minister Pieter W. Botha had sought to reform the system he had inherited from John Vorster in 1978, and in September 1984 a new constitution, based on a tricameral parliament for whites, Indians, and Coloureds, was inaugurated.

The new constitution sparked the formation of new opposition groups inside South Africa, most notably the United Democratic Front. The exclusion of Africans from the new constitution sparked a revolt that broke out in the Vaal Triangle (the industrial conurbation that includes Vereeniging, Vanderbijlpark, and Evaton, south of Johannesburg) on the very day the constitution took effect. By June 1985 this revolt had escalated into a major crisis for the government, more serious even than the Soweto uprising of 1976–77. In planning for the new newspaper, no one knew whether this revolt would spiral into civil war or whether a more repressive apartheid order would be established.

The launch of the *Weekly Mail,* on 14 June 1985, was a direct consequence of the demise of two Johannesburg newspapers— the *Sunday Express* and, more especially, the *Rand Daily Mail* (*RDM*), the last issue of which was published on 30 April 1985. A group of journalists from those newspapers, finding themselves unemployed, decided to use their severance pay to found a newspaper that would carry forward the ideals of the *RDM*.

The name they gave to the new newspaper identified it as a successor to the *RDM*. The legacy of Laurence Gandar, the best-known editor of the *RDM*, was one of dissenting liberalism and crusading social protest. He had stood for the promotion of human rights and the need for fundamental change away from apartheid. Among the triumphs of the *RDM* had been the 1965 prisons exposé and the uncovering of the Information Scandal (Muldergate) in 1978–79. In the early 1980s the *RDM* had tried to report events in the African townships, which had resulted in a loss of some white readers. With *RDM*'s circulation long in decline, its backers, especially the multinational Anglo American company, claimed they could no longer support the newspaper for financial reasons—though many believed they gave in to those who wanted the *RDM* closed for political reasons.[1]

The new newspaper would not be dependent on any such support. Anton Harber, Irwin Manoim, and the others involved in the project first had the idea of establishing a weekly magazine sold by subscription only. They anticipated they would fall foul of the Newspaper Registration and Imprint Act of 1971, which gave the authorities power to impose punitive registration fees on newspapers. The solution seemed to be to produce a publication for members of a *"Weekly Mail* Society" created for that purpose, for such a publication would not be constrained by legislation affecting the press. Harber and Manoim, who would become coeditors of the new newspaper,[2] nevertheless decided to apply for registration. To their surprise, probably because the authorities did not anticipate the *Weekly Mail* would become such a thorn in their flesh, their application was approved at the relatively modest fee of R5,000.[3] They then decided to launch a weekly newspaper that would be available both by subscription—and subscribers initially had the right to elect a member to the board of the newspaper[4]—and on the streets.

Harber, who had been a political reporter on the *RDM*, was in contact with Gwen Lister, who for some time had been trying to launch an independent alternative newspaper in South Africa's colony, Namibia, that would also train Namibian journalists.[5] Manoim had worked with the South African Student Press Union's *SASPU National*, and he had helped editorial staff to use personal computers to set up their stories.[6] In 1985 he and Harber pioneered the use of desktop technology in South Africa for layout and editing. Two Apple Macintoshes and a laser printer—arriving just in time for the first edition—made the new newspaper possible by saving time and labor and thereby reducing costs.

An initial problem was finding a press, for many owners of printing presses were not prepared to print what might be regarded as a subversive publication. It turned out that the *Springs Advertiser* would print the *Weekly Mail*, along with the right-wing Afrikaans alternatively weekly, *Die Patriot*. This was by no means an ideal arrangement: the press of the *Advertiser* could only print the *Weekly Mail* in sections, and Springs was an hour's drive from the Braamfontein offices of the *Weekly Mail* in Johannesburg. A few dedicated helpers distributed the newspaper through the night, while arrangements were made to send it from the Witwatersrand to Cape Town and other major centers.

The *Weekly Mail* belonged to a long tradition of alternative journalism. The *Guardian* and its successors from 1937 to 1963, for example, had been constantly harassed and censored for promoting democracy and the idea that political and economic rights were indistinguishable.[7] In the early 1980s a left-wing journal, *Work in Progress*, appeared erratically, as did *SASPU National*, while from 1983 a small Eastern Cape newspaper called *Saamstaan* appeared in Afrikaans. The *Weekly Mail*, however, was a more substantial, commercially viable publication that would sell mainly to a relatively affluent intelligentsia.

Some of those involved in the establishment of the *Weekly Mail* were liberals, others socialists, but their general perspective may be described as social-democratic. They believed there was scope for a newspaper that provided a wider range of reporting than was to be found in the mainstream commercial press, which reported relatively little news from the African community. They were keen to extend the kind of investigative reporting epitomized by the *RDM*. They were young—most were in their twenties or early thirties—optimistic, and brash; "a single note of realism," Manoim remembered, "may have jeopardised the entire project."[8] There was a strong sense of commitment to what was seen as an important antiapartheid cause. Many *Weekly Mail* contributors, some of whom used pseudonyms, produced material without remuneration because they believed in the newspaper's mission. Veteran journalists, such as Patrick Laurence, were willing to provide their expertise and help ensure that at least some of *Weekly Mail's* journalism was of high quality.

Though the *Weekly Mail* was born at a time when repression

had never been greater, it was also a time of hope. Harber, Manoim, and others involved sensed by June 1985 that the existing order could not last. They hoped that fundamental change might be around the corner, and that the *Weekly Mail*, which they promoted as "the paper for a changing South Africa," would contribute to the birth of a postapartheid order. Their proclaimed aim was to tell "South Africans the unsweetened truth about the country they lived in, painful or otherwise."[9]

Early Issues

The first issue established a profile for the newspaper that would be maintained for the rest of the decade.[10] A twenty-four-page tabloid that appeared each Friday, the *Weekly Mail* contained mainly political news but it also included a sizable arts section. A prominent feature was "Apartheid Barometer," which gave information about people detained and books banned. The *Weekly Mail* became in a minor way a newspaper of record.[11]

The lead story in the first issue—on links between Renamo, the right-wing Mozambican resistance movement, and the South African Police (SAP)—was not taken up by any other newspaper. The *Weekly Mail* began uncovering a network of ways in which the South African security forces were involved in covert operations to destabilize Mozambique. The story led to a visit to the *Weekly Mail* offices by former spy Craig Williamson of the SAP, though ironically the public relations division of the SAP had written to congratulate the new newspaper, and its letter had appeared in that very issue. Also in the pages of the first issue were stories on deaths in detention, forced removals, a bus boycott, "unrest" in the African townships, and the disappearance of three African activists from Port Elizabeth (the PEBCO Three).

The second issue on 21 June 1985 followed up on a number of the stories in the first issue.[12] The *Weekly Mail* also covered a right-wing indaba (meeting or conference), vigilantes in the KwaNdebele "homeland," the censorship apparatus, repression in Kimberley, a South African Defence Force raid on Gaborone (Botswana), and the question of the confidentiality of journalists' sources.

Content of this kind set the *Weekly Mail* apart from the mainstream commercial press in the mid-1980s. The newspaper sought to cover what was happening in the African townships at a time when most white South Africans remained ignorant of developments in those areas. *Weekly Mail*'s pages, for example, carried news and photographs of the mayhem in Duduza township (near Nigel on the East Rand, southeast of Johannesburg) following the funeral of four student activists killed by heavily disguised police, and it was the first to write about suspected apartheid collaborators who were killed by "necklacing."[13] The newspaper was bold enough to suggest police involvement in the rigging of hand grenades that blew up eight young activists and in the murder of Matthew Goniwe of Cradock and three other prominent Eastern Cape activists.[14]

The *Weekly Mail* deliberately set out to provide deeper coverage than the mainstream press on extraparliamentary organizations, labor and trade unions, and the nonracial sport movement. The editors believed in highlighting the problems faced by ordinary working people in black townships. The attention they paid to topics like the Release Mandela Campaign, the second consultative conference of the African National Congress (ANC) held at Kabwe (Zambia) in 1985, universal suffrage, and the abolition of capital punishment inevitably meant that the *Weekly Mail* received hostile attention from government securocrats, who at the time were being given greater power to intervene in everyday life.[15] In an era of growing state tyranny, the *Weekly Mail* rapidly acquired a reputation as a newspaper that challenged the legitimacy of the regime and documented an emerging protest culture virtually ignored by the mainstream establishment press.

State Repression

Within days of the first issue appearing on the streets of Johannesburg, the government announced the imposition of the first state of emergency since 1960. Like its predecessor, the July 1985 emergency covered only parts of the country—mainly in the Cape Province and Transvaal. The following year a countrywide state of emergency was imposed that would be renewed each year until the early 1990s. A major aim of those who imposed successive states of emergency was to control the flow of information at its source: the authorities hoped to write the ANC and the South African Communist Party (SACP) out of current news coverage and out of the experience of ordinary South Africans. The government feared the impact that "unrest" in the black townships was having on the country's international image: if incidents of "unrest" were not reported, it was hoped the international community would forget they existed.

The *Weekly Mail* therefore had to operate in a climate of harsh repression, with informants often in hiding and reporters' notes sometimes a dangerous commodity. Many regulations issued under the powers the state of emergency gave the government were designed to paralyze journalistic activity. One new emergency regulation, on average, was introduced each week during 1986 and 1987.[16] Among the forbidden topics were statements regarded as subversive by the state—stories that normalized or legitimized the liberation movement, stories about the speeches of restricted persons or officials of restricted organizations, photographs and reports on "unrest" and the activities of the security forces, stories about "restricted" gatherings, stories about certain strikes and boycotts, and stories about detainees. The result, in the opinion of veteran journalist Percy Qoboza of the *Sowetan*, was to reduce the credibility of the press, especially in the eyes of African township residents.[17]

Glenn Moss was to write of the emergency years that "any government which has as much to hide as South Africa's rulers must fear all but the most tame sections of the media. . . . the government . . . is justified in fearing what a competent media might publish."[18] Emergency censorship, very much more radical and effective than censorship regulations imposed prior to 1986, was designed to encourage self-censorship, to minimize the crisis for whites, and to create an atmosphere of normality.

The *Weekly Mail* reacted in two defiant ways to the emergency regulations. First, the newspaper sought to portray them for what they were. Harber wrote of a "sjambokracy—where the rule of law has been replaced by the rule of the whip"—and of the police now being able, thanks to the emergency, to "remove their balaclavas" (a reference to the nighttime attire of elements of the police force in African townships).[19] Second, the newspaper succeeded to some extent in getting around even the most severe of the emergency regulations. Thus it is not correct to say that the government was able to obliterate "what was left of the independent role of the newspaper in South Africa."[20]

From the beginning, the *Weekly Mail* came into conflict with the state. At the funerals in Duduza in July 1985 police harassed a reporter and confiscated his film. When a national state of emergency was declared on 12 June 1986, the police went to the offices of the *Weekly Mail* to seize copies of the newspaper for the following day. But copies had already been sent to subscribers, and others were on their way to news vendors. The police then seized copies from news vendors; copies not confiscated became very sought after and fetched up to R50.[21] This issue of the newspaper carried details of the state of emergency crackdown and the locations where police swoops had taken place. The front-page headline read "Rule of the Big Stick," and a photograph showed police armed with quirts approaching Khotso House (a building housing many antiapartheid organizations, including the South African Council of Churches, the Detainees' Parents' Support Committee, and the Black Sash) in Johannesburg, before the emergency had taken effect. The staff of the *Weekly Mail* feared at the time that the newspaper would be prevented from publication,[22] but there was still a measure of protection in the legalism of the South African state. Regulations issued under the 1953 Public Safety Act, authoritarian though they were, nevertheless required the relevant minister to exercise his discretion in such matters.

The newspaper's lawyers initially advised a policy of extreme caution. Of twenty-eight pages in the issue of 20 June 1986, fourteen contained blacked-out text or empty white space, where articles and even a cartoon had been removed. Sometimes lines were blacked out in such a way that readers could guess what had been censored and reconstruct the likely meaning. On the front page, the *Weekly Mail* proclaimed in large letters, "Our lawyers tell us we can say almost nothing critical about the Emergency. But we'll try." A box at the bottom of the page warned: "RESTRICTED: Reports on these pages have been censored to comply with Emergency regulations." A list of 1,000 detainees in the Cape and Transvaal had every name blacked out. Political commentary and even the letters page were censored in similar fashion. What was removed included a story about Soweto that began: "June 16 did not turn into a day of violence after all." A photograph was removed, but the caption remained: "Church volunteers wrap flowers with memorial cards."

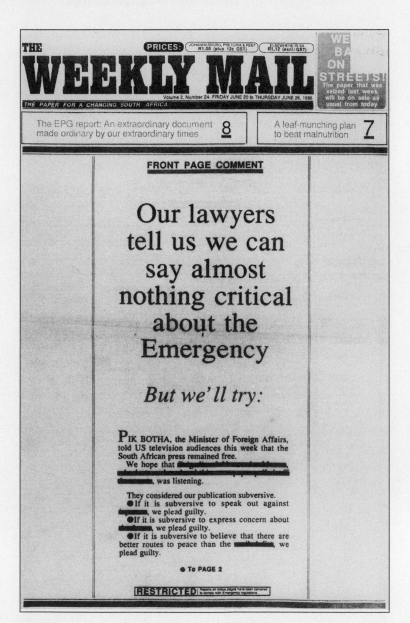

The most famous *Weekly Mail* front page was the 20–26 June 1986 edition, depicting the impact of censorship on the South African press.

The *Weekly Mail's* actions dramatically made the point that the emergency regulations were extremely harsh. But soon the *Weekly Mail's* lawyers were advising that not as much material need be censored, and the editors decided to test the emergency regulations to the limit. The following issue (27 June) contained fewer black lines, and they were restricted to a report on an expelled journalist and one letter on the letters page. On 4 July 1986 the *Weekly Mail* published a list of released detainees by area, together with some affiliations, though a photograph of the detained journalist Zwelakhe Sisulu, editor of *New Nation*, was removed. The following issue carried details of detainees' conditions and of a hunger strike. By 23 July the *Weekly Mail* was saying that the names of detainees still held would be published if families had been notified, and from 1 August it began to publish them. On 22 August the newspaper published details of the torture of a child detainee.

In its challenge to the emergency regulations, the *Weekly Mail* was greatly helped by a successful challenge in the Natal Supreme Court, where it was argued that the regulations were vague and beyond the powers of the president and the intentions of the originators of the Public Safety Act. The court set aside the government's definition of "subversive statement" and its powers of seizure and banning. The striking down of two regulations in particular—those preventing photographs of "unrest" and reporting on security force activity—provided a brief respite before the regulations were revised.[23] The *Weekly Mail* was now able to publish the censored page of 20 June 1986, and when it did so its readers found that much that had been censored had been innocuous: articles on empty streets, closed shops, and disconnected phones in Soweto, the teargassing of an Athlone (Cape Town) mosque, and loopholes in the less rigorous censorship legislation of the Bantustans. Now the front page of 8 August 1986 was reconstructed to give an account of security force action at Zwelethemba, near

Worcester in the western Cape, an example of repression in rural areas. Following the Natal judgment there was a period of relatively open reporting, such as a White City (Soweto) shooting by police,[24] though the editors pointed out that removing the black lines did not take away the censorship implicit in other legislation.

When new and tighter regulations were introduced, the effect was that "vast areas of South African life vanished from sight overnight."[25] The *Weekly Mail* felt the impact more than other alternative newspapers because it was doing more to conscientize whites about the problems of black citizens. But instead of succumbing to despair, and closing the newspaper down, the coeditors decided to look for loopholes in the poorly drafted emergency regulations. For while the ambiguities in the regulations encouraged further self censorship, they also allowed creative interpretation. *Weekly Mail* readers could sometimes read between the lines for the coded meanings of reports. Although the newspaper adopted an air of "wide-eyed innocence," in the words of coeditor Irwin Manoim, in effect the government was challenged to prosecute the newspaper. For a time this did not happen because the authorities had too much to lose by subjecting the loosely worded regulations to a court of law and by the impact that closing the newspaper down would have on international opinion. In the meantime, the police opened many dockets, and sometimes pursued charges, though relatively few cases ever came to a conclusion. It was clear that their main purpose was to intimidate.

In the face of this intimidation, the *Weekly Mail* adopted an attitude of mocking humor. When new censorship regulations were introduced, its readers were advised: "For further information telephone your Minister." The newspaper provided the minister's work and home telephone numbers. Throughout the states of emergency the *Weekly Mail* promoted the right to know. In the face of authoritarianism, the newspaper drew attention to censorship, while keeping sufficiently within the law to survive.

Censorship was tightened in particular at the end of 1986, at the time of a Christmas against the Emergency campaign launched by the United Democratic Front. In January 1987 a ban was placed on news reports and advertisements about unlawful organizations. Even blank pages were now proscribed. The issue of 9 January 1987 had such a blank page in place of an advertisement that gave the name of the ANC. This was allowed by special permission after the police phoned at 9 P.M. and said they were going to seize copies at midnight unless the advertisement was removed.

Remembering what had happened to the *RDM* after it had run a series of articles on conditions in prison in 1965,[26] South African newspapers for many years refused to touch stories relating to prisons. One of the *Weekly Mail*'s greatest scoops was a series of articles it ran by Thami Mkhwanazi on the most notorious prison of all, Robben Island. Mkhwanazi was a journalist who had been imprisoned there from 1980 to 1986. His series of articles in August and September 1987 were a major turning point in South African journalism.[27] Though not submitted ahead of publication, the authorities chose to ignore them, presumably believing that even more attention would be attracted to the Island if they responded. By this time some prisoners on the Island were allowed to subscribe to the *Weekly Mail*. Knowing of the prison series—though they were not allowed to receive copies of the newspaper containing the prison series—some prisoners feared they might lose privileges because the stories were published. For this reason, representations from the prisoners were made to the newspaper to stop running the articles, but the coeditors decided to continue the series.[28]

The *Weekly Mail* had usually submitted such material to the authorities and asked for a publishable reaction. It had done this with a story by Gavin Evans published on 16 August 1985 about his thirteen days in detention at Diepkloof Prison. The story was accompanied by a response from the liaison office of the Prisons Service on the conditions of detainees. On 6 June 1986 the *Weekly Mail* was the first newspaper in decades to publish a photograph of Nelson Mandela—this one taken twenty-two years earlier. It did so because the photograph had appeared in a Bureau for Information pamphlet, and permission was granted by the Department of Prisons in this instance, though it remained the case that all other representations of Mandela were illegal.

From Christmas 1987 the directorate of Media Relations sent the *Weekly Mail* a series of notices warning of possible closure in terms of the emergency regulations. That the newspaper was warned at all was a concession to international sensibilities. In defending itself, the editors argued that the *Weekly Mail* as a whole had to be considered, not just scattered articles or even phrases cited by the minister of home affairs. The first newspaper to be closed down under the state of emergency was *New Nation*, begun by the Southern African Catholic Bishops' Conference. It was closed from 22 March to 10 June 1988.[29] The *Weekly Mail* said this action had been taken because *New Nation* had "dared to reflect the violence of apartheid . . . because it gave a voice to the voteless majority . . . because it articulated the aspirations of millions of oppressed people." The *Weekly Mail* then published articles from the banned issue of *New Nation* on 24 March 1988, a practice later made illegal. *New Nation's* sister newspaper in the Western Cape, *South*, which had been launched in March 1987, was shut down from May to June 1988.

Although the *Weekly Mail* was threatened with similar action, its approach was different from these newspapers. The *Weekly Mail* did not appeal to its own readers but instead launched a "Wail dammit" campaign aimed mainly at influential big business, those with international contacts, and the diplomatic corps. Shaun Johnson, unlike most others who worked on the *Weekly Mail*, could look respectable and present himself well; he lobbied hard and obtained indications of support from the embassies of the United Kingdom and the United States, from the government of Sweden and from the European Union. The coeditors went to see Stoffel Botha, the minister of home affairs who was responsible, and came away convinced that he was more concerned with the way they were presenting him as stupid than with the political content of the newspaper. Robin Renwick, the British ambassador, sent letters to the government defending the *Weekly Mail* on the grounds that it did not advocate violence and presented both sides of the sanctions issue, and he argued that the newspaper should not be closed down.[30]

Nevertheless, the *Weekly Mail* was temporarily forced to suspend publication. In 1988 the police seized a copy of the newspaper that carried an article critical of Magnus Malan, minister of defense. After three warnings, the *Weekly Mail* was proscribed for one month, from 1 to 28 November 1988. Ironically, it was the same month that its Afrikaans-language counterpart, *Vrye Weekblad*, was launched.[31] That the *Weekly Mail*'s suspension was relatively short must be attributed in large part to foreign interest in its plight—especially the British government, through its high commissioner in South Africa, which helped ensure the newspaper survived.[32]

The stated cause for the suspension was the *Weekly Mail*'s publication of the ANC's constitutional guidelines, which had already been aired in the mainstream commercial press; an article on the Pan-Africanist Congress by Witwatersrand University academic Tom Lodge; a description of a visit by University of Stellenbosch students to the ANC in Maputo; and a profile of Frank Chikane, secretary-general of the South African Council of Churches. The list suggested that it was the newspaper, not particular news reports, that was the target—another case of the messenger being attacked because of the message. The *Weekly Mail* pointed out that on a previous occasion Stoffel Botha had objected to a mere 1 percent of an issue.[33] The reaction of coeditor Anton Harber to the news of the suspension was belligerent. He had already created a new verb, *to stoffel,* meaning to snuff out, and he now urged the press to stop worrying about the law and adopt the attitude of journalistic street fighters.[34]

The *Weekly Mail* remained vulnerable to government persecution after the one-month suspension was over. In August 1988 copies of an issue were confiscated on the grounds that it had covered, and therefore promoted, opposition to conscription. News coverage had included a cartoon, an advertisement by War Resisters International, and a report on 143 men who stated they would never serve in the South African Defence Force. Subsequent court action failed to bring redress.[35] In July 1989, dockets were opened against the *Weekly Mail* for contravention of the emergency regulations. Anton Harber, Jo-Ann Bekker, and Franz Krüger were charged the following month for articles printed on 20 February 1987 on the medical rights of detainees and hunger strikers, though the articles had been based on details revealed under parliamentary privilege. These charges were withdrawn later in 1989. Those who worked on the newspaper believed that some of the problems they continued to have with distribution—including copies which mysteriously disappeared between Johannesburg and Cape Town—were the result of covert police action.

Readership and Relations with the Democratic Movement

The *Weekly Mail* was a relatively expensive newspaper—its cover price of R1 in 1985 had increased to R3 in 1992—and its circulation was never large. Though the *Weekly Mail* tried to widen its circulation, which briefly increased to 30,000 when a short-lived daily edition was produced in June 1990, the newspaper generally sold fewer than 20,000 copies.[36] How many of the readers were white could never be known with certainty, for the *Weekly Mail*'s commitment to nonracialism prevented it from even trying to find out, but there is little doubt that the vast majority were white. An early readership survey revealed that the newspaper was bought mainly by "slumpies" (slightly left, upwardly mobile professionals).[37] Unhappy with the establishment press, and rejecting what they saw on state-controlled television, these readers were prepared to read heavy doses of political reportage, much of which told of the most appalling incidents and events. The *Weekly Mail*'s pages were certainly not cheerful reading.

There was considerable debate about the policy of the newspaper in an authoritarian society constrained by heavy censorship. The dominant feeling was that the *Weekly Mail* should publish a cross section of views while simultaneously maintaining a consistent and principled editorial line. There was opposition to this approach, however, by those who rejected anything that seemed to compromise with the apartheid government. A debate arose over whether the newspaper should continue to accept the Shell company's human rights advertisements, which *New Nation* refused to carry on the grounds that Shell was breaching the sanctions campaign. To *New Nation*, Shell's messages, however reasonable and acceptable they might appear, gave respectability to a sanctions-busting enterprise. But the *Weekly Mail*, dependent on advertisements and having much difficulty obtaining them, continued to carry Shell's messages.

The relationship between the *Weekly Mail* and various sectors of civil society came under stress at the end of the 1980s. Relations with sections of the Muslim community, for example, were ruptured as the result of an invitation the newspaper extended to Salman Rushdie, author of *The Satanic Verses*, to appear at its annual book week. That the Congress of South African Writers withdrew from what had been a joint project further complicated the issue. Harber was very critical of those United Democratic Front affiliates who called on the government to ban Rushdie, accusing them of hypocrisy by using the state when it suited them.[38] Unlike, say, *South*, the *Weekly Mail* retained its independent political stance and was never closely allied to the UDF.

But the *Weekly Mail* threw its support from the beginning behind the liberation movement. The newspaper was a pioneer in giving coverage to the activities of the ANC, though it was Anthony Heard, editor of the mainstream *Cape Times*, who scooped it by publishing the first lengthy interview with "listed" ANC president Oliver Tambo in November 1985.[39] Relations with the ANC became more difficult in the late 1980s. Thandeka Gqubule's exposé of the criminally violent behavior of the Mandela United Football Club in the issue of 27 January 1989—the first such exposé in a newspaper[40]—led to the reporter having to go into hiding, and the newspaper was accused of having "betrayed the struggle."[41] Here was one of the first times a left-wing publication was targeted for maintaining an ethical stance and refusing to compromise its standards when dealing with some of the less savory aspects of the liberation struggle. Some years later the Mandelas were said to have resented the way the *Weekly Mail* covered Winnie Mandela's trial and conviction on charges of kidnapping and conspiracy to murder in connection with the death of the young activist Stompie Mokhetsi Sepei.[42]

With hindsight, the *Weekly Mail* could have done more to cover ANC activities in Zambia and elsewhere—for example, by drawing on reports in the international press. While the *Weekly Mail* covered the many visits that whites and others made to the ANC in Lusaka and elsewhere from September 1985, it did not know of other talks that took place, talks made known only years later. The newspaper's importance lay not in covering the international aspects of the struggle but in giving its largely white readers an idea of what was happening in the black townships, of what blacks were thinking and how they were suffering. Editors of the mainstream press read the *Weekly Mail* and admired its courage.[43] The *Weekly Mail* was ahead of its time in reporting on many issues—while confronting the government and helping to expose the repressive nature of apartheid.[44]

There can be little doubt that the way the *Weekly Mail* harassed the apartheid regime played a part in bringing the government to the negotiating table. By early 1989 the newspaper was telling its readers, in an article entitled "Quietly Thinking the Unthinkable," that the government was nudging toward a dialogue with the ANC.[45] Later that year, the *Weekly Mail* would cover P. W. Botha's secret meeting with Nelson Mandela that had taken place in July, and how de Klerk was beginning to indicate his willingness to make the leap that Botha would not make.

The 1990s

The events of February 1990—beginning with de Klerk's speech releasing Mandela, unbanning the ANC, and other opposition groups—largely vindicated the role played by South Africa's resistance press in the last years of the apartheid era, although ultimately those events signaled the end for most alternative publications. The *Weekly Mail* responded to the new political dispensation with an abortive attempt to reposition itself as a daily.

Launched with great fanfare on 20 June 1990, the *Daily*

Mail had long been the goal of Harber and Manoim, who from the beginning had wanted a new version of the *RDM* in a daily morning newspaper format. Although the *Daily Mail* attracted excellent journalists and had a distinctive style, the new broadsheet newspaper faced too much competition to become viable—two weeks before it was launched, the *Star* had come out with a morning edition. The *Daily Mail* experienced a rerun of some of the problems that beset the *RDM*, and after only forty-four issues the daily died on 4 September 1990.[46] This had various consequences for the *Weekly Mail*. The advent of the *Daily Mail*, which coincided with a move to new premises and the acquisition of new equipment along with new staff, signaled the decline of the egalitarianism and high-mindedness that was still evident at the *Weekly Mail*.

The collapse of the *Daily Mail* left the *Weekly Mail* owing a large debt to Caxtons, a subsidiary of the *Argus*, which had printed both newspapers. The only way the debt could be managed involved a deal in which the *Argus* was allowed access to *Weekly Mail* news reports until the debt was paid back in April 1991.[47] The newspaper did briefly lose some of its independence, but by the early 1990s that did not seem to make much difference in terms of news coverage. The *Weekly Mail* had been losing money for some years, and in order to survive it had to take on more of the characteristics of a mainstream commercial newspaper. *Weekly Mail* editors were less prepared to take risks, and the newspaper itself was less prepared to challenge the authorities in the postapartheid era.

Nevertheless, the *Weekly Mail* continued with its tradition of investigative journalism. Some of this was not directly political. The newspaper illustrated the continuing secrecy of South African public life in 1991, for example, by exposing conditions in psychiatric hospitals, particularly the treatment experienced by Africans.[48] Another high-profile story exposed a slave trade in Mozambican citizens, who were being smuggled across the eastern Transvaal border. *Weekly Mail* reporters bought two such slaves for R200 each.[49]

The newspaper's most important role in the early 1990s, however, was in its coverage of the roller-coaster transition process.[50] In August 1990 it published documents obtained from a disgruntled Pretoria businessman who had failed to recover money he had spent on a military intelligence operation called Project Crist, which had involved setting up a newspaper in Gaborone (Botswana) directed against the ANC and its guerrilla army, Umkhonto we Sizwe.[51] The *Weekly Mail's* reputation for investigative reporting was enhanced when the newspaper precipitated the Inkathagate scandal in July 1991. It showed that Mangosuthu Buthelezi's right-wing Inkatha movement had been bankrolled by the South African Police to stage an anti-ANC rally and sustain the anti-COSATU union federation UWUSA (United Workers' Union of South Africa). This led to a confrontation on television between editor Anton Harber and Minister of Law and Order Adriaan Vlok—the first time an apartheid government minister was directly challenged and contradicted on the air. The scandal was interpreted as a major setback for the regime during the negotiations process.

Subsequent news reports involved the police supplying guns to Inkatha, the establishment of a military training camp for Inkatha in northern KwaZulu-Natal and the training of Inkatha recruits in the Caprivi Strip—they then returned to KwaZulu and were involved in various killings. Much of the content of these stories was confirmed when the Truth and Reconciliation Commission heard detailed evidence about those events in 1997 and 1998.[52] The *Weekly Mail* played a major role in uncovering information about this so-called Third Force and in prodding a reluctant de Klerk to take belated action to prevent the transition process from being derailed.

The *Weekly Mail* had for some time been collaborating with the British daily, the *Guardian*—most notably during the In-

Let freedom reign

Never, never and never again shall it be that this beautiful land will again experience the oppression of one by another.

I et freedom reign
God bless Africa!

— Nelson Mandela, May 10, 1994

The *Weekly Mail and Guardian* rejoices at the beginning of a new era for South Africa.

kathagate scandal, which was exposed by David Beresford, a *Guardian* writer who had worked from a desk in the *Weekly Mail*'s offices since 1985. The *Guardian*'s weekly international edition was distributed with the *Weekly Mail* from 1992 and finally integrated into one continuous newspaper. The *Weekly Mail* was renamed the *Weekly Mail and Guardian* from 30 July 1993—later shortened to the *Mail and Guardian*—although for years people continued to refer to the *Mail and Guardian* as the *Weekly Mail*.[53]

Assessment

Before the 1980s left-wing publications like the *Guardian* had exhibited a type of journalism that, in the words of Anthony Sampson, "threw light on the darker regions of South African life."[54] The *Guardian*'s investigative journalism—such as the Bethal farms exposé and coverage of the antipass campaign, the Alexandra bus boycott, the demolition of Sophiatown, and acts of police brutality—set a precedent that was to be followed by the *RDM* and the *Weekly Mail*. These newspapers clashed with the authorities because their content helped delegitimize the power of the South African state.

The *Weekly Mail* became, in the words of Keyan Tomaselli and Eric Louw, "South Africa's first-ever commercially viable leftist-press."[55] Despite the *Weekly Mail*'s social democratic approach, it was jealously protective of its editorial and financial independence, a stance that would lead the newspaper to distance itself from aspects of ANC policy in postapartheid South Africa.

Though the *Weekly Mail* was regarded by mainstream competitors during its first five years as a "fringe" newspaper, it had an influence out of all proportion to its circulation.[56] This was largely because the *Weekly Mail* represented views closer to those of the majority of South Africans than the mainstream press. Despite the fact that the newspaper sold on average perhaps 20,000 copies an issue, editor Anton Harber rejected the idea that it was a "fringe" publication. The *Weekly Mail* was central to the alternative press of the late 1980s and encouraged the birth of similar newspapers, like *South* and

Vrye Weekblad—even though they could not survive as commercial publications.

The *Weekly Mail* could perhaps have done more to train African journalists—its first full-scale training program did not take place until early 1988.[57] But in the early years the challenge of producing the newspaper while dealing with constant legal intimidation absorbed almost all the energies of the staff. The *Weekly Mail* did provide openings for African journalists, some of whom were to play important roles in the new era into which South Africa moved after 1994. One of the first journalists to receive full training with the *Weekly Mail* became sharply critical of the way the newspaper continued under white editorship.[58] A suitable black replacement, however, was not immediately apparent, and it was not realistic to expect Harber and Manoim to abandon the project they had begun.

From the outset, the quality of its reporting made the *Weekly Mail* essential reading for staff on other newspapers, and its distinct contributions to journalism were widely recognized. The *Weekly Mail* helped keep the mainstream press on its toes—filling much of the gap left by the closure of the *RDM*, reporting on issues that might otherwise have not been publicized, and offering an idea of what the new South Africa might look like. The effect of its dissident approach to journalism was to demystify the ANC for the newspaper's largely white readership and thus undermine the government's main rationale for censoring the press. The *Weekly Mail* not only worked for a new democratic order; it helped, in a small way, to bring it about.

Notes

1. On the controversial demise of the *Rand Daily Mail*, see esp. J. Mervis, *The Fourth Estate* (Johannesburg: Jonathan Ball, 1989), chap.

34; H. Tyson, *Editors under Fire* (Sandton: Random House, 1993), 325; K. Tomaselli, R. Tomaselli, and J. Muller, eds., *Narrating the Crisis: Hegemony and the South African Press* (Johannesburg: Richard Lyon, 1987), 79ff.

2. See the cartoon of the two in Tyson, *Editors under Fire*, 330.

3. *New Nation* had to pay R20,000. The government asked the *Namibian* for R20,000, which the newspaper challenged successfully in court.

4. The board of six members had five journalists on it. The idea that a subscribers' representative could "have a say in editorial decisions," as first suggested, proved impractical.

5. The *Namibian* would not appear until 30 August 1985, but Lister, who had resigned from the *Windhoek Observer* after being demoted as political editor, had for months been trying to raise funds. Unlike Harber, she was successful in getting money from the European Community and the Nordic countries. The launch of the *Weekly Mail* was a boost to Lister's efforts to get the *Namibian* off the ground. Cf. Lister's account of the launch of the Namibian in the tenth anniversary issue, August 1995. Gwen Lister, interview by Christopher Saunders, Windhoek, 1997.

6. I. Manoim, *You Have Been Warned: The First Ten Years of the Mail and Guardian* (London: Viking, 1996), 59.

7. The *Guardian* was banned three times under the mastheads *Guardian* (1952), *Advance* (1954), and *New Age* (1962). On the *Guardian* and other newspapers in South Africa's alternative journalism tradition, see L. Switzer, ed., *South Africa's Alternative Press: Voices of Protest and Resistance, 1880s–1960s* (Cambridge: Cambridge University Press, 1997). When Manoim was asked for material for this chapter, he responded that the history of the *Weekly Mail* was of no interest to him. This despite his having assembled a popular history of the newspaper in *You Have Been Warned*.

8. Manoim, *You Have Been Warned*, 3.

9. I. Manoim, quoted in R. Simmonds, "A State of Emergency: The Alternative Press under Apartheid," (unpublished paper, Department of Journalism and Media Studies, Rhodes University, 1996), 2.

10. The *Weekly Mail* had some amateurish features. It was not until vol. 1, no. 4, that the newspaper was numbered, and many of the early issues did not include the year on the front page.

11. This was the main reason why Christopher Merrett decided to index the newspaper. He was never able to interest the coeditors in the index, which he began in roneod form in 1988 (*Weekly Mail Index*, 1987). The 1989 index was the first to appear in the University of Natal Library Publication Series (1990) and indexes followed for 1990, 1990–91, 1992, 1993, and 1994. Retrospective indexes for 1985 and 1986 appeared in 1992, compiled by C. Merrett and P. Sukram, and by C. Merrett and C. Nel.

12. Further evidence on links between the South African security forces and Renamo was provided in the issue of 28 June 1985.

13. Patrick Laurence, "Death on a Sunday Afternoon," *Weekly Mail*, 16 August 1985.

14. *Weekly Mail*, 5, 12, and 19 July 1985. The information in Patrick Laurence's story about the rigged hand grenades was confirmed more than ten years later when the police responsible applied to the Truth and Reconciliation Commission for amnesty.

15. The securocrats, as they were called, included persons in the civil service, police, military, and even notables outside government service who were members of the Botha government's National Security Management System. For details on NSMS, see chap. 1.

16. A. Harber, "Finding the Loopholes: How the *Weekly Mail* Carries on Reporting," *Index on Censorship* 16, 4 (1987): 22. Cf. A. Harber, "Censorship," in J. Harker, *The Legacy of Apartheid* (London: Guardian Newspapers, 1994). On the emergency regulations and the way they affected the press, see esp. R. Abel, *Politics by Other Means: Law in the Struggle against Apartheid, 1980–1994* (New York: Routledge, 1995), 259–72; C. Merrett, *A Culture of Censorship: Secrecy and Intellectual Repression in South Africa* (Cape Town: David Philip, 1994), chap. 6; K. Tomaselli and R. Tomaselli, "From News Management to Control," *Die Suid-Afrikaan*, 1986; G. Stewart, "Perfecting the Free Flow of Information: Media Control in South Africa," *Index on Censorship* 16, 4 (1987); Simmonds, "State of Emergency."

17. Merrett, *Culture of Censorship*, 119.

18. G. Moss, editorial, *Work in Progress*, April–May 1988, 2.

19. *Weekly Mail*, 1 November 1985, 15; 26 July 1985, 12–13.

20. A. H. Heard, "Caution Is the Watchword," *Index on Censorship* 15, 7 (1986): 7.

21. Manoim, *You Have Been Warned*, 60.

22. Glenn Frankel, *Guardian Weekly*, 29 June 1986.

23. The media regulations were issued in revised form in December 1986.

24. *Weekly Mail*, 29 August and 5 September 1986.

25. Manoim, *You Have Been Warned*, 72.

26. Benjamin Pogrund wrote a three-part series in 1965 on prison conditions in Pretoria, Pietermaritzburg, and Port Elizabeth revealing a regime of general brutality, including electric shock torture and filthy conditions. In spite of the accuracy of the information, backed up by affidavits, Harold Strachan, the main informant, was banned, documents were seized, jail sentences were handed out to prison officials, the editor and the company that owned the *RDM* were fined, and Pogrund was given a suspended sentence of three months in prison. The case dragged on for four years.

27. *Weekly Mail*, 7 August to 4 September 1987.

28. Cf. Manoim, *You Have Been Warned*, 90–92. The first article in the series was about Mandela on Robben Island (7 August 1987). Mandela read the series in Victor Verster Prison near Paarl, where he was housed in the last years of his captivity.

29. This is discussed at length in Abel, *Politics by Other Means*, chap. 8 ("Censorship and the Closure of the *New Nation*").

30. For example, Department of Foreign Affairs archives, Pretoria: South West Africa, 1988, vol. 6: R. Renwick to Director-General, Foreign Affairs, 18 October 1988.

31. The first issue appeared on 4 November 1988.

32. R. Renwick, *Unconventional Diplomacy in Southern Africa* (Basingstoke, UK: Macmillan, 1997), 124. Renwick thought the *Weekly Mail* had played "an invaluable role in exposing the abuses of the security forces."

33. *Weekly Mail*, 15 January 1988, 2.

34. Merrett, *Culture of Censorship*, 137.

35. *Weekly Mail*, 10 November 1989, 4.

36. G. S. Jackson, *Breaking Story: The South African Press* (Boulder: Westview Press, 1993), 64.

37. Ibid, 57.

38. A. Harber, "The Press and the Battle," *Monitor* (Port Elizabeth, special edition on Human Rights), 1989, 167; Jackson, *Breaking Story*, 167–68.

39. The comments and opinions of persons listed under the 1982 Internal Security Act were not supposed to be quoted in the media.

Unlike Harber and Manoim, Anthony Heard could use newspaper funds to fly to London for the interview. A. Heard, *The Cape of Storms* (Johannesburg: Ravan Press, 1991).

40. Denis Beckett had been the first to write about it, in his newsmagazine *Frontline.*

41. Manoim, *You Have Been Warned,* chap. 7 ("Mother of the Nation").

42. S. Mallady, *After Apartheid* (London: Faber, 1993), 182.

43. Cf. Jackson, *Breaking Story,* 204, 259 note 11.

44. The *Weekly Mail's* Afrikaans counterpart, *Vrye Weekblad,* however, was the first publication to expose the apartheid death squads in 1989. A month earlier, the *Weekly Mail* had reported a confession by death row inmate Almond Nofomela about his involvement in death squads, but their existence had been denied by the government and the police. *Vrye Weekblad's* scoop was to secure an interview with Dirk Coetzee, who had headed the Vlakplaas death squad unit before he fled the country. *Vrye Weekblad,* 17 November 1989. The *Weekly Mail* merely reported that he had left for London. Jacques Pauw then exposed Coetzee's successor, Eugene de Kock. *Vrye Weekblad,* 24 November 1989.

45. Title of an article by M. Swilling, cited in R. Rosenthal, *Mission Improbable* (Cape Town: David Philip, 1998), 242.

46. See Manoim, *You Have Been Warned,* chap. 8 ("The Short Life of the *Daily Mail"*), for the reasons why Joel Joffe, the largest investor, pulled the plug.

47. Ibid., 140; K. Tomaselli and P. E. Louw, *The Alternative Press in South Africa* (Bellville: Anthropos, 1991), 225 (citing *Daily News,* 7 May 1991).

48. *Weekly Mail,* 28 June 1991, 2.

49. *Weekly Mail,* 16 November 1990.

50. On the events of the period 1990 to 1994, see, M. Coleman, *A Crime against Humanity* (Cape Town: David Philip, 1998); S. Friedman and D. Atkinson, eds., *A Small Miracle* (Johannesburg: Ravan Press, 1994); F. W. de Klerk, *The Last Trek: A New Beginning* (London: Macmillan, 1998); A. Guelke, *South Africa in Transition* (London: I. B. Taurus, 1999). De Klerk calls the *Weekly Mail* "a radical newspaper." *Last Trek,* 254.

51. *Weekly Mail,* 30 August 1990. The businessman's name was Abel Rudman: cf. D. Ottaway, *Chained Together: Mandela, De Klerk,*

and the Struggle to Remake South Africa (New York: Times Books, 1993), 239.

52. Cf. Truth and Reconciliation Commission Final Report, October 1998, which contains numerous references to *Weekly Mail* stories.

53. For example, Terry Bell on "The Editors," SAFM radio, 28 March 1999.

54. A. Sampson, *The Treason Cage: The Opposition on Trial in South Africa* (London: Heinemann, 1958), 171.

55. Tomaselli and Louw, *Alternative Press*, 13.

56. Ibid., 89.

57. Manoim, *You Have Been Warned*, 121.

58. This was Thandeka Gqubule. Cf. Manoim, *You Have Been Warned*, 128.

Notes on Contributors

Mohamed Adhikari is a senior lecturer in the Department of History at the University of Cape Town. His numerous publications include *"Let Us Live for Our Children": The Teachers' League of South Africa, 1913–1940* (1993); *James La Guma* (1996); and *Straatpraatjes: Language, Politics, and Popular Culture in Cape Town, 1909–1922* (1996).

George Claassen is a professor and head of the Department of Journalism at Stellenbosch University (South Africa). He was a founder and editorial member of *Beeld* in 1974 and reported from Europe, Israel, and the United States for various Nasionale Pers publications between 1975 and 1988. He has also worked as an editor and translator of documentary programs produced by Toan Films. His publications include *A History of the Low Countries* (1981) and a historical novel, *When Beggars Die* (1988). He is coeditor of the *Afrikaans Quotation Dictionary* (2d ed., 1997). Claassen is working on a history of the mainstream, commercial Afrikaans press entitled, *Quisling or Herald? Perspectives on the Afrikaans Press under Apartheid*, to be published in 2001.

David Howarth is a lecturer in political theory (Division of International Relations and Politics) at the University of Staffordshire (Stoke-on-Trent, England). Howarth's publications include "Complexities of Identity/Difference: The Ideology of Black Consciousness in South Africa" (1997), *Discourse*

Theory and Political Analysis (coauthored with Aletta Norval and Y. Stavrakakis, 2000); and *Discourse*, produced for the Open University in the series Concepts in the Social Sciences (2000).

Ineke van Kessel is a researcher at the African Studies Centre in Leiden (Netherlands), and she also works as a freelance journalist. Her Ph.D. dissertation, "'Beyond Our Wildest Dreams': The United Democratic Front and the Transformation of South Africa," has been published by the University of Virginia Press. Van Kessel received the 1985 Dutch Press Award (Prijs van de Nederlandse Dagbladpers) for her coverage of the 1984 South African elections while working for the Dutch News Agency, ANP. She has coedited a book in Dutch on Africans in the Netherlands and published articles and book chapters on various aspects of African history and politics.

Franz Krüger was until recently national editor of news and current affairs at SABC Radio (Johannesburg). He holds an M.A. in journalism from London's City University. A former secretary-general of the National Union of South African Students, Krüger has worked on newspapers in England and Namibia, as well as South Africa, and as a freelance journalist he has contributed articles to a variety of newspapers and newsletters, journals and magazines, and radio and television services in southern Africa and Britain. He launched the East London News Agency in the 1980s and was group editor of the Eastern Cape News Agency.

Peter Limb is a librarian at the University of Western Australia and has recently completed a Ph.D. dissertation on ANC history. His publications include "The ANC and Black Workers," in *Peace, Politics, and Violence in the New South Africa*, ed. Norman Etherington (1992); and *The ANC and Black Workers in South Africa, 1912–1992: An Annotated Bibliography* (1993). Limb wrote a regular bibliographical column for the *Southern*

African Review of Books and is currently a coeditor of the scholarly Internet network H-Africa.

Christopher Merrett is university librarian at the University of Natal (Pietermaritzburg). He is the recipient of the John Phillip Immroth Award for Intellectual Freedom (American Library Association, 1991) and the South African Society of Archivists Prize (1990 and 1995). His numerous publications include *A Culture of Censorship: Secrecy and Intellectual Repression in South Africa* (1994).

Mbulelo Mzamane has taught at various universities in Africa, Britain, and the United States. He was recently head of the Department of English Studies and Comparative Literature at the University of Fort Hare (South Africa), and later vice-chancellor and rector of the university. Mzamane is the author of several works of fiction, including *Mzala* (1980), *My Cousin Comes to Jo'burg* (1981), and *Children of Soweto* (1982). He has also edited books of poetry and short fiction, including *Selected Poems of Mongane Serote* (1982), *Selected Poems of Sipho Sepamla* (1983), *Hungry Flames and Other Black South African Stories* (1986), *Images of the Voiceless: Essays on Popular Culture and Art* (1988), and *Global Voices: Contemporary Writing from the Non-Western World* (1994).

Christopher Saunders is a professor in the Department of History at the University of Cape Town. His numerous publications include *Black Leaders in Southern African History* (1979), *Historical Dictionary of South Africa* (1983; 2d ed., 1999), and *The Making of the South African Past* (1988).

Jeremy Seekings is an associate professor in the Department of Sociology at the University of Cape Town. His Ph.D. was on the origins of the township revolt in South Africa during the 1980s, and he has published several articles and a book, *Heroes or Villains: Youth Politics in the 1980s* (1993), on this topic. He has recently published *The UDF: A History of the United Democratic Front in South Africa, 1983–1991.*

Les Switzer has worked as a journalist and taught at various universities in South Africa and the United States. He is currently a professor in the School of Communication and adjunct professor in the Department of History at the University of Houston. His numerous publications include *The Black Press in South Africa and Lesotho: A Descriptive Bibliographic Guide 1836–1976* (1979), coauthored with Donna Switzer; *Media and Dependency in South Africa* (1985); *Power and Resistance in an African Society: The Ciskei Xhosa and the Making of South Africa* (1993); and *South Africa's Alternative Press: Voices of Protest and Resistance, 1880–1960* (1997).

Keyan Tomaselli is a professor and director of the Centre for Cultural and Media Studies, University of Natal, Durban. He helped write the South African government's White Paper on Film and is editor of *Critical Arts: A Journal for Cultural Studies.* His numerous publications include *The Press in South Africa* (1987) and *Broadcasting in South Africa* (1989), both coedited with Ruth Tomaselli and Johan Muller, and *The Alternative Press in South Africa* (1991), coedited with P. Eric Louw.

James Zug is a journalist based in New York. His first book, *Striking the Anvil: A History of the Guardian/New Age Newspaper,* will be published by Michigan State University Press in conjunction with the Mayibuye Centre/Robben Island Museum in 2001.

Index